M000013296

SHAPING RACE POLICY

CP

PRINCETON STUDIES IN AMERICAN POLITICS

HISTORICAL, INTERNATIONAL, AND COMPARATIVE PERSPECTIVES

SERIES EDITORS

IRA KATZNELSON, MARTIN SHEFTER, AND THEDA SKOCPOL

A list of titles in this series appears at the back of the book

SHAPING RACE POLICY

THE UNITED STATES
IN COMPARATIVE PERSPECTIVE

ROBERT C. LIEBERMAN

PRINCETON UNIVERSITY PRESS

PRINCETON AND OXFORD

Copyright © 2005 by Princeton University Press
Published by Princeton University Press, 41 William Street,
Princeton, New Jersey 08540
In the United Kingdom: Princeton University Press, 3 Market Place,
Woodstock, Oxfordshire OX20 1SY

All Rights Reserved

Second printing, and first paperback printing, 2007
Paperback ISBN-13: 978-0-691-13046-0
Paperback ISBN-10: 0-691-13046-9

The Library of Congress has cataloged the cloth edition of this book as follows

Lieberman, Robert C., 1964–
Shaping race policy : the United States in comparative perspective / Robert C. Lieberman.
p. cm. — (Princeton studies in American politics)
Includes bibliographical references and index.
ISBN 0-691-11817-5 (cloth : alk. paper)
1. United States—Race relations—Political aspects. 2. African Americans—Government
policy. 3. Minorities—Government policy—United States. 4. United States—Social policy.
5. Welfare state—United States. 6. Manpower policy—United States. I. Title. II. Series.

E184.A1L478 2005
323.173—dc22   2004065771

British Library Cataloging-in-Publication Data is available

This book has been composed in Sabon
Printed on acid-free paper. ∞
press.princeton.edu

Printed in the United States of America

10 9 8 7 6 5 4 3 2

For Benjamin

CONTENTS

ILLUSTRATIONS

TABLES

PREFACE

As I WRITE, one of the more curious and cynical affairs of American politics in recent memory is unfolding in a race for the United States Senate in Illinois. Over the summer, the Republican nominee's campaign unraveled and he withdrew, handing almost certain victory to his Democratic opponent, a young state senator from Chicago named Barack Obama. Obama's father was Kenyan and his mother was white—he is black. Desperate, the state Republican establishment began flailing wildly, and quite publicly, for a replacement candidate. The candidate they eventually found was Alan Keyes, a former State Department official with a Harvard Ph.D. who had previously run twice each for president and the Senate—in his home state of Maryland. (He had never lived in Illinois before hastily agreeing to move there and run.) Keyes is also, not coincidentally, black. Like George Bush *père*'s nomination of Clarence Thomas to the Supreme Court, this selection had more than a whiff of affirmative action about it. The party whose leaders insist that American public life be color-blind, that race be kept out of matters such as employment and university admissions, evidently felt that it was a necessary qualification for the nomination and they reached halfway across the continent to find a suitable African American candidate (apparently believing that the runner-up, a black Illinoisan, was unsuitable), denying all the while that race had anything to do with it. Besides providing entertainment for politics watchers in the summer lull between national party conventions, this episode illustrates in a stark, if tragicomic, way, the central tension in American race politics and the central theme in this book: the conflict between color-blind and race-conscious approaches to the challenges of a multiracial society.

Ours is an age of paradoxes for American minorities. African Americans increasingly occupy positions of power, wealth, and prominence in the American establishment that were simply inconceivable a generation ago. Today the secretary of state and the president's national security advisor are African Americans—in a Republican administration, yet. In the business world Merrill Lynch, American Express, AOL Time Warner, and Fannie Mae all have black CEOs. A black woman serves as president of Brown University. Barack Obama himself was the first black president of the Harvard Law Review, and by the time this book is published will in all likelihood be serving as only the third African American senator since Reconstruction. Evidence abounds of political, economic, and social progress of precisely the kind that the civil rights revolution of the late twentieth century was supposed to produce.

At the same time, African Americans and other minorities remain, on average, far behind other Americans on many measures of economic well-being, social status, and political power. They remain more likely to be poor, jobless, ill housed, undereducated, and in poor health. They remain disproportionately concentrated in declining inner cities, isolated from the jobs, schools, and social infrastructure that are the essential building blocks of opportunity in modern American society. Despite real progress toward tolerance and integration, over the last decade or so a dispiriting sequence of explosive incidents belied the simplistic notion that the post–civil rights era has been one of steady, linear progress toward a truly equal society: the savage beating of Rodney King by white police officers and the racial violence that convulsed Los Angeles when the officers were acquitted of assault; similar violence in Cincinnati (and, on a smaller scale, Washington, D.C., Miami, and St. Petersburg, Florida, among other cities); the murder in Jasper, Texas, of James Byrd, a black man whose corpse was subsequently dragged triumphantly through town behind a pickup truck; accusations of police brutality in New York City, including incidents in which an unarmed black man was shot forty-one times by police officers and another was sodomized with a wooden stick in the bathroom of a Brooklyn precinct; and a running dispute over racial profiling by police and airport security officers, among other law enforcement officials.

This ominous litany tells us, among other things, that for all the progress of the past forty years, African Americans still have not achieved the full measure of inclusion and acceptance in American society that the civil rights triumphs of the past century promised. Indeed, the new century has opened with a swelling murmur of political controversy over the place of African Americans and other racial and ethnic minorities in American life: conflict over black disenfranchisement in Florida during the 2000 presidential election; over how best to represent minority voters and interests in Congress; over the declining fortunes of American cities, which are struggling to maintain even the most basic social services, crime protection, and schools for their increasingly minority populations; over whether the government should classify people by race (as in California's Proposition 54, defeated by the state's voters in 2003 but threatening to return there and elsewhere) and, if so, how (as in the Census's adoption of a new, check-all-that-apply approach to racial categories); and over affirmative action, especially in the Supreme Court's acceptance of race as a legitimate category in university admissions in 2003. All of these controversies—especially the last—centered on the nub of the question that has haunted American politics for centuries: whether we best honor our commitment to equality and inclusion by taking account of race and the ways it has built barriers to opportunity or by dismissing it as a modernist fiction whose relevance is sustained only by our own obsession with it.

This book is an attempt to understand how the United States has chosen between these two visions of race policy—the race-conscious and the color-blind—and with what consequences. The United States has long been a society divided by race, and Americans have equally long been ambivalent about how to approach this fact. Both approaches to race policy have deep roots in American politics: color blindness embodied in the egalitarian liberal tradition and race consciousness in both its sinister and more benign variants, exemplified by slavery and the civil rights tradition, respectively. How, then, do we choose? And which is more likely to work? Although the dilemma is as old as the republic and even older, the question remains as urgent as ever, and more so because it is so deeply submerged beneath the surface of contemporary American political debate.

The same questions and tensions increasingly haunt Europe as well—especially what Donald Rumsfeld, in one of his sublime moments of inadvertent clarity, called "Old Europe," the Europe whose past is equally haunted by racial obsessions. Read the news in France and Britain and you will notice a grim resemblance to American reports: rising racial tension and violence (increasing in the wake of the September 11 attacks and the Madrid bombings of March 2004), including full-scale riots in several British cities over the past few summers; racially motivated police misconduct in London; patterns of racial and ethnic inequality, exclusion, and discrimination; the continuing electoral success of Jean-Marie Le Pen in France; and the embarrassing gyrations of British politicians around issues of race. Above all, these countries, like the United States, are struggling with the fundamental dilemma of a multiracial society, the choice between color-blind and race-conscious policies and understandings.

These European stories are familiar and yet unfamiliar. Racial conflict and inequality in Britain and France, as depressingly similar as they might be to American patterns, are embedded in different political structures, policy regimes, and systems of belief; to paraphrase Tolstoy, each unequal society is unequal in its own way. How have *they* chosen their race policies? How have their choices played out? And what can we learn, about both the race policy as a general phenomenon and our own particular dilemmas and challenges, by viewing American race politics alongside these alternative histories?

What we learn above all is that context matters. Successful race policy that can move a country even incrementally closer to an ideal of fair and equal inclusion is not simply a moral endeavor, a matter of willing an ethical imperative—color blindness, for example—into existence. It is, rather, a *political* endeavor, in which moral ideals can be advanced (or frustrated) through the operation of political arrangements. Without understanding this fundamental truth, we risk choosing blindly.

These questions and concerns dovetail with a personal research agenda that emerged from my first book, *Shifting the Color Line*, in which I argued that racial conditions shaped the development of welfare policy and institutions in the New Deal and that these racially structured institutions in turn reshaped racial identities and conflicts in subsequent years. That argument, however, raised important questions that *Shifting* itself could not answer: was the episode I analyzed in that book a singular phenomenon or was it an example of a larger pattern in American political development? In the closing pages of *Shifting*, I speculated almost offhandedly that race has from the very beginning been a critical factor in American politics, shaping political institutions and practices in a variety of ways. But as I began to dwell on this possibility, what began as an idle speculation gradually developed into something of an intellectual obsession: what difference *has* it made for American politics that the United States has been a multiracial society from the very beginning? This basic intuition, that race has fundamentally shaped American political development, was the starting point for this book. But how could we tell if it was true? Political science was largely silent on this question.

Enter Britain and France. The observation that race politics in these countries seemed in some key respects similar to the American experience opened the door onto a possible route toward an answer. If racial division is always present as a background condition in American politics, then it is very difficult, if not ultimately fruitless, to identify the causal role that race might have played in shaping American political development by studying the United States—where race is, in effect, a constant—in isolation. Comparison gets around this problem. As a way of making inferences about American politics, this is something of a departure for the literature in American political development, in which implicitly comparative propositions about the consequences of particular ideological or institutional patterns are common but rarely worked out explicitly. The intellectual path along this comparative route led me to encounters with a number of other emerging research agendas in the social sciences—in American and comparative politics, and historical sociology—that both complicated and enriched the journey.

Writing a book that weaves together so many intellectual threads inescapably requires help, and I have been very lucky to have had quite a lot if it, from extraordinarily generous friends and colleagues. Ira Katznelson has been especially stalwart as an intellectual companion. His subtle readings and pointed questions, delivered always with grace and good humor, improved this book immeasurably. Tony Marx was also a peerless source of support, both intellectual and moral; he and Karen Barkey often helped to remind me that what we do is important and worthwhile, and they helped keep me sane while we all tried, often against seemingly long odds, to do it. Others at Columbia have contributed their knowledge, wisdom, advice, and support: Lisa Anderson, Alan Brinkley, Chuck Cameron, Rudy de la Garza, John Huber, Mark Kesselman, Ken Prewitt, Bob Shapiro, Jack Snyder, and Al Stepan. Beyond Morningside Heights, many colleagues have read, listened, questioned, and argued, and their efforts have saved me from errors of fact and logic and helped me understand better what I was up to. Many go unnamed, but a few deserve mention and public thanks: Sheri Berman, Mark Blyth, Frank Dobbin, Desmond King, Bo Rothstein, John Skrentny, and Rogers Smith. Careful footnote readers will notice my special debt to Erik Bleich and Randall Hansen, who generously shared their deep knowledge of French and British race politics with a novice and whose own work has been indispensable to me. Patrick Weil facilitated research in Paris, opening up his office, his apartment, and his "little black book" of contacts to me. Sean Farhang, Lisa Kahraman, John Smelcer, and Abhijay Prakash provided able research assistance. The Russell Sage Foundation, the German Marshall Fund of the United States, and the Lyndon Baines Johnson Foundation funded much of the research behind the book. At Princeton University Press, Chuck Myers has been a sensitive yet gently persistent editor. All of these people and institutions have my deep gratitude.

I have explored and developed the material in this book in a number of other publications. These works, on which this book builds, are "Race, State, and Policy: The Development of Employment Discrimination in the United States in Britain," in *Ethnicity, Social Mobility, and Public Policy in the United States and the United Kingdom,* ed. Glenn Loury, Tariq Modood, and Steven Teles (Cambridge: Cambridge University Press, 2005); "Race and the Limits of Solidarity: American Welfare State Development in Comparative Perspective," in *Race and the Politics of Welfare Reform,* ed. Sanford F. Schram, Joe Soss, and Richard C. Fording (Ann Arbor: University of Michigan Press, 2003); "Strong State, Weak Policy: Paradoxes of Race Policy in the United States, Great Britain, and France," *Studies in American Political Development* 16 (2002): 138–61; "Ideas, Institutions, and Political Order: Explaining Political Change," *American Political Science Review* 96 (2002): 697–712; "Political Institutions and the Politics of Race in the Development of Modern Welfare States," in *Restructuring the Welfare State: Political Institutions and Policy Change,* ed. Bo Rothstein and Sven Steinmo (New York: Palgrave Macmillan, 2002); "A Tale of Two Countries: The Politics of Color-Blindness in France and the United States," *French Politics, Culture and Society* 19, no. 3 (Fall 2001): 32–59.

Finally, my family deserves thanks beyond my powers to express. Lauren Osborne remains my most exacting and demanding reader. As always, she read every word, most more than once, and many more that she rightly excised. If the words that remain are the right ones, in the right order, it is a tribute to her skillful handling of both the words and their author. But the words are only the beginning; amid the accelerating chaos of our lives, she offered support, understanding, and love beyond words. Our son Benjamin, too, has acquired the family word bug. During the time of this book's writing—which occupied and preoccupied his father rather to his cost—he grew from infancy into childhood to become a reader and writer of inspiring depth and enthusiasm. With love and admiration I dedicate this book to him. Our younger children, Martha and Aaron, may know only that Daddy spends a lot of time "at the office," but they serve as constant and joyful reminders that no matter how important the work that happens there, there is someplace more important to be.

Robert C. Lieberman
New York City
August 2004

SHAPING RACE POLICY

Chapter One

CONFIGURATIONS OF RACE AND STATE: THE POLITICS OF RACIAL INCORPORATION

Rᴀᴄᴇ—particularly the color line dividing white from black (or white from everything else)—has always been central to American political life.[1] It has instigated our most harrowing political challenges, from sectional strife to Civil War, and inspired our proudest achievements, from emancipation to the civil rights revolution. Despite these achievements, however, racial division and inequality remain disturbingly present and disruptive forces in American political life—even more so today, in many ways, than in the bad old days of slavery or Jim Crow. Whereas once the color line was apparent for all to see, etched without irony or embarrassment on the nation's lawbooks, on its maps, and in its customs and social codes, now it has shifted beneath the surface of American politics. Although few will openly acknowledge the color line, its effects are everywhere, in decaying inner cities, overcrowded prisons, and substandard public schools. What has made racial division such a persistent theme in American political development despite dramatic progress in American racial attitudes and institutional practices? How is it possible that these divisions remain when Americans seemed so decisively to have exorcised their racial demons more than a generation ago, and when so much progress has been made? This question and the profound challenge it poses to the American self-image of universal equality and opportunity lie at the center of this book.[2]

In the past half-century, progress toward racial equality and integration has been nothing short of revolutionary. The immediate liberal integrationist aims of the civil rights movement have met with resounding and long-lasting success: formal, state-sponsored segregation has ended and discrimination has been outlawed across a variety of domains. Moreover, racism—the belief in the existence of biologically rooted racial categories and in the inferiority or historical underdevelopment of one or more racially defined groups—has declined dramatically in American life over the past half-century.[3]

But this revolution in legal status and public attitudes has not meant unimpeded incorporation for African Americans into all spheres of American life. Within this generally upward trajectory (although from such a low starting point that downward was scarcely possible), progress has been, to say the least, uneven.[4] In this book I zero in on one particularly jarring disjunction between the success and failure of racial incorporation in two related but distinct policy areas over the course of the twentieth century: welfare and employment. In the realm of employment, the civil rights revolution spawned, rather unexpectedly and almost despite itself, a deceptively strong and arguably successful approach to attacking employment discrimination—the cluster of policies and practices known collectively as "affirmative action." The rise of affirmative action is all the more surprising because it emerged from a resolutely color-blind antidiscrimination law that seemed to prohibit precisely the kind of race-conscious enforcement measures that it spawned. Despite its shortcomings and the controversy surrounding it, American employment discrimination policy has proven one of the country's stronger pillars of minority incorporation. By 2002, nearly one-fourth of employed blacks held professional or managerial jobs (compared to 35 percent for non-Hispanic whites), more than three times the proportion in 1960. And despite several decades of stagnation, the wage gap between black and white workers remains historically small.[5] Large inequalities remain, but the American labor market is much more diverse and more protective of minority rights than at any time in history.

The American welfare state—by which I mean here principally cash income-support programs—has quite a mixed record of incorporating African Americans into structures of public social provision.[6] Social insurance programs such as Social Security have grown in diversity over nearly seventy years. Expanding coverage and increasing benefits have both benefited African Americans, who now participate in Social Security at a rate nearly comparable to that of whites: one in seven African Americans aged fifteen or over receives some kind of benefit from Social Security (including survivors' and disability benefits).[7] The program, moreover, has incorporated minorities with surprisingly little friction or controversy and enhanced the economic prospects of a growing black middle class. At the same time, public assistance programs such as Aid to Families with Dependent Children (AFDC; since 1996, Temporary Assistance to Needy Families) have followed precisely the opposite path. The real value of AFDC benefits reached its peak in the early 1970s and has declined steadily ever since, in an era when the minority presence on the AFDC rolls has steadily increased.[8] In contrast to social insurance, American "welfare" policies have consistently treated their disproportionately minority clien-

tele as excluded from the mainstream and posed barriers to their full incorporation in American life.

These policies, then, underscore my central question: why is there success in some areas of racial incorporation and failure in others? The lump-
iness of racial progress in the post–civil rights era poses a puzzle and a
challenge. The puzzle is to explain why the civil rights revolution failed
to bring about the full-scale incorporation of African Americans into the
full promise of American political, social, and economic life. What are
the causes of racial progress and what are the barriers that stand in its
way? The challenge is to devise policy strategies for addressing these persistent imbalances, which threaten to erode, if not to undermine completely, much of the progress of the last generation. What kind of policies
will help achieve the full incorporation of minorities into American life?
One approach is to target policies at minorities in order to make up for
past discrimination, equalize opportunity, and ensure diversity in institutions such as schools and workplaces. But some critics charge that such
race-conscious approaches to achieving equality threaten instead to undermine equality by highlighting rather than submerging group differences. If American society is to live up to its color-blind ideals, these analysts argue, it must stop treating people differently on the basis of race,
ethnicity, or other group characteristics.[9] This conflict between race-conscious and color-blind policy came to a head most recently in the lawsuits
over admissions policies at the University of Michigan, in which a closely
divided Supreme Court upheld the principle of race-conscious admissions
for the purpose of ensuring diversity while restricting the range of accept-
able applications.[10] But the Michigan cases, however publicly and bitterly
fought, were merely the latest skirmish in an ideological and political
battle that has raged for a generation or more on extremely varied policy
terrain—from affirmative action to voting rights and representation to a
broad range of social policies.

The puzzle deepens when we consider that welfare and employment
policy are connected in important ways. Both are aimed, broadly speaking, at mitigating inequalities generated by market forces, whether by providing benefits directly or by ensuring access to jobs. In the American
welfare state, moreover, the labor market largely regulates access to social
benefits; workers have access not only to generous social benefits such as
Social Security and unemployment insurance but also to a range of tax-
financed and private benefits such as health insurance and pensions, while
nonworkers are relegated to public assistance programs that tend to be
punitive, stingy, and politically weak.[11] The American welfare state consequently tends to amplify rather than reduce labor market inequalities. We
might expect, consequently, that policies that successfully reduce racial
inequities in the labor market would have a similar multiplier effect in

helping to narrow racial gaps in the welfare state. Experience, however, does not seem to bear out this proposition. The rise of the policy commitment to equal employment opportunity coincided with growing class stratification *among* African Americans; some have argued, indeed, that affirmative action, which has tended to benefit relatively more advantaged members of minority groups, contributed to the growing gap between haves and have-nots among minorities.[12]

From one perspective, it is hardly surprising that racial incorporation is stronger in social insurance and employment discrimination than in public assistance. Antidiscrimination policy, ensuring what appears to be fair labor-market access, may simply substitute for more generous and inclusive social provision in the national policy mix, and thus on balance increase inequality by reinforcing the distinction between those who work and those who do not. Such, at any rate, is one prominent argument about the gender effects of the American welfare state, in which strong employment discrimination protection for women coexists with high levels of gender inequality in terms of class status and access to social provision.[13] American welfare reform in the 1990s, which explicitly required work of (mostly female) public assistance recipients, underscored this argument.

At the same time, however, the substitution argument does not translate easily and precisely to the case of racial inequality. American welfare policy and employment policy alike have been severely constrained by the politics of race. The United States rejected the grand postwar Keynesian bargain that linked active full employment policies with generous social benefits; rather, in both policy areas, broader and potentially more racially inclusive policy options have been defeated by racially structured coalitions.[14] This pattern suggests that racial barriers to inclusion cut across welfare and employment policies more generally and, consequently, that the puzzle of uneven incorporation remains unsolved; successes as well as failures need to be explained.

This account of policy outcomes hinges on the notion of "incorporation," by which I mean the extent to which a group is accorded full membership in the national community, with fair and equal access to civil, political, and social rights. This formulation obviously owes a great deal to T. H. Marshall's famous analysis of citizenship, which he decomposed into these same three components. But it also goes beyond Marshall's essentially teleological account of citizenship, in which social rights—"from the right to a modicum of economic welfare and security to the right to share to the full in the social heritage and to live the life of a civilized being according to the standards prevailing in the society"—follow in an orderly and cumulative progression from the development of civil (legal equality) and political (voting) rights. Marshall's influential formulation equates social citizenship with the existence of universal social policies that promise broad access to benefits as a counterweight to the stratifying effects of social class.[15] But this conflation of policies and outcomes is too rigid to account for the ways in which apparently universal policies can introduce or reinforce other kinds of social stratification, along other axes of heterogeneity than class.[16] Certainly the range of minority experience in American welfare and employment policy and the varying capacity of these policies to overcome racial stratification suggest that race, too, is a potentially important barrier to the full flowering of social citizenship.

The notion of incorporation is intended to specify more precisely the extent to which policies in fact offer benefits and protection to minorities and enable them to attain a measure of status within the national community. Incorporation is thus the obverse of the idea of "social exclusion," a concept that denotes not simply chronic poverty or unemployment or even exclusion from social benefits but social marginality and isolation.[17] Measuring minority incorporation in social policies thus has two components. First, it requires identifying, as far as possible, the extent to which minorities actually benefit from social policies. Second, it involves assessing the extent to which inclusion in those benefits enhances or stifles inclusion in other areas of the political economy. Consequently, my account of minority incorporation in welfare and employment policies will involve both data on minority access to benefits, capturing participation levels, and accounts of policy developments over time, capturing the propensity of policies to foster increasing inclusion.

Incorporation is more than just the lack of discrimination in awarding benefits and protecting rights; protection against deliberate, overt discrimination—differential treatment of individuals explicitly because of racial or ethnic characteristics—is a necessary but not sufficient condition for full incorporation. Incorporation also encompasses rules and procedures that allocate benefits, rights, and status. This may happen in such a way that some groups are systematically favored while others are systematically deprived. Such group imbalances may occur even in the absence of discriminatory intent through the unconscious operation of program administration, as when uniform, apparently race-neutral rules are applied unevenly to different groups. One group may be less inclined to seek benefits, for example, whether because of fear, lack of access, or cultural differences among groups. This kind of administrative discrimination also occurs within a political setting, and policies themselves can encourage such discrimination by shifting discretion over the rules and their application to lower levels of government and to front-line administrators or by adhering to standards of policy "success" that bias implementation and evaluation. Policies may thus be discriminatory even if they are applied in scrupulously neutral ways.[18] The distinction between discriminatory intent and discriminatory effects is an important one because they imply different causal mechanisms behind failures of racial incorporation. Both have operated powerfully in American social policy at various times and in different contexts. In an earlier time, openly discriminatory intentions frequently informed, and even dominated, American politics and policy-making.[19] In the post–civil rights era unequal incorporation persists despite the absence of such open discrimination. Nevertheless, past patterns and practices of deliberate exclusion shape today's more subtle and hidden limits to racial incorporation. A historical exploration of incorporation patterns is thus a necessary component of understanding and altering them.

EXPLAINING INCORPORATION

Why this curious and maddening mixture of success and failure? Two factors have dominated recent scholarly attempts in the social sciences to answer such questions about the evolution and consequences of public policies: ideas and institutions.[20] Despite their ample virtues as ways of explaining policy development, these approaches have complementary flaws that limit their ability by themselves to explain this puzzling dual outcome, in which incorporation has gone in dramatically different directions at the same time, in substantially the same ideological and institutional contexts. For the most part, however, social scientists have seen these approaches as alternatives; few, if any, have managed successfully to merge ideas and institutions into a single unified explanatory framework. An innovative approach to considering ideas and institutions together in more historically specific configurations, however, offers a more satisfying general account of seemingly contradictory incorporation outcomes.

The idea that matters most in attempting to explain incorporation is racism. Perhaps these outcomes simply reflect prevailing public beliefs and attitudes about the proper place of minorities in American society. Some observers believe that racism dominates white Americans' beliefs and that the express desire to exclude African Americans and other minorities accounts for the persistence of racial inequality.[21] More sophisticated versions of the racism thesis suggest that even though out-and-out racist expression is frowned upon, racial stereotypes remain a powerful framing device that can shape political behavior and policy debates, often in ways that remain hidden behind a norm of color-blind equality.[22] Others suggest that racial prejudice per se is less important than other kinds of beliefs in shaping white Americans' opinions about policies such as affirmative action and others that are designed expressly to benefit minorities.[23]

What these perspectives share, despite their disagreements about the prevalence of certain kinds of racist beliefs, is the view that what matters in shaping political and policy outcomes is *ideas*—not just opinions but also more deeply rooted cultural beliefs that inform the goals and desires that people bring to the political world and, hence, the ways they define and express their interests; the meanings, interpretations, and judgments they attach to events and conditions; and their expectations about cause-and-effect relationships in the political world. This view has long pervaded the most sophisticated analyses of American race relations, from Gunnar Myrdal's magisterial survey in the 1940s to President Clinton's national initiative on race and *The New York Times*'s Pulitzer Prize–winning series on "How Race is Lived in America" in more recent years.[24] It is undoubtedly true that over the course of American history, racist ideas about the inherent inferiority of racially designated groups have often played a decisive role in policy decisions.[25] It might be the case, moreover, that modulations in American beliefs about race over time can account adequately for variations in race policies and outcomes. Moments of more racism, that is, might produce more exclusionary policies and lower levels of incorporation, whereas periods when racism abates might produce the opposite.

This explanatory approach, however, faces a number of important challenges. First, racism has declined dramatically as a central force in American life. How is it, then, that incorporation has not steadily improved? Second, racial incorporation varies from policy to policy. Dramatic successes and catastrophic failures coexist. How is this possible if the general level of societal racism is the primary barrier to incorporation? We know a fair bit about how particular kinds of racial stereotypes contribute to policies that limit incorporation, as in welfare policy, or about how voters distinguish between general principles such as the idea of integrated schools and policies such as busing, which might actually enforce integration.[26] What is generally lacking in such accounts, however, is an explanation of how Americans choose among competing ideas and beliefs, resulting in concrete political and policy choices—or "why," as Sheri Berman puts it, "some of the innumerable ideas in circulation achieve prominence in the political realm at particular moments and others do not."[27]

The most robust challenge to ideas-based approaches to explaining policy outcomes stems from perspectives that focus on political institutions. Political analyses of policy-making typically and convincingly view policy choices as the consequences of institutions, a set of regularities in political life (such as rules and procedures, organizational structures, norms, or taken-for-granted cultural understandings), which shape political behavior, allocate power and regulate its exercise, and therefore affect political outcomes.[28] Institutional accounts of race in American politics typically focus on particular features of American politics—federalism and localism, pluralism, the fragmentation inherent in separated powers—to explain the persistence of racial inequality in American politics. Such works generally argue that these enduring features of American governing arrangements systematically shape the access of minorities to political power and thus affect political and policy outcomes that limit minority incorporation.[29] From this baseline, however, the challenge for institutional approaches is to account for any progress at all.

Some institutional perspectives on American race politics and policy fare somewhat better at explaining the pattern of racial progress in the United States, particularly by pointing to changes in the institutional context of race policy both over time and across policy areas. Jennifer Hochschild, for example, argues that success has come most firmly and permanently when policies are relatively straightforward and self-enforcing and when they are promulgated by policymakers with strong institutional bases to induce others to change their behavior. Taking a somewhat broader historical view, Philip Klinkner and Rogers Smith have shown that certain political conditions—wars requiring full-scale national mobilization, adversaries that inspire the invocation of America's egalitarian liberal tradition, and social movements—have been necessary to produce racial progress throughout American history.[30]

But even these more supple institutional works pose knotty analytical questions. First, how do we account for institutional changes that might, in some contexts, produce more favorable policies and prospects for minorities than the common patterns of American politics? With their emphasis on order, institutional models of politics are often better at explaining stability than at accounting for important change that goes beyond normal and regular variation. Second, institutional approaches are limited in their capacity to account for the substantive course of politics. Given the raw material—assumptions about actors' beliefs, preferences, knowledge, understanding, and expectations—institutional theories can generate remarkably accurate predictions about which outcome from among a range of contemplated outcomes is likely to occur. But precisely because institutional approaches tend to take these things as given, they are often at a loss to explain the appearance at any given moment of any particular menu of substantive choices. Why, for example, when the institutional conditions for policy change obtain, do policymakers reach for color-blind or race-conscious strategies to address racial inequality and promote incorporation? And finally, the same fundamental question that challenges ideological approaches bedevils institutional theory as well: how to explain variations in outcomes even in the same institutional context.

These prevailing approaches to American politics, rooted in ideas and institutions, fall short of explaining both the unevenness of American racial progress and the profoundly troubling persistence of entrenched racial inequality. Substantively, patterns of racial ideas and policy-making institutions do not map cleanly onto policy outcomes. Sometimes policy developments occurring simultaneously—and thus by definition in the same ideological and institutional context—have gone in very different directions and produced divergent incorporation results, as in the 1960s, when employment discrimination policy took off just as welfare policy hit yet another roadblock. Some outcomes, moreover, seem to defy *both* ideological and institutional explanations. An example is the rise of affirmative action during the 1960s and 1970s. Both ideas (the apparent triumph of color blindness in the Civil Rights Act of 1964) and institutions (the apparent weakness and fragmentation of the American state) would lead us to expect anemic enforcement of employment discrimination law. What emerged, however, was a race-conscious policy backed by the strong and consistent arms of law and state.[31] The general question that these and other episodes raise is how ideas and institutions, which separately tend to be associated with regularity and stability in politics, can combine to produce such different outcomes.

COALITIONS AND CONFIGURATIONS

The answer to this question lies in the idea of coalitions. Because policy-making involves simultaneous attention to multiple issues, policy often emerges from coalitions—often-unexpected conjunctions of political forces, the proverbial "strange bedfellows" of politics—rather than simple majority agreement on particular policy. Race policy is especially prone to this logic because it inherently pits minorities against majorities in situations where each group seeks its own advantage. Race, in fact, has at times emerged as a distinct dimension in American politics that commands the attention of policymakers not to the exclusion of other issues but in combination with them, and these are precisely the circumstances in which race policy change is most likely to occur.[32] Analyses of American politics, however, tend to presume that race policy is a matter of moral suasion rather than strategic action. I depart from this view by exploring the role of such strategic coalition politics in the evolution of race policy and racial incorporation. Coalition building entails the convergence of purposive and strategic political actors operating under common rules on particular courses of action that are collectively decided on and implemented. The process of forming coalitions necessarily involves both ideas (actors' goals) and institutions (the rules that bind them).

Ideas and institutions combine in particular configurations at distinct historical moments to shape the possibilities available to political actors to form and maintain race policy coalitions. Three factors combine to create the contexts for these processes of coalition formation. The first is the institutional setting of key policy decisions, especially the formal structures that organize policy-making: executives and legislatures, bureaucracies and courts. These institutions set the terms of legislative compromise that can shape policy outcomes and they influence patterns of implementation that can ultimately shape the capacities of states to incorporate minorities. But the formation of policy coalitions around issues of racial incorporation also entails questions about the relative capacity of minority groups themselves to participate in the process of coalition formation in order to influence policy, suggesting attention to such factors as group size, cohesion, and status; participation in electoral politics; patterns of political mobilization; and strategic alliance with other groups. A second factor, related to but distinct from the first, is the structure of linkages between racial groups and the state, which can encompass elements of the political system such as the party system, the nature of interest representation, and federalism, all of which can affect group mobilization and group-state relations. For racial minorities especially, distinctive histories of racial formation have been decisive not only in defining the political boundaries of group identities but also in shaping the links among different racially defined groups and between groups and national political institutions.[33] These historically constructed political configurations—group-state linkages as shaped by political institutions—form another central axis of comparison. A third set of factors is the cultural repertoires on which political actors draw to understand the status of racial groups in society and to define what constitutes rational solutions to problems of racial conflict and inequality. None of these factors alone is sufficient to explain patterns of race policy; together, they point toward a convincing causal explanation of race policy and of the peculiarities of racial incorporation in the United States.

In these different policy contexts, ideas and institutions have interacted differently to shape race policy coalitions. These policy coalitions emerge from conflicts over ideas about the legitimacy of race as a political category, the place of racial identities and groups in national political life, and the role of the state in addressing racial conflict and inequality. These ideological debates, in turn, occur in institutional settings that shape actors' strategies in pursuit of their goals, privilege certain actors over others, and influence policy choices. It is these processes of coalition formation that ultimately determine the paths that race policy follows: colorblind or race-conscious, coercive or voluntary, unified or fragmented, backed by strong or weak state authority. How, then, did coalitions form around particular solutions to common racial challenges, at particular moments, in a variety of settings? Accounts of these processes of coalition formation, maintenance, and change and their consequences for racial incorporation are the hinge that connects ideas and institutions in a broader causal argument about change and variation in race policy.

Forming policy coalitions involves collective and authoritative decision-making in a context where potential participants in the decision might not only disagree about the preferred outcome but might approach the situation with altogether different motives.[34] Thus, explaining the formation of coalitions requires an account of both the motivations of the disparate actors who come together to back particular outcomes and the decision-making structures and processes that allow them to do so. As in a criminal investigation, familiar to readers of mystery novels or viewers of police dramas, this means finding motive and opportunity: ideas, which underlie the goals and interests of political actors, and institutions, which shape how they can and must act to realize those goals.

As I have already suggested, neither ideas nor institutions adequately accounts for the full range of variation in race policies or incorporation outcomes. Ideas, especially widely shared and often taken-for-granted cultural beliefs about public affairs, surely shape the beliefs, understandings, and goals of citizens and policymakers and help to frame public problems and determine which policy solutions seem reasonable and rational in a given situation. Much of the most prominent and convincing work on race politics and policy in the United States (and elsewhere) has taken this approach.[35] But ideas and cultural dispositions by themselves are not decisive in explaining political and policy outcomes, especially in race policy, which generally involves conflict and contestation among competing ideas—particularly between varieties of race consciousness and color blindness. The question for race policy is which among these competing ideas win by being enacted into policy or otherwise carried into action by states; and these are questions that cannot be resolved simply by understanding the substantive content of national approaches to race. Ideas, in short, give us motive but not opportunity.

Political institutions provide the opportunity, by constraining political behavior through the operation of rules, norms, and organizational settings, as well as by structuring political openings for group mobilization and the articulation of interests. Institutional analysis typically begins with basic structural features of national governing arrangements—separated powers or parliamentary government, federalism or centralization, and the like—that frame strategic possibilities for political actors seeking particular goals. But actors' goals, while often adjusted to fit institutional circumstances, are likely to be products primarily of enduring national cultural and ideological patterns as well as shifting political and policy circumstances. Precisely because institutional approaches tend to take these things as given, they are at something of a loss to explain the appearance of any particular set of substantive choices. Institutions, then, can provide opportunity but fall short on motive.

The need to connect motive and opportunity in a more complete explanation suggests viewing policies not merely as the projections of national culture or as the mechanical outcomes of institutional forces but as the results of political conflicts in which particular elements of national cultural and ideological repertoires are mobilized and enacted into policy. These political struggles take place within historical and institutional contexts that shape policy-making not simply by organizing power but also by acting as gatekeepers for political ideas and cultural dispositions. Policy-making in democratic government is not simply a process of optimizing the choice of policy instruments to solve readily identifiable social problems.[36] Rather, it entails the formation of coalitions among actors who represent both interests vying for power and diverse policy ideas.

Race policy in particular fits this profile. It involves a clash of interests between majorities and minorities, and its outcomes hinge on matters of access to power and group cohesion, mobilization, and strategy—in short, the stuff of institutional politics. But race is also, by common assent, a cultural phenomenon, a socially and politically constructed set of categories that has often been nurtured and maintained by ideological beliefs and cultural consensus. The majorities and minorities that struggle over race policy, then, are almost by definition on opposite sides of the defining cultural dimension: color blindness. Thus the intersection of race with politics and policy-making necessarily entails a coalition-building process that combines what Hugh Heclo has called "powering" and "puzzling"— clashes of both power and culture between majorities and minorities.[37]

AMERICAN RACE POLITICS IN HISTORICAL AND COMPARATIVE PERSPECTIVE

This approach to explaining racial incorporation in the United States, however, suffers from at least one potential serious limitation. At the broadest and most general level, the problem is that the basic factors that shape race policy and incorporation—federalism, the separation of powers, the liberal tradition—are constant and so cannot explain variations in policies or their consequences. But even allowing that in their real operation these factors are not so constant—federalism and separated powers work differently as times and conditions change; and liberalism is under constant challenge from rival traditions—it is difficult to separate out the effects of ideas and institutions within the confines of a single national example. If both ideas and institutions seem to point toward the same outcome, which is the more fundamental explanation? Are both required to enhance (or suppress, as the case may be) incorporation prospects for minorities? In the 1960s, for example, both ideas (the decline of racism and the rise of liberal integrationism) and institutions (the relaxation of the Southern stranglehold on policy-making through Congress and the party system, for example) could be said to point toward more inclusionary race policy. Without examining a wider range of situations in which ideas, institutions, and outcomes vary, it is impossible to disentangle these potential causal threads.

To get around this analytical quandary, we need strategies to expand variation along all of these dimensions—ideas, institutions, policies, and incorporation outcomes—in order to find the causal connections between ideas and institutions, on the one hand, and policies and patterns of incorporation, on the other.[38] I deploy two such strategies: history and comparison. History is important to the argument for several reasons. First, all the elements of the argument vary over the broad span of time that the study covers (most of the twentieth century). For example, although American political culture and discourse have always been especially race conscious, the precise modes of expressing ideas about race and of squaring them with liberal ideals have changed dramatically. Levels of tolerance for explicitly racist ideas have also fluctuated in American political life. Similarly, although the American constitutional framework has remained basically unchanged for more than two centuries, the workings of its institutions—Congress, presidency, courts, bureaucracy, party system—have changed dramatically. Thus, snapshots of policy-making at single slices of time reveal only limited views of the politics of racial incorporation. Race policy-making under Jim Crow, Southern Democratic dominance, and the Conservative Coalition may not altogether resemble race policy-making in a less racist era of homogeneous and polarized parties, for example, even though the underlying national structures are the same.

Policies and outcomes themselves also change, and it is important to understand not just the consequences of particular configurations of ideas and institutions but also how the society moves from one state of affairs to another. Simply showing that the underlying causal conditions (ideas or institutions) have changed, producing a concomitant change in policy or incorporation outcomes, is not a sufficient account of policy change, for it begs the more fundamental question of why the conditions changed in the first place. It may, in fact, be the case that some idiosyncratic and exogenous shock to the system, such as war or depression, alters political ideas and institutional processes enough to bring about significant policy change. But it may also be the case that ideas and processes that are *internal* to the system may themselves combine to effect large-scale change. The civil rights transformations of the 1950s and 1960s, for example, might be not only the products of external events such as World War II and the Cold War but also outgrowths of the very ideological and institutional structures that constitute the American political tradition: an ideology of equal rights; political mobilization and organization; pressure on policymakers through the courts, elections, and other institutional venues.[39]

History is important, furthermore, because a large part of the motivating puzzle is the emergence over time of very different policies and incorporation outcomes from parallel exclusionary origins. Resolving this puzzle demands attention to the way policies developed over time—how events at one time shaped later circumstances, how particular sequences of events generated self-reinforcing processes that constrained available options at subsequent times, and how these processes intersected other events and processes that made significant change possible. Thus, the analysis revolves around historical narratives, organized to focus on such historically situated moments of coalition-formation. The narratives also emphasize alternative explanations for patterns of policy development, particularly "purer" applications of ideas- or institutions-based arguments, by considering alternative policy paths that might have come about. The narratives deploy several strategies toward this end in addition to the most obvious one—the comparison of historical processes. One is simply the careful historical reconstruction of the strategic choices available to political actors at key moments: how did they understand and articulate their goals and how did they perceive and exploit the political opportunities available to them? A second is the judicious use of counterfactual reasoning, asking "what if" questions about the possible consequences of choices foregone that can help reveal the causal importance of particular factors in a historical sequence.[40]

Finally, history is important because of slavery and its legacy. Appealing to the legacy of slavery is a common and intuitively appealing keynote in accounts of current patterns of racial inequality in America, in both scholarly and popular discourse (witness the recent controversial movement for the payment of reparations for slavery to African Americans).[41] Slavery has doubtless cast a long shadow over American political development—beginning in the earliest decades of European settlement in North America and persisting even after emancipation in the social and legal codes of the Jim Crow South and in the political and economic subordination of African Americans (and others whose racial identity was deemed suspect) in the class and political battles of the urban North. "As much as anything," writes Andrew Hacker, "being 'black' in America bears the mark of slavery. And in our own time, must it be admitted at the close of the twentieth century, that residues of slavery continue to exist? The answer is obviously yes."[42]

But beyond such vague assertions, it is far from clear what the legacy of slavery actually means for incorporation prospects today. Claims about the legacy of slavery in American politics tend to be long on rhetoric but short on analysis. While true at the broadest and most obvious level, they are generally deficient in two respects. First, they commonly fail to identify convincing causal mechanisms by which the "residues of slavery" have been transmitted over time to shape present-day patterns of inequality and incorporation. A variety of possible mechanisms are on offer in the vast literature on race in American life—psychological, sociological, economic, and even political.[43] These accounts, however, generally sidestep the question of how the impact of slavery can linger over long spans of time, outlasting former slaves and slave owners, and how particular patterns of racial domination and inequality persist even when the original structures and conditions of racial domination have long since fallen away. How, in short, was the racial hierarchy of slavery encoded in enduring structures—institutionalized—in ways that had long-term effects on politics, policy, and ultimately on the prospects for the political and social incorporation of racially defined minorities?

But the United States is hardly alone as a nation divided by race, and as a second and complementary analytical strategy, the book compares the American experience with that of two other countries, Great Britain and France. Comparative analyses of American politics are rare, and of American race politics rarer still. Historical and institutional analyses of American politics, moreover, are frequently implicitly comparative, advancing propositions about the causal importance of particular and often distinctive characteristics of American politics—the separation of powers, federalism, or the liberal tradition, for example—without really testing those propositions in other national settings. Much is lost, however, in the failure to treat the American challenge of racial incorporation comparatively. Building on the few outstanding examples of comparative race studies that include the United States, however, I offer a new comparative approach to understanding American race politics.[44] This strategy not only further expands the pool of observations of race policy and incorporation patterns but also permits the basic ideological and institutional background of race policy-making to vary. Britain and France, while sharing certain important characteristics with the United States, embody both different cultural approaches to race (in terms of their commitment to color blindness) and fundamentally different policy-making institutions. Setting the United States within this comparison, alongside countries that face similar race policy challenges and parallel dilemmas of racial division, thus allows us to trace the path of race politics and policies in national settings with different configurations of culture and institutions, the better to assess how our own distinctive political culture and state structure have shaped the fortunes of America's racial minorities.[45]

A brief survey of contemporary European politics easily debunks the notion that American racial conflict is unique. Moreover, the United States is not even the only country in which the processes of state- and nation-building revolved critically around racial distinctions. As Anthony Marx and others have shown, a comparison of the United States with other postcolonial, postemancipation societies such as South Africa and Brazil, among others, suggests that American racial history has close parallels elsewhere.[46] In particular, race was present at the creation of the American welfare state, limiting its scope and reach in critical ways. As with more general state-building processes, the United States was not alone in forging its welfare state in a racially heterogeneous political context. In his foundational work on the origins of the welfare state, the sociologist Harold Wilensky offered the hypothesis that such social heterogeneity—whether racial, ethnic, religious, or linguistic—might have limited or delayed welfare state growth.[47] Thus there is a firm basis for treating the United States as part of a comparative set of countries that trace their institutional roots to formative, racially structured political conflicts.

In fact, many countries were racially or ethnically heterogeneous in one way or another at the founding of their welfare states in the late nineteenth and early twentieth centuries. Among Western industrial (or industrializing) countries, this heterogeneity took a variety of forms. The United States in this period had not only a large population of African Americans—former slaves and their descendants—but also an even larger population of immigrants, many from Southern and Eastern Europe, who were considered racially distinct from "white" Americans (those of Anglo-Saxon and other Northern European descent) in the social, economic, and political hierarchies of the era.[48] Some countries, such as Canada, Australia, and New Zealand, had substantial aboriginal populations. Others—particularly Britain, France, Belgium, and the Netherlands—ruled over extensive colonial empires in Africa, Asia, and the Americas, whose populations were deemed racially distinct from Europeans. Still others faced substantial heterogeneity among their own "native" populations along lines of religion, language, or other significant cleavages that took on almost racial characteristics—Switzerland, for example, but also Britain, France, the Netherlands, and Belgium again.[49] Other European countries that also began to construct welfare states around the same time—Germany, Austria, and the Scandinavian countries, for example—were more homogeneous along racial, ethnic, linguistic, or religious lines.

Each of these heterogeneous societies developed a welfare state that deviated in important respects from the solidaristic, social democratic model, which entails generous universal benefits based on the rights of citizenship. All of these states, by contrast, restrict access to social benefits in significant ways, whether through the labor market or through other means of stratification, with important consequences for minority incorporation. These alternative welfare regimes arose principally because the conditions for social democratic coalition building—robust labor organization, working-class formation, and a state structure that fostered cross-class alliances—did not prevail. Social heterogeneity, racial or otherwise, tended to impede labor organization and working-class formation and shape the party systems of diverse countries, limiting the possibilities for fully inclusionary welfare states. Thus, such diversity poses a coalition-building challenge when demands for social and political solidarity across class lines coexist with demands for exclusion along some other axis.[50]

These considerations suggest a relatively narrow range of countries against which to compare the United States if we are interested in understanding the American trajectory from radical racial exclusion toward partial and halting incorporation. First, the comparison should include countries whose formative experiences of state building (and welfare-state development) occurred in racially heterogeneous political settings—and consequently for whom racial incorporation and exclusion have posed long-standing political challenges. This criterion excludes countries that face acute contemporary problems arising from growing racial and ethnic diversity but lack such a history: Germany, particularly, but also Sweden and Denmark, both of which are increasingly racially divided societies. Second, it should include countries where racial diversity remained a key political issue over the course of the twentieth century, thus excluding countries such as Belgium, for whom nineteenth-century colonialism did not translate into extensive twentieth-century multiracialism.

Finally, the comparison should involve countries that have included racial minorities as presumptive citizens—either automatically by birth or with minimal requirements—at least nominally (even if not always in practice) entitled to the full array of civil, political, and social rights available to full members of their societies, or at least entitled to inclusion under the broad umbrella of social protection. Thus, not suitable are countries that explicitly excluded certain racial groups from coverage. Australia, Canada, and New Zealand ("the showcase of progressive politics in the 1890s," according to one historian) all restricted old-age pensions to persons of European descent and excluded aboriginal natives from coverage in the early twentieth century. In South Africa, pensions were by law more generous for whites than for those designated "Colored," while native Africans were excluded altogether. The United States, to be sure, has not always lived up to this standard, especially in the case of immigrants from Asia and Latin America (to say nothing of Native

Americans).[51] African Americans, however, were nominally guaranteed citizenship, equal protection, and political rights from Reconstruction onwards; they were, that is, *presumptive* citizens, whose actual incorporation into social protection policies could not be directly denied but nonetheless became a subject of intense political conflict, struggle, and negotiation. This point precisely identifies the main comparative issue: the persistence of exclusion in the face of an explicit liberal democratic commitment to inclusion.

RACE IN THREE COUNTRIES

Along with the United States, Great Britain and France meet these criteria almost uniquely.[52] Britain and France may not, at first blush, seem like natural comparative foils for an examination of American race politics. In recent years, to be sure, they have experienced a rising tide of racially charged politics—race riots in Britain in 2001 and Jean-Marie Le Pen's surprising and disturbing performance in France's 2002 presidential elections being only the most recent manifestations. But in the broader sweep of British and French history, such events seem small, and they do not appear to bespeak a deep historical engagement with racial division, hierarchy, and domination, as American politics so self-evidently does. The history of American race relations, after all, is a catalogue of apparently distinctive features—a long history of racial diversity at close quarters, slavery, involuntary migration, periodic and convulsive racial violence—that seem to distinguish it decisively from the French and British cases, where racial diversity seems more recent, more voluntary, and less incendiary. But to assume and assert that these differences matter without asking why and how is to miss the point. The pertinent question is how we can understand the consequences of such factors as longevity, slavery, and violence precisely by contrasting the United States to other countries where these historical patterns vary.

Despite these important differences, however, the United States, Britain, and France are in fact well suited to a comparison of race politics and policy. First, they are among the most racially diverse of the developed countries. Racial minorities comprise 8 percent of the population of Britain and at least 6 percent in France, compared to 13 percent African Americans and more than 20 percent total nonwhites in the United States. In each country, minorities are growing in size and political importance.[53] Second, these countries share a history of rule by Europeans over others; in each case an official ideology of racial superiority was backed by state power and often violent repression, not only in recent years or even in the twentieth century but dating back to the earliest encounters between

Europeans and Africans, Asians, and others. This form of rule differed significantly: the French and British empires kept colonial subjects far removed from most metropolitan citizens while in the American South politics and society were defined by the very proximity of the races (although this occurred at some remove from the lives and sensibilities of most Northern Americans). Still, France and Britain ruled large numbers of non-Europeans in the nineteenth and early twentieth centuries, and in all three cases the definition of nationhood coalesced, in part, around exclusionary, racially defined identities.[54]

More important even than these similarities, however, are the common political traditions of these three countries. Uniquely among the great powers of the West, these countries share long-standing liberal democratic regimes, characterized politically by contested and decisive elections, increasingly broad citizen participation and popular sovereignty, and respect for the rule of law.[55] Ideologically, these political traditions share commitments to the protection of individual rights, political equality, and a universal model of citizenship that is, at least in principle, based on a set of shared civic norms rather than on blood or kinship.[56] In each of these countries, moreover, nonwhites migrated in large numbers during the twentieth century—from colonies to the European metropoles and from South to North in the United States—and in all three countries, these migrants arrived as presumptive citizens, ostensibly entitled to full membership in the national community.[57]

What makes these countries especially suitable for the comparison, however, is that against these background similarities, Britain and France differ from the United States both in the key factors that shape incorporation—ideas and institutions—and in the outcomes themselves—patterns of incorporation over time and across policy areas. To consider ideas first, within their broad regime similarities, these three countries have converged on very different varieties of liberalism and, within that ideological variety, on different political and cultural understandings of race. Britain's tradition of liberalism led it to recognize the legitimacy of subnational identities such as race and ethnicity and consequently to embrace multiculturalism as a policy framework. French republicanism, on the other hand, emphasizes the supremacy of French nationality as a political identity and eschews intervening attachments or group identities, leading it to adopt assimilation as the guiding principle of race policy (and also to prohibit the collection of racial data about the population, making the study of race in France particularly challenging). In the United States, liberal individualism has coexisted with republican and racist traditions, leading to an ambivalent embrace of race-conscious multiculturalism in the context of an aspiration toward color blindness. These ideological and cultural differences have led these countries to frame racial issues

differently and consequently to adopt different kinds of race and integration policy. French policy emphasizes the assimilation of minorities and
the ending of racism, while British policy is designed to promote the
peaceful coexistence among groups through antidiscrimination measures,
largely on the American model (although Britain has not gone as far toward creating affirmative action).[58]

These countries also differ in the kinds of institutions through which
they organize the exercise of political power (still within the broad confines of liberal democracy) and consequently the means by which minorities came to be connected with national politics. In the United States,
state power is notoriously fragmented and decentralized, characterized
by separated powers; a locally representative congress; decentralized, patronage-based nonprogrammatic political parties; a weak bureaucracy;
federalism; and strong and relatively independent courts. The multiple
veto points that inhibit coalition formation combined with the radically
localized nature of linkages between African Americans and the state have
often frustrated the political aims of minorities, who have frequently
sought the protection of the national state against the depredations of
local majorities.[59] In Britain and France, by contrast, state power is more
concentrated and centralized—in parliamentary majorities and cabinets
in Britain's system of party government, and in a strong executive and an
often-imperious administrative state in France's Fifth Republic.[60] These
systems of political institutions offer fewer (or at least differently configured) veto points, but also correspondingly fewer points of access, for
those who would influence political deliberations and policy outcomes.[61]

These national configurations of ideas about race and political institutions, however, have produced puzzling and paradoxical incorporation
outcomes in all three countries. Cultural ambivalence and institutional
fragmentation in the United States have produced weak welfare incorporation and strong antidiscrimination policy. British race-consciousness
has combined with relatively centralized, unitary political institutions
to produce stronger welfare incorporation and weak antidiscrimination
enforcement, in defiance of a strong law that actually invites something
like affirmative action. In France, color blindness and a centralized state
have combined to generate a mixed record of welfare incorporation and
particularly anemic antidiscrimination enforcement. The central question, posed initially about the United States, presents itself again on a
wider stage: why success in some areas of racial incorporation and failure in others? But viewing these outcomes across several countries deepens the conundrum even further. Clearly, race policies and incorporation
outcomes have not been consistent within countries or even within policy areas. Nor do policies and outcomes seem to follow directly from

particular cultural or institutional patterns. But it is precisely these outcomes as they developed and unfolded over the twentieth century that I seek to explain.

CAUTIONS AND LIMITATIONS

Several confounding factors pose potential problems for the comparison of the United States with Britain and France. Most important is the close connection among race, citizenship, and immigration that distinguishes European from American race relations. Unlike African Americans, who are mostly native-born citizens (although their access to the rights of citizenship was until recently severely limited), most nonwhites in Britain and France are either immigrants or the descendants of post-1945 immigrants, and many are not citizens. Thus differing levels of racial incorporation may result from political processes that make distinctions on the basis of citizenship or nativity rather than race or ethnicity per se. But in all three countries, citizenship is based primarily on residence (*jus soli*) rather than descent (*jus sanguinis*), and most immigrants or their children are able to naturalize.[62] Moreover, incorporation is in many ways weakest (or at least no stronger than elsewhere) in the United States, where citizenship is the highest, suggesting that citizenship is not a sufficient explanation for the level of incorporation.

Nevertheless, it may be the case that the fundamental problem in France and Britain is one of immigrant incorporation. Like the United States, France has historically absorbed and assimilated immigrants from many different countries, and it is plausible to suggest that France and Britain might follow the ethnicity model of assimilation, in which successive waves of immigrants successfully adapt themselves to the host society. But just as the process of racial formation in the United States has called the ethnicity model into question, there is evidence that North Africans in France and their descendants are facing steeper barriers to assimilation and naturalization than earlier groups of European immigrants, suggesting that factors other than immigration and citizenship may be playing a role. Moreover, national citizenship has become less important as a basis for incorporation in recent years, as immigrant communities have grown in size and prominence in the Western world and international norms of human rights and have increasingly defined access to civil, political, and social rights. In all three cases, the presumption behind policy, at least since the 1970s, is that immigration is a prelude to permanent settlement and ultimately to citizenship. These countries share a common goal of incorporation across lines of race, ethnicity, and even nationality, although they differ sharply in the ideological frameworks in which they embed this common aim.[63]

Another difference is the nature and distribution of racial and ethnic group identities. Although differentiation among multiple racial groups has always been an important part of American racial history, what is comparatively striking about the history of race in the United States is the dominance of a single racial cleavage. Until the very end of the twentieth century, African Americans were by a wide margin the single largest racial or ethnic minority group in the population. American social politics has largely revolved around the black-white divide, and the link between African Americans and the welfare system remains a central issue today.[64] In Britain and France, by contrast, the racial minority population comprises multiple and shifting groups of different origins and identities without a single dominant one. In Britain, nonwhites made up 7.9% of the total population in the 2001 census: of this group, 23% were of Indian background, 16% Pakistani, 12% Caribbean, 11% Black African, 6% Bangladeshi, and 5% Chinese. Moreover, nonwhites also comprised a set of distinct religious communities; a majority of nonwhites were Muslim, Sikh, or Hindu.[65] In France's 1999 Census immigrants made up 7.4% of the population, and the proportion of immigrants from North Africa grew over the 1990s. In 1990, however, more than 10% of the population lived in households headed by immigrants, suggesting a larger minority population than that captured by immigration statistics; in 1999 this figure was nearly 12%. Of this latter group, a majority had non-European origins and one-third were from North Africa. Among African immigrants and their descendants, many are Muslims, although ranging widely in levels of belief and practice, suggesting that religion and culture may be at the root of racial conflict and exclusion in Europe, a possibility that events since 11 September 2001 seem tragically to have borne out.[66]

In both countries, the concentration of Muslims has had important consequences for minority incorporation. In France, religion has been particularly important as a perceived challenge to the resolutely secular public schools, as in the long-running controversy over whether Muslim girls would be allowed to wear headscarves in school; in Britain, Islam has increasingly been a focal point of cultural conflict, especially since the controversy over Salman Rushdie's novel, *The Satanic Verses*. It is possible, then, that differences *among* racial and ethnic groups within these countries might affect their prospects for incorporation. But it is not clear how intraethnic diversity might affect incorporation. On the one hand, political elites might find a single dominant minority group more threatening and respond with exclusion and even repression, as in the pre–civil rights American South. On the other hand, diversity might produce fragmentation among minority groups, weakening prospects for broad mobilization to demand incorporation.[67] Which of these processes is invoked depends not simply on the unity or diversity of minority groups but on the political mechanisms that structure interactions among groups and the state. To resolve this puzzle, then, understanding the interlocking institutional and cultural mechanisms of incorporation is crucial.

Finally, it should be clear that my purpose is not to develop a general and complete theory of either the political effects of racial heterogeneity or the political causes behind racial incorporation or its limits. Heterogeneity is only one of many routes through which states have arrived at the modern condition of limited capacity to build political (to say nothing of human) solidarity across racially constructed lines. Rather, my purpose is to suggest how racial politics can be "built into" the structure of social policy through the construction of certain kinds of barriers to incorporation. Even when the original conditions and logics of racial conflict and exclusion have given way to new political circumstances that appear more favorable to incorporation, these historically determined patterns can still prove influential in shaping political responses to new challenges.[68] These patterns matter not because they embody primordial and timeless racial conflicts but because they affect the political possibilities available to subsequent actors, both those who wish to protect the status quo and those who seek to challenge it. Thus, although the argument applies directly only to the narrow range of historically diverse, liberal democratic states on which it is built, its conclusions about the cultural and institutional ingredients of coalition building in diverse societies may be more broadly useful in pointing the way forward not only for the United States but also for other countries that aspire to build more just and equal societies.

A Look Ahead

To investigate how these factors contributed in combination to defining distinctive national paths toward racial incorporation, I present a comparative historical exploration of the evolution of racial incorporation in the three countries, in welfare and employment discrimination policy, over the course of the twentieth century (with an emphasis on the post–World War II era). At the study's center is a historical account of the divergent paths of American race policy over the past half century, drawing on a combination of primary archival sources, quantitative data drawn principally from government statistics, and the work of other scholars. Running alongside the American story are historical accounts of the British and French experiences, which are organized and presented to show the analytical parallels across all three countries.

The argument that emerges from this comparative historical analysis is that political conditions favoring racial incorporation have arisen not from constant institutional or ideological forces but from fruitful combinations and configurations of these factors that have appeared at particular historical junctures in each country.[69] The most successful instances of incorporation presented here—laws against employment discrimination in the United States and welfare in Britain—in fact appear to share few pertinent characteristics: while American affirmative action developed in an ambivalent ideological context (between race consciousness and color blindness), with weak institutional support and a high level of minority mobilization and organization, British welfare policy evolved in an increasingly race-conscious political context and in a relatively centralized state with moderate levels of minority mobilization. Similarly, the political circumstances of the most conspicuous failures—American welfare incorporation and French employment discrimination policy—seem to have little in common.

The more successful instances of incorporation, whether in the United States or elsewhere, share common historical circumstances. Incorporation tends to succeed when political institutions either support the adoption and implementation of inclusive and egalitarian policies that overcome historical inequalities *or* provide opportunities for mobilized groups to challenge prevailing policy models and push particularly for more race-conscious approaches. These institutional processes, however, have depended on the presence of particular kinds of policy ideas and often on the organized pressure of racial minorities themselves. Thus, the possibilities for incorporation depend not on institutions or ideas alone but on historically specific, convergent configurations of ideas, institutions, and opportunities. Such openings for movement toward greater incorporation are especially wide when configurations of ideas and institutions are discordant—both with each other and with received structures of exclusion and inequality. These circumstances generate new imperatives for political actors to break out of familiar and settled habits and seek new paths.[70]

Chapter 2 begins the story by describing the emergence of the American welfare state in a racially heterogeneous political context. In the United States, race posed a steep barrier to the construction of a national, cross-class social policy coalition because the imperatives of racial rule constrained the possibilities available to policymakers. In particular, the need to include the South on its own racial terms affected both the substantive and structural features of the welfare policies that emerged from the New Deal. Different ideological and institutional configurations of racial rule, in the form of colonialism, also shaped social reform in Britain and France in the early twentieth century, affecting the nature of cross-class coalition building and producing both ideologically and structurally different welfare states that encoded historical patterns of racial domination in varying ways—centralization or decentralization, solidarity or division, direct or indirect claims on the state for social benefits and protection.

The next four chapters trace the subsequent development of the American welfare state and its variable capacity to incorporate African Americans, who increasingly sought entry into the national political economy. Chapter 3 describes in detail the institutional and ideological characteristics of the racially exclusionary American welfare state as it emerged from the New Deal, characteristics that seemed to bode ill for the future of minority incorporation. Chapter 4 examines two dramatic mid-century transformations that reshaped the possibilities for incorporation: welfare reform, particularly the American failure to expand the scope of its welfare state in the post–World War II years, and the mass migration of blacks from South to North. Contrasted with parallel development in Britain and France—more extensive welfare reforms and similar minority migrations from colonies—these developments reveal the particular configurations of institutions, group-state linkages, and cultural repertoires that would shape postwar patterns of minority incorporation in social provision.

The next chapters then chronicle these paths of incorporation in the American welfare state. Rather then covering all three countries in each chapter, I juxtapose first social insurance and then public assistance with the case that best illuminates the configuration of institutions and ideas that shaped incorporation in each sector. Chapter 5 focuses on Social Security, whose national institutional structure allowed it to overcome its racially exclusionary origins. Social Security is compared with the case of social insurance in France, where institutional and ideological differences limited minority incorporation. Chapter 6 turns to American public assistance, where institutional fragmentation and intense race consciousness severely limited the potential for minority incorporation. The contrast here is with Britain, where institutional centralization promoted stronger incorporation. Taken together, chapters 3 to 6 highlight how cultural and institutional factors constructed by early welfare state politics—particularly the tensions between color blindness and race consciousness, the divergent structural foundations of welfare policy, and the resulting processes of coalition building—combined to produce often surprising patterns of minority incorporation into the national provision of social benefits.

The next two chapters turn to employment discrimination policy. Chapter 7 explores the passage of the Civil Rights Act of 1964, and particularly the coalition-building compromise that produced an ideologically color-blind and institutionally fragmented antidiscrimination law. When contrasted with the British and French laws (and the coalitions that produced them), the Civil Rights Act seemed to create very infertile ground for strong minority incorporation in the labor force. Chapter 8 then shows how color blindness and institutional fragmentation gave way precisely to an active, race-conscious program of antidiscrimination enforcement in the form of affirmative action, while the British and French antidiscrimination efforts foundered despite their nominally stronger state apparatuses.

In addition to drawing general lessons about the cultural and institutional determinants of race politics and policy, chapter 9 returns to the particular challenge with which I began: the persistence of racial division in American society and the variable success of racial incorporation of African Americans (and other groups) in the United States. It also suggests future policy directions for Americans (and others) who seek to negotiate the universal dilemma of race politics, how to spin the flax of race consciousness into the gold of color blindness and move modern societies toward true racial equality.

Chapter Two

LEGACIES OF SLAVERY AND Imperalism COLONIALISM: RACE AND THE POLITICS OF SOCIAL REFORM

LIKE ANY FORM OF STATE BUILDING, welfare state development involves defining the boundaries of national membership: who is entitled to the benefits and social protection that the state will offer? The welfare state is, among other things, a mechanism of social solidarity, a means of linking citizens to the state through a set of social rights and to each other by ties of interdependence. Welfare states are at once inclusive and exclusive mechanisms. They embody ties among a community of citizens, but they also define a boundary between the community and outsiders, depending on who can claim social protection, and in so doing they can construct and reconstruct relations of inequality and social division within society along lines of class, sex, citizenship, and race.[1] Welfare-state making is a matter of building coalitions, particularly across class lines but also, possibly, across other kinds of social divisions. To what extent does racial heterogeneity inhibit or enable coalition building for social policy? And to what extent were racial minorities part of the coalition that enacted pioneering welfare legislation?[2]

The founding moment of a national welfare state is important, moreover, because it sets critical patterns—of policies, organizations, categories, rules, and procedures—that establish the framework in which later questions of inclusion and exclusion will be decided. If, as the political scientist E. E. Schattschneider wrote, "organization is the mobilization of bias," then policy-making is the institutionalization of bias.[3] Public policies, and particularly social policies, inherently make distinctions among people by conferring benefits and imposing costs on defined segments of a population. Race—and particularly the imperative of racial exclusion—was an important political factor in shaping American welfare-state development and, consequently, in setting the institutional terms by which policy benefits and burdens were allocated. Welfare-state development, moreover, tends to be a path-dependent process, in which early choices shape subsequent possibilities by generating self-reinforcing processes of learning, the coordination and organization of political activity, and the adaptation of expectations that tend to make national welfare systems comparatively stable over time.[4] Thus we might expect patterns of racial bias that were influential at these moments of creation to persist as welfare systems developed and matured.

If this history were unique to the United States, we might simply chalk up the deeply rooted entanglement of race and American social policy to the anomalies of American racial history. But the American version of the story—distinctive welfare-state policies arising in a racially heterogeneous political context—was actually quite common among Western countries in the early twentieth century. The politics of race, particularly the relationship between citizens at home and their colonized subjects abroad, was also instrumental in shaping welfare-state building in France and Britain in the early twentieth century. But the way bias was institutionalized—the means of racial exclusion and the role race played in structuring the building of welfare coalitions—differed in each country, in at least three particular ways. First, although political rule in each state was based on racial distinctions in the nineteenth century, the form of racial rule was different: slavery in the United States and colonialism in Britain and France (with important differences between its British and French variants). Second, different cultural understandings of racial distinctions arose in each country, although they all shared certain common elements. And finally, the institutional structure of policy-making varied across these three states. In all three, political coalitions were crucial for achieving social reform, but the importance of race in building these coalitions differed. Together, these three types of differences produced not just different kinds of welfare states but contrasting political and policy responses to the challenges of constructing them.

This chapter surveys the way each of these countries met this challenge in the early twentieth century in order to assess the role that the distinctive legacy of slavery may have played in shaping the subsequent challenges of incorporation for African Americans. Each of the three factors—structures of racial rule, ideas about race and its connection to national identity, and policy-making institutions—helped to shape the coalitions that established early national welfare policies. The coalitions built at these moments both shaped the initial institutionalization of bias in the welfare state by fashioning means of racial exclusion and created enduring welfare institutions that would critically affect subsequent incorporation possibilities for minorities.

SLAVERY, COLONIALISM, AND STATE BUILDING

Slavery and its aftermath were, of course, central in shaping the American political world of the late nineteenth and early twentieth centuries. But slavery was only one form of rule based on racial distinctions. The historian George Fredrickson argues that racism has historically encompassed not only the belief in "permanent and unbridgeable" differences between groups but also the use of power to dominate and subjugate on the basis of those differences.[5] This formula of racially defined rule defines a broad category of political practices, including slavery as well as softer forms of pervasive discrimination as well as more formally institutionalized systems of racial dominance such as apartheid (including Jim Crow in the American South), certain brands of nationalism (including nationalism's totalitarian and genocidal variants), and Western imperialism and colonialism.[6]

Writing at the height of both European colonialism and Jim Crow segregation in the United States, W.E.B. Du Bois recognized racial domination as a fundamental human problem that transcended national boundaries. "The problem of the twentieth century," he famously wrote in probably the most-quoted line ever written about race relations, "is the problem of the color line." Less well known, however, are his very next words, his definition of the color line: "the relation of the darker to the lighter races of men in Africa and Asia, in America and the islands of the sea."[7] The global dimension of racial domination was never far from Du Bois's work or thought; not only was he among the founders of the National Association for the Advancement of Colored People in the United States but he also devoted much time and energy to the (ultimately fruitless) goal of building an international pan-African movement that could effectively confront European imperialism. Du Bois understood that despite their differences, slavery and colonialism were linked by a fundamental and constitutive commitment to racial distinctions that exposed deep tensions within the Enlightenment tradition and spawned common legacies of exclusion and injustice.[8]

"Two new devices for political organization and rule over foreign peoples were discovered during the first decades of imperialism," wrote Hannah Arendt. "One was race as a principle of the body politic, and the other was bureaucracy as a principle of foreign domination."[9] Like slavery and segregation, imperialism in the nineteenth and twentieth centuries constituted rule by "whites" of European descent over "blacks," conducted through a set of formal institutions and social arrangements supported by an ideology of racial superiority. All of these forms of rule were also justified and explained by other means—economic, political, diplomatic—and a complete explanation of slavery, segregation, or imperialism would surely involve all of these. But underlying these explanations, or at least deeply intertwined with them, is what Du Bois called the color line. "It was," he wrote, "a phase of this problem that caused the Civil War; and however much they who marched South and North in 1861 may have fixed on the technical points of union and local autonomy as a shibboleth, all nevertheless knew, as we know, that the question of Negro slavery was the real cause of the conflict."[10] Similarly, imperialism and colonialism, no matter how extensively they involved other factors, constituted irreducible structures of racial rule. Colonial rule in all its varieties depended on the definition of a fundamental gap between colonizing and colonized peoples, which was then invoked to justify economic extraction and political subjugation. Colonial domination, in turn, tended to reinforce and naturalize racial distinctions between rulers and ruled by appearing to provide evidence of inferiority.[11]

The highpoint of imperialism and colonialism in Europe in the late nineteenth and early twentieth centuries also coincided with the formative period of the European welfare state and matters of race and membership were central to early social politics. In the United States, the connection between slavery and the political conditions of the late nineteenth and early twentieth centuries was not hard to discern. The Civil War brought emancipation and a series of constitutional amendments intended to establish civil and political rights for the former slaves and their descendants. These protections, however, were quickly hollowed out, initially by the Supreme Court and ultimately by the political capitulation of the North to white supremacy in the South once it became clear that the Republican Party could dominate national elections without contesting Democratic dominance in the South. Although it was often submerged as an explicit political issue in national politics for a time after the final failure to enforce black voting rights in the South, race remained a central axis of American politics in the late nineteenth and early twentieth centuries. Racial and ethnic divisions stymied working-class formation and helped to frustrate the populist attempt to unite blacks and whites into a broad working- and lower-class political coalition. Ultimately, despite the apparently revolutionary impact of the Civil War and Reconstruction, a new color line arose that strikingly resembled the old. By the time Du Bois evoked it so eloquently at the turn of the century, the new color line had been institutionalized in the repressive labor practices of debt peonage in Southern agriculture and in the legal, social, and political codes of the South through state-sponsored segregation backed by violent repression. These factors limited the scope of political pressure for social reform in the early twentieth century and, reinforced by the fragmented American state, posed steep barriers for the formation of broad, cross-class coalitions for national social policy.[12]

The European welfare state similarly traces its origins to a political moment when questions of racial inclusion and exclusion were central to national politics. This was the era that historian Eric Hobsbawm has dubbed "the age of empire," when imperial conquest and colonial rule dominated political life. These enterprises were part of the process by which European states negotiated the transition toward mass politics and democracy, which required new means for securing the allegiance of the newly enfranchised working class and creating an "imagined community" among citizens.[13] European states, liberal and conservative alike, faced the dual challenge of appeasing growing working-class political movements without capitulating to socialism and of protecting and extending colonial empires to which their working classes were indifferent if not altogether hostile. These challenges evoked in broad terms what Hobsbawm has called "the strategy of the soft embrace": programs of meliorative social reform that had varying results depending on the breadth and composition of reform coalitions—and particularly depending on whether or not those coalitions reached across classes to include both capital and labor.[14]

Thus a crucial question in the early politics of American, British, and French social reform was the relationship between race and class in the construction of reform coalitions. To what extent did the imperatives of racial rule affect the class politics of social reform? How was the politics of welfare-state building, the construction of a means of social solidarity at home, connected to the process of drawing race-based distinctions between national citizens and racially distinct subjects either across or within national boundaries? Seen in this light, the welfare state is potentially an agent of the political construction of race-based national solidarity. By linking social groups to each other and to the state through a network of social rights, the welfare state institutions that were created in this context were thus instrumental in defining the rights of differently situated, racially defined groups of citizens and subjects, including the right to state protection against what Franklin Roosevelt called "the hazards and vicissitudes of life."[15]

The relationship between race making, whether imperial or domestic, and social politics was potentially critical not only in driving the United States, Britain, and France to create welfare states but also in shaping their institutional structures, the political and procedural mechanisms that regulate access to social benefits. But these linked processes of racial rule and welfare-state formation were not uniform across countries. Ideas about racial characteristics and their connections to national identity, membership, and solidarity have clearly been critically important in the political development of modern nation-states.[16] Moreover, these three national cultures drew from a common stock of racial ideas in the nineteenth century. The puzzle, then, is to understand how certain ideas were crystallized into policies at certain historical moments, particularly at critical moments of state formation, and why national welfare states approached the challenges of racial inclusion and exclusion with such different institutional tools. Answering this question requires setting racial ideas in historical and institutional context and examining the way different paths of national development interpreted and enacted them.

COMPARING SLAVERY AND COLONIALISM:
THE EVOLUTION OF RACIAL RULE

Variations in the nature of racial rule, whether in the form of slavery or colonialism, were potentially of critical importance in shaping welfare-state formation. In particular, the domestic politics of imperial rule—the extent to which clear racial boundaries between home citizens and colonial subjects underlay the power and democratic legitimacy of metropolitan political elites in imperial powers—had important effects on the politics of social solidarity. To the extent that imperial politics demanded a hard and fast racial line between citizens at home and subjects abroad, social welfare policies were freer to insist on a high level of social solidarity among their beneficiaries. In the case of slavery, the same schema applies—the ability to draw race-based boundaries between citizens and less-than-citizens played a critical role in defining the boundaries and possibilities of social solidarity in the post-emancipation era.

In other words, the presumption of racial homogeneity among citizens allowed for the construction of welfare systems with more forceful and authoritative means of connecting individual citizens to the state. There were two reasons for this outcome. First, the challenge of racial rule demanded the protection and propagation of the ruling racial group (the "imperial race" in colonial parlance), which placed a burden on the state to ensure the health and welfare of its own citizens. At the same time, the pointed racial division between home and abroad meant that a strong, centralized, and deeply penetrating welfare state did not threaten a racial hierarchy that ordered political life within the home country. But in countries where the boundaries of imperial and racial citizenship were more permeable, the possibilities for social policy were restricted by the possibility of racial inclusion. The presence of racial diversity *within* rather than *across* home-country boundaries made the creation of centralized, national welfare states more politically dangerous. In such countries, the problem of distinguishing between those who were and were not entitled to consideration as members of the national community was a more complicated political and administrative enterprise, since one could not simply presume that social and national boundaries coincided. Rather, welfare states in these countries were more likely to take complex institutional forms, involving decentralized decision-making and administration rather then constructing direct links between citizens and the state. In these countries, the principal difference in the form of racial rule was whether racial minorities were located mostly inside national boundaries (the United States) or beyond (Britain and France). Although the United States, among these three countries, would conventionally be considered

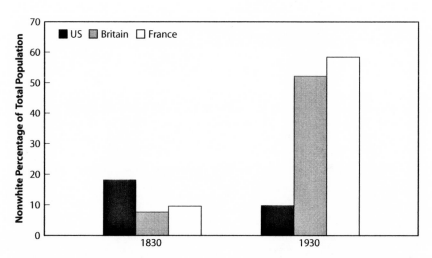

FIGURE 2.1 Nonwhite Population, U.S., French, and British Empires. Source: See note in text.

the most multiracial, many more people of non-European descent were ruled from London or Paris than Washington.

In the early nineteenth century, European colonization of sub-Saharan Africa, Asia, and Oceania had barely begun. The colonial empires of France and Britain (excluding India, which was administratively separate from the rest of the British Empire) were still relatively small and the populations under British and French rule, including those of the home countries, were predominantly European. As figure 2.1 shows, around 1830 the French and British empires remained less than 10 percent nonwhite.[17] By contrast, blacks made up nearly 20 percent of the population of the United States. Essentially all of the nonwhites in the British and French empires lived in colonies—principally Ceylon and the West Indies in the British case and Algeria in the French. Similarly, more than 90 percent of American blacks lived in the South, where they were, of course, slaves.[18]

Over the course of the nineteenth century, the size and character of the French and British empires changed dramatically, as did the American political landscape. Sub-Saharan Africa and Asia became major colonial destinations, bringing tens of millions of non-Europeans under European rule. "We are no longer a Commonwealth of white men and baptized Christians," wrote George Bernard Shaw in 1900 with a touch of disgust. "The vast majority of our fellow-subjects are black, brown, or yellow; and their creed is Mahometan, Buddhist, or Hindoo."[19] By around 1930, as figure 2.1 shows, nonwhites made up majorities of the populations of both empires. In the United States, by contrast, after several massive waves of European immigration, the black population—by an order of magnitude the largest minority group in the country until the 1960s— had dropped to approximately 10 percent of the total U.S. population (its lowest point since the decennial census began in 1790). There was a similar divergence in geographic dispersion. Near total geographic separation of the races remained the rule in the European empires, especially the French; few Europeans other than administrators and military personnel migrated to the colonies. Very few colonials lived in their respective metropoles, while very few whites lived in most colonies; colonies where whites did live in large numbers tended to have relatively small native populations (South Africa being the most prominent and important exception). In the United States, by contrast, northward migration of African Americans in the 1910s and 1920s had begun to disperse the black population. Still, in 1930, around 80 percent of black Americans lived in the South, where the immediate proximity of African Americans posed a very different set of political challenges for American whites.[20]

RACIAL RULE, COALITION BUILDING, AND THE POLITICS OF SOCIAL REFORM

The geographical and political proximity of blacks and whites did not alone determine the impact of racial rule on the welfare state. Equally important was the centrality of race to the process of building political coalitions around social reform, particularly whether or not race emerged as a significant or even dominant line of political cleavage that altered or even trumped other potential cleavages—primarily class.[21] In the United States, race helped overcome class-based political conflict and was one of the central axes around which the politics of welfare revolved. The coalition behind the American welfare state in the 1930s depended crucially on the protection of racial rule. The political imperative of uniting whites against blacks produced an approach to welfare policy that was necessarily exclusionary and decentralizing and that allowed locally dominant white elites to exclude blacks from benefits.

In Britain as well, the political construction of racial distinctions was critical in the creation of cross-class coalitions for welfare policy. But the difference between internal racial conflict in the United States and the appearance of internal racial homogeneity in Britain proved critical in pushing the two countries toward different approaches to constructing welfare institutions. In Britain in the years before World War I, social reform and imperial fervor were the twin pillars beneath a political coalition that created inclusive national welfare policies as a means of unifying Britons across class lines and against a racially defined threat from outside. By contrast, race did not come to trump or displace other cleavages in French social politics. Distinctions not only between French citizens and colonial subjects but also between racially suspect Jews and other Frenchmen and among the various provincial populations (many of whom were seen as racially distinct, even equivalent to France's African subjects) all affected the politics of state building and social reform in France. French imperialism was less consumed with constructing racial distinctions across national boundaries, and French social reform in the interwar years did not mobilize racial antagonisms to overcome class divisions, whether to inclusionary or exclusionary effect. The result was the perpetuation of the Third Republic's corporatist pattern of social provision, based on civil society attachments. In order to understand how racial differences in coalition building led to three such different policy outcomes, we must first look at the way the process of building coalitions unfolded in each country.

The United States

The challenge of building a broad, cross-class coalition for social reform faced particularly steep barriers in the United States. Over the first decades of the twentieth century, proposals for public pensions, unemployment compensation, and health insurance consistently met with frustration in national politics. When, during the Great Depression, national political and economic conditions finally provided an opening for the adoption of national welfare policy, the results, while substantial indeed, stopped considerably short of creating a unified, national welfare state that conferred broad social rights on the basis of citizenship. Rather, even in conditions of national emergency, reform possibilities were compromised by the challenges of knitting together a cross-class policy coalition while maintaining the racial hierarchy that pervaded American society.

From its formative moments the American welfare system has had to grapple with the problem of racial division, and the task of incorporating African Americans remained at the center of welfare politics throughout the twentieth century.[22] Most simply, race and welfare are intertwined because race was a significant line of social and economic cleavage and a significant axis of political power long before the development of national social policy, so that welfare policies were crafted and administered largely to avoid disrupting existing racial arrangements. Although analysts disagree about the extent to which racial politics has been the direct cause of racial imbalances in the welfare system, there is little doubt that the historically subordinate position of African Americans in the political economy has placed them at a significant structural disadvantage in the post–New Deal welfare state.[23]

The roots of this history lie, first of all, in the structure of American racial rule in the aftermath of emancipation. Even after the end of slavery, racial rule remained central to the American regime, specifically the political imperative for the control and exclusion of an African American population that was internal, regionally concentrated, and formally entitled to the rights of citizenship. Although demands for racial exclusion were fiercely contested, they did not abate and in the late nineteenth and early twentieth centuries they were gradually but indelibly encoded into both the formal and informal governing arrangements of American state and society.[24] Before the Civil War, there had been little that could be called social policy in any national sense in American politics. But the post–Civil War era coincided with the origins and growth of the American national welfare state, beginning with the national system of military pensions and culminating in the Social Security Act of 1935, which sealed the participation of the national government in social provision.[25] After emancipation, then, the status of the newly freed slaves and their descendants almost necessarily moved to the center of the politics of American social policy. It was not only the presence of African Americans within national boundaries of the United States but also their status as presumptive citizens (at least under the original intent of the Thirteenth, Fourteenth, and Fifteenth amendments to the Constitution) that posed the fundamental conundrum of social politics: how to produce welfare policy without running afoul of the South with the threat of racial inclusion.

The exclusionary political imperatives of racial rule were entirely consistent with the dominant ideological approach to race and citizenship in the late nineteenth and early twentieth centuries. Despite the rhetorical appeal of color-blind liberalism, racism—the presumption of separateness and superiority—was the ideological hallmark of the era. Although Justice John Marshall Harlan famously declared in 1896 that "our Constitution is color-blind," he did so as the lone dissenter in *Plessy v. Ferguson,* the case that finally established the legality of state-sponsored racial segregation. The majority's claim that "in the nature of things [the Fourteenth Amendment] could not have been intended to abolish distinctions based upon color, or to enforce social, as distinguished from political equality, or a commingling of the two races upon terms unsatisfactory to either" in fact reflected the dominant national belief.[26] In citizenship law as well, race and other ascriptive characteristics largely governed rules of inclusion and exclusion, leading ultimately to race-based immigration restrictions and political and cultural incentives for immigrant groups to be seen as white. This era also saw the advent of social Darwinism and scientific racism in American intellectual life. These currents of thought appeared to ground popular racism and the political imperatives of racial rule in scientific authority, further underscoring the extent to which racism suffused American political culture in this era.[27]

The historical connection between race and the politics of the welfare state arose, finally, because of the particular configuration of political institutions by which whites ruled over blacks, not only in the Southern states but also in the national government. The segregated, white-supremacist South of the first half of the twentieth century set up an elaborate set of mechanisms to disenfranchise African Americans and to undermine the rights that the Constitution seemed to protect. Although Reconstruction, the postwar military occupation of the South, ended formally in 1877, Northern Republicans continued to try to use federal power to enforce black voting rights in the South until the 1890s.[28] Consequently Southern politicians developed a very strong interest in protecting state- and local-level political autonomy from national incursions.

The South, moreover, was a one-party region and elected only Democrats to Congress (with very rare exceptions). Once in Washington, Southern Democrats, who won essentially perpetual reelection, climbed the rigid seniority ladder in Congress so that when Democrats controlled Congress, Southerners chaired committees, in an era in which congressional rules gave committee chairmen tremendous power over policymaking. Although twentieth-century Southern Democrats were more heterogeneous than is commonly recognized, they were reliably unified (and often allied with Republicans against their fellow Democrats) on civil rights and labor issues, and they used their pivotal legislative position to challenge (and usually to defeat or amend) any policy provision that they regarded as a challenge to the Southern system of racial supremacy and labor-repressive agrarian peonage.[29]

Until the New Deal, social reform at the national level was, for a number of reasons, almost nonexistent. The separation of powers made lawmaking an especially complex, multistage enterprise, especially given the pivotal veto power of the president and the option of a minority of senators to mount a filibuster. Patronage-based, nonprogrammatic political parties often provided weak support for bold and innovative policy measures. A weak bureaucracy provided neither programmatic ideas nor administrative expertise. Federalism and the locally representative structure of American governing institutions gave local and regional interests a great deal of leverage to shape national policy-making. As Theda Skocpol has shown, these institutional factors militated against national social insurance and other European-style welfare policies, as did the lack of national mobilization behind such policies. Moreover, the Supreme Court routinely blocked attempts at social and economic reform until the middle of the 1930s. Some reforms were possible, especially maternalist policies such as mothers' pensions, maternal and child health assistance, and protective labor regulations for women; but very few workingmen's social policies succeeded until the 1930s. The localized structure of most maternalist social policies, especially mothers' pensions, meant that they largely excluded African Americans. Several Southern states had no mothers' pensions at all; those that did declined to operate them in heavily black counties and used discretionary administrative tactics to direct benefits to white families.[30]

Franklin Roosevelt's New Deal, abetted by the Supreme Court's timely about-face, brought the national government into the business of social reform. Roosevelt's reform coalition, which combined Northern urban workers, Midwestern farmers, and Southern whites, was in many respects similar to the industrial-agrarian coalitions that produced social reform in many European countries, and it pursued a familiar reform agenda: social insurance, labor rights, and economic regulation.[31] But the pivotal, if not the dominant, element in the New Deal coalition was the South, whose participation in the welfare-state building enterprise was contingent on maintaining the utter subordination of African Americans, not just as low-wage workers but as political and social inferiors.

The resulting policy settlement, the Social Security Act of 1935, took the form of a race-laden institutional bargain between the Southern and Northern wings of the Democratic party over the terms and mechanisms of inclusion in the welfare state—that is, over the boundaries of social solidarity. The Roosevelt administration proposed a widely inclusive set of social policies under national control, combining fully national social insurance for all workers with financial support for state public assistance policies such as mothers' pensions, under terms that would give the federal government substantial administrative and political leverage.[32] This package—inclusive, national social policy—proved unacceptable to Southern congressional leaders because it threatened to create direct links between Southern African American workers and the national state, effectively mobilizing a class coalition against racial hegemony. The responsible congressional committees, both chaired by Southerners, altered Roosevelt's proposal by eliminating agricultural and domestic workers from eligibility for national social insurance on the one hand and removing federal controls over state public assistance on the other. Occupational exclusions eliminated more than three-fifths of the African American work force from the protection of social insurance; radically decentralized public assistance allowed wide areas of discretion to local elites in setting benefit levels and requirements. The result was a structurally limited, decentralized, and bifurcated welfare system that perpetuated African American dependence on local political and economic elites for their livelihoods. Thus at the founding moment of the American welfare state, the particular institutional configuration of racial rule effectively blocked the formation of a more fully reformist coalition, joining classes across racial lines in support of more a more broadly unified welfare state. Instead, even though African Americans were nominal partners in the New Deal coalition (although not solidly until 1936 or even after), the imperatives of racial dominance outweighed conventional class position in defining interests and cleavages in the social politics of the 1930s.[33]

The welfare system that emerged from the New Deal moved on two tracks. Social insurance policies—Old-Age Insurance (Social Security) and Unemployment Insurance—were national policies that paid benefits linked to workers' contributions as a matter of right. Although it weathered considerable uncertainty through the 1940s, Social Security was politically unassailable by the early 1950s, largely because of its contributory structure but also because of equitable professional administration and skillful political management.[34] As a result, it not only included African Americans fairly and without discrimination, it also expanded to include previously excluded occupations, including farm work and domestic labor, effectively bringing many African American workers into the national welfare state on the same terms as whites. By contrast, public assistance policies—especially Aid to Families with Dependent Children (AFDC), the program most commonly called "welfare"—which disproportionately targeted African Americans, were decentralized and parochial, placing near-complete authority in the hands of local political elites. The result was widespread discrimination against African Americans in AFDC administration, not only in the South but in Northern cities as well, especially cities dominated by traditional party organizations (machines), another setting in which African Americans were dependent on white elites for their access to benefits.[35] While regularly employed workers gained nationally protected social rights through an expanding social insurance regime, African Americans were disproportionately relegated to weaker, partial, and fragmented links with the welfare state through public assistance. Thus entering the post–World War II era, the United States had a two-track welfare state with a strong racial valence essentially built into it institutional structure, the legacy of the configuration of racial rule that structured social politics in the 1930s.

Great Britain

"The separation of the tropical Empire from the European island," wrote the Oxford geographer Sir Halford Mackinder in 1924,

> although perhaps a source of weakness from a military point of view, has had this supreme advantage, that on the one hand imperial rule in the dependencies has not corrupted freedom at home, and on the other hand those who exercise that rule, go out generation after generation with the spirit of justice and trusteeship ever renewed from their free homes and schools.[36]

In contrast to the United States, the color line in the British Empire was almost entirely a geographical one, with whites living at the center, in the British Isles, and nonwhites at the periphery, in overseas colonies and dominions.[37]

The ideological underpinnings of the British Empire in the nineteenth century depended, in fact, on the twin characteristics of physical distance and racial difference. From the earliest notions of a British empire in the sixteenth century, the notion of Great Britain as an island nation, separated from the rest of Christendom and the world, dominated imperial imagery—the "scept'red isle . . . This fortress built by Nature for herself / Against infection and the hand of war, . . . This precious stone set in the silver sea / Which serves it in the office of a wall, / Or as a moat defensive to a house, / Against the envy of less happier lands," so lovingly evoked by Shakespeare's John of Gaunt.[38] Great Britain comprised not a single national group but three—English, Scottish, and Welsh—and the forging of a distinctively *British* national identity out of these strands was the work of the ensuing centuries. That identity centered around a number of components: Protestantism (defining British identity against continental, and particularly French, Catholicism), the monarchy and its attendant pageantry, and the distinctive British tradition of liberty (again, contra French despotism)—and the common domination of Britons over imperial subjects overseas, which helped to meld the previously subordinate Scots and Welsh into the English-dominated British nation.[39]

Essential to this sense of national unity was the racial distinction between Britons and their imperial subjects. The transformation of the British Empire in the late eighteenth century from a relatively loose commercial federation centered in North America to an extended empire centered in Asia and built on military and administrative power produced increasing anxiety in Britain, particularly about the growing state apparatus necessary to rule such an empire, which seemed to many to be a projection of "oriental despotism" onto the home front.[40] By the nineteenth century, however, this anxiety had been largely been resolved within British liberal thought by identifying subject peoples as "backward" and "uncivilized," not yet ready for the benefits of liberalism and representative government but requiring the tutelage of a more civilized race.[41] The geographical distance between Britain and her colonies served to underscore this racial distinction, and to blur, if not to erase, distinctions of race and class within Britain itself—even extending to the Irish, who were considered somewhat less that Britons proper but undoubtedly more than imperial subjects. "In the minds of many," writes historian Robert Huttenback,

> "Nigger" really did begin at Calais—or Dublin. Irishmen were cursed by a double indictment, judged to be both low-class and members of an inferior—the

Celtic—race. They were condemned as dirty, emotional, shiftless, untrustworthy, undisciplined, and unstable. . . . Within the spectrum of Anglo-Saxon prejudice, it was clearly better to be English than Irish, but even more important to be white rather than black. Irishmen and other non-British Europeans might be the objects of opprobrium, but they were at least not as strange and different as the peoples of Africa and Asia.[42]

Much of the British Empire's wealth, moreover, derived from the slave trade, which was one of the linchpins of the imperial economy before its abolition in 1807. Slave ports such as Bristol and Liverpool became the great commercial centers of the empire, institutions such as the Bank of England fed on the slave trade, and slave-trading merchant families such as the Gladstones rose to prominence and power.[43] Thus by the nineteenth century, British imperialism had helped to consolidate and advance a racial conception of British identity and political destiny.

Institutionally, British politics in the late nineteenth and early twentieth centuries was evolving toward full-fledged parliamentary democracy anchored by strong and disciplined political parties. Imperial politics and racial rule were at the center of this path of development. The last third of the nineteenth century was an uncertain and unsettled period in British politics. Reform acts in 1867 and 1884 quadrupled the size of the British electorate, marking the transition to mass democracy and upending the elite patterns of British party politics.

Under the dominance of the Conservative Party, social reform lay mostly dormant, although it was kept alive by the key figure in the new Conservative majority, Joseph Chamberlain. Hardly a typical Conservative, Chamberlain was a self-made businessman from the Midlands, a former Liberal, and the first major British political leader to support old-age pensions. What united Chamberlain and his followers with other Conservatives was imperialism, support for the maintenance and strengthening of the empire; in fact it was Liberal support for Irish home rule in the 1880s that prompted Chamberlain's defection to the Conservatives. But in the new world of mass politics, empire was not an easy political sell. Despite an impressive victory in the so-called "khaki" election of 1900 during the Boer War, the Conservatives, led by Victorian aristocrats (first the Marquis of Salisbury and then his nephew, Arthur Balfour), could not easily mobilize popular support for traditional imperial aims of glory and commerce.[44]

Empire was not a popular cause among the middle and working classes in Britain. Liberals divided on imperialism. Many opposed imperial ventures for reasons of economic interest or humanitarian concern. Some Liberal imperialists had followed Chamberlain in defecting to the Conservatives; those who remained had little influence in party councils until after the Boer War.[45] The rising Labour party was similarly skeptical about the benefits of imperialism, opposing what it saw as the economic and political exploitation inherent in imperial rule, a position that remained in the party's official pronouncements for more than half a century.[46] But even the Labourites had their imperialists, the Fabians, who saw imperialism as a progressive force, bringing advancement to benighted peoples in remote corners of the world. "We are confronted [in South Africa]," wrote Bernard Shaw in the Fabians' 1900 election manifesto, "with colonies demanding democratic institutions in the midst of native races who must be protected despotically by the Empire or abandoned to slavery and extermination."[47] By and large, however, working-class opinion was concerned with the utility of empire—its capacity to produce jobs at home, as in the industries that stood to benefit from military and naval spending—and not with its ideology.[48]

As Colonial Secretary from 1895, Chamberlain pursued an imperial policy that revolved around what Rudyard Kipling famously called the "white man's burden" to lead the colonial world for both the enrichment of Britain and the betterment of imperial subjects. The notion of an "imperial race," distinguishing white Britons from nonwhite colonial peoples, was central to the politics of imperialism at the turn of the century, and it gave the imperial mission a newly heightened racial character.[49] This policy culminated in the Boer War, which was largely engineered by Chamberlain and Alfred Milner, the British High Commissioner for South Africa and Governor of the Cape Colony. Milner was an echt proconsul, a product of Balliol College, Oxford. Balliol's charismatic master in those years, the classicist Benjamin Jowett, believed that scholarship should serve to instill virtues of character, duty, and leadership in the future rulers of the empire so that they could emulate the philosopher-kings of his beloved Plato. Milner absorbed these lessons well and believed deeply in the civilizing mission of the British Empire and in the superiority of the "British race." Some years later Milner would write,

> [I]t is the British race which built the Empire, and it is the undivided British race which can alone uphold it . . . deeper, stronger, more primordial than these material ties is the bond of common blood, a common language, common history and traditions. But what do I mean by the British race? I mean all the peoples of the United Kingdom and their descendants under the British flag.[50]

But the racial mission of empire was not the only, or even the most prominent, part of Chamberlain's imperial policy. The centerpiece of that policy after the Boer War was tariff reform, a repudiation of Britain's traditional free-trade stance in favor of a system of imperial preferences: free trade within the empire and protection from outside goods, especially a tax on foreign grain. To sell tariff reform to the working class, which traditionally supported free trade because it kept food prices low, Chamberlain linked imperial preference with social reform—old-age and unemployment pensions, labor exchanges, and so forth. Thus it was the politics of imperialism that brought social reform back onto the national agenda, with clear distinctions between the kinds of policies that were appropriate for Britons at home and those for colonial subjects. Social reform appealed to imperialist politicians for a number of reasons. For Chamberlain and others, imperial strength was essential to Britain's continued prosperity and economic dominance, and hence to the welfare of the working class.[51]

The Boer War also exposed a serious domestic problem for a world military power such as Great Britain: an alarming number of army recruits were found physically unfit for service—more than one-third between 1893 and 1902. Moreover, the fact that it took three years (and a quarter of a billion pounds) for the mighty British army to defeat the vastly outnumbered Boers proved profoundly worrying to British policymakers, especially when contrasted with "armed, organized, vigorous, Imperial Germany," Britain's nemesis in the developing tensions among the European powers.[52] After the war the government appointed a Committee on Physical Deterioration to explore the reasons for this state of affairs and to recommend remedies. Although the committee was careful not to place too much weight on racialist notions of hereditary fitness, its report is shot through with worries about the protection and propagation of the race, and it constituted the opening salvo in a campaign for "national efficiency" that included a close brush with eugenics. But most of the committee's conclusions had to do not with "racial" divisions in the British population but with the execrable conditions under which most British working people lived. The national efficiency movement also increased the pressure for social reform of various kinds, ranging from physical fitness schemes (such as the Boy Scouts, founded in 1908 by Robert Baden-Powell, a Boer War hero) to education reform to welfare policies such as free meals for schoolchildren and, significantly, pensions.[53] And so, even though the immediate effect of the Boer War was to put social reform on the back burner while the government prosecuted the war, its larger effect was to make social reform more urgent than it had ever been, in the interests of preserving the "imperial race."

For others, such as the Fabian socialists and Liberal reformers, the proposition was the reverse: social reform was their primary aim, and its potential contribution to the success of the empire was a useful rhetorical and political device to advance its prospects. Like imperialism, social reform constituted a long-standing project that was by itself too weak to sustain a majority coalition. Thus by reframing social reform as an imperial policy, focused on preserving and strengthening the racialized rule of distant nonwhite peoples, social reformers returned to the center of British politics.[54]

A final consideration weighed on the gathering movement for social reform: Britain's Poor Law tradition. Under the New Poor Law of 1834, the purpose of poor relief had not been to prevent poverty but to deter pauperism. Paupers—the idle able-bodied deemed "undeserving" of charitable assistance—were consigned to demoralizing and niggardly poor relief practices such as the notoriously brutal workhouses that were the responsibility of local parishes. This emphasis on pauperism in British social policy was rapidly becoming untenable for a number of reasons. Late nineteenth-century social reformers had called attention to the widespread problem of poverty, whose afflictions spread well beyond the class of paupers. With the Boer War and the Committee on Physical Deterioration, the consequences of poverty became a national problem, linked with the problem of preserving the "imperial race" for the protection of the nation in the international arena. In this context, the local Poor Law approach was exposed as inadequate to meet this grave national need. Finally, the growing political inclusion of the working classes led to demands for social reform that would remove the stigma attached to Poor Law relief and instead offer social benefits as the "birthright of an Englishman, a part of his citizenship, not a deprivation of it," as historian Derek Fraser has put it.[55]

These imperatives combined to make social reform a national question that demanded a cross-class policy solution, on the model of the "soft embrace." Chamberlain ultimately failed to carry his tariff-reform proposal—it galvanized Liberals in defense of free trade and divided Conservatives who were reluctant to raise taxes to pay for social reform after the expense of the Boer War. But by 1908 the Liberals were in power and their government was dominated by a group of liberal imperialists for whom the goals of imperialism and social reform were inseparable—men such as Sir Edward Grey, R. B. Haldane, and Herbert Henry Asquith, a Balliol contemporary of Milner's who became prime minister. This government pursued an ambitious social reform agenda that formed the basis of the British welfare state (along with an expensive naval buildup for the defense of the empire). Again, interests alone are insufficient to account for the formation of the social imperial coalition; neither the bourgeois advocates of imperial preference and military expansion nor the working-class supporters of the welfare state could have mustered the support to prevail in the majoritarian Westminster government; combined, however, they were able to fulfill much of both programs.[56]

The keynote of these policies was the nationalization of the British welfare state. The New Poor Law of 1834 had already begun this trend, standardizing poor relief and vesting authority for certain social policy functions above the traditional parish level, and the national government in the nineteenth century increasingly began to address broader social problems such as public health and factory conditions. Nevertheless, social policy in Britain before 1908 remained overwhelmingly decentralized and locally operated. But under the leadership of David Lloyd George at the Exchequer and Winston Churchill at the Board of Trade, the Liberal government enacted a series of social reforms that undermined the Poor Law system. For Lloyd George, Churchill, and their Liberal colleagues, these steps were part of a larger agenda that linked the achievement of social peace and the extension of central government control over the economy.[57]

The Asquith government thus began to dismantle the Poor Law tradition and to build a centralized national welfare state. In 1908 the government created a system of Labour Exchanges to help the unemployed find work, and passed an Old Age Pensions Act, which created a system of noncontributory, means-tested pensions that were nevertheless reasonably universal in scope and definition. Three years later, the National Insurance Act established compulsory, contributory national unemployment and health insurance.[58] It was in the second of these, the Old Age Pensions Act of 1908, that the issues of the boundaries of national citizenship and the role of the state were most fully played out.

The Old Age Pensions Act established a weekly pension of five shillings for all British subjects age seventy and over who had been resident in the country for at least twenty years and whose annual income was £31 or less (the amount of the pension was phased down for pensioners with incomes between £21 and £31).[59] The Liberals had a commanding majority in the House of Commons (nearly 60 percent of the seats), and so they could adopt the bill without any serious obstacles. The Conservatives, the major opposition party, were reluctant to oppose the bill outright lest it recall for voters their own rather embarrassing failure to embrace social reform in the wake of the Boer War (vindicating Chamberlain's long-time advocacy). Instead, Conservative MPs used the parliamentary debates to expose what they saw as the act's fundamental flaw, its creation of social rights that potentially superseded the social control inherent in the Poor Law.

The Old Age Pensions Act sounded the death knell for the Poor Law. Pensions, Lloyd George made clear in his opening speech on the bill in the Commons, were to be a reward to workers for service to the state, and the act created a category of rights that workers could claim directly against the state rather than a set of maneuvers by which the state could enforce some kind of moral order on the lower classes. Conservatives recognized the act's nationalizing potential and offered an amendment to allow local Poor Law authorities to set pension rates, to which Asquith answered,

[T]he Bill [gives] a statutory right . . . to the enjoyment of a pension, and one of the primary objects of the Bill [is] to take away the discretionary and inquisitorial powers exercised by the outdoor relief committee of boards of guardians. If the Amendment were adopted the applicant would be in the same position as a candidate for outdoor relief, and the whole object of the Bill would be destroyed.

The bill did carry over certain Poor Law distinctions, particularly by excluding criminals and recipients of poor relief from pensions, so that the government could maintain, as Haldane did, that pensions were to be restricted to the "deserving" poor:

The Bill does not profess to introduce any new principle. It recognises that since the days of Queen Elizabeth, and perhaps earlier, there has been as part of the accepted law of the land an obligation to assist in the provision for the necessitous. This is the principle of the British Poor Law. That principle is embodied in the system which exists now and is recognised in the policy of this Bill as an old principle which we desire to carry out and adapt to modern circumstances.

But this argument fooled no one. These exclusions were merely an accounting maneuver, keeping aged paupers off the pension rolls and on the relief rolls, where they received approximately the same amount, and they lapsed quietly and unlamented two years later. The act created (or began to assemble) a *national* welfare state on the ruins of the Poor Law system and constructed direct, unmediated links between the British state and British citizens—however they were to be defined.[60]

That definition of British citizenship was itself in dispute, particularly in a debate over whether or not pensioners would have to be physically resident in the United Kingdom (meaning England, Scotland, and Wales) to receive a pension. The issue was framed in ominously racial terms. What about the case, asked Earl Winterton, "of the alien who resided in this country for twenty years. He was, perhaps, not a very desirable citizen, but he might manage to keep within the clauses of the Bill as regarded pensions, and as soon as he received a pension at the age of seventy he might leave the country and go back to Poland." In a particularly revealing comment, he "most strongly disapproved of pensions being given to such men as Polish Jews coming to England at the age of fifty and leaving at the age of seventy."[61]

Here Winterton articulated precisely the question of the boundaries of membership and territory that were to define the modern British state— whether citizenship was constituted by residence or by ties of blood, as he suggested in his reference to Jews. (Jews were just then at the center of British immigration debates and had been the particular targets of the Aliens Act of 1905, which gave the state the power to exclude would-be immigrants who were likely to become public charges and to deport aliens who went on poor relief within a year of their arrival.)[62] Conservatives saw a chance to expose the act's nationalizing logic. Conservative member John Rawlinson stated the government's dilemma quite precisely:

> [D]id [the government] mean the Bill to be . . . merely an extension of the present system of outdoor relief? If that was so, then residence within the United Kingdom was clearly a condition precedent to its receipt. . . . If that was not the intention of the Government, they should make it perfectly clear that they meant this sum of money to be payable even in the case of the Polish Jew.

With his predicament thus starkly framed, Lloyd George equivocated artfully, saying that he believed an amendment requiring residency unnecessary because the bill could already be held to do so, thus sidestepping the sensitive racial question embedded in it. The amendment was defeated by a vote of more than three to one, but the debate exposed the delicate balance that the emerging British welfare state had to manage: how to link Britons together under a national umbrella of protective rights while excluding suspect others.[63] Although the "others" contemplated were not the imperial subjects of Asia and Africa, this debate directly foreshadowed—and in fact helped to construct—the challenges that the British welfare state would face when these subjects began coming to Britain half a century hence not as subjects of an empire but as citizens of a commonwealth.

Three years later, the Parliament passed the National Insurance Act, which consisted of two parts, covering health and unemployment. These enactments consolidated the nationalization trend begun in 1908, establishing national, compulsory, contributory benefits for most of the population and finally putting the Poor Law to rest. Health insurance covered all employed workers, while unemployment insurance was initially restricted to workers in industries that were prone to cyclical unemployment, but with almost no conditions on receipt of benefits.[64] Building on the precedent of the 1908 act, these policies did not so much supersede the Poor Law as bypass it altogether, giving those who were out of work because of sickness or layoffs a direct claim on benefits from the central government. In introducing the health insurance section of the bill, Lloyd George made this purpose explicit, presenting the bill as a means for reducing pauperism.[65] Although it did not achieve the notoriety of the health insurance bill (largely because it generated less intense controversy), the unemployment insurance bill in particular was a key step in the nationalization of the British welfare state. Largely the work of William Beveridge, then a civil servant at the Board of Trade and later the architect of Britain's post–World War II welfare state, unemployment insurance was a major breakthrough for British national policy. "For the average English workman," historian Bentley Gilbert has observed, "who did not pay income tax, who stayed off the poor law, who did not serve in the army, who rarely used the post office, His Majesty's Government was a far-off, Olympian thing as unconcerned with his affairs as he was with affairs of State. Now, finally, visibly, and intimately, the government was truly his servant."[66]

Together, these policies took an important step toward centralizing the British welfare state, creating direct and unmediated links between nearly all workers in Britain (and their families) and the state by providing certain benefits almost unconditionally. By creating these centralized, national social rights, these policies constituted an important mechanism of social solidarity, underpinned as they were by a broad, cross-class coalition that brought together middle- and working-class concerns. Such national solidarity, constructed by social policies aimed partly at unifying an "imperial race," served as a counterweight against the class warfare that seemed to be tearing continental Europe apart. British social imperialists—from the Tory imperialist Milner to the Fabian socialists—believed that the amelioration of working-class conditions was necessary to forestall "divisive" socialism that would foment class conflict and undermine the empire. Like American welfare policies, then, the coalition behind these policies was built on a foundation of racial rule that served to unify Britons across classes in favor of moderate social reform. But unlike American race politics, which differentiated Americans from each other along internal, institutionally and politically constructed racial lines, British race politics constructed a national racial community against others abroad. British policymakers thus identified a national interest in welfare policy that began to unify British citizens in a network of social solidarity through the welfare state and the mechanisms of social citizenship. As Ann Orloff and Theda Skocpol have noted, Britain's political institutions—majoritarian parliamentary government system, strong bureaucracy, weak courts—better enabled it to translate social reform ideas into centralized policy than the fragmented American state; in the imperial context, these policies took on an inescapable racial valence.[67]

France

In France, as in Britain, the politics of race was primarily a matter of the distinction between the colonies and the metropole. And as in Britain, imperialism and social reform mingled in French politics in the late nineteenth and early twentieth centuries, suggesting at least the possibility of a similar cross-class social-imperial coalition that might have linked race-based imperial rule with domestic social solidarity through welfare policies. In fact, some social reformers in France explicitly invoked the importance of racial distinctions and imperial rule in support of such universalistic policies.[68] But political differences between France and Britain—in both the character of race politics and the structure of national political institutions—prevented this coalition from forming, resulting in a more decentralized welfare state rooted more directly in civil society than Britain's. Thus, unlike in Britain, race politics in France did not provide the impetus to overcome the indirect structures of social provision that had developed in the nineteenth century.

Like its British precursor, however, French imperialism was deeply rooted in notions of racial difference and superiority. At the center of the French imperial project was France's "civilizing mission" ("la mission civilisatrice") toward its colonies and, in fact, toward the rest of the "uncivilized" world. This view of the French imperial project was clearly built on the same sort of racial hierarchies that underlay British imperialism and American segregation and divided citizenship, which emphasized the backwardness of non-European peoples. In his argument for imperial expansion, Jules Ferry, France's leading late-nineteenth-century imperialist, stressed the humanitarian element of France's imperial project. The "superior races" of the West, he argued, had not only the right but also the duty to mobilize their advanced technical, scientific, and moral developments on behalf of the "inferior races" who were not yet on the road to progress. Even French opponents of imperialism tended to share Ferry's view of the French place in the racial order.[69]

But French racialism was situated in a very different ideological and political context than its American and British counterparts. Rather than coexisting with, or even helping to define, a liberal tradition, French imperial notions of racial difference were aligned, beginning in the late nineteenth century, with a universalizing republican tradition that sought to elide differences and construct a common national political culture. This had not always been so of French imperialism, however. Early French imperialism, including the conquest of Algeria in the 1830s, was associated with the enemies of republicanism—the aristocracy, the military, and the church.[70] But under the Third Republic, Republican leaders discovered the utility of imperialism as a means of political legitimation, particularly in boosting France's international prestige and also in advancing the notion that the principles of French republicanism were truly universal.

Thus, leaders of the Third Republic, from Ferry to the socialist proconsul and cabinet minister Albert Sarraut, developed a republican-imperial synthesis that linked the idea of republican citizenship, derived from the Jacobin strand of France's Revolutionary heritage, to the notion of France's international mission to rule over the unfortunate benighted masses of Africa and Asia and thereby boost the glory of *la nation française*. There remained a tension, however, between the imperial idea of racial superiority and the republican idea of universalism that gave the French imperial-republican synthesis a profound ambiguity. On the one hand, the idea of national social solidarity was fundamental to French republicanism—the French nation as an interconnected body of citizens undivided by partial or particular loyalties, such as religion or race, that might divide them from one another. This vision would seem to extend to the colonies as well as to metropolitan France itself, and in the mature version of republican imperialism this embrace of membership across boundaries was explicit, particularly in the idea of "Greater France" ("la plus grande France"), a boundaryless political and geographic entity that would encompass "a hundred million Frenchmen" across the empire. This was not an idle boast, at least numerically speaking. In the early twentieth century, the population of France proper hovered under 40 million, while the population of France's overseas possessions totaled approximately 50 million. This notion, moreover, had a long pedigree. An 1833 law granted citizenship to all freemen in the colonies (creating a theoretical explosion of citizenship when slavery was abolished in 1848), and Algeria, France's oldest overseas possession, was actually declared French territory in 1848 and later divided into three departments, subject to French laws rather than indirect colonial rule.[71]

On the other hand, the Third Republic was also the high point of a particularistic, ethnocultural notion of French national identity, which had several manifestations in turn-of-the-century French politics. Colonial subjects overseas were not the only targets of the *mission civilisatrice*. Under the Third Republic, France was undergoing a process of internal assimilation of regional and linguistic minorities who were commonly compared in official discourse to racially distinct Africans and other external colonial subjects; the historian Eugen Weber even goes so far as to suggest that "the famous hexagon can itself be seen as a colonial empire shaped over centuries."[72] French national and colonial politics thus made more of internal, racially constructed differences and consequently less of cross-border differences than British politics and in this respect found itself somewhere in between the British model (confronting the "other" without) and the American model (facing the "other" within, including, prominently, Jews).[73] This was also a period of restrictive immigration and nationality laws, which heightened distinctions between French citizens and outsiders in metropolitan France.[74]

Similarly, in the colonies, the reality of assimilation was considerably more limited than the rhetoric of the republican-imperial synthesis. The policy of assimilation itself was a matter of intense political debate for decades, and even at its high-water mark, colonial subjects were denied political rights while still being counted as members of the French national "family," linked to the metropole more by "vassalage" (*vassalité*) than by solidarity, according to Sarraut, one of the major theorists and practitioners of French republican imperialism.[75] "Here we have the core contradiction of Greater France," writes historian Gary Wilder:

> Natives were repeatedly counted among the proverbial 100 million members of this new French nation. They were identified as belonging to the "national family." But despite references to "black and yellow brothers," the implied relationship was one of paternity not fraternity. Ultimately, colonized members of "greater France" remained protégés under French tutelage: infantilized targets of a beneficent civilizing project.[76]

Finally and most ominously, French racialism and romanticism mingled in an evolving ideology of French nationalism that insisted on the unified organic, biological (and sometimes Catholic) roots of French identity, an ideology that has cast a long shadow over French intellectual and political life in the twentieth century, culminating in Vichy. Although explicitly antirepublican in its outlook, often violently so, this tendency nevertheless shared the Jacobin, republican aversion to pluralism. More recently it has resurfaced as neorepublicanism in French political discourse, shorn of its uglier tendencies but still a potent force in French political and intellectual life.[77]

Partly as a consequence of this ambiguity in the relationship among imperialism, republicanism, and national identity, French social imperialism took on a rather different cast than its British counterpart. French social imperialists tended to be opponents (or at least skeptics) of democracy. In the early years of the Third Republic, after France's defeat by Prussia and the rise and violent fall of the Paris Commune, the survival of democracy was far from certain. In a coup d'état on 16 May 1877, the reactionary president Marshall Maurice de MacMahon dissolved the republican-dominated National Assembly. Even though this crisis was resolved in favor of the republic (republicans won more than three-fifths of the seats in the new Chamber, and MacMahon resigned), monarchism remained a potent force in French politics. It was antidemocratic politicians and intellectuals such as Maurice Barrès, Léon Daudet, and Charles Maurras, the founder of the reactionary Comité de l'Action Française, who most directly advocated links between social reform and racially inflected notions of national unity. Moreover, Maurras and others supported decentralized social policy, which would place power in the hands of local elites and corporate bodies, reminiscent of feudalism, rather than the state. Other, more respectable, conservative social reformers shared this corporatist orientation and were also skeptical of the republican assimilationist approach to the colonies, often on explicitly racial grounds. At the same time, French socialists as well as social reformers such as the Radical Republican Georges Clemenceau were reluctant to embrace imperialism, not least because they worried that colonial adventures would hinder reform at home. Thus French politics struggled with both internal diversity and the possibility of external association, making the formation of a racially constructed, cross-class coalition for social reform unlikely and, by the same token, rendering social reform problematic as a vehicle for pursuing national unity.[78]

The structure of French political institutions was a further barrier to the construction of a stable coalition for national unity through social reform. The imperative of the "soft embrace" held as much sway in France as elsewhere. Third Republic political leaders sought equally to attract new voters, to ensure labor peace and forestall socialism, and above all to consolidate the growing power of what Republican leader Léon Gambetta called the "new social strata" (les nouvelles couches sociales)—the rising bourgeoisie of the professions and the civil service.[79] The Third Republic was dominated by a parliament with neither a strong executive nor a robust party system, so that despite mass suffrage, the representation of social interests beyond the republican bourgeoisie was limited. As Stanley Hoffmann puts it, "political life came close to the model of a pure game of parliamentary politics" that defended France's "stalemate society," and under these institutional conditions blocking and delaying proved particularly easy.[80] Thus even when a broad coalition that included the more moderate representatives of labor came to power behind René Waldeck-Rousseau in 1899, in defense of the republic against the anti-Dreyfusards, it proved to be short-lived and disinclined to move toward serious national social reform.[81] Thus to the extent that the raw materials existed for a coalition in favor of social reform as an agent of national social solidarity in response to the imperatives of racial rule, French political institutions were ill equipped to sustain such a coalition.

As a consequence, social reform in France was enacted not by broad, cross-class coalitions that linked the fates of middle- and working-class citizens but by an alliance principally between the business interests and the state, pointedly excluding labor. French politics lacked a strong imperative that could link French citizens together under a national welfare state. Consequently, universal welfare policies were slow to develop, and neither imperial politics nor the imperatives of racial exclusion could provide sufficient force to overcome political disagreements rooted in class divisions, despite strong republican arguments for national solidarity through social security.[82] Moreover, the push toward social solidarity did not become linked to national-level, centralized policies, which threatened to provide a platform for the broad inclusion of colonial "citizens" in social provision. This was a particular challenge in the wake of World War I, in which nearly one million colonial natives fought for France and more than 200,000 died. After the war, the deployment of the Force Noire in the Rhineland and the Ruhr enabled France to decrease its national service requirement for metropolitan French citizens to eighteen months, while colonials were required to serve three years.[83] French political leaders recognized the strong claims on French society that this service created, but were unwilling to extend social rights on this basis. This pattern contrasts strongly with the United States, where military pensions for Civil War veterans, in which African Americans were generally included on fair and equal terms, formed the basis for a proto-welfare state in the late nineteenth century.[84] Rather, on both the Right and the Left, the politics of social reform tended toward decentralization—for Republicans because they hoped to gain votes by contrast with the extreme centralization of the Second Empire, and for conservatives precisely because of the contrast with the historically centralizing tendencies of the republic.[85]

Although central to French imperial politics, race was in the end not decisive in structuring social politics at the critical moment of French welfare state building; both ambiguities in French racial ideology and the structure of French political institutions contributed to this result. The consequence of these forces for French social reform was that welfare policies developed not through the construction of national state-led policies but by the accretion of decentralized, corporatist welfare schemes that were neither state-administered nor state-financed. These policies had their roots in the nineteenth-century flourishing of *mutualité,* the tradition of mutual societies organized around occupational, fraternal, or other local attachments—an arrangement that invited homogeneity, insularity, and exclusivity among distinct groups. A series of French welfare policies took this form, from workmen's compensation to old-age pensions to family allowances.[86] Unlike Britain, France did not create centralized, state-led welfare before World War II, although not for lack of trying—a serious attempt to create national, compulsory, contributory old-age pensions failed in 1910. When national social insurance did pass in 1930, followed by family allowances in 1932, they left in place the *mutualité*-based structure of earlier welfare policies, so that attachments to the French welfare state remained mediated by civil-society attachments and contributed only weakly, if at all, to the construction of social solidarity before World War II.

CONCLUSIONS

Structures of racial rule, along with national ideas about race and national policy-making institutions, in the United States, Great Britain, and France contributed to the construction of differently configured welfare states in which citizens and culturally defined groups of citizens were connected to the state through different institutional mechanisms. Racial rule in the

United States was directed primarily at minorities at home rather than colonial subjects beyond home borders. The United States also had a deep tradition of ascriptive race-consciousness that challenged the liberal presumptions of universal (and, therefore, color-blind) citizenship. And finally, fragmented political institutions gave particular leverage to the most race-conscious actors in national politics and allowed them to engineer welfare policy to protect their interests. Race, in short, limited the possibilities for building a broad, cross-class coalition for social provision, resulting in a fragmented welfare state that did little to address inequalities created by the labor market. British welfare state institutions were similarly the product of a coalition that united whites across class to provide racially exclusionary social benefits, although these similarly drawn coalitions embraced very different prescriptions for social reform. In Britain, external rather than internal patterns of racial rule, race-conscious imperial politics, and highly centralized majoritarian political institutions produced a more comprehensive national welfare state. In France, both ideological ambivalence about the racial character of imperialism and the fragmented polity of the Fourth Republic blocked the formation of a strong cross-class coalition, delaying and limiting the evolution of the French welfare state. Thus the American and British welfare states were built more clearly on exclusionary race-conscious ground, while the French welfare system seemed to be more color-blind, if ambiguously so; at the very least, the French welfare state was not structurally committed to the exclusion of racially designated outsiders. Only Britain, however, moved toward the creation of a unified and centralized welfare state; the American and French systems of social provision remained fragmented and decentralized.

It was primarily in the United States that these early welfare state developments had immediate and direct implications for racial minorities—African Americans—who were widely excluded from social benefits in the wake of the New Deal through deliberately fragmented institutions that bore out the American welfare state's race-conscious origins. But each system created a set of institutional terms by which groups could form attachments to the welfare state and acquire rights to social provision, and these institutional patterns set in motion a number of processes that would structure the later incorporation of racial minorities into welfare systems. These subsequent paths of incorporation, moreover, did not necessarily bear out the ideologies of race consciousness or color blindness that seemed to be embedded in national welfare states. In addition to enduring welfare state institutions themselves, these moments of welfare-state formation helped to construct patterns of group-state linkage that would help to form the basis of racially constructed identities and forms of group mobilization. These institutional patterns, moreover, would help to define and redefine cultural understandings of race and its political significance.

These institutions were far from innocent of the historical legacies of racial rule that structured the politics of their creation, and none of these countries would have to wait long to see how these policy systems would respond to the challenge of increasingly multiracial societies. After World War II, structures of racial rule came under direct challenge in each of these countries, resulting in large-scale migrations of nonwhites—from rural South to urban North in the United States and from colonies to metropole in Britain and France—that dramatically changed the racial configuration of each. In each case these new migrants were presumptive citizens nominally entitled to available social rights, but they entered welfare states that were configured differently as a result of prior developments. In each country the changing racial complexion of society placed strains on the welfare state, and each country responded differently in incorporating racial minorities into national structures of social provision. The fate of postwar racial minorities in these welfare states was a function not simply of levels of racial hostility or of national ideological or cultural approaches to racial difference but also, if not primarily, of the welfare state institutions inherited from earlier developments.

Chapter Three

THE ROOTS OF WELFARE
INCORPORATION

On the eve of World War II, the conjunction of racial rule and the politics of social reform had produced a range of cultural and institutional approaches to the challenges of the welfare state. These new national configurations of welfare policy, forged in the race-laden politics of nation- and state-building efforts in the early part of the century, seemed to set the United States, Great Britain, and France on distinctive paths toward patterns of racial incorporation (or non-incorporation, as the case may be). In particular, the formation of race-based coalitions for social reform in the United States and Britain and the nonformation of such a coalition in France seemed to be linked with similar cultural and ideological models for race policy—converging, broadly speaking, on race consciousness in the United States and Britain and emergent color blindness in France.

But in the new racial environment of the late twentieth century, the encounters between racial minorities and the welfare state have produced results that do not conform squarely to the race policy models that emerged in the early part of the twentieth century and have, for the most part, persisted ever since. Despite similar race-conscious, multicultural approaches to race policy, Britain and the United States diverged dramatically in their capacity to incorporate racial minorities into social benefits. While Britain has achieved fairly high levels of inclusion for immigrants from the so-called New Commonwealth and their descendants into most welfare state benefits, African Americans in particular, but other minorities as well, have long been relegated to meager and politically weak benefits in the American welfare system. Within the American welfare state, moreover, different programs have developed differing capacities to incorporate minorities—ranging from quite strong for social insurance programs to considerably weaker for public assistance. France, by contrast, has achieved a moderate level of racial incorporation in welfare benefits.

The explanation for these puzzling paths lies in the institutional mechanisms by which the welfare state mobilized and enacted these cultural models of race, producing policies that connected racially defined groups to the welfare state in a variety of ways. In this chapter I begin to explore how welfare state institutions, constructed in racially charged political contexts early in the twentieth century, shaped the implementation of social provision policies with widely varying and often unexpected racial consequences. I begin by suggesting that the institutional structure and organization of the welfare state are crucial for shaping patterns of racial incorporation because they determine how citizens (and, by extension, groups of citizens) come to be linked to the state. Two elements of welfare state structure are especially important: the nature of the arrangements connecting the welfare state, the labor market, and citizens and families (the welfare state regime); and the degree of centralization in welfare policy-making and administration.

A survey of both the institutional and ideological structure of the early-twentieth-century American welfare state follows, showing how an ambivalent race conscious vision was embedded in a welfare state that was strictly divided according to labor-market access, highly fragmented, and partially decentralized. Parallel overviews of the British and French welfare states reveal different configurations of familiar institutional and ideological elements—in Britain, race consciousness (albeit in a somewhat different variant) embedded in a labor-market-sensitive but centralized and unitary welfare state; in France, an increasingly centralized welfare state, heavily tilted toward social insurance for workers, that has struggled to maintain its color-blind orientation. These detailed pictures of welfare state configurations provide the grounding for the following chapters, which chronicle the post–World War II transformations of both welfare states and racial contexts and then show how racial ideas and welfare institutions interacted in the postwar era to produce divergent patterns and paths of racial incorporation.

WELFARE INSTITUTIONS AND MINORITY INCORPORATION

The key question that emerges from the comparative history of welfare-state building is how the structure of welfare state policies has shaped the incorporation of racial minorities by facilitating the broad extension of social rights and, secondarily, by shaping the politics of welfare reform. These influences depend on the mechanisms by which individuals are attached to the welfare state—whether by virtue simply of citizenship or residence; through the labor market; or through occupational or other group affiliation. These mechanisms usually operate at the individual (or family) level; that is, it is *individuals* who must be judged eligible to receive old-age pensions, for example, or unemployment compensation, or family allowances. But these individual attachments cumulate into group attachments, and if these individual-level means of inclusion in social provision are not evenly distributed across racial or ethnic groups, the structure of the welfare state can work against broad incorporation, leaving minorities systematically on the outside looking in and reinforcing group inequalities.

Welfare states vary dramatically in their mechanisms of attachment and consequently in the patterns of inclusion and exclusion that they foster. Moreover they tend to cluster around a limited number of configurations of such mechanisms, or welfare regimes, each with its own policy characteristics and distinctive mode of politics.[1] None of these three welfare states fits into the social democratic category, the most universal of the welfare regimes; all three, rather, are examples of more limited regimes, in which access to social provision is conditional on a different set of factors.

The United States and Britain are both variants of liberal welfare states, which have relatively low levels of spending and benefits and emphasize need-based (or means-tested) assistance as residual benefits for those who cannot support themselves in the labor market. Politically, these welfare systems generally have weaker public support than in other regimes, making anti-welfare appeals fertile ground for conservative politicians, particularly in the post-1960s era of the neoliberal turn. This political pattern potentially creates an opening for racialized resentment to inflect the politics of welfare, making the prospects for racial incorporation into social provision highly uncertain and dependent on the more particular configurations of politics in individual welfare states.[2]

France's welfare state, on the other hand, is a version of what is variously called the conservative, corporatist, continental, Christian Democratic, or (breaking the alliterative pattern) Bismarckian welfare regime (although France fits uneasily in the category because over time it has added universal and, increasingly, means-tested programs to its income- and employment-linked social insurance core). These systems generally have higher levels of spending, which is concentrated in contributory social insurance programs such as pensions, unemployment benefits, and family allowances, to the exclusion of both means-tested cash and in-kind benefits and social services. They also tend to inhibit job growth by raising labor costs through the heavy imposition of payroll taxes on employers and to reinforce status distinctions within countries (hence the designation as conservative, even though they lean toward generosity), both through the common reliance on specialized funds for particular occupational or other groups and through the exceedingly strong link between work and benefits. Consequently, these welfare systems (as well as the labor markets to which they are linked) often construct rigid barriers between "insiders" and "outsiders" that pose particular challenges for racial and ethnic minorities whose position in the political economy may be rather precarious. Politically these systems engender strong support for the welfare state, which is furthered through more-or-less corporatist patterns of decision-making in which stakeholder organizations such as labor, employers, or occupational groups play an important policy-making role. The state's role in such welfare systems may thus be rather circumscribed, depending (as in liberal regimes) on the particular political configurations underlying welfare politics and policy-making.[3]

Welfare regimes are certainly important factors in shaping racial incorporation in social provision; to the extent, for example, that racial minorities suffer from lower levels of labor force participation and different patterns of employment, different welfare regimes will produce varying levels of incorporation. These broad institutional clusters, however, do not have uniform consequences for racial incorporation, just as they do not account for systematic differences in the way welfare states grant social citizenship to women.[4] Similarly, these welfare regimes are not sufficient to explain variations in racial incorporation for several reasons. Racial incorporation in welfare states depends not only on the general means of connecting citizens to the state but also on the state's institutional capacity to administer benefits fairly across groups. Ideological and cultural frames, moreover—the presumptions of color blindness or race consciousness that underlie policies—can also contribute to a welfare state's propensity to address racial inequalities through social incorporation.

An important structural factor affecting the welfare state's capacity to regulate group access and shape patterns of group-state linkage is the degree of centralization in the policy-making and administrative structures of the welfare state—the extent to which local politicians and administrators can control the flow of benefits, whether by setting benefit levels and eligibility rules or by exercising discretionary authority.[5] The institutional logic of the national, or centralized, welfare state is more conducive to broad inclusion than the parochial, or decentralized, welfare state. Centralized welfare systems are more likely to rely on universal rules and procedures and to exercise strict administrative control that reduces opportunities for discrimination on the part of front-line welfare workers. Central governments, especially in large, complex, and pluralistic modern states, are less likely to be "captured" by a particular racial group that might more easily achieve political dominance in a small local government. Consequently, central governments are more likely to insist on racially neutral and fair administration as being in the national interest.[6]

Decentralized systems, in which operational control of welfare policies is devolved to lower-level officials, are more likely to use their discretionary power to exclude minorities. Small political units are often more prone than larger ones to be captured by local majorities at the expense of minorities, and local officials and political elites are more likely to feel threatened by concentrated minority populations, and hence exclusion will be most likely where racial minorities are most likely to live. Spreading welfare policy authority across multiple jurisdictions can produce competition to keep taxes and benefits low and spark competition among groups for benefits. Finally, the fragmentation that often accompanies decentralized policy-making encourages a politics of blame-shifting among levels of government that can work against minority incorporation.[7]

These institutional structures of welfare states also interact with their ideological and cultural settings to produce different paths of incorporation. Two alternative conceptual models of race policy emerged from the historical legacies of racial rule in the United States, Great Britain, and France: one that accepts racial and ethnic difference as legitimate elements of society and aims to promote coexistence and manage conflict, and another that emphasizes national unity over difference and pursues assimilation. But these policy models have uncertain consequences. On the one hand, multicultural strategies invite discrimination and exclusion by categorizing social groups by race, ethnicity, or other cultural attributes. On the other hand, they can frame otherwise hidden inequalities and thereby permit or leverage special directed action on behalf of disfavored groups. Similarly, assimilationist strategies can discourage racial division by applying universalistic rules, but they can also conceal inequities behind a color-blind façade and inhibit racial and ethnic mobilization that might enhance prospects for incorporation.[8]

The history of the American welfare state suggests that institutions, which may or may not have been part of an explicit race-policy consensus, can profoundly affect the working out of color-blind or race-conscious intentions and understandings. Decentralization of policy-making and administration, for example, has exposed minorities to discrimination and exclusion in some programs, while centralization and national administration have enhanced incorporation in others. Contributory social insurance policies, which allocate benefits on the basis of social rights, are more likely to be administered fairly and color-blindly across groups, potentially overcoming the effects of race-conscious presumptions, while discretionary, need-based relief policies may be more likely to invoke racial classifications and reinforce race consciousness.[9] The American case in particular—in which policy efforts aimed at transforming the American racial structure have had variable results in a common cultural setting— thus highlights the indeterminacy of ideologically framed policy models for shaping paths of incorporation and suggests that political processes intervene between policy frameworks and incorporation. In the comparative context as well it is not simply national commitments to color blindness or race consciousness that are at issue. Rather, possibilities for racial incorporation depend as well on how these commitments are put into practice in concrete historical and institutional settings. Similarly, broad-brush institutional portraits of welfare states (such as Esping-Andersen's welfare regimes) tend to obscure the concrete racial dimension of welfare incorporation. Welfare state institutions do not simply trump either national cultural predispositions about race and race policy or the political leverage that minority groups can achieve through mobilization and organization. Rather, the encounter between racial minorities and the welfare state will be shaped by the interaction among these factors. By allocating power, institutions can constrain and channel the claims and demands of political actors and groups.

THE AMERICAN WELFARE STATE: FRAGMENTED LIBERALISM

"From the Negro's point of view," Charles H. Houston of the National Association for the Advancement of Colored People (NAACP) told the Senate Finance Committee in February 1935, the Social Security Act "looks like a sieve with the holes just big enough for the majority of Negroes to fall through."[10] In other words, Houston feared, the fledgling American national welfare state would not allow African Americans to share in the expansion of the social rights of American citizenship. Houston objected to the legislation for three broad reasons. First, he lamented that the bill's institutional framework left African Americans vulnerable. It left too much power in the hands of states at the expense of the national government and was weighted too heavily toward contributory programs for workers at the expense of more broadly inclusive policies of social provision.

Second, he worried that the bill would feed the racism that already crushed African Americans' economic and political opportunities. "There are plenty of decent people down South," he said, "but we also know from experience, in the Scotsboro case and Judge Wharton, for example, that it is the same as political suicide to take an advanced stand on racial issues in many cases." He described the racism embedded in federal public works projects such as the Tennessee Valley Authority as well as in the labor market and American society in general. "We have had the most disgusting experiences in the matter of public health," he told the senators. "If you want to know how much handicap the Negro citizen suffers, the only thing you have got to do is to try to get a job, travel, or else get sick." Across many spheres, he pointed out, the bill did little or nothing to help African Americans overcome the pernicious effects of racial distinctions. Several times he expressed "a special plea that guaranties of no discrimination be written into the bill." Earlier, George E. Haynes of the National Council of Churches had detailed for the House Ways and Means Committee the drastic imbalances in spending on whites and blacks in existing federal assistance programs, particularly in vocational education under the Smith-Hughes Act and agricultural extension work under the Smith Lever Act. The principal exception to this pattern, Haynes had pointed out, was land-grant colleges, in which federal funding (although not state funding) for black and white institutions was basically proportional to the population balance throughout the South. Unlike other federal grant legislation, however, the Morrill Act, which governed land-grant colleges, had been amended in 1890 to prohibit discrimination in the allocation of federal funds.[11]

Finally, Houston lamented the limits that the bill imposed on African American aspirations for full citizenship in the form of robust links between racially defined minority groups and the state. The Social Security Act, he feared, would do little to help African Americans gain a foothold in the structure of American politics or to offer them much leverage to advance legitimate claims on the new national welfare state. "Our flat position is we do not want to deprive the white citizens of anything but we simply want to have all citizens share in the benefits under the law. . . . We Negroes are United States citizens who have never failed to shoulder our full share of the national burden; if we have not paid you more money in taxes, it is because you have denied us equal opportunity to work."[12]

Houston's discussion offers a remarkably cogent and prescient account of the American welfare state in the immediate aftermath of the Social Security Act, particularly of its implications for African Americans and other racial minorities. (It is worth noting that Houston's testimony came *before* Congress had acted to restrict black access to welfare policies by limiting eligibility and federal oversight; he seems to have taken it for granted that it would do so.) His three categories of objection to the act, in fact, provide an ideal frame in which to set the burgeoning American welfare state to track its consequences for the incorporation of racial minorities over the subsequent generations. Each of Houston's points—about institutions, ideological repertoires, and patterns of group-state linkage—comprises an essential part of the context in which the politics of welfare incorporation would play itself out over the course of the twentieth century.

Initially embedded in a broad economic security program that emphasized jobs for those who could work and relief for those who couldn't, the act complemented programs such as the Works Progress Administration, which employed millions of people (and generally included African Americans on a reasonably fair basis), and the National Labor Relations (Wagner) and Fair Labor Standards Acts, which extended labor rights and sought to secure a reasonable standard of living for workers and their families. But the jobs component of the New Deal withered in the late

1930s and 1940s, leaving the Social Security Act as the key structural template of the new American welfare state.[13]

Institutionally, the Social Security Act constituted a critically important set of choices about how the American welfare state would be organized. In general terms, the welfare system that emerged from the New Deal embodied two distinct models of social provision. On one side were social insurance policies, which offered workers protection against certain predictable risks such as old age and unemployment. These protections were embodied principally in Old-Age Insurance and Unemployment Insurance, which promised benefits to workers in industrial and commercial jobs out of funds that pooled contributions from workers and their employers. Over thirty years, the categories of risk covered by social insurance expanded to include the surviving spouses and children of deceased workers (1939), disability (1956), and health (Medicare, created in 1965). These social insurance programs shared a number of important institutional characteristics, above all their contributory structure, under which the right to benefits depended on contributions made either by individual workers or by employers on their behalf. In addition, social insurance programs were by and large national programs whose eligibility rules and benefit structures were determined at the national level and whose administration was centralized.[14] Thus these programs established strong claims for workers and their families on the national state.

On the other institutional side of the American welfare state were public assistance programs, means-tested benefits for the needy aged, blind, and families with dependent children. These policies were intended for those not covered by social insurance and who consequently did not acquire benefit rights through work. Public assistance programs, above all Aid to Dependent Children (after 1962 Aid to Families with Dependent Children, replaced in 1996 by Temporary Assistance to Needy Families), were not only noncontributory—meaning that benefits could not be claimed as rights based on prior contributions—but also decentralized. Partly funded by the federal government, they nevertheless delegated almost all policy and administrative control to state and even local authorities, so that eligibility rules and benefits levels were matters of local decision. The parochialism of American public assistance policies was a direct legacy of the British Poor Law tradition, which lodged responsibility for poor relief squarely on the heads of local officials and which depended on the distinction between the deserving poor and undeserving paupers and on the principle of "less eligibility," which meant deliberately making relief less attractive and more shameful than even the lowest-status work. As in newly industrializing England, when local parish officials tried to subvert the Poor Laws by increasing poor rates only to find the problem of pauperism in the countryside growing rather than shrinking, this arrangement created a dilemma between the impulse toward charity and generosity and the fear of encouraging undesirable behavior ("idleness") by undesirable people, who then almost by definition remain undesirable. The Social Security Act did impose some order and regularity on the patchwork of state and local relief policies that it replaced—chief among them being mothers' pensions—but the fundamental institutional characteristics of Poor Law parochialism remained intact: means-testing, morals-testing, and local administration. This picture of institutional distinction between national social insurance and parochial public assistance does not fully describe the multi-tiered nuances of the American welfare state, in which many contemporary programs do not fit neatly into either of these categories. Nevertheless, it does capture an essential structural feature of American social policy, which had from its origins a built-in racial character, since it sorted—not accidentally—white and black Americans largely into different categories of social provision.[15]

Ideologically and culturally, the American welfare state that emerged from the New Deal was steeped in the tension between color-blind liberalism and ascriptive racialism that has long defined the American political tradition. On its face, the Social Security Act was silent about race. Although it did not prohibit racial discrimination explicitly, as Houston and others advocated, neither did it explicitly make racial distinctions among its target populations, as other countries did in their social security programs. Nevertheless, despite this surface color blindness, the act perpetuated racial distinctions that existed in the American political economy, particularly through the exclusion of agricultural and domestic labor from social insurance but also through maneuvers such as extending Old-Age Insurance benefits to survivors in 1939.[16] These moves effectively segregated the target populations of welfare policies, reserving social insurance for white working men and their families and relegating needy minorities and women to public assistance. This feature of the new welfare state was clearly recognized by African American political elites, who greeted the Social Security Act as a tremendous opportunity missed to construct social citizenship on a more racially equal basis.[17] In this regard, the act was entirely in keeping with other policy debates and decisions of the same era, which commonly perpetuated racial (along with ethnic and gender) hierarchies. It effectively framed the new social citizenship on a model that tilted heavily toward whiteness, much as immigration restriction policies and melting-pot assimilationism in the same period defined American citizenship in racially and ethnically exclusive terms. Moreover, as Desmond King argues, the narrow model of Americanism in the early part of the twentieth century fueled the growth of multiculturalism in the latter part of the century by fostering a sense of exclusivity and separateness that came to be celebrated rather than scorned. The American welfare state was born in a political context that depended heavily on racial distinctions, which were considered not only legitimate but also essential for political life—and not just in the South, where race was clearly at the root of politics, but in the North as well.[18] Thus although it would be anachronistic to call the ideological and cultural underpinnings of the American welfare state "multicultural," its underlying presumptions were undoubtedly race-conscious in that they both accepted and furthered the legitimacy of group distinctions on the basis of race.

Finally, the Social Security Act did little to reformulate the political opportunities for group-based mobilization available to African Americans in the United States. Through social insurance programs, it fostered strong direct links between workers and the national state so that beneficiaries could make strong legitimate claims both to expand their rights and protect their gains. But public assistance programs, which disproportionately served minorities, reinforced the links of dependence and subordination between local white elites and African Americans—initially in the South but increasingly in the North as well—by casting clients as supplicants to local grandees rather than as honorable claimants of rights. Meanwhile, continuing disfranchisement in the South, along with that region's brutal system of state-sanctioned white supremacy, foreclosed almost all prospects of advancing such claims for most African Americans, more than three-fourths of whom still lived in the South in 1940. Even in the North, where African Americans had the franchise, electoral politics frequently remained a weak platform for pressing group demands; rather, urban party organizations run by white "ethnics" often limited the devolution of real power to their black constituents. This is not to say that the first half of the twentieth century was a fallow one for African American political organization and mobilization. Rather, this era saw the founding of the NAACP and the National Urban League, the rise and fall of Marcus Garvey's African nationalist movement, and the organization of black labor in the Brotherhood of Sleeping Car Porters, among other developments. But these patterns of mobilization trained their efforts not on welfare rights and the institutions that oversaw those rights, but rather on the venues where a disfranchised minority could exert some leverage—such as the intelligentsia, the economy, and the courts, where Houston and his protégé Thurgood Marshall devised an ingenious civil rights litigation strategy under the auspices of the NAACP Legal Defense Fund. During World War II, African American political mobilization expanded, taking advantage of the unique wartime pressures on the American state to press claims on the central state itself and setting the stage for the civil rights movement to come.[19]

ALTERNATIVE PATHS: THE WELFARE STATE IN BRITAIN AND FRANCE

For Britain and France as well, the welfare state was to be a key element in shaping racial incorporation. In Britain, the welfare state, born in the years before World War I and completed with a flourish in the aftermath of the second, had helped to unify Britons across divides of class and region. With it welfare state in place, writes the great chronicler of British race relations E.J.B. Rose, "Great Britain, conscious that for a time it had stood alone against tyranny, seemed, for all the miscarriage of its economic plans, to be founding a just society."[20] For its part, France held its own welfare state to be an essential part of the republic, upholding the principles of solidarity and mutual responsibility, guaranteed and overseen by the state.[21] As in the United States, the shape of the welfare states created and expanded in the first half of the twentieth century would be critical in determining patterns of incorporation for racial minorities in the century's second half. In each case, the same configuration of factors—institutional structure, ideological repertoires, and the patterning of group-state relations—would fundamentally shape the encounter between racial minorities and welfare states and thus profoundly affect the paths and possibilities for full (or less-than-full) incorporation into these societies.

Britain and Its Welfare State: Liberal Exclusion

The early British welfare state, like the American, was critically divided between relatively generous social insurance policies for workers and extensive but less generous means-tested public assistance programs for nonworkers. The old-age pensions created in 1908 were initially noncontributory benefits available universally to people over age seventy of limited means. Social insurance designed to protect workers against risks that would make them unemployable—old age, sickness, industrial accidents, and economic cycles that resulted in periodic layoffs—followed soon after, beginning with unemployment and sickness insurance in 1911. Old-age pensions came under the social insurance umbrella in 1925 when the original pension scheme was replaced by a system of contributory old-age insurance, covering widows and orphans as well, for those over age sixty-five. These programs were compulsory and contributory, with contributions being equally allocated to workers, employers, and the national treasury. Modeled on German social insurance, National Insurance was itself a model for the American architects of Social Security.[22] Like American social insurance, these policies were nationally constituted and adminis-

tered and constructed an important citizenship link between British subjects and the national state based on strong individual claims on the state.

Although these acts left the British Poor Law in place, they substantially
undercut it by beginning to chip away at the distinction, fundamental to
the Poor Law, between poverty and pauperism, between deserving and
undeserving poor. In particular, old-age pensions removed the elderly permanently from the category of paupers and from the harsh local jurisdiction of parish Poor Law commissioners. Nevertheless, the Poor Law distinctions remained intrinsic to the structure of British social policy,
dividing beneficiaries of the welfare state between those eligible for national insurance benefits and those reduced to destitution for other reasons deemed uninsurable. A Royal Commission on the Poor Law and the
Unemployed appointed in 1905 had famously issued a split report in 1909
in which a majority recommended continuing the Poor Law and a small
but vocal (and publicity-savvy) minority led by Fabian reformer Beatrice
Webb recommended scrapping the Poor Law in favor of national and
preventive measures to combat poverty.[23] Between the wars the national
government continued to chip away at the operation of the Poor Law,
replacing parish authorities with local government supervision of poor
relief and creating new categories of public assistance in areas such as
public health and education.[24] But although the Poor Law, after more than
three centuries, was on the verge of dissolution, the British welfare state
retained its fundamental emphasis on work as a test of deservingness,
which was institutionalized in the distinction between National Insurance
and public assistance, in whatever form it would eventually take.

The ideological underpinnings of British welfare politics were resolutely liberal, in many respects even more so than the supposedly distinctively liberal United States.[25] Economically, Britain remained committed
to laissez-faire and free trade, having eliminated tariffs on imported grain
with the repeal of the Corn Laws in 1846 and subsequently rejected calls
for protection, including Joseph Chamberlain's tariff reform proposals of
the 1900s.[26] Politically, the Victorian values of individualism and voluntarism remained strong, reflected in the resilience of the Poor Law tradition
despite the impressive advance of solidaristic social policies. But Britain's
liberal political culture was strongly defined by the imperial distinction
between insiders—white Britons in England, Scotland, and Wales—and
outsiders—the colored inhabitants of the empire. British liberalism was
itself founded on this distinction, dependent on an incipient race consciousness that divided the world between the advanced races, who were
worthy of political liberty and capable of self-government, and the backward races, who needed their tutelage. Thus British politics was at the
very least implicitly racially ascriptive; in fact, its ascriptivism was inseparable from its liberalism, since many of its imperial policies and their suc-

cessors were built on this racialized distinction between British citizen and imperial subject.[27] In this view, British liberalism contrasts with Rogers Smith's depiction of American liberalism and ascriptivism as fundamentally at odds with one another (and it echoes several critiques of Smith's view that hold the American liberalism was built on the same distinctions of rationality and backwardness).[28]

There remained, in the early twentieth century, one prominent exception to the insider-outsider distinction in British political race consciousness, and that was the Irish. Ireland remained part of the United Kingdom until 1922, although Irish union and home rule had formed a critical dividing line in British politics for more than a generation. Irish residents of Great Britain were often considered in racially alien terms: not only were they mostly Catholic, in contrast to the Protestant self-conception at the core of British political identity, but they were also portrayed politically and culturally in classic racialized terms as lazy, prone to drink, sexually predatory, and generally somewhere between whites and Africans or Asians on the evolutionary scale of civilizations. The partition of Ireland after Irish independence, under which Northern Ireland remained a part of the United Kingdom, contributed further to the ambiguous status of the Irish in Britain; while residents of Northern Ireland remained British subjects, citizens of the Republic of Ireland lost their Commonwealth status but retained special entry and immigration privileges under the British Nationality Act of 1948 and the Commonwealth Immigration Act of 1962.[29]

Unlike American social policy, though, British social policy in the early twentieth century did not constitute an elaborate scheme to sort a certain group of people—in the case of Britain, the Irish—into separate categories of deservingness and benefit eligibility. The Irish happened to have been particularly exposed to the harshness of the Poor Law, since they were likely to be poor and unskilled, and often lacked settled roots in a local parish (one of the requirements for poor relief).[30] Thus the Irish in Britain stood particularly to gain from the nationalization of relief and the replacement of the Poor Law. But the status of the Irish in Britain, although it was an important focus of political debate, did not have the same critical regional or partisan hold on British welfare politics that the parallel status of African Americans did in American politics. In the early part of the twentieth century, Irish MPs generally supported the construction of the welfare state; later in the century, Northern Ireland, as a relatively poor region of the United Kingdom, stood particularly to gain from the nationalization of welfare policy, and the Northern Irish parliament endorsed the post–World War II reforms emanating from London. The presence of the Irish in Britain did not, it appears, impede the building of a foundation for a national welfare state that encompassed the Irish as well as other

Britons, nor did that welfare state contain any obvious mechanism by which the Irish could be readily excluded.

Thus, although the British political consciousness of race encompassed divisions at home (between British and Irish) and abroad (between British and imperial subjects), the consequence of the early development of the British welfare state was on balance to advance the latter distinction and submerge the former. To the extent that the early development of the British welfare state constituted a repudiation of the Poor Law, it served to knit together the citizens of Britain, the Irish included, into a national community of citizens. This is not to say that political carping about the Irish as feckless public charges ended with the construction of National Insurance—far from it. Irish dependence on the British dole was, in fact, a common theme of British welfare and immigration debates in the interwar period.[31] The status of the Irish thus serves to highlight the tension inherent in British social policy between liberal color blindness and ascriptive race consciousness that would remain important.

The advent of National Insurance in Britain also underscored differences in the way British citizens and imperial subjects were linked to the state. By deepening the connection between Britons at home and the new welfare state, National Insurance helped to further the construction of British citizenship, adding a social dimension to the civil and political layers that had accrued over the previous centuries.[32] These new national links between citizens and the British state came at the expense not only of local parish-based connections under the Poor Law but also of the extensive network of friendly societies, or private fraternal organizations, that often provided sickness insurance, funeral benefits, and the like to their members. By the turn of the twentieth century there were nearly 24,000 such societies enrolling more than four million members.[33] The friendly societies had long opposed national old-age pensions, and when pensions came they dealt a severe blow to the societies' prestige and independence.

These national patterns of citizenship, however, did not encompass colored immigrants to Britain, who were linked to the British imperial state not through ties of citizenship and mutual solidarity with native Britons but through subordination to the extensive imperial bureaucracy. World War I and its aftermath in particular began to reshape race relations in Britain as colonial subjects began settling in Britain in numbers large enough to attract the notice of the government.[34] The most common route to Britain for colonials in this period was British merchant shipping. Ships would recruit crews in India and the West Indies, signing local men to articles requiring that they serve for a round-trip journey. These "black" seamen held the worst jobs, were paid less than their white counterparts, and were shunned by British seamen's unions. Many remained in English ports rather than returning home, however, leaving a growing black population in port cities such as London, Liverpool, Cardiff, and Glasgow. Imperial politics and the changing demands of the imperial system shaped the British government's response to the growth of the non-European population of Britain. The Board of Trade, which oversaw commercial relations with the empire, sought to shore up the increasingly fragile imperial system and pursued these seamen as deserters in order to hold them to their contracts. Local officials wanted the means to control what they saw as an increasingly unruly population, prone to poverty and disorder. Meanwhile, the imperial bureaucracy—principally the India Office and the Colonial Office—pressed for decent treatment of colonials. The growing political and economic fragility of the empire and the strength of the imperial bureaucracy within the British government made it difficult for the government to sanction official discrimination by race. Moreover, the active participation of thousands of colonials in the war itself had heightened among colonial subjects their sense of solidarity and of the obligations that the empire owed them for their sacrifice. Nevertheless, in 1925 the Home Office issued the Coloured Alien Seamen Order, requiring colored (but not white) seamen who could not prove British nationality to register with the police as aliens. Although the order was rescinded in 1942 when Britain again needed military manpower, it laid the institutional foundation for a racial definition of British citizenship. Moreover, the order effectively institutionalized state-sponsored race consciousness. Until after World War II, the Colonial Office retained the primary responsibility for tending to the affairs of Britons designated as colored, further underscoring the racial distinctions that underlay British national identity and policy.[35]

France and Its Welfare State: Conservative Universalism

France's welfare state, like the British and American systems, developed with a strong emphasis on social insurance. In contrast with its British and American counterparts, however, it did not initially construct nationally administered, centralized social insurance. Rather, its origins lay in nineteenth-century structures of *mutualité,* mutual assistance plans, which were organized privately along fraternal and occupational lines and were neither tax financed nor state administered. The French Social Security system developed around these self-organized social insurance plans, and although political and administrative control over welfare policy was centralized and nationalized after World War II, these self-sustaining plans remain at the system's core. Unlike in Britain, where the friendly societies were ultimately unable to prevent the adoption of social insurance, French mutual assistance societies were able first to delay the passage of social insurance until well after World War I and then to influence the institutional form of social insurance to preserve the autonomy of occupational and other pension and unemployment schemes. In fact, more than one hundred of these pre-1945 occupational social insurance schemes remain in existence, albeit under the national umbrella, along with twenty other schemes for the self-employed, agricultural workers, and others, as well as a residual general scheme for those not included under any of the other schemes. Thus, rather than creating a national welfare state, the initial thrust of French social politics was to create policies under which workers' claims to benefits depended not on national citizenship but on attachments to particular occupational or civil-society attachments. Despite the administrative centralization of French politics, welfare policy was thus actually quite decentralized, with limited state involvement and oversight, in keeping with the political structure of the Third Republic.[36] Thus for minorities or immigrants, claims on the welfare state would depend on incorporation into these groups.

At the same time, unlike the United States and Britain, social insurance in France was not built on top of an extensive and deeply entrenched state-led structure of poor relief; the relief provisions in place were overseen exclusively by private organizations and local governments. In the absence of extensive public assistance, France created a far-reaching system of family allowances. An outgrowth of late-nineteenth-century conservative Catholic doctrine that called for the maintenance of traditional families through the wage system and initially implemented on a private basis by some Catholic employers as a paternalistic means of controlling their employees, family allowances were historically aimed at encouraging childbearing and keeping women out of the work force. Family allowances have subsequently grown to be universal and relatively generous, but when they were initially made compulsory for all workers in 1932, they mirrored the structure of social insurance in that they were privately financed and administered.[37] Across the whole range of policies, then, the early French welfare state tended to reinforce distinctions of status and class in French society by making claims on benefits dependent on access not only to the labor market but also to particular sectors and occupations. For those outside the labor market, the French welfare system had little to offer.

Ideologically, the politics surrounding the creation of the French welfare state was fundamentally color-blind. The Third Republic was strongly assimilationist. Its institutions—the army and the schools above all—worked to knit together a linguistically and culturally diverse population inside France proper into a common national and cultural community, dominated by Paris. And although colonial assimilationism waxed and waned over the course of the Third Republic, it was far from clear that membership in the French nation was restricted to white Europeans. At the same time, racial bias, and particularly antisemitism, were present in French politics during this period. In particular, the very institutions that were the engines of assimilation in the Third Republic—especially the army—proved to be the most hostile to Jews and the most prone to virulent antisemitism. The Dreyfus Affair, the most notorious and galvanizing instance of French antisemitism in the Third Republic, exposed quite starkly and brutally the limits of the assimilationism of French politics and society. On the one hand, France was able to absorb all manner of racially suspect peoples, even Jews, and make them French, so long as they foreswore any alternative identity and wholly adopted French culture and participated in its institutions. On the other hand, the capacity of Jews to become French remained open to question, with tragic consequences not just for Captain Dreyfus and his family but also for all French Jews under Vichy. Just beneath the surface of French politics in the early part of the twentieth century ran a current of tension between the color-blind universalism that has long been the hallmark of French republicanism and race-conscious particularism that has often taken sinister forms.[38]

Finally, the development of the French welfare state did little to disrupt patterns of group-state linkage that, despite the ideological tension between race-blind universalism and race consciousness in French political culture, were shaped fundamentally by the French republican tradition. French politics looked askance at most forms of political or social organization that might intervene between citizens and the national community. "Most Europeans," wrote Tocqueville, meaning Frenchmen, "still see in association a weapon of war that one forms in haste to go try it out immediately on a field of battle. One does indeed associate with the purpose of speaking, but the thought of acting next preoccupies all minds. An association is an army; one speaks in it so as to be counted and to be inspired, and then one marches toward the enemy."[39] The Le Chapelier law of 1791, which banned the formation of associations, still governed associational life in France, and opportunities for political organization remained severely limited. Political associations were active in Third Republic France, but under the law they were subject to control by the state. Given the assimilationist aims of the French state and the explosive hostility toward racially constructed groups, the political opportunity structure of early twentieth-century French politics militated against mobilization around ethnic and racial identities, to say the least. Moreover, given the decentralized institutional structure of the early French welfare state, the prospects for minorities in the welfare state turned even more sharply on their ability to penetrate French civil society, which was generally a matter of submerging distinctive racial, ethnic, religious, or national backgrounds into a common model of civic, secular, and unitary Frenchness.[40]

CONCLUSIONS

The American model of the welfare state was thus one of race consciousness (often masquerading as color blindness) embedded in a fragmented institutional structure, divided between national social insurance for workers and parochial public assistance for those outside the labor market. That this system was racially exclusionary was not merely incidental to its structure. Rather, it was predicated on a set of institutional mechanisms for racial exclusion, which were the consequences of the coalition building imperatives that drove its creation. Above all, the American welfare state seemed to reinforce and to fix into place the racial hierarchy of the Jim Crow era through this combination of ideological frameworks and institutional mechanisms.

The American welfare state, however, was not the only one to face the challenges of providing for a multiracial society and the American model was not the only one on offer in the first half of the century. The British welfare state also tended to reinforce racial distinctions that underlay British citizenship, which were entirely in keeping with the race-conscious tendencies inherent in British imperial liberalism. But although British policy similarly distinguished between social insurance and public assistance, these policies were part of an increasingly national and centralized welfare system that began to overturn the parochial history of British social policy, at least for those deemed worthy of full citizenship. French social policy was steeped in the color-blind tradition of French republicanism (although this stance often concealed race-conscious tendencies). This color-blind stance, however, was linked to a relatively fragmented policy structure that emphasized social insurance for workers who were connected to social provision through both the labor market generally as well as more particular sectoral, occupational, and other civil-society categories. Thus, despite the republican rhetoric of citizenship, the links forged between groups and the French welfare state was mediated by private attachments.

These institutional and ideological configurations remained in place roughly through mid-century. But then war came, first to Europe and then to the world, unsettling these arrangements and transforming much of what had been built in the liberal democratic world in the first half of the century. After Europe was devastated for the second time in a generation and the West was transfixed by the twin specters of fascism and communism, many of the fundamental political relationships of the previous era were open for reassessment—between states and citizens, rulers and subjects, center and periphery. In particular, total war (and total victory) against a regime based on ideas of racial purity and practices of racial extermination served to discredit the ideas and practices of racial rule among the world's democracies. These transformations would in turn profoundly alter the political and racial landscape of the United States and much of the world.

Chapter Four

POSTWAR TRANSFORMATIONS
OF RACE AND STATE

THE POLITICAL TRANSFORMATION wrought by World War II was profound and far-reaching. In the United States, the war proved to be a cata-
lyst for accelerating change in race relations on a variety of fronts. The
war, and the Cold War that followed, helped to raise expectations of full
participation in American society and the political economy and also to
expose the limits of tolerance and access that foreclosed that participation. In the war, the United States was allied with Britain and France
against a totalitarian regime defined by its racism, and in mobilizing their
populations for the war they invoked principles of antiracist liberalism
and inclusion that held out the promise of racial equality. The Cold War
exposed the hollowness of some of the West's claims about the superiority
of liberal democracy to communism, creating both political pressure for
more inclusive race policies and a cultural and ideological frame that privileged color blindness. Already in the 1940s important changes were un-
derway in the United States: Roosevelt's Fair Employment Practices Commission, Truman's desegregation of the armed forces and his civil rights
platform, and Supreme Court decisions outlawing whites-only primary
elections and racial covenants on property deeds. For Britain, meanwhile,
World War II meant the loss of empire, while for France it also meant
Vichy and collaboration with the Nazi regime, a legacy that French leaders hoped to purge once the republic was restored.[1]

In this chapter, I chronicle two of these transformations that are particularly pertinent for understanding the patterns of minority incorporation
in national welfare states that evolved in the postwar era. The first is the
reform of the welfare state itself, which in each case modified without
dramatically altering the institutional patterns constructed in the first half
of the century. In the United States, the immediate postwar years proved
a particularly barren moment for welfare policy, largely because of the
same race-laden political barriers that had constricted welfare state formation during the New Deal. Britain and France undertook more thor-
oughgoing welfare reforms: Britain moved toward greater universalism
but still within the liberal frame, and France toward more centralized and
uniform social insurance. None of these countries, however, fundamen-

tally reconfigured the structures of solidarity or modes of linkage between citizens and the state that they had constructed before the war. The chapter summarizes these reforms (and unsuccessful attempts at reform) and presents a broad statistical picture of the postwar welfare states into which racial incorporation was to become an increasingly pressing political challenge.

This challenge arose because of the second transformation that I treat in this chapter, the large-scale migrations of racial minorities that occurred in each country during the postwar years. Millions of African Americans moved from the rural South to the urban North in the United States in the 1940s and 1950s, both to escape the strictures of Jim Crow and to seek expanding opportunity in the North. This mass movement changed the nature of American race relations utterly and forever. In the same period, colonial subjects began to move from colonies to metropolitan Britain and France, setting in motion similar changes in British and French society. These migrants were moving from places where their rights were severely restricted to new places where they could claim the full rights of citizenship, including access to the benefits and protections of the welfare state. In each case they entered already-established welfare regimes whose institutional patterns and ideological frames would affect their capacity to absorb new entrants marked by racial difference. But at the same time, these demographic shifts altered the political geography of each country, affecting labor markets, patterns of political competition, and systems of social organization. These changes, in turn, began to reshape coalition-building possibilities around issues of race and welfare, with important consequences for the incorporation prospects of racial minorities. This chapter chronicles these changes as well, detailing the new racial context of the postwar world and setting the stage in both institutional and ideological terms for a detailed exploration of the paths of incorporation that would follow.

THE LIMITS OF POSTWAR REFORM IN THE UNITED STATES

During the war, Franklin Roosevelt began to outline a postwar vision for the expansion of social rights that would fulfill the vision of "cradle to grave" economic security he had articulated in the 1930s. Even before the American entry into the war, Roosevelt and Winston Churchill had outlined a set of common aims and principles during a meeting off the coast of Newfoundland in August 1941. In what became known as the Atlantic Charter, the two leaders declared their commitment to "the fullest collaboration between all nations in the economic field with the object of securing, for all, improved labor standards, economic advancement and social security" as well as to "a peace . . . which will afford assurance that all the men in all the lands may live out their lives in freedom from fear and want."[2] This declaration, while mainly focused on war aims, contained the kernel of a vision for the shape of the postwar world for which the Allies would fight, and that vision contained a robust notion of what T. H. Marshall would later call social citizenship.[3]

Two and a half years later, as the Allies prepared for the invasion of Europe that would begin the end of the war, Roosevelt expanded on this vision. In his 1944 State of the Union Message he called for a "second Bill of Rights," including rights to education, work, housing, medical care, and a level of subsistence commensurate with a decent life. "True individual freedom cannot exist without economic security and independence," he said. "'Necessitous men are not free men.' People who are hungry and out of a job are the stuff of which dictatorships are made." At a dark moment in world history, Roosevelt argued that these social rights of citizenship were necessary to save democratic civilization.[4]

By the war's end, however, much of the work-based programmatic impulse that had animated the New Deal reforms was spent. The Works Progress Administration had come under growing congressional pressure in the late 1930s and died a quiet death in 1942, while other organs such as the National Resources Planning Board, which tried to promote more active labor-market policies, exerted little influence under the exigencies of war. Although Roosevelt did not live to see postwar developments unfold, his successor, Harry Truman, sought in some measure to carry out his expansive program on several fronts, although with little success. The largest effort to expand the reach of American social policy after the war was the Employment Act of 1946. Originally conceived the previous year as the *Full* Employment Act, it proposed to establish a right to employment for all Americans and to empower the federal government to enforce that right largely through centrally directed government spending. That proposal drew on a reform impulse in American liberalism toward planning and economic intervention that had largely run dry by the 1940s, to be replaced by a more restricted vision of liberalism that focused on individual rights and aggregate fiscal management rather than the reorganization of capitalism. Hollowed out by the common conservative coalition of Republicans and Southern Democrats, the final act backed away from the commitment to full employment and dropped the instruments of federal economic intervention. The result was to increase the burdens and expectations on the social security system and its adjunct public assistance programs to smooth out the rough edges of the postwar industrial economy.[5]

Other attempts at social policy innovation met with similar, and even more complete, failure in the postwar years. National health insurance, which had been briefly considered and quickly rejected by the Roosevelt administration in developing the Social Security Act (largely because of the opposition of doctors), was one such proposal. It was a key element of Truman's reelection platform in 1948 and was championed in Congress by senators Robert Wagner of New York and James Murray of Montana (the key sponsor of the Full Employment bill) and Representative John Dingell of Michigan, but it also came to grief in Congress. The same congressional troika proposed an expansion of Unemployment Insurance to nationalize it completely and make it universal, but that, too, failed. Combined with the growing popularity and political strength of Social Security, these political dead ends left the field open for the full flourishing of the prewar vision of social policy with its emphasis on social insurance for workers and residual public assistance.[6]

The United States thus emerged from World War II as perhaps the archetypal liberal welfare state. Reasonably generous old-age pensions and unemployment insurance for regularly employed workers, with benefits tied to contributions, existed alongside a wide range of means-tested categorical benefits for nonworkers who were excluded from social insurance. Despite low levels of overall spending on means-tested programs, the United States relied more heavily on them than any other welfare state. Gøsta Esping-Andersen's original classificatory data show that 18.2 percent of American welfare spending in the 1970s went toward means-tested poor relief; in only two other countries (of eighteen in his study) was this figure higher than 10 percent, and the median level was less than 5 percent.[7] The United States was also at the extreme in offering few truly universal benefits or services—such as health insurance, family allowances, or childcare—that were common elsewhere. The American middle class, consequently, now relies heavily on private social provision, underwritten by tax expenditures, to finance health care and provide retirement income. At the same time, the American state does little to promote full employment, so that there is no active policy to maximize the number of people who are brought under the umbrella of the public-private system of social insurance and protection. The American welfare state is also particularly decentralized and fragmented. While social insurance programs for workers are nationally uniform, public-assistance policies are operated by states with minimal national oversight, exposing public assistance clients to the particular hazards of decentralized redistributive policy.[8]

A look at the American pattern of welfare spending over the postwar era confirms this comparative judgment. Figure 4.1 shows the total level of public spending on social protection—encompassing social insurance and public-assistance cash benefits as well as spending on social services and other in-kind benefits such as health care—for the United States, the United Kingdom, and France from 1960 through 1998 (expressed as a

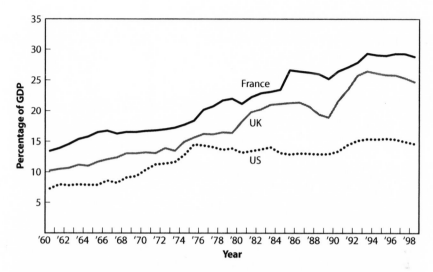

FIGURE 4.1 Social Protection Spending (including health), 1960–98. Source: OECD, *New Orientations for Social Policy*, Social Policy Studies No. 12 (Paris: OECD, 1994); OECD Social Expenditures Database.

percentage of the country's total economic output for comparative purposes).[9] Throughout the period, American social spending is lower, particularly after the 1970s, when American spending levels off while British and French spending continue to grow. By century's end, the level of American spending on social protection is only half of that in France and three-fifths of that in Britain. Lest one conclude that lagging American spending is due to the lack of national health insurance in the United States (which makes it unique among advanced industrial nations), figure 4.2 presents the same data excluding health spending.[10] The pattern over time is largely the same; if anything, the divergence between the United States and the other two countries after the 1970s is even more dramatic, indicating clearly that it is not only health care that distinguishes the size of the American welfare state from its European counterparts.

The United States has also maintained a distinctive pattern of spending within these comparatively low overall levels. Figure 4.3 charts the distribution of spending on social benefits from the late 1940s through the early 1980s.[11] Most striking is the rapid growth of social insurance in the immediate postwar years from one-fourth to one-half of social spending, a level that has been maintained since (with some fluctuation). But equally if not more significant is the prominence and recent growth of public assistance as a component of American social spending. Public assistance actually declined as a proportion of social spending from one-fifth to one-

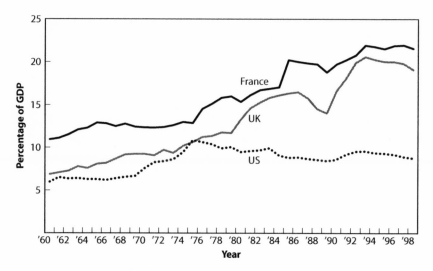

FIGURE 4.2 Social Protection Spending (excluding health), 1960–98. Source: OECD, *New Orientations for Social Policy*, Social Policy Studies no. 12 (Paris: OECD, 1994); OECD Social Expenditures Database.

eighth of all spending between the late 1940s and the early 1960s, when it began to rise, reaching approximately one-fourth in the 1980s. Two other defining features of the American social spending profile are the heavy emphasis on veterans' benefits as a separate category, especially in the years after World War II when the GI Bill offered an extensive menu of benefits to returning servicemen and their families, and the absence of family allowances, which are distinct from public assistance benefits. Both of these points emphasize the American welfare state's reliance on categorical benefits (including workers' benefits) rather than universal benefits based on citizenship or residence. Taken together, this picture of American welfare spending underscores the American welfare state's liberal profile, which has become, if anything, more pronounced in the post–World War II era, even as more solidaristic approaches to social policy became more prevalent across much of the rest of the developed world.[12]

POSTWAR REFORMS IN BRITAIN AND FRANCE

Britain: Universal Liberalism

During World War II, the British government began planning to extend and expand the welfare state to meet the aims laid out in the Atlantic Charter and to fulfill the long-held goals of British social reformers. The

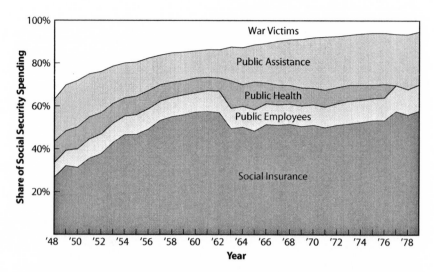

FIGURE 4.3 Social Security Spending, United States. Source: International Labour Organization, *The Cost of Social Security* (Geneva: International Labour Organization, various years).

most prominent and influential of these reformers in the interwar years was William Beveridge. As a young civil servant in the Board of Trade, Beveridge had advised Lloyd George and Churchill on the development of National Insurance and had subsequently had a prominent career as what might be called a policy intellectual, including service as the director of the London School of Economics (which had been founded in 1895 by the Fabian socialists Beatrice and Sidney Webb) and master of University College, Oxford. Early in the war, Churchill and Ernest Bevin, a Labour MP who was labor minister in Churchill's war cabinet, formed a committee to examine Britain's existing system of social provision and recommend how it might be rationalized and reformed, and he appointed Beveridge as its chairman. The committee's report, known as the Beveridge Report, was published in 1942. It promptly garnered broad political acclaim and became a national bestseller to boot, selling 70,000 copies in a day and more than 600,000 copies all told.[13] Beveridge proposed a unified social security system that would support Britons "from cradle to grave." His scheme would have provided universal social insurance encompassing old-age, unemployment, health and disability, survivors, and family allowances, with flat (hence non–income-related) benefits and contributions and minimum income levels to ensure adequacy. (In a famous series of meetings in the summer of 1942, however, his friend John Maynard Keynes convinced Beveridge to scale back the level of benefits and to suggest a long phase-in of full subsistence benefits in order to assuage anxiety at the Treasury, for whom Keynes was a consultant, about the scheme's cost.)[14]

Less than two months after the end of the war in Europe, the Labour Party won an astounding electoral victory, capturing more than 60 percent of the seats in the House of Commons. Under Prime Minster Clement Attlee, the Labour government proceeded to enact much of Beveridge's program in a new National Insurance Act in 1946, which established universal old-age pensions with standardized benefit levels designed to meet basic subsistence income. Also in 1946, the government created the National Health Service, which would provide health care universally to all Britons. Finally, in 1948, the British government sounded the Poor Law's death knell with the passage of the National Assistance act, which (as its title implied) nationalized public assistance and, nominally at least, integrated it with National Insurance to create a reasonably seamless welfare edifice.[15]

Like the United States, then, Great Britain's postwar welfare state was fundamentally liberal in that it was divided between generous social insurance programs for workers and extensive but less generous means-tested programs for nonworkers. In the context of comparatively low overall spending, the percentage of Britain's total social spending that goes toward means-tested benefits has long been comparable to the United States—in the vicinity of 20 percent in recent years.[16] Britain also relies relatively heavily on the private provision of benefits such as retirement pensions, although Britain departs from the United States in offering more universal benefits, especially health care. Like that of the United States, the British welfare state is embedded in a liberal economy and labor market with a relatively noninterventionist state, and in both countries welfare programs came under severe political attack with the ascendancy of conservative regimes in the 1980s.[17]

Where the British welfare state particularly departs from the American case is in its centralization. Britain's postwar welfare system preserves the distinction between workers and nonworkers by establishing two systems of assistance: National Insurance for workers and National Assistance for others. But unlike the American system, these two interlocking systems are both national plans, centrally organized and financed, without local or regional variation and with minimal administrative discretion. Although municipal governments in Britain often act as the front-line providers of public assistance, they act not as independent and autonomous political units but as agents of the central government, which was committed to offering nationally uniform eligibility rules and benefits.[18] By centralizing and reducing discretion, the British welfare state reduced the opportunities for inconsistent and parochial patterns of administration, and consequently offered greater potential than American public assistance for the incorporation of minorities into the welfare system.

In the first decades after World War II, Britain spent relatively little on social welfare, as figures 4.1 and 4.2 show. Until the 1970s, British levels of social spending were comparable to the United States, if slightly higher at times. Beginning in the mid-1970s, however, while American social spending leveled off and even began gradually to decline, British social spending continued to grow at quite a rapid rate, approaching French spending levels by the mid-1980s. As figure 4.2 reveals, this divergence between British and American spending patterns is not due to health spending.

Social insurance and health have long dominated British social spending, as figure 4.4 shows. These two categories combined have consistently accounted for at least seventy percent of Britain's spending on social benefits. The other notable trend in British social spending has been the growth of public assistance. From the late 1940s through the mid-1960s, public assistance made up a steady share of social spending, slightly more than 10 percent. Since then, however, it has grown steadily, reaching 17 percent in the late 1970s (toward the end of the period represented in figure 4.1) and climbing through the 1980s to more than 20 percent.[19] Britain does have a small and growing program of family allowances, but social insurance and public assistance dominate, together accounting for more than four-fifths of overall social spending. Despite higher general spending levels, then, British social policy profile strongly resembles that of the United States in its allocation of spending and in its emphasis on categorical rather than universal benefits.

France: The Triumph of Social Insurance

France, too, dramatically reformed its welfare state after World War II. After France was liberated from Nazi occupation in 1944, attention turned to the reorganization of social security as part of the postwar reconstitution of French government and politics. The principal parties of the Fourth Republic—the Communists, Socialists, and Social Catholics—all had an interest in expanding social protection, while the Right, which might have resisted, had been thoroughly discredited by the occupation and by Vichy. The leading figure in the reconstruction of the French social security system was Pierre Laroque, who as a young civil servant had been involved in the initial creation of social insurance in 1930 and had been a member of General de Gaulle's Free French administration during the war. Laroque spent most of the war in London, where he was impressed by the Beveridge report. In September 1944, Alexandre Parodi, the labor minister in the provisional postwar government, appointed Laroque to head a commission charged with recommending a social security plan.

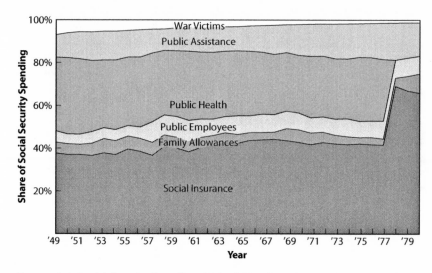

FIGURE 4.4 Social Security Spending, United Kingdom. Source: International Labour Organization, *The Cost of Social Security* (Geneva: International Labour
Organization, various years).

Laroque hoped to accomplish three things with his reform proposal. First,
borrowing from Beveridge, he sought universal protection against social
risks, based on the principle of national solidarity. Second, he proposed
to unify the multiple, *mutualité*-based social security funds into a "single
fund" under unified management and administration. And third, he advocated greater state control of social security.[20]

But Laroque ran into substantial disagreement in the chaotic politics
of the transition to the Fourth Republic. The Socialists and Communists
favored greater state control over social security, while the Mouvement
Républicain Populaire, the centrist Catholic party, preferred to retain the
prewar model of decentralized schemes and autonomous funds. Similarly,
the representatives of the existing social insurance and family allowance
funds, who were strongly represented on Laroque's commission, sought
to protect their autonomy. As these disagreements escalated into a full-
fledged stalemate, the provisional government issued a series of decrees
in October 1945 creating a single social security system and laying out a
plan to extend coverage to the entire population of French citizens living
in French territory. But under legislation passed in the Spring of 1946,
the single fund was abandoned and the French pattern of multiple social
security and family assistance schemes was retained, although now under
increased state oversight and with provision for the extension of coverage
beyond the traditional categories of workers.[21]

Since 1946, social security reform in France has focused particularly on centralizing the administration and organization of welfare and on expanding the role of the state. A 1956 law created a National Solidarity Fund, financed from general taxation rather than employee or employer contributions, to provide additional means-tested assistance to help social insurance participants avoid poverty, creating an important additional link with the national French state for workers and their families. During de Gaulle's presidency of the Fifth Republic, a series of reforms brought the social insurance funds increasingly under the administrative and fiscal control of the national government; while each specialized fund remained separate, all of the social insurance schemes were brought under uniform financial and administrative rules laid down by the central state.[22]

Even more than in the British and American welfare states, contributory social insurance for workers has come to dominate the French system; in the 1990s nearly 80 percent of France's social spending was financed by contributions, nearly twice as much as in Britain, placing it at the highest level in the European Union.[23] Coupled with family allowances, the French social security system has proven especially generous to workers while creating high barriers for the incorporation of nonworkers into the regime of social provision. This "insider-outsider" division has been exacerbated in recent decades by the high costs to employers of expensive contributory social insurance, which has contributed to slow job growth and high unemployment. In an attempt simultaneously to contain costs, reduce unemployment, and overcome growing problems of social exclusion, France has expanded the universal elements of the welfare state, creating benefits such as the Revenu Minimum d'Insertion (RMI), a guaranteed minimum income.[24]

Administratively, local governments are the front-line providers of most forms of social assistance, but they are similarly under the strong administrative control of the central government, through the agency of the departmental prefects. Even under the 1982 decentralization of the French government, which abolished the *tutelle,* the prefect's right to control local administrative action, Paris retained its hierarchically organized administrative and fiscal functions. Moreover, the prefect retained a strong hand in the local administration of welfare through the power to appoint four of nine members of the welfare administrative commission in each locality.[25] Thus the French social security system affords limited but real opportunities for variation in implementation practices—across both regions and occupational sectors. The most centralized parts of the French welfare state, in contrast with the American system, are the more universal programs that have been created by the central state in the postwar era, such as the RMI. Thus, despite the persistent legacy of its fragmented roots, the French welfare state contains strong elements of central administrative and policy control. For minorities, then, incorporation into the structures of social provision has depended not only on their integration into the civil-society and labor-market networks that provide entry into social insurance but also on their political ties to the central state, which can go some distance in enforcing solidaristic rights of social citizenship despite the French welfare state's underlying fragmentation.

France's welfare state then, departs somewhat from the liberal model of its American and British counterparts in its emphasis on social insurance and, increasingly, universalism over means-tested residual benefits.[26] It has a relatively high overall level of spending, as indicated in figures 4.1 and 4.2, which show that France has consistently spent at least twice as much as the United States on social benefits. Even with its dramatic rise in social spending over the 1980s and 1990s, Britain still lags behind France, although by a smaller margin than in the early postwar decades. Indeed, by the 1980s French social spending approached, and in some cases surpassed, that of the social democratic welfare states of the Netherlands and the Scandinavian countries. In part, the high level of spending is driven by the fragmented and highly complex structure of funds and schemes that make up the French welfare state and limit the capacity of the policymakers and managers of the national state to control expenditures without incurring substantial political costs.[27]

The breakdown of France's social spending also confirms the distinctive character—somewhere between Bismarck and Beveridge—of the French welfare state, as figure 4.5 shows.[28] The overwhelming pattern is the large and growing dominance of social insurance over everything else (except public assistance). From 40 percent in the late 1940s, social insurance's share of total social spending grew to two-thirds in the late 1970s; and although it dipped somewhat during the 1980s, it never fell below 62 percent, and it returned to the two-thirds mark in the late 1980s (not shown in figure 4.5). By the 1990s, British social insurance spending had also reached a comparable figure (especially once health spending was collapsed into the social insurance category). Realistically, however, spending on benefits for public employees should be counted as social insurance spending in France, since the French *fonctionnaires* (civil servants) belong to one of the largest of the specialized social insurance funds in the French system.[29] The inclusion of public employees brings the total level of social insurance spending to more than 75 percent by the 1990s. The prominence of family allowances, nonexistent in the United States and quite small in Britain, also distinguishes French social spending, although their relative weight has receded in the face of the relentless march of social insurance. Finally, public assistance, which was the smallest category of French social spending through the 1960s, grew somewhat beginning in the 1970s (even before the creation of a minimum

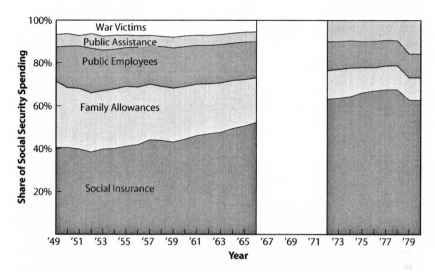

FIGURE 4.5 Social Security Spending, France. Source: International Labour Organization, *The Cost of Social Security* (Geneva: International Labour Organization, various years).

income program in 1988), although public assistance spending by the 1990s was still only slightly more than 10 percent, less than half of the American or British level.

The institutional profile of the French welfare state, decidedly different from the United States or Britain, suggests a different set of barriers and opportunities for minority incorporation, which arise principally from an exceedingly strong link between work and benefits and the resulting rigid barrier between "insiders" and "outsiders" that poses particular challenges for racial and ethnic minorities whose position in the political economy may be rather precarious.[30]

The Great Migration: From Subjects to Citizens

The second great postwar racial transformation, the great northward migration of black Americans, actually began early in the twentieth century. In two great waves, one after each of the century's world wars, American blacks left the South in staggering numbers. The second of these great migrations saw five million African Americans leave the South. "The black migration," its chronicler Nicholas Lemann has written without exaggeration, "was one of the largest and most rapid mass internal movements of people in history—perhaps *the* greatest not caused by the immediate threat of execution or starvation. In sheer numbers it outranks the migration of any other ethnic group—Italians or Irish or Jews or Poles—to this country."[31] In 1900, 90 percent of African Americans lived in the South; in 1940, slightly more than three-fourths; and by 1970, only just over one-half. By the 1960s more than three million blacks who had been born in the South lived in other parts of the country. Not only did African Americans move from the South to the North, they moved from the country to the city. At the turn of the century, three-fourths of all African Americans lived in rural areas, compared to a scant majority of whites. By 1970, four-fifths lived in urban areas, a higher percentage than for whites.[32]

The migration transformed the political geography of the United States. The black population percentage of most Southern states fell considerably. In 1910, Mississippi and South Carolina were majority black, and Alabama, Florida, Georgia, and Louisiana were more than 40 percent black. By 1970, only Mississippi had a population more than one-third black. Even more dramatic was the impact on the Northern states that were the largest destinations for African American migrants. New York, which had a net in-migration of more than 900,000 African Americans between 1940 and 1970 alone, went from having a negligible black population at the beginning of the century (around 1 percent) to 12 percent in 1970. Illinois similarly went from 2 percent to 13 percent, Michigan from 1 percent to 11 percent, and California from 1 to 7 percent. African Americans thus, for the first time in American history, became a weighty political, economic, and social presence outside of the South.

African Americans went North not simply to escape the crushing weight of Southern segregation and white supremacy but to seek the opportunities that the North's industrial economy and political democracy might offer them. Drawn initially during wartime by the increased availability of war production jobs (and pushed off the land in the South by the increasing mechanization of cotton cultivation, which in turn accelerated because of the growing labor shortage in the Southern countryside), African Americans became increasingly ensconced in the North's political economy over the decades following World War II. Economically they found jobs in the industries of the great cities of the Northeast and Upper Midwest—from New York and Newark to Pittsburgh, Cleveland, Gary, Chicago, and Detroit.[33] Politically they gained the vote, routinely denied them in the South, and became an increasingly important and even pivotal piece of the post–New Deal Democratic coalition in key states.[34]

At the same time, however, they ran up against the limits of the opportunities that migration afforded them. Discrimination and segregation were common in industrial settings, and the industrial jobs available to African Americans tended to be on the lowest rungs of the occupational ladder, without opportunities for promotion or much upward mobility. Intense and deliberate residential segregation in Northern cities meant that African Americans were increasingly crowded into ghetto neighborhoods, where poor schools and growing isolation limited their economic opportunities. Politically, African Americans in the North were often at a distinct political disadvantage despite their nominal political inclusion, particularly in cities dominated by party machines (as many of the cities in the Northeast and Midwest were). In these settings, white "ethnic" political leaders often incorporated African Americans into party hierarchies, offering patronage in return for political loyalty but without ceding a real share in local political power, at least beyond black-led "submachines" in segregated enclaves such as Chicago's South Side or New York's Harlem. More generally, despite their potentially pivotal electoral position, African Americans' increasingly tight loyalty to the Democratic party left them at risk of being taken for granted by Democratic politicians who could then seek to gain votes elsewhere by distancing themselves from African American voters and their policy concerns.[35]

In comparative terms, several important features of the great migration stand out. First, the migration constituted a movement from the periphery to the center of the American political and economic system. The South was a chronically underdeveloped region, with an economy heavily dependent on labor-repressive agriculture and paternalistic social relations and lacking much of the financial and technological infrastructure of an industrial economy. Thus in moving North, African Americans left behind a relatively narrow agrarian society for a diverse, dynamic, modernizing industrial one. Second, the migration also constituted a journey from subjecthood to citizenship for African Americans. Despite nominal constitutional protections, African Americans in the South were routinely and brutally denied citizenship rights. In the North, by contrast, these rights were available to them. They were, to be sure, quite imperfectly available (and American citizenship has long been shot through legally and politically with racial ascription). Nevertheless, there was a fundamental difference between the presumptive subordination of Southern blacks precisely on the basis of their race and the presumptive citizenship, however partially realized, of Northern blacks—not unlike the distinction between citizens at home and colonial subjects abroad.[36] The central question, then, is how this presumptive citizenship would be translated into actual practice once African Americans moved north. On what terms would they and other racial and ethnic minorities participate in American society? How would the structural impediments and opportunities embedded in the American welfare state shape the enjoyment of social citizenship rights by African Americans upon their arrival in the Promised Land?

POSTCOLONIAL MIGRATIONS: FROM SUBJECTS TO CITIZENS

In both Britain and France, mid-century welfare state reforms took place in rapidly changing societies. In the wake of World War II, decolonization redrew the map of the entire world and reshaped the political economies of Britain and France. Labor shortages in Europe created opportunities for migrants from former colonies and elsewhere, who began moving to their respective "home countries" in substantial numbers. In both countries, as in the United States to a large degree, this migration transformed the racial and political geography of empires where metropolitan whites and colonial nonwhites had once encountered each other across an imperial boundary that imposed a political and cultural as well as a physical separation. Now metropolitan societies themselves increasingly became sites of multiracial and multi-ethnic encounters on a new scale. Significantly, these were largely encounters not between rulers and subjects but among citizens of formally equal rights and status regardless of race, ethnicity, or origin. The two societies, however, reacted quite differently to these transformations.

Britain

Compared with the United States and France, Britain has a limited historical experience of immigration—waves of Irish in the mid-nineteenth century and East European Jews in the late nineteenth and early twentieth centuries were the major instances of large-scale immigration into Britain before World War II. After the war, just as Britain was reforming and expanding its welfare state, immigration from her former colonies—now independent countries of the British Commonwealth—accelerated rapidly. In particular, immigration from the "New Commonwealth"—principally India, Pakistan, the West Indies, and East Africa—began to increase as the British economy faced severe labor shortages. New Commonwealth immigration began to attract public and political notice with the arrival of the *Empire Windrush*, a former troop transport ship, which arrived at Tilbury near London in June 1948 from Kingston, Jamaica, and let off nearly five hundred Jamaican passengers. At that moment, the Parliament was debating the British Nationality Act, which would become law at the end of July. Under the act's terms, former British subjects who were now citizens of Commonwealth countries were made British citizens, eligible for British passports and consequently for free entry into and permanent settlement in Britain.[37]

The *Empire Windrush* was not, as many British political leaders feared, the harbinger of an immediate flood of non-European immigration to

Britain. Through the rest of the 1940s and into the early 1950s, several thousand immigrants from the West Indies came (and almost as frequently) went. But beginning in the mid-1950s, the pace of New Commonwealth immigration quickened dramatically, and between 1955 and the middle of 1962, more than a quarter of a million West Indians came to Britain. Similarly, migration from South Asia began to gather steam in the mid-1950s, and by 1962 more than 140,000 people had come to Britain from India and Pakistan. All told, nearly half a million immigrants from the New Commonwealth came to Britain during this period.[38]

A broad political and partisan consensus reigned on issues of immigration and race relations through the 1950s, and the Conservative governments of Winston Churchill and Anthony Eden maintained an open-immigration policy with respect to the Commonwealth, due partly to the Tory commitment to the integrity of the Commonwealth and partly to the resistance of some ministers (notably Colonial Secretary Alan Lennox-Boyd) to the possibility of race-based restrictions on New Commonwealth immigrants. But after episodes of racial violence in Nottingham and the Notting Hill area of London in 1958, the fragile consensus began to unravel and the parties began slowly to diverge on matters of immigration and race relations. In 1962 the Conservative government of Harold Macmillan passed the Commonwealth Immigration Act, which imposed severe restrictions on the entry of New Commonwealth immigrants into Britain. The 1962 act limited immigration to close family members of those already in the country and holders of work permits issued by the Ministry of Labour. The mid-1960s Labour government of Harold Wilson accepted these controls, and extended them with another, even more restrictive, Commonwealth Immigration Act in 1968. In the decade following 1962, another 300,000 New Commonwealth immigrants came to Britain.[39]

Although the movement of nonwhite immigrants to Britain was nowhere near as dramatic in sheer numbers as the great northward migrations of African Americans, these migratory patterns did substantially change British politics by bringing race politics—which had hitherto always been conducted across national boundaries—home. In 1954 there were approximately 100,000 nonwhites in Britain. By the late 1960s there were more than 850,000, and by the early 1980s Britain's nonwhite population was more than three million, nearly 6 percent of the country's total population.[40] Geographically, nonwhites in Britain were not evenly distributed across the country. They concentrated particularly in Metropolitan London and in the heavily industrial Midlands (in cities such as Birmingham) and the Northwest (including Liverpool and Manchester)—declining industrial regions that were not necessarily the areas of highest labor demand.[41]

These demographic changes had striking political consequences. Despite the apparent political consensus on immigration, partisan conflict began to erupt over internal race relations. In the 1964 election, Peter Griffiths, the Conservative candidate in Smethwick (near Birmingham in the West Midlands), defeated a member of the Labour leadership with an explicitly xenophobic and racist campaign. Griffiths's victory met with indignation from newly elected Prime Minister Wilson and befuddled embarrassment from the Tory leadership, which had long maintained a stance of genteel reserve and paternalistic distance from the sort of popular sentiment that Griffiths's campaign stirred up. For both parties, the campaign demonstrated the potential force of the incipient racial cleavage in the British electorate.[42]

Under the leadership of Home Secretary Roy Jenkins, the Wilson government pursued a policy that coupled continued immigration controls with active efforts to protect the rights and interests of blacks already in Britain. This policy was embodied in a 1965 White Paper on immigration and in the Race Relations Act of the same year, which outlawed discrimination in public accommodations (but not in employment or housing) along with "incitement of racial hatred," and established a Race Relations Board and a network of local committees to administer the law. The act met with Conservative approval, and an uneasy consensus settled over British racial politics. The consensus was short-lived. In April 1968, Tory Shadow Minister of Defense Enoch Powell, the Member of Parliament for Wolverhampton in the West Midlands, made the first of a series of notorious inflammatory speeches in April 1968.[43] Powell railed against immigrants who threatened, he intimated, to usurp the rightful place of "white" Britons in British economy and society, and he criticized both parties for ignoring the race issue. Like Griffiths, Powell created problems for both parties. Although Conservative leader Edward Heath promptly sacked Powell from the shadow cabinet for his outburst, his views clearly resonated with many voters, especially in the Midlands, England's industrial heartland, whose working-class voters normally backed Labour. Like his American contemporaries, Barry Goldwater and George Wallace, he voiced the fears of many working-class whites who saw a threat in the growing and increasingly vocal "black" population of Britain.[44] As Goldwater and Wallace paved the way for Ronald Reagan, so Powell paved the way for Margaret Thatcher.

In recent years, racial conflict has become more serious, and British racial politics has come to resemble American racial politics in many ways. In 1981, a series of serious race riots broke out in Brixton, in South London. Like a small crack in a dam, the Brixton riots precipitated a flood of similar disturbances in more than a dozen other cities, most seriously in the Toxteth section of Liverpool, Moss Side in Manchester, and Southall, an area of London with a large concentration of Indian and Pakistani residents. One four-day frenzy of racial violence in July produced more than 4,000 arrests and an estimated £45 million of damage. Like race riots in many American cities, clashes between blacks and white police officers were generally the proximate causes of these events, although the contagion of violence suggests that they sprang out of deeper grievances, as they did in a series of race riots in English cities during the summer of 2001. In ways that parallel American politics, race is at the center of many political and policy debates in Britain today. Affirmative action in employment, for example, has become increasingly controversial. The nexus of race, poverty, and urban decay has, as in the United States, become an increasingly salient problem in London and other English cities. In 1989, underclass maven Charles Murray published a cover story in the *Sunday Times Magazine* about a British underclass that catalogued the same apparent pathologies that made his reputation in the United States. Although the article makes very little mention of race, the racial subtext of the piece is unmistakable; most of the faces in the photographs accompanying the story are black; take out the proper names and the article could very well be mistaken for a *New York Times Magazine* piece about the United States. Black Britons are increasingly linked in British political discourse with many of the social problems associated with the urban "underclass," especially crime. Party politics is increasingly divided by race. Blacks are generally solid Labour voters, while Conservatives tend to oppose policies such as affirmative action that minorities often favor. At the same time, British politics has thus far avoided the development of a strong right-wing, racist, anti-immigrant party of the sort that has convulsed politics on the European continent in recent years. The far-right nationalist British National Party won fewer than 50,000 votes in the 2001 general election, although it did manage to capture a handful of municipal council seats in local elections in 2001.[45]

Even more clearly than in the United States, New Commonwealth immigration to Britain was a move from periphery to center. Immigrants left behind underdeveloped, largely agrarian economies that had long been linked to Britain through the commercial nexus of the empire and that had played a significant role in fueling England's industrial and commercial growth as suppliers of raw materials, consumers of finished products, and partners in the slave trade.[46] In the West Indies particularly, as in the American South, the post-emancipation economy was based in labor-repressive plantation agriculture that limited the economic and political opportunities available to black men and women, and even as the economies of West Indian countries were expanding, the gap between standards of living in the West Indies and Britain continued to draw migrants.[47] The journey to Britain for immigrants from the Commonwealth was also one from subjecthood to citizenship, although in practice the equal citizenship rights of black Britons were not always respected. E.J.B. Rose wrote that "the frequently quoted proposition '*Civis Britannicus Sum*,' came to mean in practice 'I am a second-class (but equal status) citizen.' "[48] Nevertheless, it is a critical comparative point that migrants to Britain from the Commonwealth, New as well as Old, came to Britain as presumptive citizens with legitimate claims on the British state for all the rights and privileges of any other British citizens, native- or foreign-born, black or white.

France

Unlike Britain, France has long been a country of immigration. As early as the first half of the nineteenth century, as many as several hundred thousand foreign-born people lived within its boundaries (although not until 1851 did the French census record the nationality of residents). During the second half of the nineteenth century, France attracted a series of waves of immigrants, mostly from elsewhere in Europe—largely from Belgium, Italy, Germany, and Switzerland in the late nineteenth century, and from Poland, Spain, and Portugal in the early twentieth and on into the interwar years. Thus by the 1930s, 7 percent of the population of France—more than 2.5 million people—had been born elsewhere. Until 1921, immigration from Africa was not even recorded in the national census—African immigrants were lumped into a miscellaneous category. Between the wars, a small number of Africans began to move to France— enough to earn their own census category but still less than 5 percent of all immigrants.[49]

After World War II, labor shortages made the recruitment and regulation of immigration a matter of the first importance for the French government. In 1945, France established its Basic Law on Immigration, creating the Office National d'Immigration (ONI) under the Ministry of Labor. The ONI was to exercise exclusive control over the recruitment of immigrant labor, with the intent to link immigration to the demand for labor in France.[50] However, these controls failed to stem immigration. Employers found it easy and preferable to skirt the ONI system and recruit foreign workers on their own, and the French government itself proceeded to negotiate bilateral labor migration agreements with several countries that had excess manpower.

At the same time, the pressures of decolonization and the increasingly fragile relations between France and Algeria, her oldest and closest colony, began to shape immigration politics. Despite the preference of some French policymakers for ethnically based immigration controls, in 1947 the government granted citizenship and free entry to Algerians. "From that date," writes Patrick Weil, the leading analyst of French immigration policy, "colonial matters dominated immigration politics, which reorganized itself around the Algerian problem. Legally, the immigrant was always Italian, Spanish, Polish, or Portugese. Politically and then socially, he became Algerian."[51] Even after independence, French officials were reluctant to limit Algerian immigration too severely. The Evian accords of 1962, which ended the French-Algerian war and secured Algeria's independence, continued the policy of free entry, a policy that lasted until 1968 when France, in the wake of its own domestic political turbulence, unilaterally limited Algerian immigration to around one thousand per month. Finally, in July 1974, as France was sliding into a deep recession, the government under newly elected President Valéry Giscard d'Estaing cut off all further immigration (although immigration, mostly for family reunification and seasonal work, continued after 1974, albeit at much lower rates than before).[52]

Between 1945 and 1974—*les trentes glorieuses,* thirty years of economic progress and expansion—more than 1.8 million immigrants entered France legally under the auspices of ONI; this figure does not even count illegal immigration or immigration under bilateral agreements with other countries. Because French population statistics record only nationality and country of origin, but not race or ethnicity, it is impossible to find even reasonably precise and consistent counts of the nonwhite population; but it is possible, by piecing together shreds of information from the sources that do exist, to gauge its relative size.[53] Algerians made up the single largest national group of postwar immigrants. Between 1949 and 1955, 180,000 people came to France from Algeria, and only 160,000 from all other countries combined. For a brief time in late 1962, in the aftermath of the Algerian war, Algerians were entering France at the rate of 70,000 per week. In all, Algerian immigration to France totaled some 700,000 during this period, along with 170,000 Moroccans, and nearly 100,000 Tunisians. By the 1980s, more than 3.6 million foreign nationals lived in France—nearly 7 percent of the population. More than half of these were non-European, including more than 1.5 million Africans (of which more than half were Algerian). In addition, by 1986 there were nearly 300,000 "Franco-Algerians," children born in France of at least one Algerian parent. Finally, by 1990, there were more than 200,000 African-born French citizens. The volume of postwar, postcolonial immigration inescapably and dramatically transformed French politics and society. As in Britain and the United States, nonwhite immigrants concentrated in a few regions in France, particularly in Paris and its suburbs, Provence (especially in and around Marseille), Lyon, and northern industrial cities such as Lille.[54]

The political consequences of nonwhite immigration have been as profound as in Britain, although with different consequences, given differences in both the institutional structure of politics and the cultural and ideological repertoires available in French political life. On the one hand, French politics remained officially color-blind. The assimilationist tendencies of French political life were amplified by memories of collaboration with a racist regime under Vichy and found expression in a new republican synthesis that sought to purge ethnic, racial, and religious distinctions from the public sphere altogether. Pointing in the same direction were the political controls to which immigrants in France were subject, most prominently the restrictions on the creation of ethnic or national associations. As a result, French political leaders and institutions have been reluctant to recognize the distinctive situation of African immigrants.[55]

At the same time, French politics since the 1960s has increasingly been occupied with the challenges of racial and ethnic diversity. When the Socialist François Mitterrand became president in 1981, he did not roll back the immigration restrictions that had been put in place by de Gaulle and his right-wing successors in the 1960s and 1970s (just as the Labour governments did not repeal immigration restrictions adopted by Conservative governments in Britain). Mitterrand's government did, however, lift the ban on the organization of ethnic associations, allowing racially and nationally identified groups to organize directly to press political demands. Mitterrand also reformed France's governmental structure, giving much more power to regional and local governments, providing a further opening for the electoral politics of race, particularly in the areas around Paris, Lyon, Marseille, and elsewhere where immigrants are most concentrated. The most important consequence of the racialization of French politics, however, has been the rise of the National Front, an explicitly racist and anti-immigrant political party led by Jean-Marie Le Pen, a former member of the French Foreign Legion who served in Southeast Asia and Algeria and whose political career began as a member of Pierre Poujade's right-wing populist movement in the 1950s. In national politics, Le Pen has consistently received between 15 and 20 percent of the first-round presidential vote, wreaking particular havoc in 2002 when he defeated Socialist Prime Minister Lionel Jospin for a place in the second-round runoff. The National Front, however, has been even more consequential at the local and regional level, where it has won several mayoralties and joined government coalitions in a number of regional governments. The National Front's success, in turn, has further fueled the neo-republican synthesis in French politics, making the "respectable" parties of both right and left reluctant to address racial and ethnic political dilemmas directly.[56]

French immigrants from North Africa (as well as West Africa and Southeast Asia), like their British and American counterparts, moved from periphery to center, from former colonies that remained underdeveloped and economically dependent to the metropolitan, industrial core of the former empire.[57] Migration from Algeria to France had an added political dimension because of the Algerian war of independence from 1954 to 1962, which accelerated immigration from Algeria and also created a distinctive class of political immigrants, the "harkis," Algerian Muslims who were recruited to fight for the French and were "repatriated" to France by the French government after the war.[58] Immigration to France also constituted a transition from colonial subjecthood to citizenship, if not for immigrants themselves then for their children born in France, who were automatically eligible for French citizenship under French nationality law (which, despite being made more restrictive in 1993, retains the principle of *jus soli,* the right to citizenship for those born in national territory).[59] Thus, like African American migrants in the United States and New Commonwealth immigrants in Britain, postcolonial immigrants to France were presumptive citizens who could claim rights from the French state.

CONCLUSIONS

These postwar developments—welfare reform and migration—set the stage for the incorporation challenges of the postwar era, principally by reconfiguring the ideological and institutional circumstances in which those challenges would arise. The United States emerged from World War II and its immediate aftermath, first of all, with its political culture of race consciousness heightened and intensified. The experience of the war itself and the mass migration that followed meant that African Americans were fast becoming a national rather than a regional presence, and persistent racial inequality was becoming an increasingly troubling political issue that posed a stark challenge to Americans' self-image of color-blind fairness and opportunity. Accordingly, tensions began to grow both between race-conscious and color-blind visions of American society and between varieties of race consciousness—on the one hand Southern (and, increasingly, Northern) racism, growing even more virulent as it came under mounting attack, and on the other hand a more benign race-conscious vision, aimed at the remedial targeting of resources and opportunities at American blacks to achieve more equal results. In Britain, similarly, postwar immigration also began gradually to promote a similar attitude of race consciousness, which gelled in the 1960s in the multicultural, "race-relations" approach to integration policy that accompanied race-based immigration restrictions. In France, postwar migration, coming as it did on the heels of the shameful race-consciousness of Vichy, tended to reinforce the official color-blindness of French political culture, although in a context of steadily rising racial tension.

Institutionally, postwar welfare reforms deepened and solidified prewar patterns along two dimensions. One was the distinction between social insurance for workers and residual public assistance programs for non-workers, and the other was the distinction between centralized and decentralized policy. In the United States, these two dimensions overlapped, particularly in the divide between national social insurance and parochial public assistance, which would prove critical in shaping the encounter between African Americans and the welfare state. Britain and France offer different configurations of these institutional elements. While the social insurance–public assistance rift is essential to all three welfare states, in Britain the two types of social protection are tied together in a relatively uniform, centralized system while work-oriented social insurance continues to dominate the increasingly centralized French welfare state, leaving nonworkers largely outside of its generous provisions.

These institutional differences, moreover, helped to construct different patterns of linkage between racial groups and the state, mediated by labor market access and state structure. In combination with both the institutional structure of national welfare states and national ideological and cultural traditions regarding race and race policy, these patterns of group-state linkage would prove essential in shaping the patterns of racial incorporation that emerged in postwar generations. In the United States, these linkages differed fundamentally across the rigid social insurance–public assistance line that divided the American welfare state, and so in the following chapters I take up these two stories—of racial incorporation in Social Security and "welfare"—separately.

Chapter Five

ENCOUNTERS WITH THE WELFARE STATE: SOCIAL SECURITY AND SOCIAL INSURANCE

THE POLITICAL SETTING for the African American encounter with the postwar American welfare state changed quite dramatically in the decades after World War II. Before mid-century, the presumption of African American inferiority was central to American political beliefs. After World War II, however, the racist presumptions of American political life began quite dramatically to recede. Over this same period, African Americans built a social movement that did perhaps more to transform American society than any other single political development of that era.

The civil rights movement sought and achieved revolutionary change in American race relations. Building on an existing organizational infrastructure rooted in churches and local NAACP chapters, the civil rights movement began with local pressure in the South for the desegregation of municipal services, public accommodations, and schools.[1] As the movement gained success, resources, and widespread support, it began to focus its attention both on the national political arena, where it pressed for the Civil Rights and Voting Rights acts, and on the North, where segregation and discrimination tended to be embedded in patterns of economic and social relations rather than encoded in law.[2] Over time, the movement's substantive focus began to shift from legal segregation and civil rights to issues of economic welfare and inequality. The 1963 March on Washington, for example, was conceived not only (or even primarily) to pressure the Kennedy administration on civil rights but also to "draw public attention to 'the economic subordination of the American Negro,' the pressing need for 'the creation of more jobs for all Americans,' and the wider goal of 'a broad and fundamental program of economic justice.' "[3] Toward the end of his life Martin Luther King's efforts were increasingly focused on economic questions, as in his Chicago campaign of 1965 or the Poor People's Campaign, which brought King fatally to Memphis in 1968.

These changes in the American political landscape substantially reshaped the context in which African Americans would encounter the welfare state in the postwar era. National social insurance, however, was relatively insulated from these forces both because its institutional structure shielded it from national debates about poverty and because, unlike public assistance, its constituency had grown less racialized over time. In contrast with "welfare," Social Security was not associated with a racially identified client population, nor was it the subject of a public, race-conscious campaign for expansion. Rather, despite its clearly racially exclusionary origins, Social Security expanded its scope and reach relatively smoothly, beginning in the 1950s. These developments occurred with minimal racial rancor and resulted from a number of interlocking factors: the program's national, centralized institutional structure; its ironic color-blind bona fides and its ability, for the most part, to fly under the highly sensitive race-conscious radar of postwar social politics; and the unshakable links of rights-based social citizenship that it conferred on its beneficiaries, based on their strong connection to the labor market.

In this chapter, I trace the fortunes of African Americans in Social Security over the postwar period and show how institutional features of the program, combined with its rather ambiguous place struggle between race-conscious and color-blind policy models, promoted the smooth and successful incorporation of African Americans. I then contrast the path of American social insurance with the case of France, which best highlights the configurational differences that produced success in the United States and less complete incorporation in France.

Despite the French welfare state's disproportionate emphasis on social insurance as a vehicle for providing social protection and despite the color-blind context of French social politics, French social policy has proven unable to incorporate minorities as fully as American Social Security. These differences stem particularly from France's particular difficulties in breaking out of its own self-imposed color-blind policy model, difficulties that are amplified by the structure of the French welfare state, which tends, like its American counterpart, to magnify distinctions created by civil society and the labor market between workers and nonworkers. Nevertheless, the presence in France of some universal social benefits, guaranteed and enforced by the central state, has mitigated some of the more inegalitarian effects of French welfare policy and protected the French welfare state from the direst failure of minority incorporation.

This comparison in particular highlights the importance of institutional arrangements, not in shaping policies by themselves but in translating the ideological content of policies—color blindness or race consciousness—into concrete outcomes. It is not self-evident how multiculturalism or assimilation, even when embedded in public policies, might affect the prospects for minority incorporation. Each might set in motion different chains of events that could result either in more or less successful incorporation. On the one hand, race-conscious strategies invite discrimination and exclusion by categorizing social groups by race and emphasizing politically constructed differences. On the other hand, they can help call attention to inequalities that might otherwise go unnoticed and thereby enable deliberate measures to redress them. Similarly, assimilationist strategies can discourage racial division by applying universalistic rules, but they can also conceal inequalities behind a color-blind façade and inhibit racial and ethnic mobilization that might enhance prospects for incorporation. The comparison between national social insurance in the United States and the social-insurance-dominated welfare state reveals this indeterminacy and displays how welfare state institutions helped to transform American race consiousness into color-blind incorporation success and to temper the perils of French color blindness through active, if covert, race consiousness.

PATHS OF DEVELOPMENT: RACE AND SOCIAL SECURITY

Despite the exclusionary race-conscious context in which it was born and grew to maturity, Social Security became increasingly racially inclusive over its first generation. Two factors in particular propelled the program toward greater racial incorporation: the expansion of coverage, which brought into the program categories of workers that had initially been left out, and the growth of benefits, which benefited all pension recipients but especially minorities and others at the low end of the wage scale. These factors, in turn, were products primarily of a set of institutional forces that allowed the program's expansionary impulse to trump the resilient ideological power of racial exclusion of racial exclusion. Had Social Security's institutional features been different—less national and centralized, less contributory, more sector- or state-specific—its capacity to advance racial incorporation would likely have been diminished. At the same time, the transformation of Social Security from an exclusive to an inclusive incorporative program was more-or-less complete before the civil rights revolution and its attendant color-blind vision reached their peak in the early 1960s. This timing suggests that it was primarily institutional and not ideological developments that made it possible for color blindness to flourish in this significant sector of the American welfare state.

Following an initial decade or more of considerable political uncertainty, Social Security's path has been one of consistent expansion and broadening inclusion. In the early years after the passage of the Social Security Act, several of the program's features came under attack, particularly its financing plan, which called for the program to build up considerable reserves in the Treasury from the collection of payroll taxes to fund future benefits. Payroll taxes were to be collected beginning almost immediately (in 1937, giving the Social Security Board time to get organized), but benefits were not scheduled to be paid until 1942. Discomfort with this financing arrangement led to the adoption of amendments in 1939 that shifted the system to pay-as-you-go financing by moving the initial benefit payment up to 1940, postponing a scheduled increase in the payroll tax rate, and creating a separate trust fund in the Treasury for Social Security receipts and expenditures.[4] This move effectively (and rather ironically, since this was not the intention of the members of Congress who initiated the amendment) helped shore up the program's shaky political support—by accelerating benefits and limiting pressure to raise taxes quickly. But it also exposed the program to political risks, particularly the prospect that general revenues might someday be necessary to cover benefit obligations.

During the 1940s, Social Security came under considerable political pressure from both the Left and the Right. On the Left, remnants of the Townsend movement, which had pushed for generous, universal, noncontributory old-age pensions in the 1930s, remained vocal and put considerable pressure on policymakers. But conservative opponents of the program were also lying in wait during the 1940s, and with the election of Eisenhower along with Republican majorities in Congress in 1952, many thought they had their long-awaited opportunity to destroy the program. The House Ways and Means Committee created a special subcommittee on Social Security, chaired by Representative Carl T. Curtis of Nebraska, who had long been a burr under Social Security's saddle. Curtis hoped to exploit a weakness in the program's structure that had been exposed by the 1939 switch to pay-as-you-go financing, namely the lack of a legally enforceable obligation for the payment of benefits. The highlight of the subcommittee's fall hearings was Curtis's attempt to browbeat recently retired Social Security Commissioner Arthur Altmeyer, testifying under subpoena, into admitting that Old-Age Insurance was not really "insurance" because it did not issue individual contracts for retirement benefits. Curtis's hostile intentions fit hand-in-glove with a proposal being floated by the United States Chamber of Commerce to recast Social Security as a truly universal program under which pensions for all elderly citizens would be funded out of current revenues (rather than out of a reserve funded by worker and employer contributions). Social Security supporters saw the Chamber proposal as a conservative scheme to do away with the program altogether. Fueling their fears, the secretary of the new Department of Health, Education, and Welfare (HEW), Oveta Culp Hobby, convened a secret advisory group of outside Social Security "experts" that was stacked with businessmen who supported the Chamber's plan. When word of the so-called "Hobby lobby" leaked to the press (through the good graces of Wilbur Cohen, the consummate Social Security insider and an estimable political operator in the corridors and backrooms of Washington—and himself later an HEW secretary under Johnson), Hobby had to expand the advisory group. The Eisenhower administration, left with considerable egg on its face, quickly and quietly abandoned the Chamber plan and instead lent its support to a large expansion of Social Security.[5]

Although this episode—the acceptance by an "opposition" president of one of the crown jewels of the New Deal—marked, in effect, the political coming-of-age of Social Security, it was actually only one in a long series of program expansions that over time helped to anchor the program as one of the fundamental and most universal sources of American social citizenship (see table 5.1). The 1939 amendment included the first such expansion, extending social insurance coverage to surviving spouses and children of covered workers who died before reaching retirement age. But it also kicked off a run of expanded coverage, driven by the program's growing popularity and the additional revenue (and deferred costs) that expansion offered, bringing categories of workers who were initially excluded under the Social Security umbrella. (In two instances, in 1939 and 1948, small groups of workers initially included were excluded; these are minor exceptions to the overall expansionary trend, however, and were later reversed.) The major period of coverage expansion was the 1950s, when the largest categories of excluded private-sector employees—farmers and farm workers, domestic employees, and the self-employed—were included. By 1960, Social Security provided essentially universal coverage for workers.

For African Americans, this expansion of coverage has had important consequences. First, two of the categories of workers excluded from coverage in 1935—agricultural workers and domestic servants—were disproportionately black. Approximately one-half of all African American workers (three-fifths in the South) were farm or domestic laborers. But the drive for program expansion, propelled by the ambitions of Social Security program executives as well as by the political logic of the policy itself (under which adding new workers who pay taxes now and collect benefits later allowed policymakers to keep taxes low and benefits high), overcame persistent resistance to including African Americans in social insurance. Significantly, the major step in this expansion came with the 1954 amendment to the Social Security Act. The amendment brought the lion's share of farm and domestic workers into Social Security and was—uniquely among the amendments of this era—adopted under unified Republican control of the presidency and Congress (when the Southern Democrats who usually wielded such powerful influence over policy-making were temporarily displaced).[6]

TABLE 5.1
Expansions (and Contractions) of Social Security Coverage

Year	Categories
1939	*Dependents and survivors* Seamen Bank and loan-association employees (Agricultural processing workers excluded)
1948	(News and magazine vendors excluded)
1950	Non-farm self-employed, excluding professionals Regularly employed agricultural workers Regularly employed domestic workers State and local government employees—voluntary Nonprofit employees—voluntary
1954	Self-employed farmers Most self-employed professionals—architects, funeral directors, accountants Remaining agricultural workers Remaining domestic workers Clergy—voluntary
1956	*Disability* Expanded self-employed professionals—lawyers, dentists, veterinarians, optometrists
1965	*Medicare* Doctors
1984	Nonprofit employees—compulsory
1986	Federal government employees
1990	State and local government employees—compulsory for those not covered by public pensions

Note: Italics indicate program expansion; parentheses indicate exclusion of groups previously covered; all other entries indicate extension of coverage to groups not previously covered.

At the same time, Congress acted repeatedly to increase the level of Social Security benefits. The first and most significant blow for more generous social insurance was struck in 1950, when the program was at risk of being engulfed by rapidly growing and popular public assistance programs for the elderly. In the amendments of that year, in addition to expanding coverage, raising payroll taxes, and ending the authorization to go to general revenues to pay benefits, Congress increased Social Security benefits (which had not changed in ten years and whose real value had

TABLE 5.2
Social Security Benefit Increases (before indexing)

Effective Date	Percent Increase
September 1950	77.0
September 1952	12.5
September 1954	13.0
January 1959	7.0
January 1965	7.0
February 1968	13.0
January 1970	15.0
January 1971	10.0
September 1972	20.0
March 1974	7.0

Source: Derthick, Policymaking for Social Security,
429–32; U.S. Social Security Administration, A Brief
History of Social Security, SSA Publication No. 21–059
(2000).

deteriorated badly) by 77 percent.[7] In addition to preparing the way for
the ultimate political triumph of social insurance as the pension paradigm
for American workers, the 1950 amendments set off a flurry of regular
benefits increases that accelerated over the next two decades as Democrats
in Congress and the White House learned the political virtues of generous
and well-timed (they always seemed to arrive just in time for elections)
Social Security increases (see table 5.2). In 1972, at the instigation of President Richard Nixon, who hoped to deprive Democrats of the perpetual
political credit they got from raising benefits, Congress instituted auto-
matic annual cost-of-living increases in benefits.[8]

Figure 5.1 traces the value of Social Security benefits from 1940, when
the first benefits were paid, to 1974, when inflation indexing began (the
1974 increase was temporary; after May 1974 benefits reverted to their
February 1974 levels, which became the base for subsequent cost-of-living adjustments). The figure shows the value of a hypothetical $100 bene-
fit in 1940 adjusted annually for inflation and periodically for legislated
benefit increases. During the first decade, benefits lost more than 40 percent of their purchasing power, until the 1950 amendments—the dramatic
first upward move in the figure—restored them to their original level. The
1954 amendment for the first time brought benefits to a substantially
higher level, approximately 17 percent above the original baseline, and

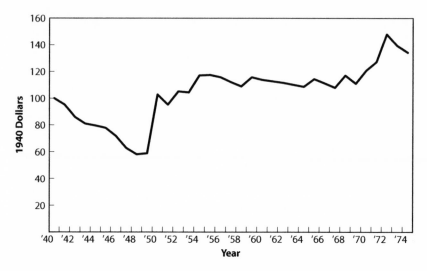

FIGURE 5.1 Real Social Security Benefits (real value of $100 benefit in 1940). Source: U.S. Social Security Administration, *A Brief History of Social Security*, Publication No. 21-059 (2000).

established a plateau that Congress maintained for the next fifteen years with periodic (and increasingly frequent) increases. Beginning in the early 1970s, benefits took a sharp move upward, as the Democratic Congress and the Republican president very nearly fell over each other in their efforts to claim credit for expanding Social Security (fueled in part by House Ways and Means Chairman Wilbur Mills's short-lived campaign for the 1972 Democratic presidential nomination).[9] By the mid-1970s, benefits were nearly 40 percent higher than in 1940, and they have since grown with inflation.[10]

For African Americans and other minorities, this pattern of development has meant growing inclusion in Social Security, within the limits of their participation in the labor market. Since the beginning of the program, minority participation has grown steadily. Figures 5.2 and 5.3 show the overall growth of nonwhite participation in Social Security from 1940, when the first Social Security benefits were paid, until 2000. These data were compiled from the annual data reported by the Social Security Administration (and its predecessor, the Social Security Board), in the *Social Security Bulletin* and its annual statistical supplement. They include benefits paid to retired workers only (excluding benefits for spouses and other dependents as well as disability benefits), both because this is the most straightforward measure of the reach of retirement pensions and because these were the data most consistently available over the entire life

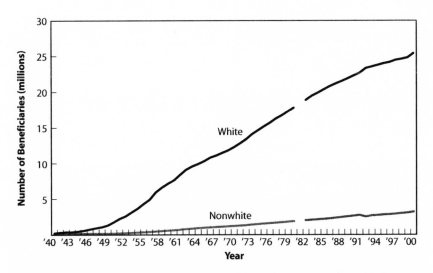

FIGURE 5.2   Social Security Retirement Beneficiaries by Race, 1940–2000. Source: *Social Security Bulletin, Annual Statistical Supplement.*

of the program. Data on the race of Social Security beneficiaries come from self-reported designations on Form SS-5, the application for Social Security numbers. The inclusion of a race question on this form was mildly controversial in the 1930s; the NAACP opposed it, on the grounds that the information could be used to discriminate, but they lost the fight and the Social Security Administration has collected and reported aggregate race data every since. The original Form SS-5 allowed applicants to check one of three racial categories: white, negro, or other. Since the early 1980s, following the Office of Management and Budget's Directive No. 15, issued in 1977, the race question on Form SS-5 has included a broader set of categories: Asian, Hispanic, non-Hispanic black, non-Hispanic white, and American Indian.[11] But because Social Security numbers are issued either at birth or early in a person's working life, almost all of the people currently receiving benefits filed applications with the old categories; consequently, benefits data are divided simply into white and non-white categories. These data are thus a rather blunt instrument for gauging the precise racial consequences of Social Security benefits. Nevertheless, they are useful in chronicling the broad transformation of the program from a whites-only benefit to a reasonably universal one. The Social Security Administration did not report data for 1981 due to computer problems, hence the gaps in these figures as well as those in Figure 5.4.

In 1940, approximately 5,500 nonwhite retirees were among the 132,000 people who began receiving Social Security checks, and the num-

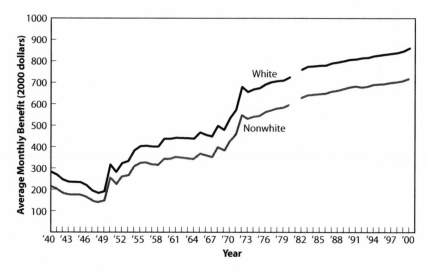

FIGURE 5.3 Social Security Retirement Benefits by Race, 1940–2000. Source: *Social Security Bulletin, Annual Statistical Supplement.*

ber of nonwhite beneficiaries has grown steadily since. Nonwhite beneficiaries have always received smaller pensions, on average, than whites because benefits are tied to the wages a beneficiary earned when he was working. But over time, as more categories of workers have been included in Social Security benefits and as minorities have entered the work force in greater strength (although within limits), the relative position of minorities in the Social Security system has improved. Figure 5.4 shows nonwhite beneficiaries and benefit levels as a percentage of white levels and reveals steady growth, as the labor-force participation of African Americans and other minorities has grown and as they have earned social insurance rights accordingly. Consequently, as Social Security has played a central role in binding the American middle and working classes to the national state by providing social benefits based on rights, this development has included African Americans to the extent that their position in the political economy brought them under the national welfare state's protective umbrella.

Amid this picture of steadily growing incorporation, there are some signs that the status of African Americans and other minorities is rather more ambiguous. Minorities are more likely either to work irregularly or to be out of the labor force altogether and hence to fall between the cracks of social insurance protection. Those minorities who do work earn lower wages, on average, and because Social Security payroll taxes are regressive (a flat percentage of wages from the first dollar earned up to a limit and

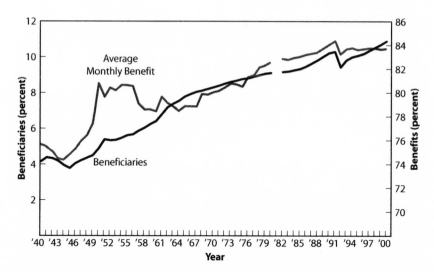

FIGURE 5.4 Nonwhite Social Security Beneficiaries and Benefits as a Percentage of White, 1940–2000. Source: *Social Security Bulletin, Annual Statistical Supplement.*

no taxes on earnings above the limit) are thus likely to pay a higher percentage of their earnings in Social Security taxes. On the benefits end, African Americans are likely to earn lower average benefits because benefit levels are related to wages earned while working. Moreover, African Americans have lower life expectancies than whites, making it more likely that they will die before retirement age and, should they reach retirement age, likely that they will receive less over the course of retirement.[12] On the other hand, benefits are somewhat progressive because there is a minimum benefit that favors low earners while the benefits of high earners are capped at a maximum level. Overall, however, these considerations do not alter the powerful conclusion from the history of Social Security: it is the closest thing to a truly color-blind program of social provision and social citizenship that the United States has known.

RACE AND WELFARE IN FRANCE: CONSERVATISM AND THE IRONIES OF COLOR BLINDNESS

Dominated as it was by social insurance, the French welfare state seemed poised to emulate the American pattern of smooth and seamless minority incorporation into this realm of social provision. For French workers, including the new postwar immigrants and their families, the welfare state provided strong connections to the state through generous, rights-based benefits. But both the institutional and ideological contexts of French social policy differed from those of the United States, producing substantially different political dynamics and different incorporation results. The conservatism of the French welfare state meant that, despite similarities on the social insurance side of the ledger, residual public assistance policies for those left out of the labor market were limited (at least until relatively recently). The trend toward centralization of the welfare state meant greater uniformity in benefits and administration, although it was reversed somewhat by decentralizing reforms in the 1980s. The color-blind orientation of French policy seemed to reinforce the prospect of strong incorporation by offering policymakers and administrators no grounds for making racial distinctions in defining policies or awarding benefits. But France's official color blindness did not alone determine the welfare incorporation prospects for French minorities. On the one hand, it did not prevent local forces, especially municipal authorities, from discriminating in the allocation of benefits and the provision of social services. On the other hand, neither did it prevent the central state from taking notice of incorporation outcomes or from stepping in to protect minorities, even to the point of taking affirmative steps to ensure incorporation prospects. As in the United States, institutional structures—particularly the pattern of centralization in the welfare state—proved crucial in translating the ideological content of policy into concrete results.

The large-scale immigration of North Africans and other nonwhite postcolonial migrants presented France and the French welfare state with a profound dilemma: how to target integration efforts and resources on these new immigrants without violating the strong political and cultural bias against recognizing racial and ethnic distinctions.[13] In the first decade after World War II, French policy toward immigrants was quite haphazard and laissez-faire. Not only did the government exert very little actual control over the immigration flows into the country, but it also took little or no direct action to address problems of living conditions for immigrants or of their more general incorporation into French society.[14] Unable to find housing, many immigrant workers in France lived in steadily worsening conditions, often in tin and cardboard shantytowns, known as *bidonvilles*, at the edges of major cities.

In 1958, when the statist Fifth Republic replaced the chaotic Fourth (which came to grief largely over the Algerian crisis), the state stepped in and the Labor Ministry created the Fonds d'Action Sociale (FAS) to oversee and finance efforts primarily to improve housing conditions for Algerian workers in France.[15] Most of the FAS's funding came, in effect, from immigrant workers themselves. More than 70 percent of the FAS's revenue in its early years came from the Caisse Nationale d'Allocations Familiales, the family allowance fund, which in turn paid reduced allowances to immigrants whose children had stayed behind. (It also received funds from a tax on employers who failed to spend an obligatory 1 percent of their payrolls on workers' housing and from the state.) In its early years its budget was small—11 million francs in 1959—and it was primarily a housing agency. As late as 1967, more than four-fifths of its budget went to finance the construction of housing for immigrant workers, mostly hostels for single men but also family housing.[16]

Over time, however, the FAS broadened its scope and expanded its activities to include education, job training, and welfare and social services, to the point where it became the linchpin of the French state's effort to "insert" immigrants into French society. By the 1990s its budget was more than a billion francs annually—a ten-fold increase since 1970—approximately evenly divided among housing, education, and social and cultural services. It now funds more than three thousand projects, many of which are undertaken by minority organizations, especially since organizing restrictions were relaxed in the early 1980s.[17] The FAS embodies the dilemma inherent in the French model of minority integration, in which a centralized state attempts to manage minority incorporation at the individual level, without recognizing or validating ethnic, racial, religious, or other communities. But to accomplish this, the state has increasingly relied on policies that target minorities, granting them both benefits and legitimacy, a stance that has become increasingly controversial and politically risky since the rise of Le Pen and the National Front in the early 1980s.

As power was decentralized in the 1980s and the FAS turned its attention away from housing and toward other issues, local authorities gained more control over the location and allocation of low-cost public housing as well as other welfare state resources. Hence, local officials had greater incentive to save money by restricting the settlement of the poor in local public housing, thereby limiting welfare spending and other costs they feared would be associated with the presence of low-income minority residents. Armed with this new authority, mayors began increasingly to use their new authority to sort racially defined immigrants and their descendants into the least desirable units in the least desirable areas, and even in some instances to refuse them housing altogether. Moreover, because nearly half of France's North African immigrants lived in public rental housing as recently as the early 1990s (compared to one-third of all immigrants and less than one-fifth of the total population), racial minorities are particularly exposed to such political manipulation. One effect of this manipulation of housing access has been to create concentrated minority pockets of dependency on state-provided income, particularly rent subsidies and other income support—especially in the notorious *banlieues*, the outer-ring suburbs of Paris, Lyon, Marseille, and other French cities, where large concentrations of minorities live in conditions of isolation and deprivation.[18]

As in the United States, institutional factors made the critical difference in promoting racial incorporation. First, policy centralization worked to protect minorities. The central state, through the FAS (whose very existence belied the French state's official color blindness) as well as the traditional ministries and the prefect system, actively intervened in some areas to protect minorities from exclusion and discrimination. Decentralization, conversely, tended to limit the French welfare state's integrative capacity by rendering policy more prone to capture by local public officials with racially exclusionary aims. Second, the structure of political parties and group mobilization in the French political system tended to inhibit minorities per se from participating in the formation of policy coalitions. This was particularly true at the local level where, unlike in the United States, minorities had fragile political linkages, minority organizations were generally weak (if present at all), and the respectable political parties of both the Right and the Left shied away from addressing issues of race and integration directly for fear of baiting the National Front.[19]

The Socialist governments of the 1980s responded by creating a number of programs to provide targeted assistance to areas with high concentrations of poverty and social need. The most prominent of these programs has been Educational Priority Zones (ZEP), created in 1981 to provide additional resources to schools in depressed areas—"zones where social conditions constitute a risk factor or even an obstacle for the scholarly success of the children and adolescents who live there and therefore for their social insertion."[20] In effect, as was widely recognized but rarely acknowledged outright, this meant high concentrations of immigrant and minority residents; students of foreign nationality were overrepresented in the ZEP by nearly three to one in the mid-1980s (28.9 percent of students in ZEP schools were non-French, compared to 10.8 percent of students in all schools). "The proportion of foreign elementary students appears," wrote one analyst, "to have been a criterion determining the choice of ZEP."[21] To some degree this assessment is true; the proportion of foreigners is one in an unprioritized list of possible selection criteria issued by the Education Ministry.[22] Concurrently, the national government created a special urban policy to assist targeted areas, which coincided to a great degree with ZEP.[23]

Like the FAS, the ZEP embodied the tension in race and welfare politics in France—and elsewhere—between the cultural imperative of assimilationism and the political imperative to address problems of racial and ethnic incorporation directly. Layered atop this dilemma in the French case was the tension between the rather forced republican consensus that increasingly dominated French political life, on the one hand, and the centralized, statist institutional architecture of the Fifth Republic, which gave national political leaders the power to address instances of racial inequality and imbalance when they were so inclined.

In some instances, the central state has intervened directly in the administration of the French welfare state to promote the integration of minorities. In one celebrated incident in 1990, the right-wing mayor of the Paris suburb of Montfermeil tried to exclude immigrants' children from the local *école maternelle,* or nursery school, only to be overruled by the departmental prefect, the central government's representative, at the behest of Education Minister Lionel Jospin. This highly publicized episode was only one in a series of instances in which decisions by local authorities to exclude immigrants or racial minorities from benefits were reversed by the national government; the incidents involved a range of social benefits including family leave, family allowances, and birth allowances.[24]

Direct evidence of the effects of such political maneuverings on nonwhite incorporation into the French welfare state is maddeningly sparse because France, in keeping with its republican assimilationist political tradition, prohibits the collecting and storing of data about the racial and ethnic characteristics of individuals.[25] (This prohibition itself and the lengths to which the state has to go to promote minority incorporation suggest the limits that political institutions face in circumventing the color-blind cultural and ideological frame of French politics.) What evidence there is, however, suggests a mixed picture. As in the United States and Britain, there are substantial disparities between native French and immigrants from Africa and Asia in employment and earnings. Rates of immigrant unemployment in the 1990s in France were nearly twice total unemployment rates (more than twice among men), and unemployment among immigrants from Africa (both North and West) and Turkey was nearly three times as high as among the general population. The disparity also affects the children of immigrants regardless of citizenship. In the early 1990s, only 30 percent of young men of Algerian descent had steady employment for a year after leaving school, less than half the figure for the population as a whole and approximately half the figures for Spanish and Portuguese immigrants and their children. North African immigrant families were also more than twice as likely to have incomes below 90,000 francs (about $17,000) than native-born families, and less than half as likely to have incomes above 160,000 francs (about $30,000).[26]

Some of these barriers to economic success and social integration result from factors such as disparities in education and mastery of the French language. In addition, noncitizens are legally barred from public-sector employment and from certain professions, restrictions estimated to exclude immigrants from more than five million jobs. Beyond these effects, however, there is also ample evidence of intentional racial discrimination in the French labor market, affecting recruitment, hiring, firing, promotion, pay, and working conditions. Much of this discrimination occurs through outright differential treatment of immigrants and *Français de couleur*—discriminatory hiring and promotions, lower pay for similar jobs, longer hours, smaller bonuses, and so forth. But subtler forms of discrimination occur through nepotism and other kinds of recruitment networks, which tend to restrict minorities' access to many jobs, as well informal segregation and even racial and ethnic harassment in workplaces.[27]

Although these patterns of inequality are no more severe than elsewhere, the French welfare state, which places such heavy emphasis on employment as a source of social rights, probably amplifies their effects. During *les trentes glorieuses,* immigrants came to France from North Africa and elsewhere—often skirting national immigration laws with the help of employers—to fill labor shortages in the French economy. But beginning in the 1970s the economy tightened, reducing employment opportunities especially for immigrants, and in the early 1970s the French government tried to end new immigration, whereupon France found itself, somewhat to its surprise, with a large and growing permanent, economically and socially marginal, and increasingly racialized population of immigrants and their children who were entitled to claim French citizenship. Consequently, the pattern of social and economic integration for recent immigrants from North Africa and other non-European colonies and possessions seems to be following a different trajectory than for previous waves of European immigrants into France.[28]

The lack of citizenship has not itself been a barrier to participation by minorities in the French welfare state. Formally and legally, French income support and social service programs treat all legal residents of France equally, whether immigrants or natives, citizens or noncitizens.[29] This principle of territoriality developed gradually in the postwar era, from a 1946 law that imposed long waiting periods before immigrants could qualify for social benefits to a series of laws and administrative rulings in the 1980s that granted broad social rights to all residents regardless of nationality. Along the way, in 1974, France ratified an International Labour Organization convention requiring equal treatment of citizens and noncitizens in social security.[30] Today the only income support program that treats immigrants differently from citizens is the Revenu Minimum d'Insertion (RMI), a minimum income program, for which new immigrants are ineligible for three years.[31] Some state services in fact have as one of their principal purposes the integration of new arrivals into French society. An example is the *écoles maternelles*, which immerse children in French language and culture as well as providing childcare.

Thus immigrants who came to France in the postwar decades and worked steadily acquired durable social insurance rights. In more recent decades, however, racial and ethnic minorities increasingly find themselves excluded from the social insurance system—outsiders in the insider-outsider game of the conservative welfare state—because they are disproportionately excluded from the labor market. This lack of connection to either the labor market or the core of the welfare state feeds the growing phenomenon of social exclusion, a term that denotes not simply chronic poverty or unemployment but social marginality and isolation.[32] Thus the structure of the French welfare state has helped to fuel the racial dimension of social exclusion in France.

The flip side of this story of growing social exclusion driven by the tight connection between work and social insurance is the growing trend toward centralized, universal policies—some means-tested but some not—that offer greater opportunities for forging links between racial minorities and the welfare state. Unlike the U.S. Social Security system, in which claims to benefits depend on attachment to the labor force and are enforced through a fragmented network of partial and particular occupational affiliations, these programs were created and are administered by the national state and are often aimed precisely at achieving "insertion," or incorporation, of people who fall outside the mainstream of the French political economy. Chief among these programs is the RMI, which was created in 1988 precisely to help address the social exclusion that was compounded, if not created, by the conservative structure of the French welfare state. In the legislative debates on its creation there was no mention of race or immigrants nor any direct acknowledgment of the racial targeting that such a program would entail; all the talk was of social solidarity and the republican ideal of the rights of man, of the "new poverty" that was afflicting France, and of the imperative of "inserting" the excluded into French society. The problem of social exclusion was closely linked to growing numbers of minorities and their increasing isolation from the mainstream of society. Minorities, however, were not part of the coalition-building processes that produced the RMI or other "insertion" policies, once again because of both the pervasive color blindness of French social politics and the structure of French political parties and associational life. Not surprisingly, however, a tabulation of the demographic characteristics of RMI recipients in the early 1990s showed that non-French, non–European Union nationals made up 10 percent of the RMI rolls (a figure that probably understates the proportion of minorities because nonwhite French citizens are counted as French and not distinguished by racial or ethnic background).[33]

French civil society also provides its own distinctive opportunities and limitations for minority access to social benefits through the welfare state.

Although there are several hundred private organizations in France devoted to assisting immigrants and minorities, until 1981 the formation of "foreign," or ethnically based, associations by minorities themselves was illegal. The integration of minorities into other local organizations, such as labor unions, varied considerably from place to place within France, and unions themselves varied considerably in the commitment to integrating minorities and advancing their interests. Because most minorities in France were, for much of the postwar period, immigrants without French citizenship, they had little political leverage with which to demand equitable treatment. Moreover, the exclusion of noncitizens from the civil service and other sectors of the economy (such as the large and powerful railroad industry) limits minority access to the privileged social insurance systems of these groups, forcing them to rely more heavily on general welfare programs for support. Even the relaxation of these nationality requirements for public-sector employment under the European Union in the 1990s has not improved this situation; if anything, it has sharpened the distinction between European and non-European (or non-European-appearing) immigrants.[34]

Nevertheless, there is evidence to suggest that minorities in France receive many public benefits on a reasonably equal basis, due to a combination of organized assistance and central enforcement of welfare rights. Immigrants, for example, were only slightly less likely than French citizens to receive unemployment benefits when they were out of work in the 1970s. Communities where immigrants are concentrated rely heavily on welfare assistance—from family allowances to the national minimum income, housing assistance, and free medical coverage, among other programs; one study of immigrants in a suburb of Lyon in the early 1980s, for example, found that approximately 75 percent of new cases at the local welfare office were families of African origin. Moreover, the French welfare state, despite its corporatist origins and fragmented structure, contains universal elements—the RMI, family allowances, and others—that help to mitigate the stigma attached to government assistance and limit the development of overlapping structural sources of exclusion and inequality that have come to characterize black exclusion in the United States.[35]

Minority incorporation into the French welfare state, then, appears to be a rather ambiguous achievement, limited on the one hand by the difficult entry of minorities into the French economy and civil society, but furthered by its strongly centralized institutional structure and partial universalism. The French political tradition of color-blind republicanism can only partially account for the pattern of minority incorporation in French society. Group-state relations in France are shaped not only by this cultural and ideological legacy but also by a set of welfare state institutions that tug at both ends of the integration-exclusion spectrum.

CONCLUSIONS

The institutional and ideological contrasts between social insurance in the French and American molds highlight the importance of combining institutional and ideological factors to explain incorporation outcomes, and particularly of institutional forces in channeling ideological ones—for these are, in effect, two color-blind cases (or at least as close as the United States gets to true color blindness) of work-based social insurance that have come out quite differently. The key distinction that emerges from these cases is an institutional one: centralization. It is the most centralized aspects of each welfare state that are best able to protect minority social rights and promote incorporation. In the United States, this is without question Social Security; in France, ironically, this has tended to be the so-called residual parts of the welfare state that do not depend on the labor market, such as income supports, family allowances, and state schools.

Institutional structures, it turns out, can overcome exclusion in a variety of ideological contexts. They can, moreover, decisively influence patterns of incorporation even in similar ideological and cultural settings. The same institutional contrast, between centralized and decentralized policy, also lies behind the differences between the two tracks of the American welfare state—social insurance and public assistance, which have had extremely different incorporation trajectories. Even more starkly than in the French case, this divergence in the American welfare state highlights the importance of institutions, not only by themselves but also as sites where different racial ideas are invoked and mobilized. For those African Americans who were relegated to the margins of the American political economy and the residual element of the welfare state, the distinctively American combination of fragmentation and race consiousness proved nothing short of disastrous.

Chapter Six

ENCOUNTERS WITH THE WELFARE STATE:
PUBLIC ASSISTANCE AND "WELFARE"

THE RISE OF THE CIVIL RIGHTS movement and its spread into the cities of the industrial North meant that the practices and outcomes of the welfare system, already suspect for blacks and whites alike, would come under increasing scrutiny, with important implications for the incorporation of minorities into social provision. The emergence in 1967 of the National Welfare Rights Organization, an offshoot of the civil rights movement, led to a large rise in applications for public assistance especially in Northern cities and to concurrent pressure on local and national welfare authorities to address growing problems of black urban poverty.[1] But the increasingly assertive race-conscious presumptions that lay behind these changes clashed with the color-blind rhetoric and aspirations for social citizenship within American liberalism that the civil rights revolution also embodied. Finally, these conflicting ideological and organizational currents were situated in an institutionally fragmented welfare state that shaped the system's receptivity to claims for incorporation.

Parochial public assistance—particularly Aid to Families with Dependent Children, the principal component of "welfare" in the United States—was thus thrust onto the front lines of the civil rights conflict because of its entanglements with local structures of political power. But this very localism made the politics of reforming welfare complex and treacherous even in the face of powerful demands from mobilized minorities themselves. In particular, this intersection of institutional fragmentation and rising race consciousness posed acute coalition-building challenges for welfare reformers and defenders alike. These challenges emerged during the civil rights crescendo of the 1950s and reached a climax in the linked legislative battles over civil rights and poverty in the 1960s, which, despite important achievements, failed fundamentally to strengthen the patterns of linkage between poor African Americans and the American welfare state.

In this chapter, I examine the politics of racial incorporation in the "welfare" component of the American welfare state and show how the combination of decentralization and race consciousness shaped this doleful path. To emphasize the role of institutional fragmentation, I contrast the American story with the politics of racial incorporation in the British welfare state. Britain's welfare state shares many key features with its American counterpart, particularly its liberalism, denoting the relative prominence of residual public assistance schemes as a complement to work-based social insurance, and its race-conscious ideological setting. What especially distinguishes the two systems from one another are the relative institutional unity and centralization of the British welfare state, which have allowed Great Britain to channel its race-conscious policy impulses into more racially inclusive policies and practices and to place the British welfare state on a path toward greater incorporation, in stark contrast to the American story of isolation and exclusion.

THE AMERICAN ENTANGLEMENT OF RACE AND WELFARE

The political trajectory of public assistance following 1935 was quite different from that of social insurance. The first blow to public assistance was the 1939 Social Security amendment, which removed survivors of working men—the "worthy widows" for whom public assistance was generally thought to be intended—from the public assistance rolls. This move fundamentally changed the character of Aid to Dependent Children, shifting its focus to an entirely different and more politically suspect population, defined increasingly by behavior rather than misfortune. ADC rapidly acquired its familiar character as a punitive program, governed by often intrusive rules about its recipients' activities regarding work, sex, and child rearing and plagued by confrontational encounters between clients and the state. In the South, the administration of ADC was quite evidently discriminatory; in the North, it rapidly developed into a patronage tool that white political leaders could use to ensure the political loyalty of a growing black population. In other respects, the period between the 1930s and the 1960s was a relatively stagnant one for American welfare policy outside of Social Security. Congress adjusted the formula for matching state spending with federal money, and during the Eisenhower years it began to develop a cautious social policy agenda based on the theme of vocational rehabilitation. But in general, ADC spent its first twenty-five years flying below the radar of national politics.[2]

But while it was out of sight and mind, ADC was changing rapidly, mostly as a result of the Great Migration. During the 1950s, the proportion of African Americans on the Aid to Dependent Children rolls grew markedly, particularly as Southern blacks moved to Northern cities. By 1962, 30 percent of ADC recipients were African American, and the proportion had already reached a majority in many cities as early as the 1940s. In the 1950s and early 1960s, there was a series of crackdowns, investigations, and purges of ADC rolls by state governments. One prominent crackdown mechanism that expanded in the 1950s was the introduction, or stiffening, of "suitable home" rules governing the receipt of ADC benefits, provisions that were often used to target African American recipients. Several of these racially directed state and local welfare episodes—most notably by Louisiana in 1960 and Newburgh, New York, in 1961—gained national notoriety, drawing attention to the increasingly interconnected politics of race and welfare.[3]

In the 1960s, Americans "rediscovered" poverty, and John Kennedy's attention to it in the 1960 presidential campaign placed the issue squarely on the national political agenda. After Kennedy's assassination, President Johnson declared "war" on poverty, committing his administration to a program of welfare state expansion on a scale that deliberately recalled the New Deal, but imprinted with Johnson's own grandiose political vision.[4] But Johnson's War on Poverty overlapped another commitment, to racial equality and equality of opportunity. Even before the passage of the Civil Rights and Voting Rights Acts, the civil rights movement was shifting its sights away from Jim Crow in the South and onto the deplorable economic conditions of African Americans throughout the country. The politics of race and welfare, already intertwined before the War on Poverty, came together more explicitly and explosively than ever before, and they were connected in particular ways that reflected both the institutional structure of earlier social policy and the changing status of African American citizenship. The link between civil rights and welfare was well understood and clearly articulated by many of the participants in the policy debates of the 1960s. The opening section of the report of the 1966 White House Conference on Civil Rights, for example, called for a restructuring of welfare programs as a key element of a civil rights strategy. As then structured, the report noted, public assistance programs such as AFDC not only failed to provide adequate benefits but also placed their disproportionately black clients in a subservient relationship to often capricious and unprofessional state and local governments. The report called for substantial nationalization of welfare programs to overcome these structural barriers.[5] While it represented an important new thrust in the politics of social provision, the War on Poverty was still waged in the long shadow of the New Deal, a social policy regime whose gaps and silences had enormous consequences for the definition of African American citizenship and political identity.[6]

The tumultuous 1960s were indeed a watershed for the politics of welfare. The welfare state grew in the 1960s, not only through the proliferation of new programs but also through the growth of established programs. By the time the modestly expansive 1962 Public Welfare Amendments were adopted, ADC had already entered a period of dramatic growth. Between 1960 and 1962, the number of families receiving ADC grew almost as much as during the entire decade of the 1950s; over the next five years the rolls would grow by nearly 40 percent. Real spending on ADC benefits would double between 1960 and 1967. But underlying the apparent explosion of welfare in the 1960s were trends that had begun in the outwardly stable 1950s and merely continued through the following decade. Increasingly, ADC recipients lived in cities—from 40 percent in 1950 to more than half in 1960 and nearly three-fifths by the end of the decade. In particular, they were increasingly found in Northern cities. And the racial composition of the ADC caseload was changing as well, but the African American share of the recipient population grew much more dramatically in the 1950s than the 1960s. Even the 1962 act, hailed as the first comprehensive national welfare reform since the New Deal, essentially adopted and expanded the Eisenhower era's approach to welfare, based on vocational rehabilitation.[7]

Unlike these earlier efforts, the War on Poverty amounted to an unprecedented attempt to reconfigure the institutional architecture of the American welfare state away from its parochial roots and toward a more national structure. Through national action, the War on Poverty aimed at expanding the reach of social citizenship, embracing many who had been excluded from the social rights of the New Deal. Those left out of the national structures of New Deal social provision and relegated to its parochial structures were disproportionately black; the War on Poverty thus necessarily entailed a push toward national social citizenship for African Americans. In its substance, the War on Poverty addressed many of the same themes as did earlier welfare reform efforts, dramatically expanding educational, vocational, and rehabilitative programs for the poor.[8] But it did so not by adding increments to the existing welfare structure but by attempting to recast altogether the institutional logic of the welfare state and, as a result, the substance of social citizenship.

Two battles of the War on Poverty embodied this new welfare direction: the Economic Opportunity Act of 1964 and the AFDC amendments of 1967. In each case, the administration sought to reestablish social citizenship on national grounds, and in each case a wide range of possibilities for strategic choice in building coalitions existed. But the institutional legacy of New Deal social policy, under which African Americans were attached disproportionately to the parochial structures of AFDC, constrained the choices available, so that different coalitions formed in response to the impulses—both ideological and organizational—to expand social rights for African Americans.

Race, Coalitions, and the Politics of Congress

The struggle for expanded social rights in the 1960s played itself out not only in the streets but also in the halls of national power, especially in the shifting partisan and regional coalition-building possibilities in Congress. Because of the inherently fragmented structure both of American political parties and of Congress itself, building legislative coalitions for national policy-making has always been a difficult enterprise. During the 1940s and 1950s, Congressional coalitions were generally constructed from two of three broad blocs: Northern Democrats, Southern Democrats, and Republicans. But during the 1960s, the relatively stable alignments of regions, parties, and interests of the New Deal era began to disintegrate, making coalition-building even more volatile and complex. Political scientists Keith Poole and Howard Rosenthal, in fact, describe this mid-century alignment as "the only genuine three-party system in American history." In the wake of Martin Luther King's Birmingham marches and the murder of the NAACP's Mississippi field secretary Medgar Evers in the spring of 1963, Democratic leaders in Congress found it increasingly difficult to hold their members together even to pass routine bills. House Majority Leader Carl Albert told President Kennedy that the issue of civil rights was "overwhelming the whole program" and undermining the majority's cohesion.[9]

Northern Democrats, especially those from major cities, were increasingly pulled in multiple and contradictory directions. They were closely tied to organized labor, which was a powerful force in Democratic party politics in the postwar era, especially in the major manufacturing cities of the Northeast and Midwest. But unlike European labor unions, which used their positions in government coalitions to usher in a grand postwar bargain of full employment and generous social benefits, American unions were primarily concerned with safeguarding the limited bargaining rights that they had won in the 1930s and nearly lost in the 1940s and with protecting the system of social insurance created in 1935. At the same time, Northern urban Democrats were increasingly dependent on African American votes as the Great Migration redrew the electoral map. While the economic agenda of unions did not threaten the interests of African Americans, neither did it do much to benefit them, because African American union membership was low and they did not yet benefit extensively from social insurance programs. As long as civil rights and expansive anti-poverty programs were kept off the national agenda, labor and blacks could join together in a modestly liberal coalition. Finally, Northern Democrats were closely tied to the urban party organizations that dominated many Northeastern and Midwestern cities' politics and formed an essential part of the New Deal coalition. These traditional party organizations sought above all to keep control of federal programs that were channeled through local governments. These elements of the Northern Democratic mix began to come into conflict with one another as early as the 1940s and 1950s, especially as African Americans began to articulate political demands that clashed with the settled interests of unions and machines: greater access to jobs and housing, a more generous welfare state, an end to police brutality, and so forth. These tensions escalated in the 1960s, when issues such as affirmative action pitted unions and blacks directly against one another. Thus when Northern liberals began to urge the national government to action on racial equality, they did not necessarily speak with a unified or unequivocal voice.[10]

Nevertheless, the increased insistence of Northern Democrats on racial equality as national policy pried open the incipient regional split in the Democratic party that had been obvious at least since 1948. Southern Democratic interests in the maintenance of white supremacy were clearly under attack as early as the 1940s, but the national enactments of the 1960s sealed the bargain between the national Democratic party and African American voters, leaving the once-solid South increasingly isolated. Southern Democrats in Congress retained their historic power as committee chairs through the system of seniority and strong committees that had prevailed since the early part of the century, but even Southern power in Congress was increasingly under attack from within the party. In 1957, Senate majority leader Lyndon Johnson, a Texan with presidential ambitions, deftly engineered the passage of a civil rights act that was substantively weak but symbolically important not only because it was the first federal civil rights law passed in eighty-two years but also because it showed the possibility of breaking the Southern stranglehold on the Senate that had long impeded civil rights legislation.[11] Toward the end of the 1950s, the House Rules Committee, which controls the flow of legislation through the House, became the central site of the intraparty struggle. The committee had a Democratic majority of eight to four, but two Southern Democrats, chairman Howard Smith of Virginia and William Colmer of Mississippi, joined with the committee's Republicans to create a persistent blocking coalition against much liberal legislation. Upon John Kennedy's election to the presidency, House Speaker Sam Rayburn (also a Texan but a fierce protector of the House's legislative capacity) moved to expand the committee in order to break the conservative logjam and won by picking off twenty-two Republican votes, just enough to counter the sixty-four Democrats—all Southerners—who voted against the proposal.[12] By 1964, Southern Democrats were unable to block the passage of the Civil Rights Bill; the pivotal players were now Republicans.

At the same time, the "party of Lincoln" was beginning to splinter. While most Republicans in the early 1960s upheld the party's historical commitment to nationally protected civil rights, others began to move away from that position and steer toward the siren song of Southern white votes.[13] Electoral disaffection among white Southerners offered Republicans an opportunity to marry their traditional opposition to national government power with an anti–civil rights stance. Barry Goldwater represented just such a possibility: a solid conservative with a strong libertarian streak, he opposed the Civil Rights Act in the Senate even after most Republicans had climbed aboard. He also won five Southern states as the 1964 Republican presidential nominee. Although the dual transformation of the Republican party to an anti–civil rights party and the white South to a predominantly Republican electorate would not be consummated for decades, both trends were clearly evident by the mid-1960s.

In this institutional context, the trajectory of welfare policy would be shaped largely by the dynamics of coalition-building among these shifting elements. In the 1960s, these dynamics led to different kinds of coalitions and consequently different outcomes. The dramatic demise of the Economic Opportunity Act came about because, in the end, white Southerners *and* urban Northerners equally resisted its nationalizing thrust—each for their own reasons, but each for reasons having to do with the convergence of institutional parochialism and racial politics. On the matter of AFDC, by contrast, the urban North tended to support greater national power.[14] In this case, however, Northerners were defeated by the parochial coalition of Southerners and Republicans. The fate of African Americans in the War on Poverty thus depended on the configuration of institutional legacies and coalitional possibilities in place in the mid-1960s.

The War on Poverty: The Economic Opportunity Act

The Economic Opportunity Act attempted to create a new national basis for social citizenship. Its programs deliberately bypassed the elaborate tangle of state and local officials that had controlled even federally funded public assistance under the New Deal. The Community Action Program, through its doctrine of "maximum feasible participation" of a community's poor people in devising and administering the programs that were to serve them, thus linked new national policies directly to citizens. At the national end, the act created the Office of Economic Opportunity (OEO), a new agency in the Executive Office of the President, outside the ambit of the traditional welfare bureaucracy, to oversee the new welfare regime. This new nexus of local participation and federal money and power helped many poor people—especially African Americans in the rural South and urban North—reduce both their reliance on AFDC and their dependence on the paternalistic patronage of local political authorities. While the Community Action Program and the other weapons in the War on Poverty's arsenal brought the federal government into direct action on social welfare, by their very nature they challenged entrenched local structures not only of economic status but also of race and political authority as well.[15]

It was precisely the institutional architecture of the Economic Opportunity Act that was the central flashpoint of controversy, both in 1964 and when it was amended the following year. Controversy revolved particularly around the division of authority between the federal government and state and local agencies. Republicans and Southern Democrats were skeptical of the bill because of its potential to introduce the direct provision of welfare services by the federal government to the poor, effectively expanding the compass of national social citizenship. Southern attacks on the mechanics of the program successfully reduced the federal government's authority over the antipoverty effort. With the civil rights movement surging ahead and the traditional racial structure of Southern society crumbling in its path, Southern members of Congress took the threat of "maximum feasible participation" very seriously. The reliable segregationist Howard Smith, who had opposed federal control of ADC in 1935, warned that the NAACP could receive antipoverty money under the terms of the bill, as could the Ku Klux Klan or a "nudist colony."[16] In 1935, when the party of Lincoln still claimed the allegiance of African Americans, it was an Ohio Republican, Thomas Jenkins, who sparred with Smith about his racial motives. But in 1964, the presidential nomination of Barry Goldwater marked the end of a century of Republican claims to be the party of civil rights, and another Ohio Republican, William A. Ayres, joined Smith's chorus, warning that "there won't be any white people" in the new antipoverty programs.[17]

In contrast with the Civil Rights Act passed by the same Congress, the Equal Opportunity Act did not gain the support of Republicans, presenting Johnson with a different strategic choice: either accommodate powerful white Southerners or concede. Facing defeat by the conservative coalition, Johnson, ever the legislative strategist, brought the South on board. To allay Southern fears, the administration arranged for Philip Landrum of Georgia, a stalwart conservative Democrat, to sponsor the bill in the House rather than Adam Clayton Powell, Jr., of Harlem, whose Education and Labor Committee was responsible for its passage. The administration also agreed to a governors' veto over any antipoverty grants to groups in his state, an important change considering that men such as George C. Wallace and Orval Faubus occupied Southern state houses. Sure enough, of the five governors' vetoes exercised in 1965, four were by Southern governors, including one by Wallace, who rejected a community action grant to a biracial group in Birmingham, Alabama.[18]

Wallace's veto came in May, just as the House Education and Labor Committee was working on the reauthorization bill for the Economic Opportunity Act, and it prompted a mini-revolt among committee Democrats, who voted the following day to strip governors of their veto power over OEO programs. The Johnson administration, the *New York Times* reported, was "quietly jubilant," but governors, both Northern and Southern, were appalled. Governor Nelson Rockefeller of New York warned in a telegram to the committee that rescinding the veto would "open up another serious avenue through which Federal and local officials can bypass state governments." A week later the committee backed down and adopted a compromise known as the "Rockefeller plan," which restored the veto but gave OEO the power to overrule "arbitrary" vetoes that appeared to be based on racial prejudice or "political considerations."[19] Thus even the legendary Eighty-Ninth Congress, elected in Johnson's 1964 landslide, could not repeal the governors' veto entirely, settling for a cumbersome procedure almost guaranteed to increase tension among national, state, and local politicians and administrators. The War on Poverty was thus created by the same coalition that created the Social Security Act—the New Deal coalition of urban North and white South. By the time of the War on Poverty, however, African Americans were an essential part of the Democratic political base in the North, giving the Northern wing of the party both a stronger inclination and a greater necessity to challenge the power of the segregationist South.[20] But in the end, the logic was the same: the administration had to accede to Southern institutional demands in order to expand the national welfare state.[21]

Ultimately, the Great Society's vision of fully inclusive, national social citizenship for African Americans failed, and this failure served to underscore and entrench the partial, parochial social citizenship of the New Deal welfare state. What finally brought the War on Poverty, and particularly the Community Action Program, to heel was a telling opposition coalition between parochial forces—segregationist Southern Democrats and Northern mayors—who were accustomed to exercising control over public assistance. This reversal of the expansionary coalition of the New Deal was partly, but not wholly, based in racial politics. Provoked by the activities of the Child Development Group of Mississippi, an early-childhood education program that served poor black families, Mississippi Senators James Eastland and John Stennis denounced the War on Poverty as a thinly disguised, federally sponsored civil rights effort, and successfully reduced its funding in 1965. Eastland, Stennis, and other Southerners were rather transparent in their race-based opposition.[22]

At the same time, mayors such as Richard Daley of Chicago were not in principle opposed to providing welfare benefits for African Americans; in fact, in the early years of ADC, Chicago and other cities had used the parochial structure of ADC to direct benefits toward African Americans as a patronage tool. At a private meeting with leading civil rights lawyer William Coleman and White House staffer Carl Holman in November 1965, one black leader argued that

> some means must be found of breaking the hold of city machines on . . . the welfare programs which they have used as a political instrument. . . . So long as this condition persists, the city political bosses will continue to oppose any action to organize the masses, since, if they are organized, they can only be organized to fight the *status quo*. (The machine in city "x" builds up frustration which ultimately leads to violence because, if you are on relief, they have their thumb on you, if you are in a public housing project, they have their thumb on you, if you are a social worker, you cannot deal with a client unless the precinct captain then the alderman recommends this client to your attention.)

The War on Poverty threatened this source of patronage by seeking to remove state and local officials from the welfare loop, and suddenly Daley and other mayors found themselves confronted with federally backed, community-based welfare agencies that they could not control and that created sturdy political platforms for black political organization in opposition to local elites. Behind Daley's leadership, mayors protested to the Johnson administration, which quietly began to retreat from its insistence on "maximum feasible participation" and its strategy of doing an end-run around local officials. Thus, institutionalized structure and racial politics converged to shape a coalition that sought to preserve the racialized parochial structure of welfare.[23]

In much New Deal social legislation, this coalition of Democrats from the urban North and rural South had been forced to overcome its internal splits, finely engineering national and parochial welfare institutions to accommodate regional differences over issues of race and labor.[24] In the Great Society congresses—the Eighty-Eighth in the wake of the Kennedy assassination and the Eighty-Ninth with its overwhelming Democratic majorities—these differences receded in the face of national tragedy, presidential commitment, and social unrest. But after the Republicans regained forty-seven seats in the House in the 1966 elections, this unsteady alliance once again found itself anchoring the Democratic governing coalition. Only this time, the two partners were in uncharacteristic agreement in their opposition to national institutions of social citizenship that would empower African Americans. In the wards of Chicago and the Mississippi Delta alike, white local elites feared the disruptive potential of CAP agencies and their bureaucratic patrons in the Office of Economic Opportunity.

In 1967, the Johnson administration won a substantial reauthorization of the War on Poverty, but to gain this victory the administration had to bargain away the remnants of national control of the Community Action

Program.[25] The House Education and Labor Committee accepted an amendment sponsored by Representative Edith Green of Oregon giving local mayors control of CAP agencies. On the House floor, Republican Charles E. Goodell of New York offered a substitute to the reauthorization plan that would have "spun off" the various poverty programs from the OEO—which Goodell called "a monument to administrative asininity"—to traditional line agencies of the federal government that were more susceptible to Congressional oversight and control. But Goodell and the Republicans opposed the Green amendment, which "might as well be called the bosses and boll weevil amendment because it is an amendment for the big city hall bosses and for the southerners to completely denude community action of its potential." James Gardner of North Carolina objected to Goodell's reference to "boll weevil" southerners. "In the South," Gardner said, "we are perfectly able to take care of our own problems," a thinly veiled reference to race relations. Goodell was not fooled. "I must say," he replied, "I have very little confidence that southern local governments will undertake the innovation and the new approaches necessary to help the downtrodden Negro in the South."[26] But it was not only Southerners who championed the Green amendment; Northern urban representatives such as Roman Pucinski of Daley's Chicago and Hugh Carey of Brooklyn, both generally liberal on racial issues, joined Goodell, Green, and others in defending it on the House floor. Augustus Hawkins, a black Democrat from Los Angeles (whose district included Watts), offered a last-ditch amendment to strike the Green amendment but it was defeated, and the presence of the Green amendment kept Southern Democrats in line with the party leadership on key votes. In the end, the Democrats hung together, defeating Republican attempts to redirect OEO funding and passing the bill.[27] It is one of the biting ironies of the 1960s that the great institutional innovation of the War on Poverty, an attempt to realize the New Deal ambition of national, inclusive social policy, was brought down by a variant of the same coalition—rural South and urban North—that created the American welfare state in the first place.

The War on Poverty: AFDC Reform

Although reform of AFDC was not formally part of the War on Poverty, the conflict between national and parochial visions of social citizenship spilled over into a new round of debate on AFDC. In 1967, at the height of the War on Poverty fray, President Johnson proposed legislation to increase Social Security benefits. At the same time, he proposed a welfare reform package that called for nationalizing reforms of AFDC that echoed the nationalizing impulse of the Economic Opportunity Act. In a message to Congress on children and youth in February 1967, Johnson called for nationally mandated minimum payments, a provision that had been rejected at the behest of Southern senators in 1935.[28] Johnson also proposed several other national mandates aimed at standardizing and strengthening AFDC programs, including financial incentives for work and training opportunities, benefits for unemployed parents, and income set-asides so that AFDC recipients could earn some income without having their assistance payments reduced. Constrained by the program's preexisting federal structure, the Johnson administration could not simply bypass the states as the War on Poverty sought to do. But the thrust of Johnson's welfare reform proposals was to require states to enact nationally determined social rights.

Like the main War on Poverty programs, Johnson's welfare proposals were not explicitly racially targeted. If anything, they were defined in class terms, aiming at bringing a previously excluded poor population under the umbrella of an increasingly national welfare state. But in the political context of the 1960s, they effectively constituted a drive for national citizenship for African Americans. This was true not only because the beneficiaries of these reforms would disproportionately be poor African Americans but also because the proposals came from the administration that was responsible for national action in civil and voting rights for African Americans. Johnson himself, moreover, had framed the Great Society's aims in racial terms, most prominently in his commencement address at Howard University in June 1965, in which he famously declared, in the wake of the Civil Rights and Voting Rights acts, that the Great Society was

> the next and more profound stage of the battle for civil rights. We seek not just freedom but opportunity. We seek not just legal equity but human ability, not just equality as a right and a theory but equality as a fact and equality as a result. For the task is to give 20 million Negroes the same chance as every other American to learn and grow, to work and share in society, to develop their abilities—physical, mental and spiritual, and to pursue their individual happiness.[29]

There could be little mistaking the thrust and likely consequences of the administration's welfare proposals.

In the months immediately following Johnson's welfare message, the country exploded. As Congress was taking up both the welfare reform and OEO reauthorization bills, riots broke out in a dozen American cities, including major clashes in Newark in mid-July and Detroit in late July. The Detroit riot was particularly brutal, lasting five days and resulting in forty-three deaths, more than seven thousand arrests, and tens of million of dollars of property damage.[30] The response to the riots among the public and policymakers was highly polarized between calls for repression on the one hand and expanded social spending on the other. The Johnson administration was acutely aware of this dilemma and the threat it posed to its already-precarious domestic policy strategy (made even more precarious by the growing conflict over the war in Vietnam). The White House had, in fact, been taking private soundings of black urban frustration with the poverty program and welfare policy and worried about their connection with urban unrest as early as 1965. Inside the White House, however, the immediate response to the 1967 riots among Johnson's inner circle was to rally to the defense of the poverty and welfare programs on the premise that the remedy to urban violence was increased social intervention on the part of the federal government.[31] In the midst of the Detroit riot, White House aide Joseph Califano reported to Johnson that the White House had received more than 100 telegrams supporting the poverty program as a response to the riots.[32] A special Gallup poll conducted in July for the White House revealed that although the public was losing confidence in Johnson's handling of racial issues, support for the poverty program remained high, and surprisingly so in the Midwest and the South, suggesting, as Fred Panzer told the president, "that rural and small town poor people may like the program much more than their Congressmen suspect."[33] Johnson also responded favorably to a suggestion that the administration create a special team "composed of Negro federal employees who can talk the language of the ghetto" to disseminate information in inner cities about federal assistance programs as well as create channels of communication between urban blacks and the administration.[34] By early September, OEO Director R. Sargent Shriver was circulating a memo on "myths and facts about OEO" to defend the poverty program from accusations that it was responsible for inflaming tensions and igniting violence in American cities.[35]

While the White House was gathering its forces to mount a defense of its poverty and welfare programs, Congress was sharpening its knives. Unlike the War on Poverty, which fell under the jurisdiction of the liberal Education and Labor Committee, both Social Security and AFDC were controlled by the revenue committees of Congress—House Ways and Means and Senate Finance—which remained under the control of two powerful Southerners, Representative Wilbur Mills of Arkansas and Senator Russell Long of Louisiana. The Ways and Means Committee merged the administration's proposal with a concurrent plan to increase Social Security benefits, which virtually ensured passage, but also substantially reframed the welfare section of the bill. Two new features in particular threatened to undermine rather than expand nationally instituted social citizenship: a freeze on federal AFDC spending for cases of parental absence from the home (as opposed to parental death or unemployment), and a requirement of state participation in work-training programs for AFDC recipients. Under the latter provision, states would be allowed to drop welfare recipients who refused to participate in work or job training.[36]

These provisions amounted to an extension of the parochial structure of welfare, and the intense debate they occasioned in Congress pitted contending institutional visions of welfare and citizenship against one another. Supporting the restrictions were the parochial forces that derived political benefits from AFDC's decentralized structure, particularly Southerners. Opposing them was an administration committed to a nationalizing approach. Northern urban liberals were caught in the middle: they worried about the loss of local political control but desperately needed federal funds to flow freely as they saw their welfare rolls increasing and their cities under siege. The welfare provisions aroused the spirited opposition of the NAACP and the National Welfare Rights Organization, a short-lived but influential movement of mostly black women that sought better access to welfare benefits through both protest and legal action. But none of these opposing forces could halt the advance of the new welfare restrictions, which passed the House almost unanimously and slid through Senate after a failed liberal filibuster. In the end, the Social Security Amendments of 1967 (as the final legislation was called) perfectly captured the divergent paths of Social Security and AFDC: the act simultaneously raised Social Security benefits an average of thirteen percent and placed new restrictions on the lives and prospects of AFDC's beneficiaries.[37]

The 1960s were, in many ways, a pivotal moment for the American welfare state. After the 1967 reforms and the subsequent failure of President Richard Nixon's Family Assistance Plan—a proposal for a guaranteed minimum income—the liberal, fragmented structure of the welfare system was solidified and the political impulse to alter that structure substantially spent. Despite a series of Supreme Court decisions in the late 1960s and early 1970s that limited certain local controls over welfare recipients and established an inviolable right to assistance under certain circumstances, American public assistance remained not only a residual program available only to those who remained outside the mainstream of the political economy but also a decentralized program subject to the vagaries and particular pressures of state and local politics in a federal system.[38] Under the terms of decentralized public assistance, states come under competitive pressure to keep taxes and benefits low in relation to other states, tending to drive redistributive benefits downward. Decentralized public assistance also exposes minorities to state and local politics and administration, which has long proven more conducive to group conflict, majority dominance, and discrimination than the national political

arena, at least in the social policy arena.[39] Under the political pressures of
the 1960s (which included civil-rights and welfare-rights mobilization as
well as the political imperatives of the war on poverty), both AFDC caseloads and benefits grew. By the early 1970s, however, the national caseload began to level off; the real value of AFDC benefits peaked in the mid-
1970s and began drifting downward as the pressures of the 1960s for
broader and more generous benefits receded.[40]

For African Americans, these developments deepened the challenges
that had long arisen from AFDC's parochial structure. By the 1960s and
through the 1970s, as figure 6.1 shows, African Americans made up more
than 40 percent of the AFDC caseload.[41] Thus African Americans were
increasingly and disproportionately reliant on politically weak ties to
local governments for benefits that were eroding and were more often
than not inadequate to reduce poverty and inequality. A series of studies
covering the 1970s and 1980s have shown that states with higher concentrations of black residence and welfare recipients have had significantly
lower benefit levels. Increasingly, public perceptions of welfare politics
came to focus not just on African Americans as recipients but on the black
ghetto poor, those who were concentrated in urban ghetto neighborhoods
plagued with multiple social, economic, and political ills. Although the
ghetto poor never constituted more than a small fraction of the American
poor population, media and political attention to poverty and welfare
issues focused almost exclusively on them. This pattern contributed to the
erosion of political support for AFDC over the 1980s and 1990s. Although Democrats in Congress has risen to the program's defense in the
face of Ronald Reagan's proposed budget cuts in the early 1980s, by the
1990s the growing polarization of American political parties, the rise of
the grass-roots Right, and the explosion of budget deficits made the defense of AFDC an increasingly untenable position.[42]

When Bill Clinton came to office promising to "end welfare as we know
it," his proposals to supplement the devolution of welfare to the states
with increased federal spending on welfare-to-work programs, job training, child care, and health insurance fell on deaf ears, particularly after the
Republican takeover of Congress in 1994. When he signed the Personal
Responsibility and Work Opportunity Reconciliation Act (PRWORA) of
1996 (after vetoing earlier versions of it twice in order to extract some
concessions from Republicans in Congress), Clinton thus accomplished a
further denationalization of welfare, leaving public assistance recipients
even more subject to the difficulties of decentralized welfare policy. While
it may be too soon to tell what the 1996 welfare reform will mean for
African Americans and other minorities, early returns suggest that whites
have been more successful than African Americans or other minorities at
leaving the welfare rolls in the wake of the PRWORA. Figure 6.2 shows

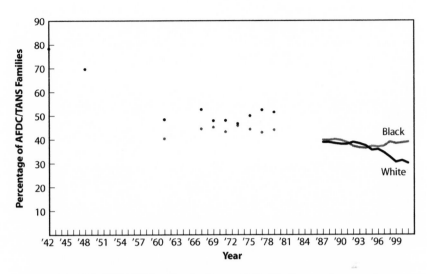

FIGURE 6.1 AFDC/TANF Families by Race, 1942–99. Source: See note in text.

that while African American levels on the welfare rolls have remained steady since the 1980s, welfare reform notwithstanding, white welfare levels fell steadily in the late 1990s. During this period, the Latino presence on the rolls grew steadily to nearly 25 percent. Finally, early evidence also suggests that states with more racially and ethnically diverse populations—diversity here comprising African Americans and Latinos—have been more likely to adopt stricter and more punitive welfare provisions under Temporary Assistance to Needy Families, the program that replaced AFDC in 1996.[43] These most recent events merely underscore the importance of institutional structures in shaping racial incorporation. While Social Security was quietly expanding, shielded by its national structure from the racial tumult of the postwar era, public assistance and its beneficiaries were the victims of institutional parochialism and the fragmented, localized patterns of group-state linkage that it produced.

Race and Welfare in Britain: Race Consciousness and Centralized Liberalism

Like American welfare policy, the British welfare state was divided between social insurance for workers and means-tested public assistance for others—National Insurance and National Assistance. And like its American counterpart, Britain's welfare system was embedded in a race-conscious political culture, which initially emphasized racial distinctions in

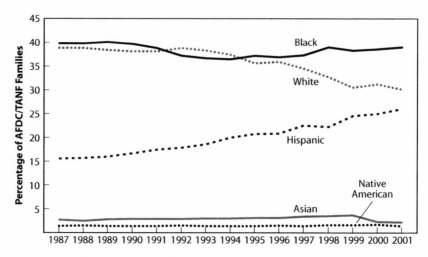

FIGURE 6.2 AFDC/TANF Families by Race, 1987–2001. Source: See note in text.

extending rights rather than universal, color-blind access to citizenship. But rather than being institutionally divided and politically antagonistic, the two parts of the British welfare state were unified into a single, national, centralized scheme, under common administrative control. This institutional structure enabled the British state to channel the race-conscious impulses of British politics, driven first by residual imperial paternalism and later by more liberal impulses, toward the protection of racial minorities and ultimately toward a stronger incorporation path than in either the United States or France.

In the early part of the twentieth century, when merchant seamen from Asia and the Caribbean began to enter Britain, the Colonial Office acted to protect them against exploitation and discrimination (and from the more restrictive impulses of bureaucratic rivals, particularly the Home Office). But as empire devolved into commonwealth and especially as imperial subjects, who previously needed the special protection of the government, became British citizens, the state's interest in their protection declined. During World War II, the Colonial Office had set up a special section to deal particularly with the welfare-related problems of colonial immigrants, but this section shut down in 1951. This closure signaled the beginning of a shift in the British government's stance toward Commonwealth immigrants, away from colonial paternalism and toward the integrationism that would ultimately be embraced and written into law more than a decade later. By 1952, the government took the position that "Commonwealth immigrants were not the responsibility of the Colonial Office while they were in Britain. As British citizens the responsibility was entirely with the local authority where they lived." Over the 1950s, as the Conservative party fended off internal dissent on the question of race-based immigrant restrictions, the government disengaged almost entirely from any special concern for the welfare needs of Commonwealth immigrants and insisted that they should and would be treated just like any other British citizens in their dealings with the state.[44]

Connections between communities of nonwhites in Britain and local political and social elites were not new in the 1950s. As early as the 1920s, local groups began forming to address the challenges of multiracial communities. These were not organizations of nonwhites, but rather civic organizations of local white citizens who generally sought to "protect" their communities from what they saw as an influx of undesirable migrants. An example was the Association for the Welfare of Half-Caste Children in Liverpool, which sponsored studies that drew attention to the poverty and poor living conditions of nonwhite seamen and their families in Liverpool and other port cities but supported deporting them to West Africa.[45]

By the late 1940s, however, local organizations more genuinely concerned with the welfare of nonwhite immigrants began to form—for example, in Leeds in 1949, Birmingham and Bristol in 1951, Liverpool in 1952, and Nottingham in 1955. The creation of local race relations and welfare committees accelerated after the Nottingham and Notting Hill disturbances of 1958. By 1960 local committees existed in at least seventeen cities, and by the late 1960s approximately fifty such committees were in operation.[46]

Although these were mostly private initiatives (and most accounts of these developments portray this period as one of state disengagement from race relations issues), the government was a key participant in constructing this network of organized assistance for nonwhites. In 1958 the London Council of Social Services created an immigrants department, with its membership drawn from both the government and the voluntary sector. During this period the Home Office, which had traditionally been concerned with restricting immigration and monitoring and controlling the immigrant population in British territory, began to grow concerned about the strain on social services and the welfare state, which seemed to some to be resulting from New Commonwealth immigration. In 1956 the British Caribbean Welfare Service, a collaboration between the British and Jamaican governments, was formed to help prepare West Indian immigrants for their new lives in Britain and, once they arrived, to assist them with a variety of incorporation issues, including welfare. In June 1962, shortly after the passage of the Commonwealth Immigrants Act, Home Secretary R. A. Butler appointed the Commonwealth Immigrants Advisory Council to oversee local authorities' arrangements for assistance to nonwhite immigrants and to advise them on incorporation issues, particularly those having to do with welfare and social provision. Two years later, the National Committee for Commonwealth Immigrants (NCCI) was created particularly to oversee the work of local race relations com-mittees and assist them in facilitating welfare support.[47]

As race became increasingly visible in British politics—especially fol-lowing the violence of 1958 and the racist Smethwick campaign of 1964—it was becoming increasingly clear that the local, voluntary ap-proach was inadequate to cope with the challenges of incorporating non-whites into British society. The new Labour government elected in Octo-ber 1964 began to address the issue at the national level. The Race Relations Act of 1965 outlawed discrimination in public accommoda-tions, established the Race Relations Board to address discrimination claims, and reorganized the NCCI (now to be chaired by the archbishop of Canterbury), which was to continue its welfare and integration work, still overseeing local committees. Later that same year, a government White Paper, *Immigration from the Commonwealth,* announced further limitations on immigration by reducing the number of work permits that would be issued for entry into the country. Together these measures out-lined an emerging policy consensus on race and immigration issues in British politics that combined strict immigration controls with at least minimal protection of minorities against discrimination. Despite the ap-parent commitment of the national government to managing race rela-tions and protecting the rights of minorities, however, nonwhite Britons remained primarily linked to the state through the local connections—local governments and liaison committees—that had evolved in the de-cades since the war.[48]

Compared to the United States, however, this pattern of localized politi-cal linkages between minority groups and the state had limited repercus-sions for their incorporation into the British welfare state. While welfare benefits and services were administered at the local level, the decentraliza-tion of welfare did not extend, as in the United States, to fundamental program characteristics such as eligibility rules and benefit levels. Al-though some immigrants registered dissatisfaction with their treatment by local welfare offices in the early years, for the most part nonwhite immigrants seem to have received fair treatment. Both the national struc-ture of National Insurance and National Assistance and the strong norms of equal treatment that prevailed in welfare agencies militated against racially discriminatory treatment. As one welfare agency employee put it, "With regard to [National Insurance] claims, our only interest is in proof of residence and in the contributions record; with regard to [National Assistance] this is simply a financial calculation. . . . The area for discre-tion is in reality very small and is carefully codified in the instructions to staff."[49]

TABLE 6.1
Estimated Per-Capita Spending on Social Services, UK, 1961–66 (1961 £)

	Health/Welfare	Education/ Child Care	Nat'l Insurance/ Assistance	Total
1961				
Total	18.5	12.4	31.2	62.1
Immigrants	18.4	13.3	19.2	50.9
1966				
Total	18.6	12.1	31.7	62.4
Immigrants	17.4	13.9	17.4	48.7

Source: K. Jones, "Immigrants and the Social Services," *National Institute Economic Review* 41 (August 1967): 33–35.

Thus by the 1960s, when the British government began to address race relations policy, the pattern of universal social provision had taken hold, and nonwhites had been substantially incorporated into the welfare system. In 1961, as table 6.1 shows, total per capita spending on welfare and social services in the United Kingdom was £62, while spending for immigrants was only £51. This difference, however, is entirely accounted for by the difference in National Insurance benefits, the work-dependent part of the welfare state. In these categories, overall spending was £31 per person, while spending for immigrants was £19 per capita. In other areas of public social provision—health care, welfare services, education, and child care—spending on immigrants and the rest of the population was the same. Figures for 1966 show the same pattern.[50]

From the perspective of individual clients rather than aggregate spending, patterns of welfare use look quite similar across racial and ethnic groups, within the limits imposed by the labor market. Unlike the United States, Britain does not regularly and systematically report data on welfare receipt by race or ethnicity, so data are not available to present as complete a picture over time. But the few indicative bits of information that are available suggest that the racial imbalance between social insurance and public assistance is not as acute in Britain as in the United States. The best sources of data on welfare benefits by race are the periodic surveys conducted by the Policy Studies Institute (PSI, formerly Political and Economic Planning, PEP), an independent research organization. PEP and then PSI have done four national surveys on race relations. The first, conducted in 1966, was commissioned by Home Secretary Roy Jenkins (through the NCCI) to help build a case for stronger race relations legislation; subsequent surveys were done in 1974, 1982, and 1994.[51] The first two surveys were concerned mostly with documenting racial discrimination in employment and housing, but the later studies were more broadly directed at depicting the full range of minority life in Britain.

The 1982 survey is thus the first to contain data about British non-whites and the welfare state, and table 6.2 presents the proportions of white, West Indian, and Asian households receiving cash benefits.[52] The table reveals a much less dramatic split between whites and nonwhites in terms of the kind of benefits they receive (and rely on) than in the United States. Nonwhites were considerably more likely to receive certain means-tested benefits—especially Supplementary Benefit (as National Assistance was renamed in 1966)—and also more likely to collect Unemployment Benefit than whites, while whites were more likely to receive social insurance old-age pensions (Retirement Benefit). Nonwhites also received universally available child benefits at a much higher rate than whites. But when the data are broken down demographically according to family circumstances, most of the racial differences disappear; nonwhites are not markedly more likely than whites in similar family circumstances to receive various categorical means-tested benefits. Retired whites are more likely to get retirement benefits, but this disparity reflects the structure of contributory old-age pensions, which are available only to those who have worked enough to qualify, a criterion that disproportionately excludes nonwhites (both because of higher unemployment rates for nonwhites and because as immigrants they may not been in the country long enough to build up sufficient credit to qualify for benefits).[53] These data suggest a reasonably successful pattern of incorporation of nonwhites into the British welfare state that at least does not exaggerate racial distinctions that arise in the labor market.

The 1994 PSI survey similarly shows that there is not a great disparity between whites and nonwhites in their receipt of welfare benefits.[54] Table 6.3 presents the proportion of white and nonwhite families with no wage earners receiving various public benefits. Once again, whites are substantially more likely to receive National Insurance benefits ("State Pension"), while nonwhites are more likely to receive means-tested income support ("Income Support," as National Assistance, later Supplementary Benefit, is now called). Unlike the 1982 survey, the report of the 1994 survey does not categorize families by family type (families with children, pensioners, and so forth), but the disparities are consistent with, if not smaller than, those reported in 1982 (although it is hard to compare the 1994 data on families with no wage earners with the 1982 data, which include all families, with and without earners). Moreover, in 1994 the incomes of families that depended entirely on public benefits were relatively similar across ethnic groups, ranging from £118 per week for Caribbeans to £149 per week for Pakistanis and Bangladeshis, compared with £135 for whites

TABLE 6.2
Proportion of Households Receiving Welfare Benefits, UK, by Race (1982)

	All Households			Extended Households			Lone Parents			Others with Children			Pensioner Only		
	White	West Indian	Asian	White	West Indian	Asian	White	West Indian	Asian	White	West Indian	Asian	White	West Indian	Asian
Child Benefit	34	60	75	45	47	78	98	95	97	99	97	98	—	—	—
Unemployment Benefit	7	17	16	15	17	21	7	11	10	9	15	18	—	—	—
Family Income Supplement	1	5	3	3	3	2	6	15	7	1	4	2	—	—	—
Supplementary Benefit	14	20	11	15	19	14	45	50	45	7	10	8	25	(31)	(26)
Retirement Benefit	35	6	6	—	—	—	—	—	—	—	—	—	95	(80)	(74)

Source: Brown, Black and White in Britain, 242.

TABLE 6.3
Proportion of Households with No Wage Earner Receiving Welfare
Benefits, UK, by Race (1994)

	White	Caribbean	Indian/ African-Asian	Pakistani/ Bangladeshi
Child Benefit	14	29	31	50
One-Parent Benefit	3	11	2	1
Disability Allowance	8	5	10	6
State Pension	43	19	12	6
Unemployment Benefit	4	6	6	10
Invalidity Benefit	6	7	7	5
Income Support	24	44	39	50
Housing Benefit	33	63	26	31

Source: Modood et al., Ethnic Minorities in Britain, 154.

(although because nonwhite families tend to be larger, these figures translate into larger per-person income for whites than for other groups).

Some analyses of British welfare policy have found that nonwhites are somewhat less likely than whites to claim welfare benefits to which they are entitled, often because of language barriers or lack of information in minority communities about benefits rights. There is also some evidence that nonwhites experience particular difficulties in benefits offices—hostile intake workers, steep and rigidly applied qualification requirements, and the like—that result in a low take-up rate.[55] Some groups, ethnographic research has shown, are more likely to decide *not* to claim benefits for which they are eligible because claiming would evoke negative feelings from their own communities. This seems to be true particularly for Pakistanis and Bangladeshis; other groups, however—Caribbeans and Indians, especially—seem to attach no such stigma to claiming benefits and in fact have highly developed community and kinship networks that support benefits claiming.[56]

Despite this research there is also evidence that take-up rates do *not* differ that sharply by race. A PSI survey of low-income families in the early 1990s found that take-up of universal benefits such as retirement pensions and child allowances is effectively 100 percent for all groups. For means-tested income support benefits, take-up rates for whites and Asians were both approximately 60 percent, while the reported rate for Caribbean blacks was somewhat lower (although this finding is based on a very small sample and is therefore less than reliable). Finally, the national Department of Social Services has undertaken an outreach effort

TABLE 6.4
Sources of Income, Manchester, UK (1968)

	Employment	Rent, Dividends, Interest	Social Security Benefits	Total
New Commonwealth	85.9%	8.1%	6.0%	100.0%
West Indies	85.5	8.4	6.1	100.0
Indigenous	77.6	10.8	11.6	100.0

Source: Manchester Survey, *National Income and Expenditures,* 1968, reported in K. Jones and A. D. Smith, *The Economic Impact of Commonwealth Immigration* (Cambridge: Cambridge University Press, 1970), 92.

to inform minorities about benefits available to them, often in languages other than English, although some observers are skeptical about the results.[57]

Other data, some quite sketchy and all quite imperfect, also suggest the reasonably proportional incorporation of nonwhites into the British welfare state over time. A survey of residents of Manchester in 1968 showed that nonwhite immigrants derived rather less of their income from public benefits than native white Britons (table 6.4), but this difference is attributable to the slow maturation of social security claims, which must be based on long-term contributions by workers. By the 1980s, whites and nonwhites in Britain had relations with the welfare state that were considerably more similar than whites and nonwhites in the United States. British whites and nonwhites, for example, had almost identical patterns of unemployment insurance claims and used government job centers to search for work at similar rates, as tables 6.5 and 6.6 detail. Nonwhites claim a wide array of social benefits, although they rely more heavily than whites on means-tested income-support benefits and proportionately less on social-insurance benefits such as old-age pensions that depend on claims derived from past work. Among households not receiving public benefits, Indians and African Asians were twice as likely as white households to be poor (defined as having incomes below half of the national average); among households receiving some kind of public benefits, however, this ratio was only 1.4 to 1 (albeit at considerably higher levels of poverty all around). Finally, whites and nonwhites use Britain's most universal social benefit—the National Health Service—at identical rates (controlling for self-assessed health status, on the presumption that people who believe themselves to be in poor health will visit the doctor more often, all other things being equal; see table 6.7).[58]

In general, these data suggest the relative success of minority incorporation into the British welfare state. The pattern of equality in universally available services and disparities arising principally from work-related

TABLE 6.5
Percentage of Unemployed Claiming Unemployment
Benefits, UK (1988–90)

	All	Male	Female
All	60	73	40
White	60	73	40
Minority	58	70	39
African-Caribbean	58	73	42
African Asian	58	—	—
Indian	55	65	39
Pakistani	73	80	49
Bangladeshi	69	—	—
African	41	—	—
Other/Mixed	49	58	39

Note: Dash indicates too few cases for reliable percentage.
Source: UK Labour Force Survey, 1989–1990, reported in Trevor Jones, *Britain's Ethnic Minorities: An Analysis of the Labour Force Survey* (London: Policy Studies Institute, 1993), 134.

benefits—almost the reverse of the American pattern—suggests that the lack of full minority participation in social security was due not to welfare exclusion per se, but to inequality in the labor market, which limited access to National Insurance. This inference is consistent with the available evidence on racial inequality in employment. Minority unemployment— particularly for people of Bangladeshi, Pakistani, and Caribbean origin— has consistently been higher than that for whites, across all educational levels, regions, and occupational categories. Nonwhites are also more likely to be unemployed for longer stretches of time. Those employed have generally been in lower-status, lower-paying jobs (often, but not always, as a result of lower levels of education and training).[59] In fact, nonwhites fared worst in the area of public provision that was most decentralized: public, or council, housing. Despite the official "no discrimination" policy in the allocation of council housing, as early as the 1960s minorities were considerably less likely to rent homes from local authorities than whites.[60] It is not clear whether the racial disparity in council housing resulted from lower demand on the part of nonwhites or from discriminatory allocation, but public housing stands out as a unique domain of weak welfare state incorporation in an otherwise strong picture.

TABLE 6.6
Use of Job Centers as Main Method of Seeking Work, UK

	1984–86	1988–90
All	38	29
White	37	29
Minority	40	28
African-Caribbean	43	30
African Asian	45	32
Indian	40	26
Pakistani	40	34
Bangladeshi	37	22
Chinese	23	—
African	40	26
Other/Mixed	33	20

Note: Dash indicates too few cases for reliable percentage.
Source: UK Labour Force Survey, 1989–1990, reported in Trevor Jones, *Britain's Ethnic Minorities: An Analysis of the Labour Force Survey* (London: Policy Studies Institute, 1993), 133, 136.

TABLE 6.7
Percent Visiting NHS General Practitioner, by Self-Assessed Health, UK (1994)

	White	Caribbean	Indian/ African-Asian	Pakistani/ Bangladeshi	Chinese
Good/Excellent	24	32	27	35	19
Fair	48	50	55	66	—
Poor/Very Poor	69	81	83	89	—
Total	33	42	39	51	23
N	2856	1555	2055	1124	388

Note: Dash indicates too few cases for reliable percentage.
Source: 1994 PSI Survey, reported in Tariq Modood, Richard Berthoud, et al., *Ethnic Minorities in Britain: Diversity and Disadvantage* (London: Policy Studies Institute, 1997), 253.

Despite all this, racial and ethnic inequality in Great Britain continues to be an important line of social division. In the early 1990s, one-third of the nonwhite population (and even more of those under 65) was in the lowest income quintile. Although there is no official poverty line in Britain as in the United States, more than 80 percent of Pakistanis and Bangladeshis in Britain had incomes below half the national average, compared with approximately 40 percent of other nonwhites and slightly more than one-quarter of whites. Earlier studies of household income and living standards revealed similar patterns of substantial racial disparities in income, employment, and living conditions. Moreover, nonwhite disadvantage is likely to be highly spatially concentrated. Three-fifths of the minority population in 1991 lived in neighborhoods that were in the highest quintile of unemployment rates in the country, continuing the long-standing pattern of residential concentration. These patterns of inequality in status in the labor market and the political economy more generally might suggest limitations on the incorporation of nonwhites into a regime of social provision that relies heavily on the distinction between workers and nonworkers to define welfare categories.[61]

Moreover, racial conflict continues to be a serious challenge in British society. In 1993 Stephen Lawrence, a black teenager, was stabbed to death while waiting for a bus in Eltham, a South London neighborhood, in an apparently racially motivated murder. The Metropolitan Police thoroughly botched the investigation and were never able to convict the white teenaged suspects. After several years of mounting criticism, the Home Office convened an inquiry led by retired judge Sir William Macpherson to investigate the murder and assess the ensuing investigation. Macpherson's report, issued in February 1999, concluded that "pernicious and persistent institutional racism" infected the Metropolitan Police and blocked the successful investigation of the Lawrence case.[62] In the summer of 2001, violent racial disturbances that injured hundreds and caused millions of pounds of property damage broke out in Oldham and Burnley in Lancashire and Bradford in Yorkshire. The Home Office's inquiry into the violence reported that investigators were "particularly struck by the depth of polarisation of our towns and cities" and suggested that "the programmes devised to tackle the needs of many disadvantaged and disaffected groups, whilst being well intentioned and sometimes inspirational, often seemed to institutionalise the problems."[63] The racist, right-wing British National Party, while still a tiny fringe group, has begun to make life uncomfortable for Britain's major political parties on range of race and immigration issues. That they have not made further inroads, like the National Front in France, is largely a consequence of the structure of British political institutions, which, as in the welfare state, has managed to protect Britain's minorities against the worst consequences of a race-conscious society.

CONCLUSIONS

Despite the dramatic shift in racial attitudes and minority mobilization in the second half of the twentieth century, the prospects for minority incorporation in the United States have proven to be highly variable, ranging across a variety of political, economic, and social domains.[64] American social policies, too, have developed differing capacities to incorporate African Americans, depending on the institutional structures of particular policies. Several institutional mechanisms have been crucial in establishing the capacity of American welfare policies to incorporate African Americans and other minorities on equal terms. In particular, the structural gap between national social insurance programs for workers and residual decentralized means-tested programs for those cut off from the labor market has had imbalanced effects on minorities. These effects derive both from the liberal, market-conforming character of the American welfare regime and from its institutional fragmentation, embodied in the division between nationalism and parochialism in its organizational structure. Thus the American welfare state's liberalism—especially its tendency to reinforce success and punish failure in the labor market—interacts with the decentralization of its public assistance arm to pose high barriers for minority incorporation, and consequently it works to amplify rather than to overcome preexisting patterns of racial inequality.

Clearly the British welfare state has not effectively prevented the evolution of racial segregation and hierarchy either. Serious racial problems remain in British society that the welfare state cannot solve by itself—and was not designed to solve. But the British welfare state has not played the same role as the American welfare state in constructing these patterns of race-based separation. As in the United States, the liberalism of British welfare policy tends to reinforce racial inequalities that arise in the labor market, where racial minorities are disadvantaged both by poor skills and discrimination. But the British welfare state largely avoids amplifying those inequalities by relegating public assistance to weak, decentralized venues, and minorities have fared comparatively well in the British system. These patterns further underscore the importance of institutional arrangements in shaping racial incorporation outcomes. Britain and the United States share an emphasis on race consciousness, which might be expected to lead to similar limitations in the possibility of full incorporation of racial minorities into national structures of social provision. Certainly many of the same barriers to incorporation apply in both countries—the gap between social insurance and public assistance and inequalities in the labor market harm minorities disproportionately in both systems. But the centralized uniformity of the British public assistance system has allowed the British welfare state to avoid the extreme racial disparities of the American system (even though questions about racial barriers in the British system remain salient). The cultural tendency toward race consciousness, then, does not by itself determine patterns of group-state relations; rather, institutional structures help translate this tendency into actual outcomes.

The consequence of an American welfare state divided along coincidental lines of race and class is a society in which race is a central axis of inequality. Race remains stubbornly at the center of any account of American inequality despite the overthrow of state-sponsored segregation and the dissolution of "Jim Crow" racism. Since the late 1950s, African Americans have consistently been between 2.5 and 3.5 times more likely to be poor than whites, and more than twice as likely to be unemployed or disengaged from the labor market altogether.[65] Poor African Americans, especially those living in segregated neighborhoods in inner cities, experience a piling-on of economic and social difficulties that is unmatched in other welfare states, suggesting the particular failure of their weak incorporation into the American welfare system. To some extent, then, the failure of welfare incorporation for African Americans is a consequence of their poor incorporation into the labor market, in which blacks have long been the victims of severe discrimination, along with other barriers to employment such as educational inequities. The common emphasis on employment in the American, British, and French welfare states suggest that integration into the labor market—and state efforts to protect and promote minority employment—are themselves critical elements of minority incorporation, both as means of access to the social rights conferred by the welfare state and as important aspects of social citizenship in their own right.

Chapter Seven

THE DEVELOPMENT OF EMPLOYMENT DISCRIMINATION POLICY

IT IS CLEAR from the discussion of the welfare state that the labor market is central to shaping paths of minority incorporation. In each of the welfare state configurations in the United States, Great Britain, and France, the attachment of individuals and families to the labor market determines, to a greater or lesser degree, eligibility for social benefits and links to the welfare state. Consequently, the labor market's openness to minority participation and the state's ability to maintain that openness are at least as important as the structure of the welfare state in shaping a country's capacity to achieve full inclusion for racial minorities in society.

Work is central to modern conceptions of citizenship. For T. H. Marshall, "The basic civil right is the right to work, that is to say the right to follow the occupation of one's choice in the place of one's choice." Under the British Poor Law, civil right became social obligation, and claims to rights came to depend on work. After the brief Speenhamland interlude of the late eighteenth and early nineteenth centuries, in which the guarantee of a minimum wage severed the link between work and social rights, the New Poor Law of 1834 made wage labor the linchpin of claims to citizenship. "The Poor Law," Marshall writes, "treated the claims of the poor not as an integral part of the rights of the citizen, but as an alternative to them—as claims which could be met only if the claimants ceased to be citizens in any true sense of the word. For paupers forfeited in practice the civil right of personal liberty, by internment in the workhouse, and they forfeited by law any political rights they might possess."[1] In the United States as well, paid work, as Judith Shklar notes, has been an essential defining element of citizenship, distinguishing citizens from both idle aristocrats and degraded slaves. The dignity of free labor, moreover, was one of the critical ideological lines that distinguished whites from blacks and ultimately divided the country in the nineteenth century. For Abraham Lincoln, in fact, the equal right of African Americans freely to earn their livelihoods was at the very core of the crisis of the 1850s. While he shared the common view of his time that blacks were inferior in most respects, he argued forcefully that "in the right to eat the bread, without leave of anyone else, which his own hand earns, [the Negro] *is my equal and the equal of Judge Douglas, and the equal of every living man.*"[2]

Despite the reconstruction of social rights in the twentieth century and the receding of Poor Law strictures, work has remained central to citizenship, and particularly to social citizenship, in all three countries. Access to jobs remains one of the most important sources of group inequality in modern industrial economies, and it is one that consistently divides societies by race and ethnicity. In the United States, black joblessness has reached crisis proportions. One recent study found that only 51.8 percent of black men between the ages of 16 and 64 in New York City were working in 2003, and black men are convicted of crimes and incarcerated at an alarming rate, effectively removing them from the job market and often stripping them of the basic political right of citizenship, the franchise.[3] In most modern welfare states, moreover, particularly the liberal and conservative variants, the labor market serves as a filter for deservingness; labor-market exclusion thus limits the welfare state's reach in extending and universalizing social citizenship. Work, in short, remains one of the touchstones of incorporation into citizenship, not only for racial and ethnic minorities but also for any marginalized or previously excluded group.

Historically it was labor migration that brought minorities to the centers of American, British, and French societies. The push of underdevelopment in the periphery and the pull of greater opportunity at the center were the twin forces that provided the impetus for millions of African Americans and colonial subjects to travel thousands of miles to make new lives for themselves, in places where they were strangers but also nominal citizens, entitled to certain rights and to the protection of those rights by the state. To what degree would these rights be fulfilled, and how would these states go about securing them, especially when they appeared to conflict with the rights of white citizens?

Employment discrimination policy, moreover, is by definition explicitly racial, rather than clandestinely so, as welfare policy so often is. It is a case where states adopt and implement policies with the explicit aim of managing racial conflict and addressing problems of racial discrimination and inequality. Such policies rest on a recognition that racial or ethnic characteristics have become arbiters of differential access to the labor market and on the conviction that using such distinctions in this way is illegitimate. Thus, although antidiscrimination policies may entail very different definitions of what constitutes "discrimination" or "equality," the very existence of such policies presumes the presence of race as a factor in society and politics (although not, it hardly need be said, as a biological reality). Simply put, without race there could be no notion of racial discrimination in employment and there would be no policy to prohibit it.

Therein lies the fundamental dilemma of employment discrimination policy, which mirrors and magnifies the dilemma of welfare incorporation: achieving color-blind incorporation inherently requires some level of race consciousness.

In this chapter, I explore how the United States addressed this dilemma in devising its employment discrimination policy. There are several paradoxes embedded in the history of American antidiscrimination policy. First, the Civil Rights Act of 1964 represented the triumph of color blindness over the alternative American tradition of ascriptive, discriminatory race consciousness. Second, American antidiscrimination policy has proved surprisingly and distinctively robust. As policy adoption gave way to implementation, color blindness quickly gave way to race consciousness through affirmative action, which offers compensatory advantages to members of historically or currently disadvantaged groups. Finally, this active (and arguably successful) approach developed even though the institutions mobilized to implement and enforce American antidiscrimination policy were characteristically weak and fragmented.

During the 1960s and 1970s, Great Britain and France also adopted major antidiscrimination policies that both resemble American policy and differ from it in unexpected ways. Like the United States, France enshrined in law a color-blind approach to identifying and combating employment discrimination, stressing equal treatment of individuals without regard to racial characteristics. British policy, by contrast, took a more explicitly race-conscious approach that recognized the legitimacy of group-level diagnoses and race-conscious remedies.[4] Similarly, neither France nor the United States vested power in a concentrated, unified arm of the state to enforce antidiscrimination law (although they in fact took quite different institutional approaches), while Great Britain created a single agency to oversee antidiscrimination enforcement.

These divergences in the mobilization of state power are particularly important because they highlight the configurations of ideas and institutions that underlie these national policy paths. In each case, policy was the product of a debate among conflicting views about how to conceive of and organize a national antidiscrimination effort. But these debates took place among different institutional contexts that shaped their outcomes. In the United States, fragmented and decentralized politics produced a fragmented and individualistic enforcement regime. The multiple veto points that inhibit coalition formation, combined with the radically localized nature of linkages between African Americans and the state, frustrated the more comprehensive, race-conscious designs of civil rights advocates and produced a circumscribed, color-blind law. In France, by contrast, it was centralized executive-led policy-making that initially frustrated the aims of supporters of race policy. Once the government changed its mind, however, a policy was adopted quickly, with little debate and only minor alterations from the advocates' original design. The result was legislation that created strong sanctions but relied on existing arms of the state or enforcement rather than seeking to create a dedicated antidiscrimination agency. In Britain centralized party government similarly facilitated the adoption of a strong statute that sought not only to attack discrimination in color-blind terms but also to promote peaceful coexistence and equality among racial groups. Moreover, the British act also created new state capacity to oversee this process.

The parallel narratives in this chapter underscore the centrality of these processes of coalition building—shaped by political institutions, cultural repertoires, and patterns of group-state linkage—for understanding the emergence of national employment discrimination policies. I begin by tracing the evolution of the culturally rooted ideas about discrimination that framed policy debates in each country. I then turn to the legislative debates that led to the enactment of employment discrimination policy, in which these ideas were refined and crystallized into concrete policies under the constraints imposed by state institutions and patterns of mobilization.

THE RISE OF COLOR BLINDNESS: IDEAS OF DISCRIMINATION IN THE UNITED STATES

Ever since emancipation, exclusion from the labor market has been one of the dominant shapers of African American life. In the late nineteenth century, the Southern states developed full-blown systems of racial segregation and stratification that depended on near-total separation of the races and exclusion of blacks from jobs, schools, public accommodations, and other sources of power, privilege, income, and wealth. As African Americans moved north in the twentieth century, competition between blacks and whites for jobs became increasingly intense, resulting in the hardening of the color line in the North's industrial political economy. In the first half of the twentieth century, racial discrimination and exclusion in the labor market became the norm around the country and across sectors of the economy—in private industry, labor unions, and the public sector.[5]

Exclusion from jobs has also been at the center of the African American struggle for full inclusion in American society for much of the twentieth century. Whether or not to challenge segregation and exclusion from predominantly white professions and economic sectors was a central point of conflict among African American elites around the turn of the twentieth century, exemplified in the public struggle between Booker T. Washington and W.E.B. Du Bois for primacy in the national African American community. Washington represented an accommodationist commitment to black advancement within the confines of Jim Crow, Du Bois a more confrontational challenge to the racial status quo.[6] Du Bois and his camp mostly won the battle to voice the political aspirations of African Americans, which were articulated in the Niagara Movement of the 1900s and instantiated in organizations such as the National Association for the Advancement of Colored People (NAACP), founded in 1909, and the National Urban League, founded the following year. The fight against legally sanctioned segregation and differential treatment in employment as well as other spheres was central to these organizations and came to define the civil rights struggle later in the twentieth century.

In the middle of the twentieth century, rising levels of black-white competition in American industry—accelerated by the increased hiring of African Americans in defense industries during World War II—produced widespread discrimination and, perhaps more important, an increasingly acute awareness of discrimination among African Americans, particularly in the North. In 1941, A. Philip Randolph of the Brotherhood of Sleeping Car Porters threatened to organize a march on Washington to protest discrimination in defense plants. To prevent the march, President Franklin Roosevelt issued an executive order creating a federal Fair Employment Practices Committee (FEPC) to monitor and investigate claims of discrimination in defense production and requiring a nondiscrimination clause in federal defense contracts. Although the direct effects of the FEPC were limited, it occasioned the beginnings of a debate about the substantive direction of antidiscrimination efforts as civil rights advocates and public officials concerned with racial equality began to ponder whether race-conscious means were necessary to achieve the manifestly color-blind ends of nondiscrimination. The FEPC also accelerated action by states to create antidiscrimination agencies that had already begun with the New York State Commission on Discrimination in Employment, created by Governor Herbert Lehman several months before the federal FEPC. By the early 1960s, twenty-five states had employment discrimination laws on the books and their own civil rights enforcement bodies in operation.[7]

The FEPC expired after the war and Congress declined to take up President Harry Truman's invitation to re-create it on a permanent, statutory basis. Nevertheless, its brief career flagged discrimination as a matter of federal concern and marked the beginning of a period of federal government antidiscrimination activity that would culminate in the passage of the Civil Rights Act of 1964. It was, wrote Gunnar Myrdal, "the most definite break in the tradition of federal unconcernedness about racial discrimination on the nonfarm labor market that has so far occurred."[8] In December 1946, a month after the Democrats lost control of Congress, Truman appointed a Committee on Civil Rights to explore how the government might act to combat discrimination and protect civil rights. The committee's report, *To Secure These Rights,* appeared in October 1947 and advocated a vigorous and wide-ranging program, which included enforcing voting rights, banning lynching, desegregating the armed forces (which Truman ordered the following year), and attacking discrimination in part by establishing a permanent FEPC. Truman moved cautiously to address these matters, hoping both to gain enough African American votes to win reelection and reverse the Democratic losses of 1946 and to avoid thoroughly alienating Southern Democrats. But when the 1948 Democratic National Convention, behind the leadership of Minneapolis mayor and senate candidate Hubert Humphrey, adopted a stronger civil rights plank than originally proposed, Southern delegates walked out and nominated South Carolina governor Strom Thurmond for president. After Truman's reelection in 1948, he was understandably skittish about making further moves toward antidiscrimination enforcement, but civil rights was by then squarely on the federal agenda.[9]

During the late 1940s and 1950s support for federal action on civil rights, including equal employment opportunity, was gradually growing. This growth was a response both to shifting public opinion and to the international pressure created by the Cold War, which particularly exposed the tension between the United States's liberal democratic stance in the world and the illiberalism of racial segregation at home.[10] At the same time, Southern opposition to federal action was hardening, as exemplified by the Southern Manifesto of March 1956, which declared opposition to the Supreme Court's decision in *Brown v. Board of Education* and support for resistance to "forced integration."[11] The Civil Rights Act of 1957 created both the United States Civil Rights Commission, which was primarily supposed to investigate and publicize civil rights matters, and the Civil Rights Division of the Justice Department. The establishment of the Civil Rights Division, originally charged with enforcing voting rights, elevated the institutional status of civil rights enforcement, which had previously been undertaken by a section of the Justice Department's Criminal Division, operating without explicit statutory authority. Not a week after President Dwight Eisenhower signed the bill (on 9 September), Arkansas Governor Orval Faubus called out the state's national guard to prevent the enrollment of black students at Central High School in Little Rock. Several weeks later, Eisenhower federalized the national guard and sent additional regular army troops to Little Rock to enforce the law, further escalating the federal government's involvement in protecting civil rights and enforcing nondiscrimination.[12]

By the beginning of the 1960s, then, two patterns had been established. One was ideological: the primacy of a liberal, color-blind view of discrimination as the fundamental paradigm for civil rights law and policy.[13] In this view, discrimination meant simply differential treatment of individuals on account of their race, and this was deemed the fundamental problem of race relations that demanded government action. The second pattern was the gradual incursion of the state into antidiscrimination policy. At the same time, African Americans themselves were organizing and mobilizing, strategizing and acting, building a social movement that would topple Jim Crow and impel both of these developments—the ideological and the institutional—farther than nearly anyone had contemplated.

MULTICULTURALISM AND ASSIMILATION: IDEAS OF DISCRIMINATION IN BRITAIN AND FRANCE

Britain

In Britain, the notion of discrimination as a political concept was slow to arrive. For the first two postwar decades, the primary orientation of British race politics and policy was not toward the differential treatment of individuals but the integration of minority communities into British life in a variety of spheres. This was a period in British race politics that Ira Katznelson calls a "pre-political consensus," in which race was not a matter of central concern on the surface of British national politics and "both parties were in substantial agreement if not on what to do at least on what not to do."[14] What they agreed not to do, in essence, was recognize at the level of state policy that race was becoming a real and troublesome category in British society:

> This, then, was the essence of the pre-political consensus: colour would not be treated as a relevant political category. That there were any problems of discrimination, prejudice, integration, and social deficiencies, was implicitly denied. The dominant political attitude . . . "was that there was no great problem and that things would right themselves in the end."[15]

Race relations were not invisible in British politics and society, even before the 1958 riots in Nottingham and Notting Hill brought them sharply into view. The central consequence of this lack of attention to race policy on the part of the central state was not invisibility but, rather, the relegation of race politics to the local level. Local political and community leaders, left largely to their own devices by the disengaged central state, developed a set of race policy practices that focused on the reception of minority communities and their adaptation to life in Britain. This approach was exemplified by the numerous local committees that sprang up in British cities from the late 1940s into the 1960s. These committees began life, in most instances, with a paternalistic concern for the well-being of Commonwealth immigrants born often of the vestiges of colonialism and the missionary work of local churches. "For all," wrote two analysts of the local committees, "the immigrants were regarded as another disadvantaged group to be helped, like handicapped children and the aged."[16] Over time the committees evolved away from such outwardly paternalistic norms toward an approach that emphasized community relations, especially as minority communities began to organize at the local level and to define their own community boundaries. The community relations approach was formalized and given some measure of sanction and oversight by the national state in 1964 with the creation of the National Committee for Commonwealth Immigrants.[17]

Despite their relative success in many areas—not least in facilitating the incorporation of minorities into the British welfare state—the local committees and the community relations approach were decidedly nonpolitical, at least from the point of view of the minority communities themselves. Rather than providing foci of political mobilization and participation, they focused attention on horizontal links among communities, leaving local power relations intact. Race relations, their presence announced, were not matters for the institutions that wielded power in British society—Parliament and the Cabinet—but for these quasi-public organizations that provided minorities little access to or leverage over public decisions. Consequently, they focused attention away from those issues that drew attention to power imbalances between whites and nonwhites in British society, such as discrimination in employment and other spheres. By the same token, Britain does not share the American pattern of long-term, national organization and mobilization of minorities around a common political identity that, in the United States, helped to promote the concept of discrimination as a central focal point of race politics. At the same time, the evolution of the community-relations approach punctured the veneer of color blindness that covered British race politics before the mid-1960s by beginning to frame race not as a problem of the integration or assimilation of blacks into a white society but as one of accommodation and adjustment among communities whose integrity as communities was increasingly being taken for granted as a legitimate part of the British political landscape.[18]

The idea of discrimination as a frame for race policy was not absent during this period, but it came primarily from a different source than it did in the United States: political elites. As early as 1957, before Nottingham and Notting Hill, the Labour Party convened a Working Party on Racial Discrimination, which began to formulate policy ideas around the notion of sanctioning and preventing acts of discrimination against individual members of minority groups. In the late 1950s and early 1960s, a number of Labour backbenchers in Parliament introduced a series of antidiscrimination bills in the Commons, led by Fenner Brockway, a long-time left-wing Labour MP who was defeated in the 1964 election in a campaign that had similar racial overtones as the notorious Smethwick campaign of the same year, although substantially more muted.[19]

Brockway's defeat—and the drubbing administered to his fellow Labourite, frontbencher Patrick Gordon Walker, in Smethwick—were rather ironic not simply because the Labour Party won a slim majority in 1964 and formed a government for the first time in thirteen years but also because in the previous year Harold Wilson, the party leader who became prime minister, had committed the Labour Party to antidiscrimination legislation on Brockway's model. Labour had opposed the 1962 Commonwealth Immigration Act but had edged away from support for its repeal, and instead tried to neutralize race as an issue by accepting immigration controls while insisting on legal protection for minorities. Another source of influence on Labour's race-policy moves was the American experience, which was a familiar point of reference for one influential group of Labour advisors on race relations, who imported both the American focus on discrimination and the American legal approach to remedying it, which focused on civil law and administrative enforcement rather than criminal penalties. The result was the Race Relations Act of 1965, which outlawed racial discrimination in a limited sphere of activity and created the Race Relations Board to oversee conciliation efforts in cases of discrimination.[20]

Despite its weakness—Katznelson describes it as "primarily declaratory"—the 1965 act brought the policy model of discrimination, which was necessarily based on the acceptance of majority-minority group distinctions, into the purview of the British state, along with the notion that it was up to the state to address the problem.[21] Far from taking race off the agenda, as many Labour leaders had hoped, the act generated nearly immediate dissatisfaction from those who wanted to see it strengthened and broadened to include areas such as employment and housing that had been left out of its scope. Not least among these was Roy Jenkins, who became Home Secretary in December 1965. It was under Jenkins's supervision that the first Political and Economic Planning report was commissioned "to assess the extent of discrimination in Britain in fields not covered by the Race Relations Act—i.e., employment, housing, and insurance, credit facilities and financial services."[22] In addition to a survey of Commonwealth immigrants and interviews with "people in a position to discriminate" (employers, real estate agents, public housing officials, and bank managers, for example), the PEP study featured "situation tests" (also known as audit studies), in which testers of different races but with other relevant characteristics controlled were sent to apply for jobs, housing, and bank loans in order to test for differential treatment on the basis of race. The results of the study, published in April 1967, provided ample systematic evidence of racial discrimination in British society and had an important impact on British opinion. These results helped propel the passage of the 1968 Race Relations Act, which extended the 1965 act to cover employment as well as housing and commerce, although it retained the weak conciliation mechanisms of the 1965 act.[23]

Thus by 1970, when the Conservatives regained power, racial discrimination was squarely on the British national political agenda. On the one hand, the ideological model of discrimination that had come to dominate British political discourse on race and race policy was very similar to the American paradigm—liberal, color-blind, and based on individual acts of differential treatment. The American paradigm, in fact, was a model for British policy; British intellectuals and policymakers have quite explicitly seen their own evolving problems of racial conflict as similar to American ones and sought to emulate American successes and avoid American mistakes in making race policy.[24] But the evolution of antidiscrimination as a policy paradigm occurred in a very different political context in Britain than in the United States, a context marked by a more centralized, top-down policy-making apparatus and the absence of a strong social movement aimed at challenging discrimination from the bottom up.

France

In France, the notion of discrimination took hold even more slowly than in Britain. After World War II, the principal concern of French political and intellectual elites was to eradicate the vestiges of the collaborationist Vichy regime. "After the Liberation," Pierre Birnbaum has written, "the need to refound the Republic and to restore a brilliance tarnished by so much dark plotting was widely felt."[25] Although many French officials who had served under Vichy stayed on to serve the Fourth Republic, including future president François Mitterrand, the imperative of eliminating the racist antisemitism to which France had so easily, even eagerly, succumbed during the Nazi occupation prevailed. In April 1939, the French government adopted the Marchandeau decree (named for the justice minister who promulgated it), which banned racial defamation in the press, an owl-of-Minerva moment if ever there was one. The Vichy government abrogated the decree in August 1940. After the Liberation, French popular racist antisemitism was rampant—a majority in 1946 believed Jews to be a distinct race and expressed antipathy toward Jewish inclusion in the French nation—and the Marchandeau decree was restored, signaling the French government's commitment to banning expressions of racism that might undermine the renewal of the French model of republican citizenship.[26]

In the late 1940s and 1950s antisemitic racism remained prominent in France, and it spawned the beginnings of a counter-movement, principally with the formation of the Movement against Racism and Antisemitism and for Peace (MRAP), which in 1977 became the Movement against Racism and for Friendship among Peoples. MRAP began to press for more vigorous enforcement of the Marchandeau law and, failing that, the passage of new laws to combat racism. Initially these proposals focused on expanding the scope and reach of the prohibition against public expressions of racism, focused mainly on antisemitism. But gradually, as antisemitism declined and the nonwhite immigrant population grew, MRAP's proposals came to include a prohibition against differential treatment on the basis of race as well.[27] Although the MRAP proposals did encompass the idea of discrimination, based on the recognition of racial differences, the thrust of French antiracism remained rooted in the republican tradition of color-blind assimilationism that sought to erase such differences from public discourse and deny them political legitimacy.

Through the 1950s and 1960s, as colonial immigration accelerated and the nonwhite population of France grew dramatically, issues of access to jobs, housing, schools, and public services, became increasingly prominent. But the same political impulse toward color blindness that produced the attack on racist expression tended to delegitimize a policy approach toward such issues that recognized discrimination as a matter of differential treatment rather than a failure of integration. Policy responses such as the Fonds d'Action Sociale (FAS) sought precisely to obviate the need for antidiscrimination policy by helping immigrants become French and thus to facilitate their incorporation into French society as individuals and not as collectively conscious minority groups. Ironically, the FAS and other such targeted integration efforts, which embody the dilemma between universal color blindness and racial and ethnic targeting, helped to construct the social and political isolation that in the United States and Britain made discrimination more salient as a political concept, and yet French politics lacked the vocabulary to make the same move toward discrimination as a policy frame. The prohibition of ethnicity- and race-based organizing, moreover, stifled a potential source of political agitation for the recognition of discrimination per se as a problem in French society.[28]

Beginning in 1959, MRAP offered a series of legislative proposals to address both expressions of racism and discrimination, which were introduced into the National Assembly by Robert Ballanger, a Communist deputy. Although MRAP's proposals were continually blocked during the 1960s, pressure for the state to address racism and discrimination grew. Without the acquiescence of the government—meaning the prime minister and the president under the strong executive institutions of the Fifth

Republic—such legislative proposals were unlikely to succeed. Such acquiescence was not forthcoming during the 1960s. The government insisted that racism was not a serious problem in France, that French law and policy already treated all persons as equal, and that racial discrimination was consequently not a necessary target for legislative action.[29] Meanwhile, in 1971 France ratified the International Convention to Eliminate All Forms of Racial Discrimination, which had been adopted by the United Nations General Assembly in 1965, committing the French government at least nominally to antidiscrimination measures, if rather vaguely specified.[30] Thus by the early 1970s racial discrimination was making its way onto the French political agenda, although it was subsumed in a broader discourse of antiracism and dampened not only by a political tradition hostile to the very category of racial discrimination but also by a seemingly indifferent government.

THE TRIUMPH OF COLOR BLINDNESS: THE CIVIL RIGHTS ACT OF 1964

The evolution of ideas about discrimination, however, goes only part of the way toward explaining the three countries' policy approaches toward the issue. The other half of the story involves the legislative battles around transforming these ideas into policies in each country—battles that were shaped by distinctive national processes of coalition building. In the United States, the struggle for passage of the Civil Rights Act of 1964 reflected the country's characteristic race-laden institutional configuration. The fundamental problem facing civil rights supporters was assembling a supportive coalition that would pass a bill in both houses of Congress, over the absolute objections of most Southern Democrats and the ambivalence of many Republicans. The challenge was particularly acute in the Senate, where a filibuster was all but certain. At the same time, the political imperative for Northern Democrats to pass serious civil rights legislation was growing stronger, due largely to African American pressure applied through both protest and politics. Escalating conflict in the South and the peaking civil rights movement were the major stimuli behind the drive for a new civil rights law; the growing strength of African American voters within the Democratic party also made civil rights an increasingly important issue for Democratic politicians at all levels. At the same time, however, the Democratic party's tightening embrace of civil rights was already threatening to erode the party's fragile coalition and to isolate African American voters. For the Kennedy administration, civil rights had become an urgent if perilous domestic issue by the spring of 1963.[31]

Building on these shifting party alignments, the imperatives of coalition formation in Congress clearly shaped the construction of antidiscrimination law. Title VII of the Civil Rights Act of 1964, which outlawed racial discrimination in employment and created the Equal Employment Opportunity Commission (EEOC) to enforce the new law, joined the two issues—civil rights and labor—on which Southern Democrats reliably formed a cohesive bloc and often combined with Republicans to form a conservative blocking coalition.[32] As Congress debated Title VII, many civil rights advocates envisioned the creation of a new agency that would wield powerful and concentrated enforcement authority. In passing the Civil Rights Act of 1957, Congress had rejected a similar approach, deleting a provision proposed by the Eisenhower administration that would have authorized the Justice Department to file civil suits to combat discrimination across a wide range of areas, including education, employment, and public accommodations (foreshadowing the scope of the 1964 act).[33] By the early 1960s, civil rights proponents favored a similarly concentrated enforcement approach, but one that relied on executive, regulatory power rather than litigation. Such an agency—a super-FEPC—backed by statute and appropriated funds, would wield powerful and comprehensive authority over job discrimination, including the power to conduct investigations and impose sanctions on employers. This vision of administrative power involved both a streamlined structure, in which a newly constituted agency would consolidate the functions that were scattered throughout the federal and state governments, and a strong agency, empowered not merely to mediate individual disputes but to identify and regulate broader, collective patterns of discrimination. Both of these institutional paths were frustrated by the compromise that broke the logjam in Congress and allowed the Civil Rights Act to become law.

The EEOC began its gestation as a full-fledged regulatory agency, modeled on agencies such as the powerful National Labor Relations Board and the Federal Trade Commission—an independent board, whose members were not subject to presidential removal, with the power to issue blanket regulations and enforce them by ordering noncompliant employers to cease and desist their discriminatory activities. Under pressure from civil rights leaders, riding high after Martin Luther King's spring 1963 victory in Birmingham, and from Representative Adam Clayton Powell, Jr., of Harlem, who was threatening to move legislation to create such an agency, the Kennedy administration resisted, favoring instead a more moderate approach that would give statutory authority to the already extant President's Committee on Equal Employment Opportunity (PCEEO). But on 1 October 1963, two weeks after the bombing of the Sixteenth Street Baptist Church in Birmingham, House Judiciary chairman Emmanuel Celler engineered subcommittee approval of a bill including a strong agency provision in defiance of an agreement with the administration and committee Republicans on a more centrist bill. Attorney General Robert Kennedy and his deputy, Nicholas Katzenbach, orchestrated a compromise that dropped the EEOC's cease-and-desist authority and gave it instead the prosecutorial authority to file lawsuits against recalcitrant employers.[34]

Although as late as January 1964 White House vote counts suggested that there was majority support in the House for a civil rights bill containing a strong agency provision, it was clear that the prospects for passage in the Senate were remote. The Senate rules, which required a two-thirds vote to end debate, further empowered Southerners to stall legislation; the filibuster had long been a formidable tool for Southerners in blocking civil rights bills. With twenty-one Southern Democrats nearly unanimously opposed to any civil rights legislation and forty-six Northern Democrats nearly unanimously in favor, support of a substantial majority of the thirty-three Republican senators was necessary to achieve the sixty-seven votes necessary to end the inevitable Southern filibuster. Indeed, the Senate debate on the Civil Rights Act of 1964 famously lasted three months and filled more than 60,000 pages of the *Congressional Record*.[35]

Republicans, in the tradition of the party of Lincoln, had long been more liberal on racial issues than Democrats, but that pattern was beginning to change in the early 1960s and was, at the very moment of the civil rights debate, under conspicuous challenge in the presidential candidacy of Senator Barry Goldwater, a civil rights opponent who was one of the leading Republican strategists seeking to turn the Republican party toward a Southern strategy for contesting national elections.[36] Nevertheless, Republicans and non-Southern Democrats in the Senate were ideologically indistinguishable on civil rights issues as measured by Keith Poole and Howard Rosenthal's NOMINATE scores. On Poole and Rosenthal's second dimension, which denotes a scale of liberalism to conservatism on racial and sectional issues, the mean scores of Republican and non-Southern Democratic senators are identical (-0.182 for the former and -0.183 for the latter, a statistically insignificant difference). On the first dimension—corresponding to a basic liberal-conservative scale on economic and regulatory issues—however, Republicans and non-Southern Democrats were quite far apart (means of 0.305 and -0.367, respectively). Thus the key to obtaining Republican votes for civil rights was not principally swaying them toward civil rights protection but rather moderating the bill's economic and regulatory impact.[37]

The bill's most vehement Republican opponents—a small group of extreme conservatives—objected precisely to the bill's supposed creation of excessive federal power. Goldwater, the most prominent among them, had supported local integration efforts in Arizona and never disavowed the principle of integration. But, bolstered by the advice of constitutional experts William Rehnquist (then a Phoenix lawyer and Republican activist) and Professor Robert Bork (of Yale Law School), he opposed the bill on constitutional grounds. Title VII in particular amounted to "the loss of our God-given liberties," he said on the Senate floor in the closing days of the debate, and would "require the creation of a Federal police force of mammoth proportions" as well as an "informer psychology" among Americans—"the hallmarks of the police state and landmarks in the destruction of a free society."[38]

With Goldwater and his cohorts securely in the opposition, the focus of negotiations was on a slightly larger group of conservative Republican senators with moderate civil rights leanings, who might, it seemed, be induced to accept the bill were it shorn of its more egregious expansions of state power; among this group were men such as Wallace Bennett of Utah, Norris Cotton of New Hampshire, Bourke Hickenlooper of Iowa, Karl Mundt of Indiana, and minority leader Everett Dirksen of Illinois. These senators occupied the pivotal point in the strategic legislative setting with the power to grant or withhold the critical votes for passage and thus to control the terms of a compromise.[39]

It was Dirksen who brokered the compromise that finally ended the filibuster through a long series of negotiations with Senate Democrats and a Justice Department team led by Katzenbach on behalf of the administration. The Dirksen compromise included important language in Title VII to ensure that only intentional discrimination would be a violation of the act, "to make it clear that it is not an unlawful employment practice to discriminate inadvertently or without knowledge of the pertinent facts," as a White House report on the compromise put it.[40] The amended bill also stated that

> nothing contained in [Title VII] shall be interpreted to require any employer . . . to grant preferential treatment to any individual or to any group because of the race, color, religion, sex, or national origin of such individual or group on account of an imbalance which may exist with respect to the total number or percentage of persons of any race, color, religion, sex, or national origin employed by any employer . . . in comparison with the total number or percentage of persons of such race, color, religion, sex, or national origin in any community, State, section, or other area, or in the available work force in any community, State, section, or other area.[41]

This language made clear that only direct, purposive, individual acts of discrimination were to be outlawed, and not so-called statistical discrimination (inferred from numerical imbalances). Even the bill's most ardent supporters embraced this interpretation. "If the Senator can find in title

VII," Senator Hubert Humphrey offered in an exchange with Virginia's A. Willis Robertson, father of televangelist Pat Robertson, "any language which provides that an employer will have to hire on the basis of percentage or quota related to color, race, religion, or national origin, I will start eating the pages one after another, because it is not in there."[42] This provision seemed to rule out any kind of compensatory, targeted, race-conscious policy to promote equal employment opportunity and appeared to resolve American ambivalence about color blindness and race consciousness in favor of color blindness.[43]

Two other important elements of the Dirksen compromise directly concerned the structure of the EEOC and the scope of its power. One stripped the EEOC of the power to file antidiscrimination lawsuits directly, reserving this power for the Justice Department—and then only in "pattern or practice" cases where it could document systematic, rather than simply individual, discrimination—and at the same time substantially scaled back the EEOC's investigative power. The other required that the EEOC defer to state fair employment agencies in disputes over jurisdiction.[44] These provisions effectively did two things. They lowered the EEOC from its proposed status as first among equals, the lead agency in the field of job discrimination, and they stripped it of any effective enforcement power, limiting its role to mediating in individual cases.

A further institutional constraint shaped the development of antidiscrimination policy: the characteristic fragmentation of the American state. One source of this fragmentation was simply the constitutional limitation on the federal government's authority to restrict the actions of private employers, as opposed to government contractors (as well as direct government employment).[45] In the latter case, the government's authority was less ambiguous, and the executive branch had already begun to try to enforce antidiscrimination rules on both contractors and the government's own departments and agencies, mostly through the PCEEO. Banning private discrimination, however, required congressional action, which placed it on a separate institutional track from public-sector regulation.

The congressional compromise over antidiscrimination policy, then, was a product of both the institutional structure of American politics and policy-making and the distinctive pattern of agreement and controversy surrounding civil rights in the 1960s. Substantively, the Civil Rights Act embodied a compromise convergence on color blindness as the ideological frame for antidiscrimination policy and on a vision of civil rights enforcement that emphasized compensatory remedies for deliberate individual acts of discrimination; except from the South, there was little dissent from these conclusions.[46] The disagreement that had to be resolved in order to form a winning coalition in Congress was thus not over integration as a policy goal but over the form and strength of the state power that would be deployed to achieve it.

The compromise version of Title VII embedded color-blind antidiscrimination policy in an institutional structure that had three important characteristics. First, it failed to create a coordinated civil rights enforcement structure, instead muddying the civil rights waters further by establishing the EEOC in the midst of an already fragmented and confused executive environment. Second, although the EEOC was nominally charged with enforcing Title VII, the act withheld enforcement power from the commission. The EEOC's weakness and its ensuing rivalries with other agencies for primacy in the realm of antidiscrimination enforcement meant that the commission's effectiveness depended heavily on its ability to persuade rather than coerce, and on its links with other actors in the civil rights establishment—particularly nongovernmental organizations and the courts—became increasingly important in shaping its effectiveness. Finally, the EEOC was particularly vulnerable to struggles for political control and accountability, both between the White House and Congress and within the executive branch itself. In the years following the Civil Rights Act, each of these characteristics would prove influential in shaping the enforcement and development of employment discrimination policy, setting the stage for the ambivalent embrace of race-conscious remedies, despite the color-blind frame of 1964.

POLICY DEVELOPMENTS IN BRITAIN AND FRANCE

Britain

Britain's approach to the problem of race relations was on the surface quite similar to the liberal integrationism of the Civil Rights Act. But British policy arose out of a very different political and institutional context. Although British patterns of localized links between racial minorities and the state very much mirrored the American model, these linkages did not match so serendipitously the political opportunities offered by the more centralized structure of the British party and parliamentary systems. As a result, British minorities and their advocates, while they were successful in achieving antidiscrimination legislation, found themselves without the leverage in national politics and policy-making that would have allowed them to make the most of a race relations law that on paper offered very strong inclinations toward collective, race-conscious enforcement.

By the late 1960s, Britain was already developing a tradition of local race-relations activity that tended to emphasize integration of communities rather than assimilation of individuals. As in the United States, the chief organizational and political linkages between British minorities and the states arose at the local level. In both countries, Ira Katznelson argues, "these organizational linkages structured participation, created persistent, well-defined patterns of access, and established orderly procedures for reaching the migrant population *on elite terms,* leaving the distribution of political power largely intact."[47]

As a consequence of these predominantly local political ties, minorities were only weakly integrated into the centralized structure of British party politics. Like African Americans, who since the 1960s have consistently voted Democratic (mostly more than 90 percent), British minorities consistently and overwhelmingly vote for the Labour party—more than 80 percent in the case of Afro-Caribbeans and in the vicinity of 70 percent in the case of Asians through the 1980s and 1990s. British minorities are also less likely than white voters to abandon Labour for the Liberal Democrats as their socioeconomic status rises, despite long-standing support by Liberal Democrats for strong race relations policy and their consistent opposition (more consistent than Labour) to immigration restrictions. Minorities, however, tend to be concentrated in urban areas where Labour is politically dominant, and hence in extremely safe Labour parliamentary constituencies, so that their electoral influence is diluted (although residential segregation is rather less acute in the United Kingdom than in American cities). The party discipline of the British parliamentary system makes intraparty splits less prominent as strategic openings for policy-making. Thus the Labour party has made relatively little progress in incorporating British minorities, whether by offering policy concessions, forging links with leaders of immigrant communities, or working to mobilize minority voters. For example, it resisted for a long time calls for formation of "black sections" within the party organization to represent and mobilize minority voters, and it has been slow to recruit minority members and elect and appoint blacks and ethnic minorities to national or local offices.[48]

Nevertheless, electoral politics played a role in spurring the British government toward antidiscrimination legislation. In the early 1970s an uneasy interparty consensus on race and immigration began to break down, and race began to move up the public agenda. In the first of two general elections held in 1974, neither party won a majority in the House of Commons. In a second election some months later, Labour won a three-seat majority. Some analyses suggested that nonwhite voters, who were beginning to favor Labour, had provided the margin of victory. Whether or not these voters were decisive, the Labour leadership felt compelled to advocate stronger state protection for racial minorities, at least as compensation to the party's left wing for its continued acceptance of strict immigration restrictions.[49]

Thus when the government proposed a new Race Relations Act in 1976, it was responding not only to increasing racial tension but also to increasing partisan pressure to take strong action on race relations, much like that the Johnson administration had faced a decade earlier. The political imperative was, quite similarly, to attack discrimination in employment, education, and public accommodations, and generally to ensure equal treatment to all regardless of race. In introducing the act to the House of Commons in March, Home Secretary Roy Jenkins announced that the principles on which the government's policy were founded were (along with immigration restriction) the permanence of racial minorities in the United Kingdom and the imperative of affording them equal treatment.[50] Racial division in British society would not go away, Jenkins said, and the government ought to address it forthrightly. Jenkins's approach to the race relations challenge did not insist on color blindness as an absolute policy standard. "I do not think," he had said on becoming Home Secretary for the first time in 1966, "that we need in this country a 'melting-pot', which will turn everybody out in a common mould, as one of a series of carbon copies of someone's misplaced version of the stereotyped Englishman. . . . I define integration, therefore, not as a flattening process of assimilation but as equal opportunity, accompanied by cultural diversity, in an atmosphere of mutual tolerance."[51]

In making and implementing antidiscrimination law, however, the government faced very different institutional pressures than had the Johnson administration in 1964. Most important, the government did not face the same coalition-building problems. Under the British parliamentary system, which nearly always produces majority governments (as opposed to minority or coalition governments), the process of policy-making does not depend on the piecemeal assembly of legislative coalitions, nor does it, as a rule, allow either concerted minorities or fragments of the majority party to block government-sponsored legislation. Thus the government had no opponents, whether within its own party or on the opposite benches, who could block the march of legislation. Jenkins and Prime Minister Harold Wilson (and James Callaghan, who became prime minister after Wilson's resignation in April) could enact the government's favored policy without complicating amendments. Thus, despite a similar ideological background, British race relations law departs substantially from its American counterpart. Nevertheless, the parliamentary debates on the Race Relations Act of 1976 reveal disagreements over issues of institutional structure and power similar to those that shaped American antidiscrimination policy debates of the 1960s.

As in the United States, arguments over the structure and power of the antidiscrimination enforcement agency were at the center. Rather than creating a fragmented set of enforcement institutions, the act consolidated two older agencies into a new Commission for Racial Equality (CRE), which was charged with the comprehensive enforcement of antidiscrimination law in employment as well as other areas. Moreover, the CRE was to have fairly extensive powers—at least on paper—to address collective discriminatory patterns in addition to remedying individual claims of discrimination. In both respects, the British institutional pattern departed from the American model, despite the similarity of general approach.

Jenkins emphasized both aspects of the bill, arguing particularly that the greater coordination and more extensive power represented by the new commission would allow the government "not only to combat discrimination and encourage equal opportunity but also to tackle what has come to be known as racial disadvantage." The act explicitly defined discrimination to include "not only deliberate and direct discrimination but also unjustifiable indirect discrimination. A particular practice may look fair in a formal sense," Jenkins explained, "or at least neutral in its original intent, but may be discriminatory in its operation."[52] The CRE was empowered to investigate and sanction employers who engaged in such collective discriminatory practices, as well as to help individuals bring cases in the courts. Moreover, there was little problem of overlapping jurisdiction or fragmented authority concerning race relations in the British government; the CRE was given sole authority over these matters, to some extent coexisting with but largely preempting the locally oriented community-relations approach.

Both of these aspects of the CRE were controversial. Although the Conservative frontbench supported the act, Shadow Home Secretary William Whitelaw worried that the new commission's powers would "be used in a bureaucratic and harrying manner." Other Conservative members were more direct. "We do not want hordes of officials instructing people in what they may or may not do," said Dudley Smith, a leading party spokesman on race and immigration issues. "That would invoke the hostility of elements in the white community. People of all colours, white and black, are wary of the constant proliferation of officialdom in our national life." Even proponents of the legislation disagreed over whether the commission's new powers should emphasize collective or individual authority. Evan Luard, a Labour member from Oxford, argued that the commission should be primarily concerned with helping individuals make complaints. Others worried that the Home Office, which was to oversee the CRE, was notoriously disorganized and overloaded, and suggested that a more modest individual approach might get better results. Similarly, some members opposed combining the existing Community Relations Commission and the Race Relations Board into a single body, largely on the grounds that they served two different purposes (enforcement and education, respectively) that should remain separate.[53]

On the government's side proponents of the newly configured CRE argued that it was precisely this consolidated, collective power that would render the CRE effective. Alexander Lyon, the Minister of State for the Home Office and the government's leading spokesman on race relations (and former parliamentary private secretary to Jenkins), explicitly cited the American EEOC's experience in support of these goals:

> One of my concerns has been that the Commission should not be burdened to anything like the same extent as is the Equal Employment Opportunity Commission in the United States of America, by individual investigations of complaints. If, for instance, the Race Relations Commission decides that it wants to do a strategic investigation into the employment, promotion and general conditions at, say, Ford of Dagenham, and comes to the conclusion that a system of discriminatory practices has grown up, based upon racial grounds, within Ford, and then issues a nondiscrimination notice putting an end to these discriminatory practices, it will affect the lives of thousands of people by one decision, whereas the Race Relations Board in the whole of its life considered 7,000 complaints most of which in the end had to be rejected.
>
> The individual complaints system is important for the individual. I do not minimise it, and we have made a provision for it. But the real test will be what the Commission does in its strategic investigation. It is for this reason that [this bill] is more than a brushing up of the 1968 [Race Relations] Act. . . . It is a completely new approach to problems of dealing with racial discrimination.

Lyon went on to explain that resource constraints would not allow the government actively to pursue both the individual and the collective routes to antidiscrimination enforcement, and that the government had chosen to emphasize the latter, in direct contrast to the direction the United States took in the Civil Rights Act of 1964.[54] Thus the contrasting institutional contours of the legislative process led to two different outcomes from similar ideological impulses.

The resulting legislation was, on paper at least, among the strongest antidiscrimination laws in Europe, stronger in many ways than the American Civil Rights Act in terms of the power it conferred on the state.[55] In fact, unlike the Civil Rights Act, which seemed explicitly to rule out collective, race-conscious employment practices (at least for private employers), the Race Relations Act of 1976 seemed to invite them, by defining discrimination to include indirect discrimination, endowing the CRE with strong regulatory enforcement power, and even enabling (though not requiring) limited forms of "positive action." Although the law distinguished clearly between "positive action"—action to expand minority employment opportunities—and "positive discrimination"—compensatory preferential treatment for members of minority groups—its definition of discrimination deliberately went well beyond the Civil Rights Act's explicit disavowal of indirect, statistical discrimination.

France

Unlike the Civil Rights Act, the French law against racism of 1 July 1972 was not the product of an intense compromise necessary to construct a winning legislative coalition from among fragmented and diverse interests and ideological factions. The postwar era was a period of institutional transition and instability for the French republic, and these changes had important implications for minority politics. Under the Fourth Republic, parliament was dominant, but a fragmented system of political parties rooted in local constituencies and narrow social interests produced a series of short-lived and often indecisive governments—more than twenty-five in twelve years.[56] Among the most divisive issues during the Fourth Republic, and the one that eventually brought it down, was the civil war in Algeria, which led to Algerian independence in 1962. In addition to military and foreign policy, the treatment of Algerians in France was a highly contested issue, particularly the creation of internment camps for those suspected of terrorism on behalf of the National Liberation Front. This issue divided the Socialist Party, whose parliamentary deputies split badly on the bill creating the camps.[57] The Socialists had shown some interest in courting North African voters during the 1950s, but the structure of parliamentary government in the Fourth Republic placed a premium on elite bargaining and centralized party discipline at the expense of mass mobilization and local electoral imperatives. This tension contributed to the limited development of mass party organizations in French politics, limiting opportunities for the forging of electoral linkages between the Socialists and new immigrants and displacing issues of integration onto other organizations, such as labor unions.[58]

In the Fifth Republic, policy-making power shifted away from the legislature and toward the executive—the president and ministers—particularly by giving the government strong legislative powers. Thus policy-making under the Fifth Republic was increasingly centralized in the hands of the executive, providing relatively few points of access for influence on national policy, especially when superimposed on the persistent administrative centralization that has long characterized the French state.[59] Executive dominance, in turn, made for less fluid coalition-building; what mattered above all in policy-making was the executive's position, and the sort of inter- and intra-party bargaining that both African Americans and their opponents were able to exploit to build majorities in the United States was largely closed as a path to policy-making. Combined with legal restraints on immigrant and ethnic political organizations, this feature of French policy-making institutions both limited the options for ethnic minorities to influence national policy and focused those options on a small number of political actors. Moreover, the weakness of the Socialists in national politics during the 1960s and 1970s and the dominance of French national politics by the Gaullist Right during those decades further restricted the potential for minority influence on policy.

It is important not to overstate the centralization of French politics in the Fifth Republic, even before the decentralizing reforms of the 1980s; centralization did not preclude the effective capture of the state by powerful private interests. As in earlier regimes, many national parliamentary deputies were also local officials such as mayors (under the *cumul des mandats,* the custom of allowing politicians to accumulate offices), injecting a healthy dose of local interest into national politics. But this means of influence did little for ethnic minorities in France. Many of the areas in which North African immigrants were concentrated—especially the south and the industrial north—were strongholds of the Left, which was out of power at the national level from the 1950s until 1981. At the same time, these were also the regions of the country where anti-immigrant and racist right-wing political movements, from the Poujadists of the 1950s to the National Front of the 1980s and 1990s, had their strongest support.[60]

Rather than an elaborate, finely calibrated compromise, the law that passed was essentially the same as the proposal that MRAP had originally drafted and presented to the legislature as early as 1959. MRAP, along with the Communist Party, presented its proposals anew to each legislature through the 1960s without success. The critical turning point in the law's progress toward enactment was the government's change of heart, which came in a period of increased racist violence in France. In the fall of 1971, President Georges Pompidou and Prime Minister Jacques Chaban-Delmas signaled, through a letter to MRAP from presidential assistant Jacques Chirac, that the government would entertain the idea of passing an antiracism law in the coming legislative session. The executive's change of mind was utterly decisive; by contrast, even after presidents Kennedy and Johnson supported civil rights legislation, the law's road to passage was arduous and uncertain. In the French case, the only uncertainty concerned whether the government would back up its private communications with public action, which it did when it announced on 15 April 1972 that it intended to adopt an antidiscrimination law.[61]

The legislative deliberation on the law was, accordingly, short and unexceptional. Deliberations took place behind the scenes, among the government, the National Assembly's Law Committee, and two major antiracist organizations, the MRAP and the International League Against Antisemitism (LICA). The controversy revolved around several points, chief among them being the status of antiracist groups as "civil parties," empowered to bring antidiscrimination cases on behalf of individual claimants. This was a particularly important provision—a "fundamental innovation," the MRAP called it, "meant to compensate for the failure of public prosecutors"—and the law's most important institutional innovation.[62] The government was not pleased with this provision at all. Justice Minister Ren Pleven indicated during the floor debate in the Assembly that the government considered the provision a significant departure from standard French legal practice and was accepting it only with great reluctance. In the final run-up to passage, an alternative bill was introduced in the Senate that would have limited the "civil party" power to groups officially recognized as "public interest" ("utilit publique") organizations, a restriction that would have excluded both MRAP and LICA. The Law Committee adopted this amendment, only to reverse itself mere hours before debate was to begin in the Assembly, substituting a limitation of the "civil party" power to organizations that had been in existence for five years or more and a stipulation that organizations could not intervene in individual cases without the individual's consent. Striking the only discordant note in the floor debate, Socialist deputy Michel Rocard objected to the five-year rule, hinting that it had been deliberately concocted to rule out groups formed in the wake of the 1968 protests. Pleven, in response, suggested that Rocard and his fellow leftists should take what they could get.[63]

Beyond this disagreement, very little in the legislation occasioned any serious controversy, or even much public notice. The enacted law closely resembled the MRAP's original proposal of thirteen years earlier. It made direct and deliberate racial discrimination in employment illegal and it also outlawed racist public utterances and banned groups that promote racism. Like the Civil Rights Act, the French law defines discrimination extremely narrowly, prohibiting only refusal to hire or dismissal "on account of" race. The word "discrimination," in fact, does not appear.[64] But in contrast with the American case, the law did not create any new institutional capacity, whether unified or fragmented, dedicated to regulating or punishing racial discrimination. Rather, it relied on preexisting government institutions—the criminal justice system and the national system of Labor Inspectors—to enforce antidiscrimination law. Finally, the French law made discrimination a criminal rather than a civil offense, subjecting accusations of discrimination to a very exacting standard of proof in individual cases while largely eliminating the possibility of regulatory pursuit of more collective forms of discrimination.

Although the French legislative debate, more than either the British or American, did contain references to the need for the state to "implement a program of mental hygiene," as one member of the National Assembly put it, to combat racism in French society, there was, in fact, much more emphasis on the need for effective enforcement of the law. In his opening speech on the bill to the Assembly, Alain Terrenoire, the bill's chief sponsor, emphasized that "a true antiracist politics . . . demonstrates the will of the public authorities to assure the effective implementation of an equality that, far from being the reduction of all to a single model, will come to be the acceptance of their differences." Another deputy also insisted on the importance of enforcement, not just principles, in combating discrimination. "Contrary to what too many citizens believe in good faith, democratic institutions . . . are not sufficient to ensure human liberty and dignity. For it is not enough to protect the individual against the abuse of public power. The state is obligated not only to respect the rights of man but also actively to guarantee them." And, perhaps most tellingly, Lopold Helne, the deputy from Guadeloupe, spoke of the importance of addressing material discrimination against French citizens of African descent. "Indeed," he said, "Guadeloupeans leave their archipelago because of its underemployment and economic underdevelopment. Having arrived in the metropole, they find themselves confronted with problems of employment, of housing, of insertion into our difficult metropolitan society. All discrimination concerning hiring, firing, refusal of service, housing, appears to them a provocation, an injustice, a crime."[65] There was thus substantial agreement on the importance of attacking such material acts of discrimination as well as rooting out racism from public discourse, and the law provided apparently strong, coercive sanctions: imprisonment of up to a year and fines of up to 20,000 Francs (approximately $4,000 in 1972).

On the other main characteristic of the enforcement mechanism—criminal as opposed to civil or administrative law—there is no evidence of any disagreement. Even before the passage of the 1972 law, victims of discrimination could sue for civil damages, but this remedy was complicated and expensive to pursue and hence rarely, if ever, used. The leaders of MRAP had pushed for the criminalization of racial discrimination in their earliest legislative proposals because it offered more reliable and effective instruments to punish and deter acts of discrimination than civil approaches (which remain part of the French enforcement structure, particularly through the system of labor inspectors). Many French lawmakers and others regarded the criminal law as the strongest possible protection against discrimination because of the force and decisiveness of criminal sanctions. Making racial discrimination a criminal offense has important consequences for enforcement and administration of the law. On the one hand, it raises the standard of evidence required to establish discrimination, placing the burden on the plaintiff to show that he was deliberately refused a job, for example, because of his race. This is a particular problem for enforcement during times of high unemployment, when employers necessarily turn away many job seekers without giving reasons. Many judges are reluctant to impose heavy penalties upon convictions, in the belief that the fact of conviction is more important than the extent of the sanction. One French commentator worries that the use of criminal sanctions for racial discrimination will tend to make martyrs of those who are convicted. On the other hand, the criminal law gives the state, rather than the individual, the primary responsibility for pursuing the complaint, placing the weight of the state and its coercive apparatus more firmly behind the antidiscrimination cause.[66] However, in the absence of an agency dedicated to antidiscrimination as its primary mission, there is little institutional capacity or inclination in the French state to pursue racial discrimination cases with any vigor.

CONCLUSIONS

If France and the United States approached problems of racial discrimination from such historically different cultural perspectives, why did they adopt such strikingly similar laws? Why did Great Britain, whose cultural frame for race policy resembled that of the United States, take such a different approach? The cultural framing of race and the ideological underpinnings of antidiscrimination policy clearly cannot by themselves explain these national policy-making outcomes. Rather, the answers to these puzzles lie in the institutionally rooted politics of minority incorporation. In each country, color-blind ideals of individualism and citizenship contended with collective, race-conscious notions of political identity for dominance in the shaping of antidiscrimination policy. For their own reasons, American, British, and French policymakers enacted policies that sought to define and outlaw discrimination, but they did so through very different means and in very different political contexts. Despite substantial overlap in the policies they enacted, this close comparison of the three national experiences and the critical moments of race policy-making reveals that configurations of culture and institutions—patterns of centralization and fragmentation, opportunities for political mobilization, points of access to the levers of political power—have led similarly framed policies in very different directions by creating both opportunities and constraints for political action.[67]

Once on the books, these policy enactments helped to redefine what constitutes legitimate and sensible antidiscrimination action. Laws rule certain kinds of behavior in and out, create rules, procedures, and venues for enforcement, and consequently help to reframe subsequent understandings of policy. The cultural frames and ideological paradigms in which policy is shaped, then, may in fact be moving targets, as much the product of politics as a cause (as Martin Schain has shown in the case of France's vaunted republican model).[68] Even more important, however, are the consequences of these policy enactments for subsequent patterns of enforcement and, ultimately, for the prospects of minority incorporation into national labor markets. On this front, the three national trajectories diverged significantly both from each other and from their ideological and institutional origins—the ambivalent but resilient American embrace of race-conscious remedies for discrimination, the French insistence on color blindness in the face of persistent and even mounting discrimination, and the British reluctance to pursue the race-conscious approach clearly contemplated in its legislation. These puzzling paths, even more than the enactment of antidiscrimination policies, demand explanation.

Chapter Eight

WEAK STATE, STRONG POLICY: PARADOXES OF ANTIDISCRIMINATION POLICY

In June 2003, the United States Supreme Court upheld race-conscious university admissions, holding not only that race-based action to ensure diversity is consistent with the equal protection guaranteed by the Fourteenth Amendment but also that race-conscious approaches need not be regarded as second best to color-blind procedures. Although diversity in employment per se was not at issue in the case, the need to prepare a diverse work force for American business formed part of the justification for the court's decision. In support of this claim, the court cited *amicus curiae* briefs filed by General Motors and more than sixty other major American corporations in support of race-conscious admissions policies.[1] This ruling, a decisive defense of race-conscious affirmative action, marked an important milestone on a remarkable odyssey that began with the passage of the pointedly color-blind Civil Rights Act of 1964.

The transformation of American employment discrimination policy from color-blind law to entrenched race-conscious enforcement practices presents a profound puzzle. Neither ideas (the apparent triumph of color blindness in 1964) nor institutions (the apparent weakness of the civil rights enforcement apparatus) predict the emergence of affirmative action. Both approaches would lead us to expect anemic enforcement at best, color blindness because it seems to rule out collective, compensatory hiring policies and institutional weakness because it provided the state with little or no coercive power to enforce the law.

In this chapter, I show how the "weak" American state not only proved paradoxically stronger at enforcing antidiscrimination law than the "strong" British and French states but also managed to challenge most extensively the color-blind presumptions of its own law. The fragmented structure and local orientation of American political institutions, particularly Congress, forced civil rights law toward the color-blind center of American liberalism. But that law ironically proved a strong instrument for the pursuit of affirmative action, in part precisely because it was the product of what David Mayhew has called "strenuous, dramatic, and crystallizing" public political actions that promoted compromise across contending ideologies, parties, and institutions.[2] The very fragmentation and decentralization that produced this compromise meant that struggles over implementation took place in multiple venues, away from the institutional core and the cultural center, giving freer play to the diverse approaches to race policy that were part of the American cultural landscape. Advocates of affirmative action and other race-conscious policies had (and still have) political venues in which to pursue their aims and multiple points where deftly applied pressure can produce results.[3] Not only are Americans fundamentally divided about the virtues of color blindness, but the fluidity of American politics also gives wide scope to social forces that would exploit that ambivalence, and those actors have seized the strategic opportunities that American politics gives them.

The more overtly race-conscious approach written into Britain's law was subsequently undermined by the very structure of centralized party government that enabled its adoption; when government power changed hands three years later, an alternative approach took hold. Moreover, British politics offered fewer opportunities for organized pressure away from the policy-making center (particularly in independent courts) that could impel the state toward stronger enforcement. Patterns of minority political organization and group-state relations in Britain did not match the structure of political opportunities closely enough to affect the direction of policy. Britain's potentially more capacious conception of race policy was, in the end, undermined because the political conditions that nurtured it proved too elusive and transitory to sustain it. In France, greater state centralization and coercive capacity allowed policymakers to pass antidiscrimination law swiftly, with little compromise of its supporters' initial color-blind vision. But these very institutional features of French politics combined with the particular character of French group-state relations to foreclose any possibilities for more concerted enforcement. Unlike the American state and the American law, the French system provided few avenues of access for those seeking alternative policy approaches. As a result, centralization and the concentration of policy-making authority reinforced a single conception of race policy that, once enshrined in policy, proved hard to dislodge.

FROM COLOR-BLIND TO RACE-CONSCIOUS: THE EVOLUTION OF AFFIRMATIVE ACTION

Institutional Challenges: Coordination, Authority, and Control

The first challenge that the Civil Rights Act posed to the Johnson administration was the coordination of civil rights enforcement. Coordination was a challenge in a double sense: vertical and horizontal. First, the act dramatically (and quite reasonably) raised expectations about the federal government's role in attacking discrimination in all the areas covered by the law: voting, public accommodations, education, and federally funded programs as well as employment. Politically, these expectations fell particularly on the president, who would be held largely responsible for both successes and failures in civil rights enforcement. Lyndon Johnson had been a conspicuous if moderate champion of civil rights legislation, and the bill's passage presented him with a political dilemma. Vigorous enforcement would please the act's supporters and assuage the still-vibrant forces of the civil rights movement, but would displease his fellow Southerners and other skeptics of strong state civil rights authority. On the other hand, a White House task force in June 1964 doubted "that the bill will make for sufficient or sufficiently rapid progress as far as the Negro and a good part of the white community is concerned to placate the forces that have gathered over the past years." Thus for the White House, the ability to control the civil rights activities of the executive branch—vertical coordination—was essential to managing these considerable political risks, especially in the face of presidential runs by both Goldwater and George Wallace.[4]

The administration recognized these risks even before the act passed. As early as May 1964, when the Senate compromise was still in doubt, presidential aide Hobart Taylor suggested to Johnson that "it is all important that we get control of this very ticklish field because now we are beginning to reach the hard core people," that is, Southern whites.[5] In a mid-June memo, William L. Taylor, general counsel of the Civil Rights Commission, outlined the impending coordination problems, which he worried would impede the expeditious implementation of the act. He proposed a well-staffed White House office charged with coordinating executive-branch civil rights enforcement. He also counseled speed, especially in setting up the EEOC, arguing that although "implementation of the Civil Rights Bill and concrete results are bound to come slowly," it was important to "show that the Government is making a prompt good faith effort to meet its responsibilities."[6]

As much as any element of the new civil rights regime, the start-up of the EEOC exposed the president's political dilemma and the White House's drive for political dominance of the federal civil rights apparatus. Although the EEOC's enforcement powers would not begin until one year after the act became law, William Taylor recommended that the president move quickly to appoint EEOC commissioners. White House aide Lee White also counseled speed but cautioned against doing anything that might stir up trouble for Johnson's reelection campaign. "There is," White wrote in September, "good reason to get the Commission going as quickly as possible but . . . it is hard to find any compelling reasons for doing this prior to the election. Should it be done before the election this would focus attention on a difficult area and could arouse criticism over the selection of members for the Commission. Again in this case, there has not been any criticism over the failure to have named the members." Johnson did not get around to appointing commissioners until May 1965.[7]

In addition to this problem of "vertical" coordination, there was a problem of "horizontal" coordination among the alphabet soup of federal and state antidiscrimination agencies. Bureaucratic confusion could frustrate even the strongest presidential commitment to vigorous enforcement.[8] While the EEOC was supposed to enforce Title VII, it was not clear how its activities were to fit in with those of other agencies with similar jurisdiction. The President's Committee on Equal Employment Opportunity (PCEEO) coordinated antidiscrimination activities in the executive branch itself and it operated a program called "Plans for Progress," which sought to encourage large government contractors to practice nondiscrimination. Moreover, the PCEEO was chaired by the vice president, and vice-presidential nominee Hubert Humphrey, a civil rights champion, could be expected to cling to this role after taking office. Dirksen actually proposed, only half seriously, abolishing the PCEEO; intended as a dig at the administration, this move might, ironically, have strengthened the EEOC's hand. The Justice Department's role also posed coordination problems, as did the mandated deference to state agencies. In the days and weeks surrounding the Civil Rights Act's passage, the executive branch was awash in memos and meetings on the problem of civil rights coordination, with officials of the Bureau of the Budget, the Justice and Labor Departments, and the PCEEO all weighing in. The matter of the EEOC-PCEEO coordination was on the agenda of the PCEEO's first meeting after the act was signed, with the assistant attorney general for civil rights scheduled to lead the discussion.[9]

After the election, Johnson asked Humphrey to oversee the coordination of civil rights activities, and in a long memorandum to the vice president-elect, Acting Attorney General Nicholas Katzenbach laid out the basic challenges: central direction of policy from the White House and the growing number of entities with overlapping functions, especially in the area of employment.[10] To address the first, Katzenbach proposed a presidential committee, chaired by Humphrey, to set and oversee civil rights policy. To address the second, he laid out a strong argument for abolishing the PCEEO and lodging all employment enforcement power in the EEOC. He went on, however, to recommend retaining the PCEEO to avoid offending its members and supporters (including, of course, Humphrey himself). Thus Katzenbach's proposal to improve coordination boiled down to the creation of yet another committee without streamlining or abolishing anything.

Humphrey and Johnson took up Katzenbach's suggestion, and in January 1965 the President's Council on Equal Opportunity was created, chaired by the vice president.[11] Not surprisingly, the new council did not last long. Rather than providing coordination, it merely confused matters, and by summer the White House was already looking for ways to reorganize civil rights enforcement again and entertaining a variety of proposals. By August, the decision to "demolish the VP's Council" had been taken; the only question was when.[12] In mid-September Humphrey was still clinging to his role as civil rights enforcement czar, but a memo to the president suggests that coordination efforts had gotten nowhere. "It would be most embarrassing to the Administration," he wrote, "if [the various agencies'] efforts are not carefully and closely coordinated. *While initial cooperation has been good, there is still room for substantial improvement.* . . . Coordinated action by the [EEOC], by the Attorney General in bringing pattern or practice suits, and by the Contract Compliance System enforcing the Executive Orders applicable to Government contractors, could make a significant contribution."[13]

Humphrey's plea went unheeded, and the following week the White House maneuvered him into publicly calling for the dismantling of his own committees. Humphrey's memo was released to the press along with the text of Johnson's Executive Order 11246, which transferred their enforcement responsibilities to the Civil Service Commission and the Departments of Labor and Justice, scarcely mentioning the EEOC, a move that greatly dismayed the civil rights community.[14] Humphrey's committees had failed to fulfill their coordination role, but now it seemed as though the White House was giving up on coordination altogether. In fact, Executive Order 11246 led directly to the creation of the Office of Federal Contract Compliance (OFCC) in the Labor Department, setting up the most important jurisdictional battle of the EEOC's brief career.

The EEOC bumbled through its first few years, running through four chairmen in five years, beginning with the frequently absent and universally disliked Franklin D. Roosevelt Jr. During these years the commission's enforcement efforts ran up against the limits of both its statutory power and its position in a fragmented executive establishment. Unable to marshal full regulatory power, largely because pieces of this power had been parceled out elsewhere, the EEOC began inching pragmatically toward affirmative action, based on the notion of statistical discrimination. Meanwhile the OFCC also began working toward a pragmatic strategy to police discrimination in the construction industry, and particularly in construction unions working on federally funded projects. This strategy was unsuccessful under the Johnson administration. It came to fruition, ironically, only after Richard Nixon's election, in the first federal affirmative action mandate, covering construction unions in Philadelphia (and known, accordingly, as the Philadelphia Plan). Despite its obscure origins and relatively subordinate place in the executive hierarchy, the OFCC had what the EEOC lacked: an effective sanction against non-compliant employers (or, in this case, unions), namely the power to with-hold federal contracts.[15]

In the later years of the Johnson administration and into the Nixon administration, the initial concerns about the coordination of federal civil rights enforcement began to disappear from White House discussions. As Louis Martin of the Democratic National Committee aptly put it in 1967, "The unhappy fact is . . . that every time we seek to coordinate programs we usually wind up with another bureau which is itself full of red tape."[16] Moreover, the urban riots of the mid-1960s came increasingly to occupy the attention of the White House, and attempts at general coordination gave way to more ad hoc arrangements to coordinate particular responses to urban violence, such as attempts to foster cooperation between the EEOC and the Labor Department to target federal assistance to riot-torn cities.[17]

In the earliest months of the Nixon administration, White House aide Bob Brown urged White House coordination of minority affairs and pro-posed an elaborate scheme to create a single White House office for mi-nority affairs, not to "direct policy, but [to] assure that all relevant Agen-cies which should participate in a decision are apprised of this fact and operating under similar policy assumptions." Brown's concern (shared by Nixon) was to "reinforce the activities of moderate blacks" and to "re-mind the country as a whole that many blacks are seeking to progress within the system and are succeeding on the merits."[18] The thrust of Brown's coordination proposal was less to direct federal civil rights ef-forts and ensure vigorous enforcement than to make sure that executive civil rights activity conformed to White House goals and to allow Nixon to reap maximum political benefit among those minority Americans whom analysts were dubbing the "silent black majority."[19] In a December 1969 report to the Office of Economic Opportunity entitled "Reluctant Guardians," the A. Philip Randolph Institute took the executive branch to task for its flagging commitment to civil rights enforcement, citing lack of coordination as a key problem. Although a copy of the report found its way into the files of White House domestic policy aide Bradley Pat-terson, it apparently fell on deaf ears; after 1969, civil rights coordination as a substantive problem that might impede effective enforcement of anti-discrimination law disappeared from policy discussions.[20]

The "horizontal" coordination problem among civil rights agencies sty-mied the EEOC, forcing it to compete for resources, authority, turf, and White House attention. As the various White House schemes to organize civil rights enforcement centrally fell apart, the focus of attention in both the White House and Congress shifted increasingly toward the EEOC and its problems.[21] More grave than the problem of fragmented authority was the commission's lack of power, which threatened to bring it into direct conflict with other federal agencies. Unlike the Justice Department, it could not sue discriminatory employers. Unlike the Labor Department, it could not threaten to withhold government contracts from them. Above all, it lacked the regulatory power to issue authoritative cease-and-desist orders against them. Without these powers, it was reduced to a role as conciliator in individual cases and sideline cheerleader (and sub rosa advisor) in discrimination suits in federal courts.

Even before the passage of the Civil Rights Act, civil rights supporters and opponents alike recognized that the limits on the EEOC's power would be a contentious issue. In March 1964, Senator Strom Thurmond warned that state fair-employment agencies tended aggressively to seek expansion of their coercive power and worried that the EEOC would follow the same pattern. Thurmond's fears proved accurate almost immediately. Within weeks of taking office, EEOC Chairman Roosevelt testified before a House labor subcommittee (chaired by his brother, James) that without enforcement power, conciliation would be ineffective (representatives of the NAACP and the AFL-CIO took the same position).[22]

In the fall of 1965, following the Voting Rights Act and the Watts riots, the Johnson administration began to plan its civil rights program for the coming year, and the idea of granting the commission cease-and-desist power drew support from White House aides, the attorney general, the Civil Rights Commission, the Bureau of the Budget, and the EEOC itself. Attorney General Katzenbach outlined two options: granting cease-and-desist authority in individual cases, and expanding the EEOC into a full-blown regulatory agency with the power "to prescribe general rules and practices having the force of law." Katzenbach favored the first option, partly because it would preserve the Justice Department's power to file "pattern or practice" suits, foreshadowing more serious turf battles to come between the EEOC and Justice. Moreover, he argued, the latter "represents much more serious political problems. I cannot conceive of Senator Dirksen's going this far."[23] The administration's civil rights task force recommended granting cease-and-desist authority but expressed reservations about giving it more sweeping regulatory powers. Nevertheless, the administration never threw itself fully even behind cease-and-desist authority. Indeed, Katzenbach's political judgment proved correct; although the House passed a bill in April 1966 granting the EEOC cease-and-desist authority by more than three to one, the bill died after a desultory Senate filibuster (prompting Roy Wilkins of the NAACP to ask Johnson to support a reform of the Senate's cloture rule). The administration again proposed cease-and-desist authority for the EEOC in 1967, but the legislation went nowhere in the Ninetieth Congress, which instead passed open housing legislation in 1968 (somewhat surprisingly, given the conservative drift of the Congress after the 1966 elections).[24]

Another possible avenue of expansion for the EEOC was contract compliance. As the OFCC grew more vigorous in its enforcement efforts, civil rights advocates began to take notice and to recognize the potential that lay in merging its coercive instrument with the EEOC's legal and political stature. In 1966 the administration's civil rights task force concluded that the consolidation of OFCC and EEOC functions in a single agency "warranted further consideration"; two years later another interagency civil rights task force headed by Attorney General Ramsey Clark recommended that the contract compliance function be transferred to the EEOC.[25] The primary benefit of this transfer, the task force argued, would be to "transform [the EEOC] from a conciliator into an effective law enforcement agency" by giving it a legitimate and powerful sanction with which to back its attempts at conciliation. The task force also touted the benefits of coordination and efficiency that such a transfer might bring, although it also noted that this merger might hinder the EEOC's drive for cease-and-desist power. The proposal also drew support from liberal Democrats in Congress. These proposals arrived in the waning months of the Johnson administration, and although the White House briefly considered issuing an executive order consummating this transfer, the proposals, too, died on the vine.[26] Rather than merge the two agencies, the Nixon administration used OFCC to revive the Philadelphia Plan, leaving the EEOC isolated, weak, and drowning in a growing backlog of unresolvable cases.

The issue of enforcement power for the EEOC arrived in the Nixon White House almost as soon as Nixon himself did. Nixon's approach to civil rights was framed by his political position as a Republican seeking to pry Southern voters loose from their long-standing Democratic allegiance but also facing a dominant liberal regime with an increasingly settled commitment to civil rights.[27] Treading carefully through this minefield, Nixon took a characteristically moderate position on equal employment opportunity. Outright opposition to enforcement would have brought opprobrium from the civil rights mainstream, while overly enthusiastic support would have put at risk the electoral gains he sought among disaffected white Democrats in both North and South. Nixon did face skepticism from liberals about his commitment to civil rights enforcement. In his scathing April 1969 letter of resignation as EEOC chairman, Clifford Alexander accused the administration of a crippling lack of support. "The public conclusion is inescapable," Alexander wrote; "vigorous efforts to enforce the laws on employment discrimination are not among the goals of this administration." A group of liberal

Democratic congressmen wrote to Nixon several months later to protest that "years of civil rights progress . . . have been seriously compromised by your administration."[28]

Despite Nixon's temporizing, equal employment opportunity remained on the congressional agenda. Within weeks of taking office, Nixon's domestic policy staff began to collect and assess a variety of proposals, including contract compliance, cease-and-desist power, and the authority for the EEOC itself to file antidiscrimination lawsuits in federal court, a relatively new entrant into the policy mix that the Johnson Justice Department had understandably resisted.[29] When the drive for equal employment opportunity legislation resumed in 1969, the Nixon administration supported the court-enforcement option over cease-and-desist power, although not without internal dissent. Assistant Attorney General for Civil Rights Jerris Leonard, who opposed the court-enforcement option partly because it would diminish the Justice Department's enforcement role, suggested tempering cease-and-desist power by creating an independent general counsel in the EEOC that would separate prosecutorial and judicial functions (as in the National Labor Relations Board) and by establishing more rigorous judicial review of EEOC orders. Leonard also reported that Republican congressional leaders seemed more-or-less amenable to such a solution (some more, such as House Minority Leader Gerald Ford, and some less, such as Dirksen). New EEOC Chairman William H. Brown III objected, suggesting that this approach would fuel fears that the administration was soft on civil rights enforcement and risked handing a victory to liberal Democrats who could take full credit if a stronger enforcement bill passed (not to mention, as White House aide Kenneth Cole derisively noted, that these compromises would "dilute his power").[30]

Opponents of cease-and-desist included Counselor to the President Arthur Burns, Robert Hampton of the Civil Service Commission (which feared losing its jurisdiction over EEO programs in the federal government), and White House aide Bryce Harlow, who scrawled on a memo, "cease & desist authority is *dynamite*; I deplore it," and warned that an empowered EEOC "could well become an *ogre* over time, à la NLRB . . . would likely be a disaster." A memo summing up the decisive White House meeting on EEO legislation in early May 1969 noted that although some in the administration (as well as the civil rights leadership) "considered the cease and desist power to be central to any workable equal employment opportunity scheme . . . it seems to us questionable whether the executive branch of the government should assume the role of permanent advocate for aggrieved individuals in equal employment cases."[31] When the administration came down on the side of court-enforcement over cease-and-desist authority, the EEOC's Bill Brown fell in line and publicly supported it, although his flip-flop was duly noted in Congress and the press. When he claimed that court enforcement would, in fact, be a stronger weapon in the EEOC's hands than cease-and-desist authority, his predecessor, Clifford Alexander, called the administration's proposal "a cruel hoax."[32]

When the Senate passed a cease-and-desist bill in October 1970, the administration was thrown into confusion. Some presidential advisers argued that the administration should be prepared to accept cease-and-desist power but press for mitigating amendments, such as an independent general counsel or more rigorous judicial review, for fear that outright opposition would mark the president as "anti-enforcement." Others, including Bill Brown and White House aide Leonard Garment, continued to support full cease-and-desist power. Such support, they argued, was by then essentially cost-free for the administration because the Ninety-First Congress was running out of time and the administration had what Cole described as a "hold" on the legislation in the House—essentially an understanding with House Rules Committee Chairman William Colmer of Mississippi that the bill, which had been approved by the House Education and Labor Committee, would die. Parliamentary maneuvers to discharge the bill from the Rules Committee did, however, raise some worries in the White House.[33]

But the Senate's approval of the cease-and-desist bill, which the House had passed in 1966, raised the specter of passage in the next Congress, and the White House immediately began to plan its strategy for the coming onslaught. The EEOC's Brown continued to press the White House to support cease-and-desist power, threatening to resign otherwise—"my own position would become impossible should the Administration react in the negative," he wrote Garment in November 1970.[34] Once again, however, the administration supported the court enforcement approach, although in the early months of 1971 administration strategists and their congressional allies were pessimistic about the prospects of stopping cease-and-desist and again reluctant to oppose it too openly for fear of being cast as anti-enforcement. Much administration strategizing focused not on stopping cease-and-desist altogether but on finding concessions that it could extract from Congress in return. Leading the effort to find such compromises was Undersecretary of Labor Laurence Silberman, who suggested trying to limit EEOC's statutory authority to issuing cease-and-desist orders in individual cases while keeping contract compliance for Labor and lawsuits for Justice (both were slated for transfer to the EEOC in the legislation under consideration). Silberman pointed out that the business community was growing critical of the administration because of its apparent dithering and that the AFL-CIO supported transferring contract compliance to the EEOC as a way of undermining the Philadelphia Plan (on the assumption that the program would be less effective under the EEOC than under the Labor Department).[35]

The administration's circling was based on the assumption that cease-and-desist had unassailable support in both houses of Congress, but that assumption proved false. On 16 September 1971, the House, by a vote of 202 to 197, approved a court-enforcement plan offered by Representative John Erlenborn of Illinois in place of the cease-and-desist bill. The Senate first rejected the court-enforcement option in January 1972 by a 48 to 46 vote, but did an about-face a month later after a Southern filibuster threatened the entire bill, accepting court-enforcement, 45 to 39, behind the familiar coalition of Republicans and Southern Democrats.[36] Civil rights supporters were generally satisfied, although Tom Wicker of the *New York Times* wrote that "both the Southern Senators and the Administration can now plainly be seen wearing the same old Confederate uniforms."[37]

Once again, the imperatives of coalition-building in Congress and the presidency had channeled the substantive course of policy-making by adjusting the institutional tools for civil rights enforcement. Although the Senate decisively rejected two amendments offered by Sam Ervin of North Carolina to prohibit reverse discrimination, the Equal Employment Opportunity Act of 1972 did not abandon the color-blind premises of American civil rights policy, which remained embedded in Title VII. By failing to ban racial quotas in employment the act did not endorse them, nor did it settle the question of race-conscious remedies for employment discrimination.[38] What the act did settle was the question of the institutional location of antidiscrimination enforcement: the federal courts above all, the federal contracting process to some degree, but not direct regulatory authority.[39] The culmination of nearly ten years of civil rights legislating was a limited, hybrid enforcement structure with an ambiguous substantive mandate: not on its face a system conducive to robust enforcement, but one that left a great deal of room for political, administrative, and legal maneuvering.

The EEOC was also quite openly exposed to the vagaries of presidential leadership and suffered periodically from weak White House support in a contentious political environment, particularly involving hostile or skeptical members of Congress. By the time the 1972 act passed, concerns were growing within both Congress and the administration about the EEOC's competence and political responsiveness. From its very beginnings, the EEOC had been a common target of criticism, beginning with reports of Chairman Roosevelt's penchant for frequent yachting trips and suspicions that he was contemplating running for governor of New York.[40] Appointed in 1969, Brown was the commission's fourth chairman in five years. By then, the EEOC's caseload had grown well beyond its capacity to respond; its backlog of complaints was in the thousands, and there was a delay of as much as two years in processing complaints.[41] The commission's congressional relations were growing ever more antagonistic, resulting in chronic fiscal problems as Congress consistently cut back the agency's funding requests, despite regular White House intervention. Although this was fairly standard budget politics, it further exacerbated the EEOC's operating difficulties.[42]

More serious charges of mismanagement also began to surface. A 1969 management audit by the Civil Service Commission described the EEOC as a "chaotic and demoralizing management environment," and a year later the Office of Management and Budget (OMB) again found serious management problems.[43] As a result, skepticism and mistrust of the commission mounted both in Congress and the administration and became an issue in deliberations over expanding its powers. "Addition of OFCC to the present badly-managed EEOC," wrote OMB's Dwight Ink, "would serve only to bungle two Federal programs dealing with civil rights issues and clientele."[44]

In May 1972, even Leonard Garment, who had long been EEOC's champion in the White House, conceded that "the EEOC still has significant internal management problems" and suggested spreading the word that "the President wouldn't be inclined to sign any appeal letters on EEOC's budget until EEOC produces a management record more convincing to the House Appropriations Committee, and which looks better on the record than this one."[45] Indeed, Nixon did not intervene on the EEOC's behalf in that year's budget battle as he had done in previous years. The following year, the Civil Service Commission issued yet another negative report on the EEOC's management that received considerable publicity and sowed further discord within the administration over the EEOC's role (as well as within the EEOC itself).[46] Finally, as historian Hugh Davis Graham writes, "Nixon followed up his victory in the Equal Employment Opportunity Act of 1972 by turning up his campaign rhetoric and directing it against the institutions he was empowering and the purposes they were furthering."[47] By distancing himself from the civil rights enforcement effort even after forging the compromise that enhanced it, Nixon further compounded the EEOC's already tenuous position in the fragmentary and disconnected American institutional universe.

Strength out of Weakness

Even within its own limited horizons, the EEOC very quickly showed its limitations. In its first year of operation, it received nearly 9,000 discrimination complaints and resolved almost three-fourths of them, by completing an investigation and brokering a settlement between the parties or

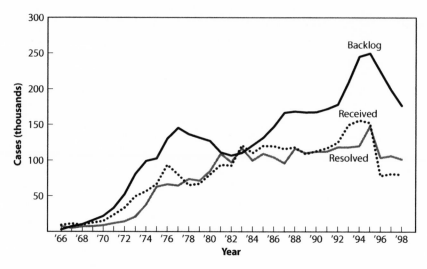

FIGURE 8.1 EEOC Caseload, 1966–98. Source: EEOC Annual Reports.

issuing a ruling (either that there was sufficient cause for the complainant to file a federal lawsuit or that there was not) or by referring cases to a state agency where appropriate. The first year's work thus left a backlog of nearly 2,500 cases unresolved (in violation of the sixty-day time limit specified in the law for resolving cases), and things only got worse from there as the EEOC entered a period of Malthusian challenges. Over the next several years the number of cases filed grew exponentially, doubling ever three or four years through the mid-1970s (see figure 8.1).[48] At the same time, the growth of the number of cases resolved every year was linear, so that by the early 1970s the commission was resolving fewer than half the number of cases it received each year. The consequence was an exploding backlog of unresolved cases that reached 10,000 in 1969, 20,000 the next year, 50,000 in 1972, and 100,000 in 1975. Not until the Carter administration was the EEOC able to begin to make up some of its lost ground: under the chairmanship of Eleanor Holmes Norton, whom President Carter appointed to lead the commission in 1977, the backlog was reduced from 145,000 to 106,000 even as the commission was fielding an average of 75,000 new complaints each year. But under the chairmanship of Clarence Thomas, appointed by President Ronald Reagan to succeed Norton in 1982, the commission fell behind again, largely because complaints rose to more than 100,000 per year. By the mid-1990s, the EEOC's cumulative backlog of cases was nearly a quarter of a million.

The commission's institutional and operational limitations, however, proved a double-edged sword. On the one hand, the EEOC's relative weakness and political vulnerability reflected the general limits on administrative power in American government. On the other hand, these very same institutional constraints created a great deal of slack in the commission's political and administrative environment. Limits on its power forced it to seek other means of influence, particularly by collaborating with other institutions, both inside and outside the state. This imperative drove the problem of antidiscrimination enforcement into the same fragmented and decentralized political arena that had produced the EEOC's incapacity in the first place. The struggle for enforcement would be fought out not in terms of administrative power emanating from Washington but in multiple arenas and jurisdictions around the country; in this political context federalism, usually seen as a constraint on civil rights enforcement and protection, was actually empowering.[49] In this setting, the EEOC sought to play what role and forge what alliances it could as it sought pragmatic rather than ideological or coercive solutions to the problem of fulfilling its mandate in constrained environment.

Among the EEOC's key partners in this endeavor were African Americans themselves, who were organized in a powerful national social movement that remained deeply rooted and active in local political and economic arenas through local organizations. The flourishing of local political organization among African Americans, in fact, was one of the important enduring consequences of the civil rights movement, and these organizations gave African Americans enhanced political leverage in many parts of the country.[50] In particular, federated organizations such as the NAACP could collaborate with the EEOC in pursuing race-conscious remedies for employment discrimination in a variety of local-level forums. The principal arenas for these activities were collective bargaining between union locals and employers as well as lawsuits in the federal courts; both of these arenas allowed the EEOC to get around its lack of coercive authority. In particular, the EEOC's relationship with the federal courts (especially after the 1972 amendments) proved empowering, because it gave the commission access to a politically and organizationally independent means of deciding discrimination cases and enforcing remedies. But beyond this structurally determined opportunity, the more historically contingent relationship that the EEOC was driven to forge with certain elements of the waning civil rights movement in the late 1960s and 1970s helped it to have an impact beyond its apparent institutional means. These elements of the EEOC's universe—also consistent with the characteristic shape of American administrative institutions—enabled it to participate in the development of policies that transformed American antidiscrimination policy beyond its color-blind legislative origins.

Hamstrung by its limited coercive power and its restricted institutional position, inundated in short order with an overwhelming caseload, and limited by the legal requirement of proving discriminatory intent in individual cases, the EEOC turned to a variety of tactics to pursue its aims. It was able to exert entrepreneurial influence through several channels, ranging from very informal to more formal, precisely because it could exploit the organizational slack in the federal government, because its exact role in the pantheon of enforcement agencies was so ill defined, and because it was able to find outside partners and allies.

To bolster and supplement its weak formal powers, the EEOC essentially did six things. First, it used its limited formal powers to further individual cases filed with it under Title VII. When an employee filed a discrimination case with the EEOC, the commission was supposed to investigate the merits of the claim and rule within sixty days whether there was sufficient evidence of discrimination to warrant a lawsuit in federal court (which could then be filed by the plaintiff).[51] Thus the EEOC did have the power either to advance or stymie actions against alleged discriminators. Although the EEOC very quickly developed a large backlog of cases, numbering in the thousands within a year, and almost never met the sixty-day statutory limit, it could and did use probable cause findings strategically to aid the prospects of private litigation, as it did in numerous complaints against U.S. Steel's plants in Birmingham, Alabama.[52]

Second, it collected information from employers on the racial composition of the work force, firm by firm. This is did through its form EEO-1, on which it required (under the general administrative rule-making power of federal agencies) employers covered by Title VII to report data on their employees by race and ethnicity. The data that the EEOC compiled from this form would prove a key weapon in the shift toward race-conscious enforcement.[53] But it is essential to note that the reporting system alone was not sufficient to produce affirmative action. Under the terms set by Title VII, the data it generated could not constitute prima facie evidence of discrimination and the EEOC had to make creative use of them in order to render them effective.

Third, the EEOC used the power of publicity to expose discriminatory practices and induce employers to change their behavior. It held a series of high-profile hearings on employment practices in New York City, for example, that targeted prominent service industries such as banking and other white-collar industries that depended heavily on their civic reputations in the nation's most liberal city. These hearings also shone a rather embarrassing spotlight on the *New York Times*, among other employers. In early 1969, another set of hearings, this time in Los Angeles looking into the motion picture industry, raised congressional hackles (particularly Dirksen's, who threatened to oppose Nixon's appointment of William Brown as commission chair because of his participation). Yet another round of hearings in Houston in the spring of 1970 brought a protest to the White House from the Republican candidate for Senate in Texas, Representative George H. W. Bush, who feared they might pose problems for his candidacy.[54] Such hearings had no legal force, but they did serve to increase public awareness about the extent and sometimes surprising venues of racial discrimination.

Fourth, it developed legal interpretations of Title VII and practical guidelines for employers. In the U.S. Steel discrimination cases in Alabama, for instance, the commission helped to formulate guidelines on seniority, which was a particularly sticky question in declining industries such as steel, where shrinking employment meant layoffs; and layoffs usually meant that African Americans, who had been hired more recently and were lower down on job ladders, would be the first to be let go. It also helped to develop guidelines for the use of occupational tests. Such tests, used as a qualification for hiring and promotion, had often worked against black workers and job applicants. In general, too, the EEOC's legal staff worked hard to develop legal interpretations that would help the commission address its fundamental dilemma: how to enforce the law in a meaningful way in the absence of any real coercive power. Meaningful enforcement, for the EEOC's legal staff, meant going beyond the piecemeal, one-at-a-time, individual-complaint approach and finding strategies that would attack discriminatory practices more generally.[55] The commission's guidelines and legal interpretations had no binding force, but they did influence the thought and behavior of other actors with different means of power and influence at their disposal; these actors were the targets of the EEOC's two other sets of activity.

Fifth, the EEOC filed briefs as amicus curiae in federal antidiscrimination lawsuits, which were often allowed to go forward on the basis of EEOC probable-cause findings in cases originally brought as complaints to the commission. Through its briefs, the EEOC was able to argue for its interpretation of Title VII before different federal judges in a variety of places on multiple occasions, even though it was legally barred from bringing these suits itself. Thus, for example, the EEOC filed an amicus brief in *Griggs v. Duke Power,* the case in which the Supreme Court ultimately ruled that employers could not use even ostensibly race-neutral tests or other occupational qualifications that tend disproportionately to bar minority applicants, unless the employer could show that they were a bona fide qualification for the job in question. The commission's brief and the testing standards and legal interpretation that it offered were cited explicitly both by the dissenting judge on the Fourth Circuit appeals panel that found for Duke Power and by Chief Justice Warren Burger, who wrote the Supreme Court's majority opinion reversing the judgment and finding for the plaintiffs.[56]

Finally, the EEOC cooperated closely behind the scenes with private nongovernmental organizations, such as the NAACP and its Legal Defense Fund (LDF), which took the lead in representing plaintiffs in antidiscrimination suits, as well as the Congress of Racial Equality and other groups involved in combating job discrimination in a variety of settings and places. EEOC staff members convened strategy meetings with LDF attorneys and others to work through disputes with employers. They offered advice about legal strategy (which was not always accepted—the commission's deputy general counsel John Pemberton advised the LDF's Jack Greenberg not to appeal *Griggs* to the Supreme Court). They shared data and helped devise legal arguments that plaintiffs' lawyers could use in arguing cases.[57]

In particular, these links with the NAACP and the LDF were the linchpin in advancing collective, race-conscious enforcement of Title VII. Neither bureaucrats nor courts, either by themselves or in combination only with one another, could have achieved this result. The EEOC certainly could not; it had neither the power to coerce nor the power to file suits; nor could the courts—although they had the power to issue decisive and authoritative rulings in the cases that came before them, these cases had to come from somewhere. Alexander Bickel, outlining what he called the "paradox of all paradoxes concerning the [Supreme] Court," wrote that "the Court may only decide concrete cases and may not pronounce general principles at large; but it may decide a constitutional issue only on the basis of general principle."[58] It was the linkages between the EEOC and the LDF that gave the courts both the cases and the principles that they ultimately used to validate the practices and principles of affirmative action. It was the LDF, with the help and background advice of the EEOC, that filed cases strategically to present issues of discrimination in the most legally promising light before receptive judges. And it was the EEOC that took the lead in developing the legal interpretations and doctrines that backed up those arguments and, ultimately, persuaded judges.

This pattern of policy and political development was dependent not only on the forging of relationships among bureaucrats and judges but also on the collective action of African Americans, organized into a movement that sought and exploited opportunities offered by the American political system. Although rooted in a national social movement, the NAACP was organized in a federated structure that mirrored the federal structure of the American state—with local, state, and national branches—and so was able to operate in multiple venues and with varied strategies at once. For the NAACP and the LDF, the courts and the EEOC were not simply the upper reaches of a hierarchy whose dicta, pronounced from on high, were law. Rather, they were opportunities to be exploited, points of access to the structure of state power, openings that could be entered to try to pry policy loose and to advance an approach to antidiscrimination enforcement that some (although by no means all) African American leaders and organizations and their allies in the worlds of law and government had spent a long time developing.[59]

At least as much as the EEOC's other maneuvers, these links forged with the LDF were the key to the commission's role in nudging forward an interpretation of Title VII based on "disparate impact," collective employment patterns that were unfavorable to blacks. These informal links, the products partly of the commission staff's entrepreneurship but also of the organizational slack in the federal government that allowed staff members to be enterprising, meant that the development of affirmative action was not simply a top-down imposition by meddlesome and imperious bureaucrats and courts, contemptuous of legislative intent and public opinion, as some interpreters suggest.[60] Rather, it was equally a bottom-up effort, facilitated by the configuration of actors, institutions, and ideas prevailing at the time. The flip side of institutional fragmentation has been a level of improvisatory suppleness that has made the EEOC and the rest of the American race-relations establishment remarkably effective. These institutional opportunities, in turn, were the result not simply of the structure of American political institutions but of the way in which African Americans had been incorporated in those institutions through the historical processes of political development.

THE LIMITS OF "STRONG" STATES: ENFORCEMENT IN BRITAIN AND FRANCE

Britain

The consequences of the Race Relations Act were quite limited in comparison with the ironic development of affirmative action in the United States. Like the EEOC, the Commission for Racial Equality (CRE) was empowered to hear complaints of discrimination from individuals and to try to conciliate disputes but not to sanction employers who were found to have discriminated. Under the Race Relations Act of 1968. Hearing individual complaints and trying to resolve them had been the main activity of the Race Relations Board, and between 1968 and 1977 (when the CRE took over its functions) the board had received nearly 4,500 employment discrimination complaints and found evidence of unlawful discrimination in only 441 cases.[61] Under the Race Relations Act of 1976, however, the CRE deemphasized individual complaints, which complainants could then bring directly to industrial tribunals, specialized courts that adjudicated employment and industrial relations disputes. Unlike American courts, industrial tribunals did not have general, cumulative policy-making authority; decisions in individual cases had no broader application to other cases, a key institutional difference that limited both the reach of British antidiscrimination law and the capacity of minorities to pursue more active enforcement. Many people in Britain were reluctant or unable to litigate cases on their own in the absence of CRE assistance, and Britain did not have either an extensive network of civil rights legal organizations such as the NAACP Legal Defense Fund or a great deal of public-interest legal activity. The CRE was, in fact, the country's main repository of anti-discrimination law expertise. The commission, accordingly, has used its own complaints procedure to offer help to individuals in litigating their cases before industrial tribunals, ranging from providing full legal representation by the CRE's own lawyers to advising applicants in preparing their cases and drafting complaints. In its early years, the CRE had hoped to undertake a promotional and training campaign to encourage other, private organizations to develop the expertise to offer legal advice and representation to individual plaintiffs in discrimination cases, but resources constraints generally prevented the commission from doing this on a large enough scale to have an impact. Consequently, the commission's complaints procedure became one of the principal channels by which race discrimination cases came before industrial tribunals.[62]

Even so, the number of complaints that the CRE received was not exceedingly large. Figure 8.2 charts the number of individual complaints brought before the CRE in its first twenty years.[63] Despite a generally steady increase, complaints did not consistently reach 1,000 annually until the mid-1980s and leveled off at approximately 1,700 per year in the mid-1990s. Employment cases generally comprised approximately two-thirds of these complaints. Although a very high percentage of the complaints resulted in some kind of advice or assistance, very few applicants were granted legal representation for their cases before industrial tribunals (and the bottom line in figure 8.2 includes both cases granted full legal representation and cases where some lesser form of legal assistance was offered; the two categories were not differentiated after 1986).

The main forum for the resolution of individual discrimination cases is industrial tribunals, which have the authority to award damages in the case of a finding of discrimination. By the 1990s, industrial tribunals—which adjudicate the entire range of labor relations matters, not just racial discrimination—heard around 1,000 race discrimination cases each year. Very few of these cases reached the trial stage (most were dismissed or settled), and of those that did, very few resulted in an award to the plaintiff, generally fewer than 20 percent—only a few dozen awards annually. The awards, moreover, were small. In 1992–93, the median award was £3,333 (approximately $5,000), and, until 1994, damages were capped at £11,000.[64]

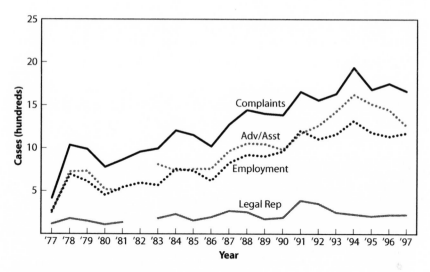

FIGURE 8.2 CRE Individual Complaints, 1977–97.
Source: CRE Annual Reports.

The CRE has participated in several hundred industrial tribunal cases each year (see Figure 8.3). In the early years, eighty or ninety percent of these cases in which the CRE was involved were either withdrawn or decided against the plaintiff, as a member of a parliamentary committee caustically noted in 1981.[65] In a small number of cases—around twenty a year in the late 1970s, increasing to about twice that by the 1990s—plaintiffs with CRE representation won their cases outright. In other cases, the parties reached a settlement, and this category grew dramatically so that very few cases reached a final judgment by the tribunal. By the 1990s, plaintiffs either won or settled 80 or 90 percent of the time, and only a few dozen pro-employer judgments were handed down each year. Despite this growing rate of success, the total number cases of involved has remained very small; in only one year did the CRE win either victories or settlements in more than 200 of the cases it took to tribunals.

Neither the CRE nor other observers, however, considered individual complaints to be the main thrust of the commission's work. Rather, the commission's authority to initiate formal investigations of employers or industries it suspected of engaging in widespread collective practices of discrimination and then to issue nondiscrimination orders was the main institutional basis for the CRE's power. The commission launched its first three formal investigations in its very first year of operation and quickly added more, initiating forty-five through 1980 (of which more than half concerned employment; the others covered housing, public accommoda-

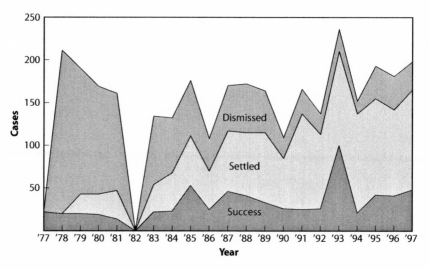

FIGURE 8.3 CRE Industrial Tribunal Cases, 1977–97.
Source: CRE Annual Reports.

tions, and education). In 1978, the commission completed its first investigation, into Genture Restaurants Ltd. Most reports took longer, largely because of budget and staff limitations (or so members of the commission's senior staff reported to a House of Commons committee in 1981).[66] After 1980, however, the commission dramatically slowed down both its initiation and completion of investigations; as of 1990 it had completed only fifty-two investigations and completed only four more in the next three years (although the number of completed reports began to increase somewhat in the mid-1990s). Formal investigations came to occupy a less prominent place in the CRE's annual reports as the commission grew frustrated and disappointed at the anemic results that they seemed to achieve. "The Commission has always been concerned with results," the 1986 annual report declared, "but in 1986 the earlier emphasis on establishing, through investigations and individual complaints, how discrimination occurs and on proposing ways to prevent this, has been accompanied by a renewed emphasis on outcomes. Increasingly, the questions asked of any set of practices or of an institution have been less concerned with how they have come to be in the situation they are in, or what procedures have or have not been adopted in the past, and more concerned with what can be done within what time-scale, to put things right."[67]

Like the EEOC, the CRE lacks strong coercive powers to sanction employers directly. Its investigative power seemed sharply to distinguish it from the EEOC, but it was unable to use this power effectively to expose offending employers and lead them toward more collectively race-conscious hiring programs. But it was precisely the institutional fragmentation of the American state that gave the EEOC and other affirmative action advocates in the United States the opportunity to find other coercive means, particularly through the courts and the peculiar political independence of the administrative agencies like the EEOC itself. Dealt a weak hand and forced to find policy solutions that worked, the EEOC was able to maneuver through its institutional environment to pursue a policy that was never explicitly enacted into law. The CRE, on the other hand, although it had legal sanction to pursue and enforce certain kinds of "positive action," seldom did. In the mid-1980s, the commission's annual report expressed some frustration that the positive action provisions of the Race Relations Act were not being put to greater use, and it even prepared a booklet on positive action, launched in 1985 (preparing the way for the greater emphasis on "outcomes" that the commission announced the following year). And finally, British companies have been considerably slower than their American counterparts to adopt their own internal equal employment opportunity structures and practices, despite the CRE's efforts (which have been largely hortatory).[68]

A number of institutional factors constrained the CRE from pursuing even the limited forms of "positive action" that fell within its statutory purview. First, disagreements within the Home Office and the Labour Party over the role of the state in acting against racial discrimination made it difficult for the CRE to act vigorously. Even before the Race Relations Act was passed, a Cabinet shuffle forced Alex Lyon, the Labour minister who had been the leading government advocate of strong antidiscrimination power, off the frontbench, in part because he had clashed with Home Office civil servants about, among other things, race relations and immigration matters.[69]

Moreover, the government's indifference, if not outright hostility, to vigorous antidiscrimination enforcement increased further when Margaret Thatcher's Conservatives swept into office in 1979. The Labour government had intended to increase the CRE's budget by nearly 25 percent in 1979, suggesting a strengthening commitment to enforcement; Thatcher's increase was less than 5 percent, and her government actually cut the CRE's budget in real terms over the next six years.[70] In 1981, the commission complained to a Commons Home Affairs subcommittee that "the reluctance of central Government to declare full commitment to equal opportunity and to take action to back this up" was a "major constraint" on the commission's effectiveness.[71] The commission's chairman, David Lane, also complained of micromanagement by the Home Office and said that he would like the commission to have "greater room for manoeuvre," while Conservative members of Parliament accused the CRE of acting in a partisan manner, favoring Labour.[72] For its part, the Home Office kept the CRE at arm's length. A Home Office official dismissively referred to the CRE as a "fringe agency" while projecting an air of supreme indifference to the commission's substantive work while taking it to task for not running in a more business-like (that is, economical) way.[73] Meanwhile, Lyon took both the commission and the Home Office to task—the former for foot-dragging ("What have you done with the law enforcement powers we gave you?" he asked Lane. "We gave you the biggest powers in the Western world in relation to law enforcement. What have you done with them?") and the latter for not caring.[74] The Thatcher government also repeatedly ignored proposals that the CRE be given expanded powers.[75]

Perhaps most important, the British political system provided few openings for alternative routes to positive action, and the integration of British minorities into this nonreceptive polity was weak. Only marginally integrated into the party system, without institutionalized recourse to other sources of power, and without the backing of a social movement on the scale of the American civil rights movement, British minorities were unable to convert the potential embodied in the Race Relations Act into actual outcomes. In particular, the British judicial system, which is not predisposed to grant claims based on constitutional rights as are courts in the United States, is a weak vehicle for advancing antidiscrimination claims. To the extent that the courts did involve themselves in antidiscrimination enforcement, their effect was to impose limits on the commission's powers through judicial review of its procedures rather than to provide a point of access for aggrieved individuals or groups to seek redress for harms done them. The rigidity of executive control under the British parliamentary system and the rapidity of the Conservative takeover after the creation of the CRE produced very unfavorable conditions for strong state action against collective patterns of discrimination or for the pursuit of "positive action"; in fact, even before the Tories' 1979 victory, MPs from both sides came to condemn the principle of positive discrimination. Some years later, the Home Office considered and rejected a contract compliance system for public contractors, modeled on the successful American practice, leaving it instead to local government to pursue such policies at their own option.[76]

Finally, and most paradoxically, the relative centralization of British antidiscrimination policy actually hindered the consolidation of the CRE's enforcement authority. The British pattern of localized race politics had relegated racial issues to lower levels of government without the crushing injustice of institutionalized white supremacy as in the American South. This development had important advantages for the pursuit of antidiscrimination enforcement and other policies for racial incorporation: it offered more proximate opportunities for active coalition-building with white elites and for partnerships across party lines in support of local developmental policy that could assist natives and immigrants alike.[77] The CRE itself occupied an uneasy position in this central-local nexus. Its parent department in the central government, the Home Office, had "little knowledge of, or contact with, local Government, which provides the bulk of the services." But when the CRE, on its own, tried to promote and oversee race-relations work by local governments, it ran afoul not only of the Home Office but also of the locally based community relations establishment, which saw its traditional role being usurped. The CRE's work with local authorities, the National Association of Community Relations Councils told Parliament, was "fundamentally misconceived. . . . The Commission currently sees *direct contact* with individual local authorities as a major priority in spite of the fact that this is also the main function of local CRC's. By its present policies the Commission is conducting what is essentially a parallel programme in which the selection of areas to visit pays little or no attention to the level of success of local CRC's."[78]

In addition to mandating national action, the Race Relations Act did require local authorities to take steps to eliminate racial discrimination, leading to a flurry of activity by local antiracist organizations, Community Relations Councils, party organizations (especially Labour), and other groups at the local level. These efforts have resulted in gains for minorities, especially in public-sector employment and the adoption of equal opportunity policies by some local authorities, but these have not come without conflict nor have they been uniform.[79] But such local attachments have corresponding disadvantages for minorities, especially the susceptibility to domination and exploitation by local majorities, which can be heightened by the lack of access to and leverage over national political institutions.[80] In the United States, the particular configuration of historical and political circumstances in the 1960s and 1970s—including significantly the heightened level of minority political mobilization—gave African Americans and their allies such leverage, allowing them to exploit openings in American political institutions from their highly localized positions when more centralized avenues were closed to them. In Britain, by contrast, local attachments, which were often locally empowering, proved nationally disadvantageous because the structure of British politics did not provide a foothold for locally attached minorities to enter into national processes of coalition-building and policy-making.

France

There are two principal institutional means available to the French state to enforce the antidiscrimination provisions of the 1972 French law against racism. One is through local police commissioners, who are actually officials of the national government. Bringing a criminal complaint of discrimination to the police results in a long, opaque procedure that is unlikely to be a high-priority matter for the police. The ability of organizations to bring complaints on behalf of individuals certainly helps matters, but not surprisingly, convictions are extremely rare. The other is through the Ministry of Labor's corps of Labor Inspectors, who are responsible for regulating all matters concerning the workplace. But although they have ample coercive power at their disposal, Labor Inspectors are generally more likely to use conciliation than coercion. Each inspector must deal repeatedly with the same employers in his territory and so can ill afford to antagonize them needlessly; moreover, an inspector's superiors in Paris want him to deal with disputes on his own, without dragging them in by resorting to formal reports, hearings, and the like.[81] Thus Labor Inspectors are ill equipped to deal with as potentially explosive a problem as racial discrimination in employment. The institutional problem is that there is no part of the supposedly "strong" French state that has as its primary raison d'être the prevention or punishment of racial discrimination.

In contrast with developments in the United States, the consequences of the 1972 law have been somewhat disappointing. Successful prosecutions for racial discrimination have been very few since the passage of the law. Between 1975 and 1984, approximately 160 cases were reported to the Justice Ministry. From 1984 to 1988, the annual number of convictions for race-related offenses fluctuated between 66 and 95. Annual convictions in the 1990s continued at a similar level, ranging between 61 and 95 between 1993 and 1997. The more precise data available for these years, however, reveal that approximately 90 percent of these convictions were for acts of racist expression rather than discrimination; only 7 of 380 convictions in that period were for employment-related discrimination. These figures contrast sharply with the number of employment discrimination actions brought in the United States. Since its creation, the EEOC has received more than 2.5 million complaints from individuals, and more than 260,000 private employment discrimination cases have been filed in federal courts since 1977.[82] These figures are not strictly comparable—convictions on the one hand and total complaints on the other—but even so they indicate an extreme imbalance in the amount of enforcement activity between the two countries.

Not only has the legal enforcement of the prohibition against individual discrimination been carried out on a substantially smaller scale in France, but the institutional structure of French politics and policy has not encouraged minorities and their allies to circumvent the proscription of other forms of action. The political opportunity structure of the Fifth Republic, especially in the 1960s and 1970s, was not conducive to minority mobilization. Until 1981 French law prohibited the formation of ethnic- or race-based associations without government approval. Moreover, the centralized focus of French politics provided few points of access for geographically concentrated minorities. Consequently, race- and ethnic-based demands were often deflected onto nonstate organizations such as labor unions; even where these organizations were more hospitable than others, they provided rather weak links to the mainstream of French policy-making. In the major wave of French protest activity during this period, the events of May 1968, mobilization was organized around political identities that could exploit political opportunities at the center of French politics and policy-making: students (in both universities and secondary schools, both state-run), salaried workers and public employees, farmers, and the working class. Despite sporadic protest activity and fledgling communal consciousness and organization by ethnic minorities in the same period (especially concerning the housing conditions of immigrant workers), questions of racial and ethnic identity were not central to the 1968 protests in France. This was the case not simply because racial and ethnic political identities were marginal to the cultural repertoire of French politics in this period but because the structure of political opportunity imposed high barriers and offered few rewards to ethnic and racial mobilization. In the early 1980s, immigrant workers were at center of a series of strikes in the automobile industry in which official recognition of Islam at the workplace was among the issues at stake. But these strikes came at a moment when the National Front was gathering strength, and Prime Minister Pierre Mauroy dismissed the strikers as foreign religious agitators who were connected with the ayatollahs of Iran. Thus neither the French state nor the structure of French politics afforded many opportunities to those interested in vigorous antidiscrimination enforcement, despite the gradual rise of antiracist politics and ethnic political orientations, along with ample evidence of widespread job discrimination in France.[83]

The high barriers against criminal convictions for racial discrimination, along with the minimal punishments generally imposed (the highest fine recorded between 1993 and 1997 was 10,000 Francs, approximately $1,700) made criminal prosecutions unlikely to provoke employers to change their hiring practices. Similarly the limited mobilization and organization of minority groups and their limited access to policy circles further restricted the possibilities for a move toward broader enforcement. The main avenue for organized pressure is through the civil party power of antiracist organizations, which allows them to intervene in discrimination cases and often to publicize employers' misdeeds in addition to imposing punishments. But the code-based French legal system, unlike the Anglo-American common-law system, does not recognize the binding power of higher-court decisions on other cases, so that legal action in the

French system has no cumulative force and little policy-making function. Finally, in response to EEOC activity, many American employers have internalized antidiscrimination law, creating equal employment opportunity offices to ensure compliance with nondiscrimination rules. In France, by contrast, hiring in private firms seems to be rather less institutionalized and to hew more closely to informal network practices that can produce systematically imbalanced results.[84]

It is clear that the institutional structure of French antidiscrimination law—both its choice of criminal law as the enforcement vehicle and its lack of a dedicated antidiscrimination bureaucracy—are centrally related to the disappointing and rather paradoxical results of the 1972 law. The structure of French political and administrative institutions guided the choices of political actors in enacting and carrying out these antiracist impulses. The rigid politics of the French parliament ruled out a broader role even for established antiracist organizations in enforcing antidiscrimination law, and the possibility of erecting a dedicated antidiscrimination bureaucracy seems not even to have occurred to French policymakers.[85] Lacking the improvisatory suppleness of the American race-relations establishment, the French institutions charged with tackling racial discrimination in employment did not mobilize the full coercive power of the French state in their pursuit of this goal.

Conclusions

The comparative histories of the implementation of employment discrimination laws particularly highlight the indeterminacy of conventional institutional understandings of policy evolution. The "weak" American state produced the most active and, comparatively speaking, the most vigorous antidiscrimination enforcement regime. The "strong" British and French states, by contrast, were able to adopt forceful laws, unadulterated by legislative compromise, with relative alacrity. Similarly, the comparison argues against accounts of policy development that rely centrally on ideological or cultural traditions. National commitments to race consciousness or color blindness were not decisive by themselves in shaping outcomes. Rather, the role that these ideological and cultural traditions play in shaping policy must be understood in relation to the structure of national political institutions and the capacity of groups to mobilize and use those institutions as leverage to further their particular policy visions. Together, these three clusters of factors shape the context for strategic political action. It was, in short, neither American liberalism nor any of its challengers that produced the distinctive American pattern of race-conscious affirmative action emerging from color-blind premises, nor was this policy simply a mechanical reflection of fragmented American political institutions. Rather, these policies resulted from the interplay among these factors, the particular ways in which citizens made use of elements of multiple political traditions and brought them to bear in distinct institutional and historical settings.

As an account of American affirmative action, moreover, this picture upends conventional views of civil rights enforcement on a number of dimensions. First, the EEOC, despite its lack of formal regulatory power, was not as anemic as it is often portrayed. It was able to marshal substantial resources that helped dramatically to shift the grounds of Title VII enforcement in a relatively short time. But it did not accomplish this through conventional command-and-control means of regulatory enforcement, using powers directly and explicitly delegated to it by Congress. Rather, it accomplished this by means of strategic alliances with private civil society groups who were, in effect, enlisted in a project of public regulatory activity.

Second, the centrality of the NAACP and the LDF to these enforcement efforts suggests strongly that the view of affirmative action as the product of a cabal of judges, bureaucrats, and civil rights lawyers to subvert the color-blind premises of the Civil Rights Act are mistaken. "Post-1968 civil rights law has notably been imposed on American democracy from the top down," writes legal scholar Andrew Kull. "Little disposed to reclaim the burden of self-government in an area offering only hard choices, the nation has largely acquiesced in policies chosen by administrators and judges."[86] This is simply not so. Administrators and judges indeed played critical roles in the evolution of antidiscrimination policy, but their actions were enabled and sustained by the wide-ranging democratic forces of the civil rights movement and its organizations. The development of employment discrimination policy was, in fact, an exercise in self-government, in which previously powerless citizens, motivated by a vision of a better future, mobilized to exploit opportunities posed by the structure of the American state to advance their cause and to push American society toward broader incorporation for all of its citizens. As the histories I have recounted in this book suggest—of welfare states and employment regimes, in the United States and elsewhere—such opportunities are often unexpected and all too rare.

Chapter Nine

TOWARD A COLOR-BLIND FUTURE: VARIETIES OF COLOR BLINDNESS AND THE FUTURE OF RACE POLICY

COLOR BLINDNESS, as both a philosophical proposition and a policy prescription, is enormously appealing and compelling. For Americans (and others) of nearly every political stripe it captures the fundamental aspirations of democratic politics and the liberal tradition. Martin Luther King, Jr., famously distilled the color blindness of the American political tradition to its essence in his dream that his children would "one day live in a nation where they will not be judged by the color of their skin but by the content of their character."[1] This color-blind vision animated the great achievements of the civil rights era and King's words have long since become a mantra to American citizens and political leaders alike. Despite King's own growing radicalism in the 1960s—his turn toward issues of poverty and economic inequality and his opposition to the war in Vietnam, for example—his phrases were increasingly taken up in the decades after his death by those who believed that color blindness itself was enough to reverse racial discrimination and inequality, that prohibiting discrimination would remove the barriers to the full incorporation of minorities into American society and obviate the need for more active measures to address racial disparities. This position found expression from voices as politically disparate as Nathan Glazer, Arthur Schlesinger, Jr., and Todd Gitlin. One conservative commentator even appropriated King's own words as a book title.[2]

Color blindness, however, is not self-enforcing, as these analyses supposed. Nathan Glazer, one of the prophets of color blindness in the 1960s and 1970s, came gradually to a skeptical view of his own erstwhile enthusiasm:

> Was more necessary to assist the rise of blacks? Twenty years ago, one could believe, and I did believe, that more was not necessary—that the measures banning discrimination in employment, education, housing, government programs, were sufficient, that the agencies policing these measures were competent, that the civil rights groups watching the agencies were vigilant, that the courts which would respond to their complaints on effectiveness of enforcement were sympa-

thetic. One could believe that American blacks would follow the path of European immigrants, now that state-imposed restrictions were lifted and private discrimination in key areas was banned. . . . These views, whatever evidence could have been collected to support them in the middle 1970s, now strike me as complacent.[3]

If the comparative analysis of race policy reveals anything, it is that Glazer's confessional intimation is fundamentally right. Color-blind intentions, even when crystallized in policy, are not enough to guarantee color-blind results. By the same token, the path to a color-blind future need not begin from color-blind policy. Just as it is not inevitable that color-blind policies bring about color-blind results, neither do race-conscious policies necessarily produce racially biased consequences. But in renouncing the naïve optimism of his characteristically American faith in color blindness, Glazer also zeroes in on the essential things that made color blindness insufficient to secure full incorporation for African Americans: civil rights groups, agencies, courts—in short, the institutional settings in which intentions are translated into actions and, ultimately, results.

COALITIONS AND RACIAL INCORPORATION

The course of race policy in the twentieth century clearly depended centrally and above all on processes of coalition formation and on the ability of racial minorities to participate in policy-making coalitions.[4] The principal settings for these processes of coalition formation are national political institutions, which are not only the principal sites of national policy-making but also important determinants of a country's capacity to manage deep social cleavages (racial, ethnic, religious, or linguistic, for example) by limiting the majority rule and providing mechanisms by which minorities can protect their interests. Not only the fundamental structure of policy-making institutions—the separation of powers or parliamentary government, centralization or federalism—but also more fine-grained institutional characteristics such as party systems and patterns of government formation, electoral arrangements, and courts are crucial in shaping policy and outcomes.[5] These institutions are important in these cases precisely because they regulate the state's capacity to incorporate minorities into political processes by which coalitions are built and sustained. The state's propensity to include minorities in coalition building, in turn, depends partly on the points of access that the state's organizational structure affords to minorities to enter into the policy-making process.

The American state famously offers multiple points of access to groups who seek to influence policy, one of the principal consequences of its fragmented and decentralized institutional structure—not only separated powers but also bureaucratic fragmentation, federalism, and powerful independent courts. But this structure is a double-edged sword, both posing barriers to the creation of decisive and durable policy coalitions and offering all manner of minority groups the means to redirect and expand the scope of political conflicts, especially when they find themselves (at least temporarily) on the losing side.[6] Multiple points of access, accordingly, have not been uniformly empowering for American minorities. British and French institutions generally limit group access and consequently restrict minority leverage over policy-making. At the same time, the same institutional features that limit access also create the possibility for more decisive and forceful state action relatively untrammeled by the imperatives of coalitional compromise.

But although national institutions are crucial in determining the avenues through which minorities can potentially participate in policy-making coalitions, this participation also depends heavily on other factors. In particular, minorities can best advance their case for incorporation when they can organize and forge links with the state on the basis of their racial identity and also when they can find congenial ideological and cultural openings to exploit. The potential leverage and tactics of groups depend partly on groups' own characteristics but also on the structure of political opportunities and points of access offered to them by political institutions and contexts. But institutional points of access are of little use to groups that are not organized to exploit them. For one thing, it is well established to the point of being axiomatic that groups do not organize to do so spontaneously or evenly across the political spectrum. For another, the "fit" between group organization and state structure is crucial in shaping the capacity of groups to participate in coalitions, affect policy outcomes, and gain inclusion in the benefits of citizenship.[7] Thus, for example, minority groups organized primarily at the local level will generally have little opportunity for leverage over centralized national policy-making but may be more likely to find avenues of influence when policy-making is decentralized and scattered in multiple venues.

In the United States, the fundamentally locally oriented history of African American political involvement, characterized above all by patterns of dependence and clientelism both in the South and the urban North, limited their capacity to join coalitions and affect policy for much of the twentieth century, compounding African American exclusion from social citizenship. In the middle of the twentieth century, however, African Americans managed to mobilize at multiple levels, forging a national social movement out of local organization and bringing down Jim Crow, first locally across the South and then nationally, claiming civil and political rights that had long been denied them. In the wake of the Civil Rights

Act, the local orientation of African American politics proved empowering, affording access to courts and other fragmented institutional sites
and enabling the emergence of affirmative action. In Britain, by contrast,
the similar local orientation of minority politics effectively isolated minorities from influence in Britain's more centralized policy-making institutions, while legal and historical limitations on minority group organization in France also severely restricted opportunities for minority influence.
These limitations, however, did not uniformly restrict minority incorporation outcomes, as the British and French welfare state cases suggest.
Rather, patterns of group-state linkage and their potential impact depend
not only on political opportunities but also on the framing and legitimacy
of claims for racial incorporation.

National ideas about race, in particular tendencies toward color-blind
and race-conscious approaches, are thus also important in shaping national policy responses to the challenges of racial conflict and inequality.
The clearest case of this phenomenon is France, in which the fundamental
color blindness of French political culture has come to inflect nearly every
aspect of the country's race policy, from the refusal to collect ethnic and
racial statistics to the limitations on racial and ethnic group organizations
and the lack, at least explicitly, of racially targeted policy. But the French
case is also the most deceptive, because this bird's-eye cultural view of
French race policy conceals the roles that other factors—the shape of
French state institutions, the party system, the changing contours of group
mobilization—have played in defining France's race policy path. Moreover, a closer look at the actual components of the French welfare state
in particular suggests that French policy is not as color-blind as its mythol-
ogy suggests, no matter how artfully the state's official rhetoric describes
it. Even more starkly than France, the United States and Britain display
the ultimate indeterminacy of culture in defining race policy. In Britain, a
developing convergence on multiculturalism as a political and cultural
frame for policy may have contributed to the relative success of welfare
incorporation, but it has neither advanced the cause of vigorous antidiscrimination enforcement nor prevented the growth of racial isolation, de-
spair, and violence. And in the United States, fundamental ambivalence
in the face of multiple political traditions has produced not a political or
cultural consensus on race as a category of public life but rather an ongo-
ing, ever-changing conflict in American political and intellectual life between color-blind and race-conscious visions of policy, citizenship, and
national identity.

It is far from self-evident, as Glazer's reflections on his own intellectual
journey suggest, how a given set of national cultural presumptions—
whether color-blind or race-conscious—will translate into policy or, more
important, into incorporation outcomes. What is clear, however, is that

this process of translation depends on the dynamics of coalition building and the means that minorities in different national political settings had at their disposal to confront the particular modes of exclusion that their societies had historically constructed. The fluidity and openness of American coalition-building processes posed particular risks for American minorities, risks that have been powerfully and tragically apparent for much of American history. But they also created—and may again create—surprising and often liberating moments of opportunity and possibility.

THE AMERICAN DILEMMA REVISITED

These conclusions, about the political mechanisms by which patterns of racial division and hierarchy are reproduced and sometimes overcome, cut to the heart of my central motivating puzzle, the peculiar persistence of racial inequality in many realms of American political life even though it has dwindled dramatically in other areas of society and politics. Most observers of American race politics—including, most famously, Gunnar Myrdal—have viewed this puzzle in terms of the dilemma between color blindness and race consciousness.[8] This dilemma is clearly a universal feature of the politics of multiracial societies. Nevertheless, it has long been particularly acute in the United States, and its resolution particularly uncertain and ever changing. Some say that the problem is the incomplete triumph of color blindness and the perverse persistence of race consciousness. There are Left and Right variants of this position. On the Left are those who believe that racism of the old-fashioned kind remains a serious barrier to racial advancement and incorporation, while those on the Right argue that multiculturalism and group-based policies such as affirmative action unwittingly and condescendingly perpetuate racial classifications. Others defend race consciousness either as a necessary step toward the full flowering of a color-blind ideal or, more positively, as a desirable end for policy on its own terms.[9] Common to all these views is the presumption that these approaches are, in effect, self-executing, that either color blindness or race consciousness, if conscientiously and consistently applied, would produce obvious and predictable consequences.

This proposition is simply false. No matter how ideologically tidy and coherent such policy models might be, they simply do not determine the consequences of race policies for the fortunes of minorities in multiracial societies. Policies motivated by color blindness and designed around its precepts do not necessarily produce color-blind outcomes. By the same token, race-conscious policies are not necessarily doomed to perpetuate racial oppression and inequality.

This conflict, between what might be called the "pure" theory of color-blind policy and a more context-sensitive understanding of the way policy translates into outcomes, was precisely at issue in the recent United States Supreme Court case over affirmative action at the University of Michigan. The plaintiffs were white applicants who claimed that the university's admissions process, which was designed to produce a racially diverse student body, violated their right to equal protection because it identified applicants by race and thus violated the precepts of color blindness. But in her majority opinion in the critical case, Justice Sandra Day O'Connor rejected the premise that race-neutral policies had an absolute claim to priority, arguing instead that racial diversity is a legitimate, even compelling goal, and that race-conscious admissions policies are a reasonable way of achieving that diversity (especially given that race-neutral alternatives have demonstrably failed to achieve comparable levels of incorporation for minorities at the university). The court's reasoning in this case was fundamentally sound; the majority understood that color-blind policy is neither necessary nor sufficient for minority incorporation.[10]

It is not, first of all, self-evident what color blindness means in a policy context. Equal treatment across the color line, that is, might ignore or sidestep other circumstances that systematically differentiate between racially defined groups in such a way that color blindness does not, in fact, amount to equal treatment. Anatole France waggishly described the "majestic equality of the law, which forbids rich and poor alike to sleep under bridges, beg in the streets, and steal bread."[11] Similarly, policies that treat blacks and whites (or any other racially or ethnically defined group) in scrupulously identical terms might willfully disregard racial distinctions that make supposedly equal treatment decidedly unequal. Such beneath-the-surface race consciousness is, in many instances, not merely an accidental or incidental consequence of color-blind arrangements but an integral part of their makeup. Examples of such policies include Social Security in its original formulation, in which apparent color blindness concealed careful racially exclusionary institutional engineering. Voting restrictions in the Jim Crow South such as poll taxes, literacy tests, grandfather clauses, and the like, are another; these were discriminatory devices framed out of necessity in color-blind terms to conform to the Fifteenth Amendment to the Constitution.[12] Other policies, by contrast—antidiscrimination laws regarding public accommodations, for example, or even Social Security as it has evolved—might be considered more truly color-blind.

At the same time, color blindness is not self-fulfilling, as the comparative analysis clearly shows. Rather, the idea of color blindness requires fleshing out in concrete contexts, and the working out of color-blind policies can actually paper over and perpetuate quite real racial distinctions and inequalities. Again, the American welfare state provides an example of policies that are color-blind on their face but have had quite dramatically racially imbalanced consequences—in particular the deepening racialization of welfare in the United States and the contribution of policies such as AFDC to the political and economic isolation of African Americans.[13] French welfare policy, too, has displayed something of a similar dynamic, in which color-blind policy has compounded the economic and social divide across the racial line. Social Security, by contrast offers an example of a policy in which color blindness ultimately triumphed, although this triumph was a long time coming and had as much to do with the program's institutional structure than with its explicit color blindness. In the American employment discrimination case, color-blind policy on its own terms quickly ran up against its own limitations, particularly the limited power it conferred on the state to remedy racial inequality. Color blindness, in fact, almost by definition means a passive state, at least with respect to attempts to adjust racial imbalances. From this perspective, color blindness may represent something of a failure of nerve, a reluctance to enlist the state in an active effort to enforce racial incorporation; such, at least, was the case in the institutionally driven bargain that produced Title VII of the Civil Rights Act. All of this suggests that the institutional and political conditions in which color blindness is deployed are at least as important as color blindness itself in determining the success or failure of color blindness as an incorporation strategy.

The flip side of these patterns is race-conscious policy, which has its own risks and rewards. On the risk side of the ledger, race consciousness can clearly be pernicious, at the extreme producing segregation and apartheid, or worse. Even in cases where democratic politics imposes limits on such repression and where state-sponsored racial distinctions embody a more benign intent, race-conscious policies risk reifying precisely the existing racial distinctions that they are intended to overcome. But just as color-blind policies are not self-fulfilling, neither do race-conscious policies and policy contexts necessarily perpetuate or construct divisive racial distinctions, at least on balance. Again, affirmative action in the United States is an instructive example. Many observers have challenged it on the grounds that it effectively segregates minority workers or students by tainting their achievements. It is also a matter of some controversy whether affirmative action has actually improved the economic position of African Americans, women, or other minority groups. Some economists and others have suggested that the gap between black and white incomes had been narrowing since the 1940s, and that government enforcement and affirmative action had little if any impact independent of trends that were already in place well before 1964. But James Heckman and his colleagues have argued that Title VII enforcement efforts, as part of a broad federal assault on racial segregation particularly in the South, had a demonstrable effect on black employment and wages in the decade or so after 1964. Derek Bok and William Bowen show that affirmative action at selective colleges and universities has significantly benefited black students who through it gained access to those institutions and, later, to opportunities that had been historically closed to them. William Julius Wilson argues that affirmative action has, in fact, been so successful at solidifying the black middle class that it has contributed to growing class inequality among African Americans and played an unwitting role in the isolation of the black ghetto poor.[14] At the very least, the race-conscious premises of affirmative action empowered minorities, in the distinctive American political and organizational context of the 1960s and 1970s, to take an active part in shaping policy aimed at their own incorporation, and the state, in response, took an active rather than a passive role in promoting that incorporation.

Race consciousness, in this case as in others, served the color-blind ends of removing race-based barriers to social and economic advancement and equalizing opportunities across racial lines. This progress came about not through the self-fulfilling properties either of race consciousness or color blindness as ideas but rather through the concrete meanings and practices that these ideas engendered in particular institutional contexts. The rules of the race-conscious game, moreover, are changing, both in the United States and elsewhere. The new multiracial categories created by the 2000 United States Census, which allowed respondents to indicate more than one racial affiliation, have the potential to change the race policy land-scape dramatically, especially by vastly expanding the number of racial categories that might potentially lay claim to legal and political protec-tions, backed by state power, that the policies of the past generation have secured. The substance of race-conscious claims has also evolved, from demands for social justice for the disadvantaged to the fashionable man-tra of "diversity" (ratified in the Michigan cases by the Supreme Court with the backing of the business community, the military, and even the Bush administration).[15] How these changing perspectives on race con-sciousness will interact with the institutional dynamics of American poli-tics to reshape race policy remains an open question.

Beyond Black and White: Color Blindness, Race Consciousness, and Latinos

Not only are the meanings and consequences of "color-blind" and "race-conscious" policy not self-evident, but the very contours of "race" as a political category are themselves subject to change. The black-white color line has been fundamental to American political development in myriad ways, and the historical and comparative analysis in this book only adds weight to this conclusion while also eliciting some of the political mechanisms that have made this so. Nevertheless, the meaning of race in American politics has undergone significant transformations over the course of American history, particularly in the twentieth century. In the early part of the century, the politics of race revolved particularly around the distinction between Americans of northern and western European (particularly Anglo-Saxon) heritage and others, especially African Americans, but also more recent immigrants from southern and eastern Europe, who were viewed as racially distinct from the native white majority. Legitimated and advanced by intellectual developments that purported to give scientific grounding to such racial categories, these distinctions generated a series of important political consequences—race-based immigration restrictions, the movement to "Americanize" immigrants, and the consolidation of a white racial identity that once again set African Americans apart. Once again, in the late twentieth and early twenty-first centuries, the definition of race in American politics has been significantly broadened and complicated both by the growth particularly of the Latino and Asian population (in the wake of the reopening of America's borders to immigration in 1965) and by the heightened status of multicultural identities and minority rights in American politics.[16] Questions about the incorporation of racial minorities into American society therefore need to be broadened beyond the black-white color line, and the ability to account for incorporation patterns of a variety of groups is an important test of any explanatory approach to race policy and its consequences.

Latinos now rival African Americans as the largest minority group in the United States. In the 2000 census, the black and Latino populations were of approximately equal size, each around 35 million people, or one-eighth of the country's total population. Latinos are also the fastest-growing group in the population; their numbers increased by more than 60 percent between 1990 and 2000, and the U.S. Census Bureau has projected that the Latino population will double over the next thirty years, becoming by a wide margin the country's largest minority group. The barriers to incorporation facing Latinos in the United States, moreover, are in many ways different from those that have historically faced African Americans and are parallel to those facing European minorities in that they encompass not only racial discrimination and exclusion but also questions of immigration status, citizenship, and language.[17] Moreover, the broad category "Latino" embraces an extremely diverse and heterogeneous group of Americans. (All of this is also true of Asians, a smaller but also fast-growing group.)

Recent patterns of Latino incorporation into American social provision and labor markets show a rather mixed picture. Like African Americans,

Latinos have come increasingly to benefit from Social Security. Between 1983 and 2000, the Latino share of Social Security beneficiaries more than doubled, reflecting the growing presence of Latinos among eligible workers. Also like African Americans, Latinos tend to receive somewhat lower benefits than white recipients, reflecting their concentration in relatively low-wage jobs. Latino benefits have also deteriorated slightly in relative terms in recent decades. In the early 1980s, the median Latino benefit was consistently more than 80 percent of the overall median, while black benefits lagged several percentage points behind. Since the mid-1990s, however, these figures have been reversed, indicating that while African American benefits seem to be gaining ground relative to whites, Latinos are beginning to fall behind. Despite the very recent trends, these patterns are consistent with the strongly integrative, color-blind policy structure of Social Security; on balance, in fact, Latinos and African Americans alike benefit particularly from Social Security's progressive benefit formula and its defined-benefit structure.[18]

These patterns are also consistent with recent trends in income inequality. Figures 9.1 and 9.2 show trends in family income and poverty by race and ethnicity in the postwar era (since 1975 for poverty). These figures show persistent economic inequality between whites on the one hand and African Americans and Latinos on the other, although Latinos have consistently been better off in the aggregate than blacks. Since the late 1970s, the economic gap between whites and these minority groups has widened as the recessions of the 1970s and early 1980s hit them particularly hard. Despite absolute gains since the mid-1990s, however, Latino economic progress has been slower than that of other groups, and the gap between blacks and Latinos in the aggregate has disappeared.[19]

Latinos, however, have been consistently less reliant on public assistance than African Americans. Figures 9.3 and 9.4 show recent trends in welfare recipiency and dependence, as defined by the Department of Health and Human Services.[20] Welfare recipiency measures the percentage of all families who receive any federally funded, means-tested benefit, such as AFDC or TANF, Medicaid, or Food Stamps. Both African Americans and Latinos have, not surprisingly, been considerably more likely than whites to collect such benefits, and recipiency rates for all groups fell in the 1990s. Welfare dependence denotes families who rely on these benefits for 50 percent or more of their total income. While white dependence rates are negligible and quite flat over time, black and Latino rates of dependence have been rather volatile, rising in the early 1990s and falling dramatically since then. At the same time, because of their increasing share of the population, Latinos make up a growing proportion of the TANF rolls, as figure 6.2 reveals, and the work requirements and other provisions of the post-1996 welfare regime have left Latino families particularly exposed to benefit cutbacks and discrimination.[21]

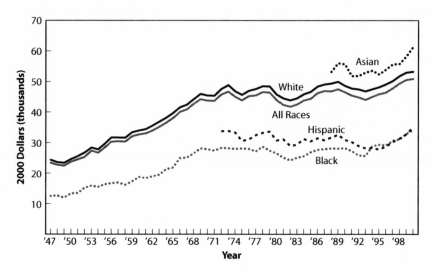

FIGURE 9.1 Median Family Income by Race/Ethnicity, 1947–2000. Source: U.S. Bureau of the Census, *Current Population Survey, Annual Demographic Supplement* (various years).

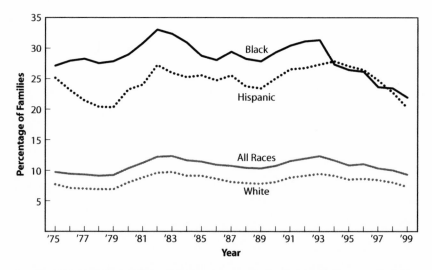

FIGURE 9.2 Families below the Poverty Level by Race/Ethnicity, 1975–99. Source: U.S. Bureau of the Census, *Current Population Survey, Annual Demographic Supplement* (various years).

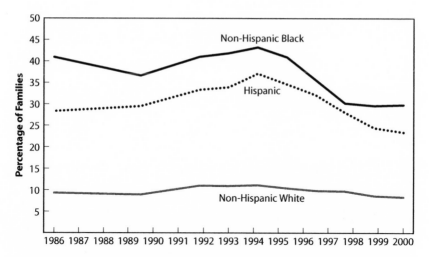

FIGURE 9.3 Welfare Recipients by Race/Ethnicity, 1987–99. Source: U.S. Department of Health and Human Services, *Indicators of Welfare Dependence: Annual Report to the Congress* (various years).

In the labor market, Latino levels of unemployment have consistently been higher than white levels but lower than black, and Latinos tend to be even more concentrated in service and low-skilled occupations. Latinos have also faced substantial job discrimination. Like African Americans, Latinos—particularly Mexican Americans in the Southwest—have historically been subjected to coercive labor practices in agriculture as well as mining and other occupations. A number of studies have documented that a large portion of the occupational and earnings gaps between Anglo and Latino workers cannot reasonably be attributed to anything other than ethnicity, strongly suggesting the prevalence and persistence of discrimination—although a recent study by Alfred Blumrosen (a long-time employment discrimination lawyer who was an early EEOC staff member) suggests that the risk of discrimination for Latinos is somewhat lower than for blacks.[22]

Like African Americans, Latinos are protected from discrimination by Title VII of the Civil Rights Act, and since the late 1960s they (along with women, Asian Americans, and Native Americans) have benefited from affirmative action in employment. Thus, Latinos can file discrimination claims with the EEOC, sue employers for alleged job discrimination, and claim group-based protection in employment, education, and other spheres. A series of studies in the 1980s and 1990s, however, have shown that Latinos have been substantially underrepresented in the EEOC's en-

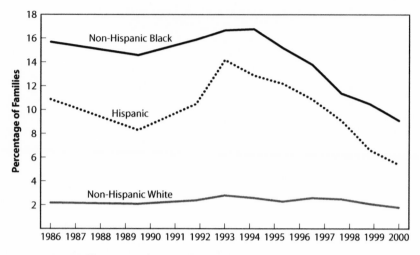

FIGURE 9.4   Welfare Dependency by Race/Ethnicity, 1987–1999. Source: U.S. Department of Health and Human Services, *Indicators of Welfare Dependence: Annual Report to the Congress* (various years).

forcement activities. Very few of the individual claims filed with the EEOC are brought by Latinos, Latino cases are more likely than others to be dismissed, and relatively few of the EEOC's own lawsuits involve Latinos.[23] Enforcement of antidiscrimination law thus seems to be less heavily focused on Latinos than on African Americans and women.

In sum, the incorporation pattern of Latinos into the American political economy is rather different from that of African Americans, and it is something of a mixed picture. On the one hand, the economic position of Latinos in the aggregate is improving and remains, in many respects, better than that of African Americans. In particular, Latinos are much less likely than African Americans to live in highly segregated urban neighborhoods that compound problems of spatial, economic, and political isolation. In some ways, Latinos in the United States seem to be following the classic script of immigrant incorporation, in which successive generations achieve greater political, economic, and social success. On the other hand, these aggregate tendencies mask tremendous variation in Latino incorporation, especially between the growing middle class and those left behind—the working poor, the growing welfare population, the residents of urban *barrios,* and immigrants. As with African Americans, this picture of Latino incorporation suggests a changing landscape that varies over time and across policy areas and substantive realms, and it is this diverse pattern of incorporation that demands explanation.[24]

Although I do not offer such an explanation here, I suggest that the analytical framework advanced in this book can help frame a convincing account of these outcomes. Culturally, the status of Latinos in American politics has always been rather ambiguous. Guaranteed American citizenship by the Treaty of Guadalupe Hidalgo of 1848, Mexicans in the Southwest were largely excluded from political rights and consigned to subordinate status in the labor market through patterns of local coercion parallel in many ways to the subordination of African Americans in the post–Civil War South. Nevertheless, the status of Latinos in the complex American racial palette has been variable and ambiguous, navigating between colorblind and race-conscious models but rarely as persistently and deeply racialized as the status of African Americans. Institutionally, Latinos have been subject to the same structures of fragmented and decentralized authority, which have similarly limited their access to electoral power and their capacity to participate in policy-making coalitions. Unlike African Americans, however, Latinos were not concentrated for much of American history in a repressive region that so dominated American politics as the white-supremacist South did through much of the formative period of American state building. Thus, although Latinos have undoubtedly been politically disadvantaged by the structure of American politics, the terms of that disadvantage have generally been more fluid and less systematic than for African Americans. Finally, patterns of group-state attachment have been different for Latinos and African Americans. Concentrated in particular states and cities, their political leverage is uneven, depending on group size and cohesiveness and local levels of political competitiveness. Patterns of group organization and mobilization, moreover, are uneven. Although national organizations such as the National Council of La Raza lobby on behalf of Latinos as a whole, Latinos have not organized cohesively at a mass, national level. Rather, heterogeneity among Latinos—by class, national origin, and geographic location within the United States—have meant that group mobilization around Latino political identities has tended to be variable and local. Finally, many Latin American immigrants have retained political ties to their countries of origin, limiting their resources for political leverage in the United States.[25]

These three clusters of factors—cultural boundaries of race, institutional structures, and patterns of group-state linkage—have shaped the incorporation of Latinos in different ways than that of African Americans, expanding their political possibilities in some respects (more fluid racial classifications, less direct repression) and restricting them in others (less sense of shared fates, weaker and more fragmented mobilization, and hence greater political invisibility). These analytical fragments, then, might be assembled into a coherent, historically grounded account of Latinos and their place in American national politics and policy. Such an account would explain the particular pattern of incorporation into the welfare state and protection from discrimination—their relatively weak attachment to public assistance and antidiscrimination enforcement, despite modest economic success, for example—in the context of their distinctive patterns of assimilation and group identity. Aristide Zolberg and Long Litt Woon have argued that it is Latinos in the United States rather than African Americans whose experience is the most directly comparable to that of immigrants, especially Muslims, in European societies where cultural incorporation is the primary challenge for ethnic and racial minorities.[26] But my approach underscores common processes of minority incorporation revolving around political power and opportunity that are important for different groups within countries as well as across national boundaries. Cultural boundaries—language, religion, and so forth—are surely important as frontiers of incorporation, but they are not isolated from considerations of political power and opportunity and need to be built into a more complete model of the politics of minority incorporation.

RACE POLICY IN THE TWENTY-FIRST CENTURY: POSSIBILITIES AND PROSPECTS

Race remains a critically important and salient political issue in all three countries. In Britain, the Stephen Lawrence case revealed serious racial imbalances in the criminal justice system and demonstrated a growing level of mistrust and suspicion between black Britons and the government. The Lawrence case remained in the news through the summer of 2002 (nine years after the murder and more than three years after the Macpherson Report), as two of the suspects were convicted of a racist attack on a London police officer. Race riots in Bradford, Burnley, and Oldham in the summer of 2001 were only the most recent and extensive outbreaks of racial violence in Britain in recent years, and they too exposed serious friction and inequality between white and minority communities. Meanwhile, British political leaders continue to grope for ways to ease racial tensions and inequalities while addressing racially defined communities that seem increasingly at odds with each other. During Britain's 2001 general election campaign, Conservative Party leader William Hague made a number of remarks about race—claiming that the Macpherson Report inhibited crime prevention by branding police officers as racist, warning that Britain was in danger of becoming a "foreign land"—that led Prime Minister Tony Blair and others to accuse him of playing the race card. Just weeks before the election Hague was forced to rebuke one of his own MPs, John Townend, for saying that Commonwealth immigration was undermining Britain's "homogeneous Anglo-Saxon society." Around the same time, Foreign Secretary Robin Cook raised eyebrows when he said in a well-publicized speech that "chicken tikka massala is now a true British national dish." Intended as a defense of British multiculturalism, Cook's comments were taken by many as a lament for a lost British identity and further fueled the campaign dustup over race.

In France, too, race remains a critical dividing line in politics. Jean-Marie Le Pen's unexpected performance in the first round of the 2002 presidential election and the National Front's strong showing in regional elections in 2004 demonstrated the persistent power of his racist appeal to win votes and to hold French electoral politics, at least sporadically, in his thrall. Racial discrimination, isolation, and exclusion, meanwhile, remain serious challenges for French policymakers, particularly in the infamous banlieues, the suburbs that ring many French cities where disadvantaged minorities are increasingly concentrated. Most recently, in the wake of the terrorist attacks of 11 September 2001 and the subsequent war in Afghanistan and Iraq, growing tensions between the Western and Islamic worlds have made even more acute the cultural and political friction among racial and ethnic groups in France as well as elsewhere in Europe.[27] Violence along racial and ethnic lines is on the rise in Europe: increasing attacks against Jews and Muslims and their places of worship, the assassination of the anti-immigrant populist Dutch politician Pim Fortuyn in 2002, the bombing of commuter trains in Madrid in March 2004. One particularly revealing incident was a soccer match between the national teams of France and Algeria in October 2001, the first time these teams had ever met. The match had to be stopped in mid-play because of rising tensions between the teams' fans. This incident marked a sobering contrast with the self-congratulatory euphoria with which France greeted its World Cup–winning team of 1998—the team of "blacks, blancs, beurs" ("blacks, whites, Arabs")—whose heroes included one player born in Marseille of Algerian parents and others from Ghana and Guadeloupe.[28] If anything, it seems, the racial situation in both Britain and France is growing more dire and divisive and calls for new political approaches and new policy solutions.

What these solutions will look like and how Britain, France, and other countries will approach continuing challenges of racial conflict and inequality remain open questions. But it is clear that diverse national policy approaches will continue to emerge from the enormous and changing variety of institutional structures, group profiles, and cultural repertoires of European countries. Already, in fact, there are signs of new directions in European race policy. During the 2002 French presidential campaign, for instance, both Jacques Chirac and Lionel Jospin explicitly announced support for policies of "positive discrimination" such as the zones d'éducation prioritaire (ZEP) (although Jospin did so with an apology for the "Anglo-Saxon" term), in contrast to Le Pen's charge that the ZEP amounted to "state racism." And in the fall of 2002 Prime Minister Jean-Pierre Raffarin announced a new government integration policy that recognizes, among other things, the presence of a significant, permanent citizen population of racial and ethnic minorities. "Several generations of youth descended from immigrants are French with full privileges," he said, "which some people seem not to have understood."[29] In Britain, a new Race Relations Act, passed in 2000, extends the protections of the 1976 act to cover public authorities, broadening the responsibility of the British state to promote racial equality and further empowering the Commission for Racial Equality to enforce these protections. At the same time, the rash of racial violence in the summer of 2001 has further highlighted the need to address growing substantive problems of racial inequality and segregation in British society.

Meanwhile, the European Union has taken up the issue of racial discrimination. Under the Treaty of Amsterdam, which came into force in 1999, the EU guarantees the citizens of its member states protection against discrimination on racial (as well as other) grounds. Accordingly, in June 2000 the EU Council adopted a directive establishing a legal and administrative framework for combating racial and ethnic discrimination across a wide range of activities, from employment and education to social welfare and public services. The directive basically adopted a race-conscious, Anglo-American approach based on the presumption of racial and ethnic diversity rather than integration. It seeks to construct a minimum level of protection against discrimination that will apply in all member countries, and its mandate is very broad. Not only does it enjoin discrimination in many spheres both public and private, it also covers both direct and indirect forms of discrimination and explicitly allows for compensatory positive action, and it calls on member countries to designate government agencies charged with the promotion (although not necessarily the enforcement) of equal treatment. The EU's entry into the field opens up the possibility of increasing uniformity in European race policy, as minorities can bring racial equality claims based on European law to be enforced by Europe-wide institutions such as the European Court of Justice. The directive states a set of antidiscrimination principles in the strongest possible terms, but much of its language is permissive rather than mandatory. For example, although it allows for positive action it does not require it, and while it places the burden of proof on respondents in antidiscrimination actions, it exempts criminal procedures from this provision. It is not clear, moreover, how its nondiscrimination principles are to be applied and enforced prospectively, as in the provision of public services such as welfare, rather than retrospectively through judicial proceedings. Finally, due to French negotiating pressure, the directive shies away from explicitly establishing statistical data as evidence of indirect discrimination and from requiring member states to collect racial statistics. Thus, it seems that the EU policy leaves ample room for diverse national approaches to the challenges of race policy and for the operation of the national cultural, institutional, and political factors that shaped race policy throughout the twentieth century.[30]

In the United States race also remains a deep fissure in national politics, and the future of race policy is in many ways as uncertain as in Europe. Race, in fact, lies at the center of some of the most divisive and seemingly intractable disputes in American politics at the beginning of the twenty-first century, not least concerning electoral politics and the fairness and representativeness of the American political process itself. More than a generation after the Voting Rights Act, minorities' access to the vote remains a matter of dispute and questions about the procedural requirements and substantive meanings of minority representation abound in the American political system. Among the swirling controversies in the turbulent aftermath of the 2000 presidential election, for example, was the apparent exclusion of many African American voters in Florida and elsewhere through alleged purges of voting rolls, obsolete equipment, and even outright intimidation and fraud. Even where minority voting itself is not at issue, the use of race as a category in designing systems of representation in American elections—particularly the drawing of majority-minority districts under the terms of the Voting Rights Act to maximize the presence of African Americans and other minorities in Congress—remains highly contentious and controversial. The disagreement is twofold: both whether race should be considered a legitimate factor at all in devising electoral systems and whether or not such race-conscious schemes in fact serve minorities' political interests.[31]

Direct racial confrontations, often violent, also remain a serious challenge in the United States. The 1990s and early 2000s saw substantial outbreaks of racial violence in American cities, most notably in Los Angeles in 1992 and Cincinnati in 2001. Other incidents, such as the brutal dragging of an African American man from the back of a pickup truck in a Texas town in 1998, or the fraudulent drug arrests of one-tenth of the black population of another Texas town in 1999, have also attracted national attention. Much of this controversy revolves around the criminal justice system. Issues such as imbalanced sentencing rules (for example, the imposition of stiffer sentences for offenses involving crack cocaine, which are more likely to involve African American defendants, than powder cocaine, more likely to involve whites) and the uneven imposition of the death penalty suggest to many observers that the nominally color-blind American legal system operates in a perniciously race-conscious fashion. The extraordinarily high incarceration rates of African American men have dramatically reshaped the social structure of black communities, especially in cities, and further fuels suspicion about the system's fairness.[32] Instances of apparent police brutality as well as patterns of systematic bias such as racial profiling have incited controversy in New York City, New Jersey, Los Angeles, Detroit, and elsewhere.

Also in recent years a movement for the payment of reparations for slavery has grown in the United States. Fueled by the settlement of a lawsuit in which the United States government agreed to compensate Japanese Americans whom it interned in camps during World War II, the reparations movement and the often derisive reaction to it have served to underscore the depth of the color line in American society and the mistrust that still deeply informs American race relations, even as more African Americans have joined the middle class. The reparations debate, which has grown particularly heated in recent years especially on college and university campuses, hinges precisely on the dilemma between color blindness and race consciousness as ways of understanding and remedying past and present patterns of inequality.[33]

Race also remains a critical axis in American debates about welfare, poverty, and inequality. By most measures—income, wealth, employment, and other indicators of economic and social well-being—disparities between whites and nonwhites have not disappeared and in some cases have remained steady and even widened, despite overall improvements for all groups during the economic boom of the 1990s. The welfare reform legislation of 1996 has not significantly changed the racial and ethnic imbalance in welfare recipiency, and there is evidence that the work requirements and other provisions of the act as well as its devolution of public assistance to state and local authorities have posed particular problems for African Americans and other minorities. Minorities receive less protection from newly devolved public assistance programs, both because policies are more punitive in places where they tend to live and because local administration works against them. They are also less successful at negotiating the welfare-to-work transition that lies at the center of welfare reform. While minorities have been just as likely as whites to leave welfare for work, African Americans have been significantly more likely to report being forced off the public assistance rolls for administrative reasons. African American and Latino welfare leavers, moreover, have been significantly more likely that whites to return to welfare. At the same time, the racial dimensions of such patterns of inequality have been rather submerged in the American political landscape. Although some commentators have celebrated the color blindness of recent American politics, Lawrence Bobo and others have argued that this turn in political discourse is more apparent than real. The very disappearance of more flagrant and obvious forms of racism, Bobo suggests, paradoxically legitimates racial inequality because whites come to believe that black-white gaps in economic performance reflect actual group differences in ability or effort rather than barriers imposed by discrimination.[34]

Finally, affirmative action has also been a flashpoint of political controversy in recent years. In 1995, President Clinton, under political fire from Republicans on the question of racial preference policies, initiated a review of federal affirmative action policies, resulting in his typically Clintonian "mend it, but don't end it" speech. The following year, California's Proposition 209 passed in a referendum vote, outlawing racial preferences in public programs, notably including university admissions, while a federal appeals court struck down the University of Texas's race-based admissions policies.[35] In 2000, Florida governor Jeb Bush ended affirmative action in university admissions and state contracting by executive order. Meanwhile, the Michigan cases were working their way through the federal court system, culminating in the June 2003 Supreme Court rulings, which upheld the principle of race-conscious policy although without quelling the controversy. In October 2003, California voters decisively rejected a ballot initiative to prohibit state and local government, including state universities and other public institutions, from collecting racial statistics (à la France), a move that would have rendered affirmative action and other race-conscious means to diversity nearly impossible. Despite this defeat, the measure's sponsors plan to take the battle for official color blindness to other states, including Michigan, in the future.

All of these policies and the political controversies surrounding them involve, to a greater or lesser degree, the dilemma between color blindness and race consciousness as the basis for political decision-making and policy design. Characteristically, however, the dilemma poses distinct challenges for each that reflect both historical legacies and present circumstances. The future of American race policy and its prospects for success in promoting the full incorporation of minorities into national life depends not only, or even primarily, on changing Americans' minds about race and ethnicity. For one thing, both race consciousness and color blindness are permanent features of the American political landscape, and despite dramatic change in American racial attitudes over the last half century, neither will give way to the other.[36] But more than that, attitudes, beliefs, and cultural patterns themselves do not alone determine policies or their consequences, and to move toward a color-blind future, American public policy will need to attend carefully to the kinds of political possibilities and coalition-building opportunities that particular varieties of color blindness or race consciousness present.

Affirmative action, in particular, has become a cultural battleground on which these contending visions of American society struggle. By pitting race-conscious and color-blind notions of policy and society against each other, affirmative action seems to involve a titanic clash of opposing cultural and ideological forces that are girding for a final battle of apocalyptic proportions, in which the forces of good (whichever side that happens to be) will vanquish the forces of evil. This view is particularly entrenched among those opponents of affirmative action who view it as a fundamental violation of American tenets of color-blind individualism and meritocracy and, by extension, as an antidemocratic or countermajoritarian imposition on the polity—witness the backbiting and finger-pointing on the Right immediately after the Supreme Court's Michigan decision.[37]

But as it has evolved and is practiced, affirmative action involves less cataclysmic conflict over grand principles on the national stage than careful adjustment and compromise that is played out repeatedly in many places and institutions. Thus, affirmative action is likely to remain resilient despite its origins outside of the mainstream of legislative and electoral politics and even in the face of widespread opposition that seems bent on destroying it in the name of color blindness. This is so because it is sustained not by a fragile ideological or cultural consensus but by a dense web of decentralized but interlocking political and institutional mechanisms, both public and private—involving courts, labor unions, universities, corporations, and governments at all levels, many of whom have come to rely on affirmative action's principles and processes for political or market advantage. Moreover, affirmative action invokes the fundamental ambivalence of American race politics, which makes it both endlessly controversial and probably necessary as a way of harnessing the irreducible race consciousness of American political life in the service of color-blind aspirations.

Welfare and poverty, too, are likely to remain key battlegrounds in the struggle for racial equality and incorporation. Here, too, the tension between race consciousness and color blindness frames the debate and the challenge. Despite the surface color blindness of welfare reform, there is simply no escaping the fact that public assistance disproportionately affects the lives and prospects of African Americans and other minorities. As Congress considered the reauthorization of the 1996 welfare reform legislation, much of the debate was conducted in nonracial, color-blind terms, an extraordinary event in the history of American welfare reform. And yet the persistence and even widening of white-nonwhite economic gaps under the new welfare regime highlighted the vulnerability of minorities under an increasingly work-based, decentralized system of public assistance. Minority organizations such as the NAACP, the National Urban League, and the National Council of La Raza were among the most vocal and active in urging Congress to soften the proposed ratcheting up of work requirements for state TANF plans above the initial 1996 provisions. Especially as the American economy enters a period of uncertainty (at best), the prospects for serious diminution of racial inequalities in the economy depend heavily on policy choices around public assistance and welfare-to-work issues, and it is far from clear that color blindness is the most fruitful strategy for addressing this challenge. In particular, the American formula of decentralized, liberal, and officially color-blind welfare policy has ill served racial minorities. Parochial, market-conforming welfare practices have exposed them to a variety of disadvantages in policy-making and implementation and have distorted the surface color blindness of welfare policy. Consequently, in the absence of more targeted policy, centrally directed welfare policy that facilitates stronger links between minorities, the national state, and the labor market seems more likely to be racially inclusive and to address the particular risks that minorities face in the American welfare state.

The dilemma affects other issues as well, including education, housing and community development, and election reform, among others. In each of these issue areas, policy choices and outcomes will have consequences for the incorporation of minorities into national life. In each of these policy areas as well as others, strong claims are made about the virtues of color blindness both as a cultural and political ideal and as a policy strategy.[38] But such blanket claims need careful empirical investigation to uncover the ways in which color blindness might or might not perpetuate racial inequalities through political mechanisms. As with affirmative action and welfare, these political mechanisms have racial implications whether we acknowledge them or not, and the simple assertion that color blindness trumps all does more to hide those implications than to expose them. Thus, the consequences of policy choices on a broad range of issues will follow not only from the racial intentions that lie behind policy-making, nor from the cultural model of race policy that the policy represents, but from the concrete ways in which these ideas and visions are enacted and implemented. Color blindness, in other words, may have decidedly race-laden consequences. Furthermore, resolving ideological and cultural disputes over color-blind or race-conscious policy models will not prevent policies from shaping future racial incorporation outcomes in unexpected and unintended ways.

In the spring of 1997, President Clinton announced a new national initiative on race. The initiative would, he hoped, "begin with a candid conversation on the state of race relations today and the implications of Americans of so many different races living and working together as we approach a new century." Clinton appointed a panel, chaired by the eminent historian of race relations John Hope Franklin, to lead this initiative, and charged it to help educate Americans about the facts surrounding issues of race, to promote a dialog in every community of the land to confront and work through these issues, to recruit and encourage leadership at all levels to help breach racial divides, and to find, develop and recommend how to implement concrete solutions to our problems—solutions that will involve all of us in government, business, communities, and as individual citizens.[39]

While many white American politicians, especially those with national aspirations, spend their careers ducking candid discussions of racial issues, Bill Clinton, a prodigiously talented politician who habitually ducked candid discussions, was at his best when addressing issues of race. And yet Clinton's well-meaning race initiative, for all the effort that went into the commission's deliberations and discussions, came to very little precisely because it focused too much on the rhetorical and cultural questions of race consciousness and color blindness and not enough on the more concrete, if more mundane, questions of policy, politics, and power that ultimately shape racial outcomes.[40] Better, instead, to have focused attention on the very real inequalities of power and resources that stymie racial progress. Still, Clinton's initiative and his general willingness to confront the challenges of race in American society far outstripped his successor's staggering lack of attention to questions of racial division. Beyond its misguided support for color blindness in the Michigan cases, the George W. Bush administration has pursued other nominally color-blind policies—massive tax cuts for the wealthy, privatizing Social Security, relaxing wages and hours standards for low-status workers, ratcheting up work requirements for welfare recipients, among others—that will undoubtedly fall hardest on Americans of color and further impede the process of incorporation across the color line.

The United States remains inescapably a race-conscious society guided powerfully by color-blind ideals. Resolving the tension between these two cultural poles is neither possible nor necessarily desirable. The question that confronts Americans and others who value both diversity and equality is how to move toward our color-blind aspirations without sacrificing what we value in our racial, ethnic, religious, or other affiliations and identities. This task will not be accomplished by arguing from first principles about the virtues of multiculturalism and liberalism, although such arguments are critically important in clarifying ideals and values. Instead we must work backward, in a sense, from a vision of a fairer, more equal society, and unpack the processes and policies that might lead us closer to that vision.

NOTES

CHAPTER ONE

1. It goes without saying—although I am saying it anyway to underscore the point—that "race" has no intrinsic political, or indeed scientific, meaning. Rather, it is a category that acquires meaning in particular historical circumstances because people assign it meaning, which can then be reproduced and reinforced by some set of social or political processes that ascribe significance to "racial" differences. See Barbara J. Fields, "Ideology and Race in American History," in *Region, Race, and Reconstruction: Essays in Honor of C. Vann Woodward*, ed. J. Morgan Kousser and James M. McPherson (New York: Oxford University Press, 1982); Thomas C. Holt, "Marking: Race, Race-making, and the Writing of History," *American Historical Review* 100 (1995): 1–20; Robert C. Lieberman, "Social Construction," *American Political Science Review* 89 (1995): 437–41.

2. The politics of "race" in the United States has come to involve a more diverse and complex set of categories than black and white. Nevertheless, African American exclusion has been one of the central conflicts throughout all of American history. Black-white conflict remains one of the most acute challenges of American society and black-white racial distinctions are still the subject of heightened legal and political scrutiny. Consequently, I focus particularly on the politics of African American incorporation. My arguments about the factors that shape black incorporation, however, are potentially applicable to other racially defined minorities; I address such potential applications in the conclusion.

3. Howard Schuman, Charlotte Steeh, Lawrence Bobo, and Maria Krysan, *Racial Attitudes in America: Trends and Interpretations*, rev. ed. (Cambridge: Harvard University Press, 1997); Benjamin I. Page and Robert Y. Shapiro, *The Rational Public: Fifty Years of Trends in Americans' Policy Preferences* (Chicago: University of Chicago Press, 1992), 62–63, 68–81.

4. Jennifer L. Hochschild, "You Win Some, You Lose Some: Explaining the Pattern of Success and Failure in the Second Reconstruction," in *Taking Stock: American Government in the Twentieth Century*, ed. Morton Keller and R. Shep Melnick (Washington, D.C.: Woodrow Wilson Center Press; Cambridge: Cambridge University Press, 1999).

5. Jesse McKinnon, *The Black Population in the United States: March 2002*, Current Population Reports, Series P20–541 (Washington, D.C.: U.S. Census Bureau, 2003); *The Social and Economic Status of the Black Population in the United States: An Historical View, 1790–1978*, Current Population Reports, Special Studies, Series P23–80 (Washington, D.C.: U.S. Census Bureau, 1979), 75; John J. Donohue III and James Heckman, "Continuous versus Episodic Change: The Impact of Civil Rights Policy on the Economic Status of Blacks," *Journal of Economic Literature* 29 (1991): 1603–43; Kenneth Crouch and Mary C. Daly, "Black-White Wage Inequality in the 1990s: A Decade of Progress" (Federal Reserve Bank of San Francisco, 2000)

6. Robert C. Lieberman, *Shifting the Color Line: Race and the American Welfare State* (Cambridge: Harvard University Press, 1998); Jill Quadagno, *The Color of Welfare: How Racism Undermined the War on Poverty* (New York: Oxford University Press, 1994); Michael K. Brown, *Race, Money, and the American Welfare State* (Ithaca: Cornell University Press, 1999); Sanford F. Schram, Joe Soss, and Richard C. Fording, eds., *Race and the Politics of Welfare Reform* (Ann Arbor: University of Michigan Press, 2003).

7. *Social Security Bulletin*, Annual Statistical Supplement, 2001, 143.

8. U.S. Department of Health and Human Services, Office of the Assistant Secretary for Planning and Evaluation, Office of Human Services, *Aid to Families with Dependent Children: The Baseline* (June 1998), 75; Steven M. Teles, *Whose Welfare? AFDC and Elite Politics* (Lawrence: University Press of Kansas, 1996), 24–26.

9. On these dilemmas, see Will Kymlicka, *Multicultural Citizenship: A Liberal Theory of Minority Rights* (Oxford: Oxford University Press, 1995); Brian Barry, *Culture and Equality: An Egalitarian Critique of Multiculturalism* (Cambridge: Harvard University Press, 2001); Ronald Dworkin, *A Matter of Principle* (Cambridge: Harvard University Press, 1985), pt. 5.

10. *Gratz v. Bollinger*, 539 U.S. 244 (2003); *Grutter v. Bollinger*, 539 U.S. 306 (2003).

11. Gøsta Esping-Andersen, *The Three Worlds of Welfare Capitalism* (Princeton: Princeton University Press, 1990); Christopher Howard, *The Hidden Welfare State: Tax Expenditures and Social Policy in the United States* (Princeton: Princeton University Press, 1997); Jacob S. Hacker, *The Divided Welfare State: The Battle over Public and Private Social Benefits in the United States* (Cambridge: Cambridge University Press, 2002).

12. William Julius Wilson, *The Declining Significance of Race: Blacks and Changing American Institutions*, 2d ed. (Chicago: University of Chicago Press, 1980); Reynolds Farley, *Blacks and Whites: Narrowing the Gap?* (Cambridge: Harvard University Press, 1984), chap. 6.

13. Julia S. O'Connor, Ann Shola Orloff, and Sheila Shaver, *States, Markets, Families: Gender, Liberalism and Social Policy in Australia, Canada, Great Britain and the United States* (Cambridge: Cambridge University Press, 1999); Suzanne Mettler, *Dividing Citizens: Gender and Federalism in New Deal Public Policy* (Ithaca: Cornell University Press, 1998).

14. Peter A. Hall, ed., *The Political Power of Economic Ideas: Keynesianism across Nations* (Princeton: Princeton University Press, 1989); Margaret Weir, *Politics and Jobs: The Boundaries of Employment Policy in the United States* (Princeton: Princeton University Press, 1992); Lieberman, *Shifting the Color Line*.

15. T. H. Marshall, "Citizenship and Social Class," in *Class, Citizenship, and Social Development* (Garden City, N.Y.: Doubleday, 1964), 72; Michael Mann, "Ruling Class Strategies and Citizenship," *Sociology* 21 (1987): 339–54; Bryan S. Turner, "Outline of a Theory of Citizenship," *Sociology* 24 (1990): 189–217; Walter Korpi, "Power, Politics, and State Autonomy in the Development of Social Citizenship: Social Rights During Sickness in Eighteen OECD Countries," *American Sociological Review* 54 (1989): 309–28; Esping-Andersen, *Three Worlds of Welfare Capitalism*.

16. Again, this argument has been most carefully elaborated in the area of gender and the welfare state. Ann Shola Orloff, "Gender and the Social Rights of Citizenship: The Comparative Analysis of Gender Relations and Welfare States," *American Sociological Review* 58 (1993): 303–28.

17. The concept of social exclusion originated in Europe, where poverty and income inequality are generally less acute than in the United States. Consequently, the challenge for social policy is less one of material deprivation than isolation from the political and economic mainstream. The concept has yet to develop much traction in the United States, where poverty and isolation more commonly coincide. Despite their coincidence, however, they are analytically distinct. René Lenoir, *Les exclus: Un français sur dix* (Paris: Seuil, 1993); Hilary Silver, "Social Exclusion and Social Solidarity: Three Paradigms," *International Labour Review* 133 (1994): 531–78; Martin Evans, "Beyond the Rhetoric: The Institutional Basis of Social Exclusion," *IDS Bulletin* 29 (1998): 42–49.

18. Robert C. Lieberman and John S. Lapinski, "American Federalism, Race, and the Administration of Welfare," *British Journal of Political Science* 31 (2001): 308; Richard Lempert and Karl Monsma, "Cultural Differences and Discrimination: Samoans before a Public Housing Eviction Board," *American Sociological Review* 59 (1994): 890–910; Sanford F. Schram, "Contextualizing Racial Disparities in Welfare Reform: Toward a New Poverty Research," *Perspectives on Politics* (forthcoming).

19. Rogers M. Smith, *Civic Ideals: Conflicting Visions of Citizenship in U.S. History* (New Haven: Yale University Press, 1997).

20. These categories do not, of course, exhaust the possible explanations for such outcomes. Such factors as class relations, macrohistorical forces, and exogenous events might also shape policy outcomes and have all been the basis of serious scholarly attempts to explain policy-making. But explanations focusing on ideas and institutions are particularly prominent both in general accounts of American policy-making and in explanations of American race policy.

21. Derrick Bell, *Faces at the Bottom of the Well: The Permanence of Racism* (New York: Basic, 1992); Andrew Hacker, *Two Nations: Black and White, Separate, Hostile, Unequal* (New York: Scribner's, 1992).

22. Donald R. Kinder and Lynn M. Sanders, *Divided by Color: Racial Politics and Democratic Ideals* (Chicago: University of Chicago Press, 1996); Martin Gilens, *Why Americans Hate Welfare: Race, Media, and the Politics of Antipoverty Policy* (Chicago: University of Chicago Press, 1999); Tali Mendelberg, *The Race Card: Campaign Strategy, Implicit Messages, and the Norm of Equality* (Princeton: Princeton University Press, 2001); Lawrence D. Bobo and Ryan A. Smith, "From Jim Crow Racism to Laissez-Faire Racism: The Transformation of Racial Attitudes," in *Beyond Pluralism: The Conception of Groups and Group Identities in America*, ed. Wendy F. Katkin, Ned Landsman, and Andrea Tyree (Urbana: University of Illinois Press, 1998).

23. Paul M. Sniderman and Thomas Piazza, *The Scar of Race* (Cambridge: Harvard University Press, 1993); Paul M. Sniderman and Edward G. Carmines, *Reaching Beyond Race* (Cambridge: Harvard University Press, 1997); Paul M. Sniderman, Gretchen C. Crosby, and William G. Howell, "The Politics of Race," in *Racialized Politics: The Debate about Racism in America*, ed. David O. Sears,

Jim Sidanius, and Lawrence Bobo (Chicago: University of Chicago Press, 2000). See Maria Krysan, "Prejudice, Politics, and Public Opinion: Understanding the Sources of Racial Policy Attitudes," *Annual Review of Sociology* 26 (2000): 135–68.

24. Gunnar Myrdal, *An American Dilemma: The Negro Problem and Modern Democracy* (New York: Harper & Brothers, 1944); *One America in the 21st Century: Forging a New Future*, President's Initiative on Race, Advisory Board's Report to the President (Washington, D.C.: U.S. Government Printing Office, 1998); correspondents of *The New York Times*, *How Race is Lived in America: Pulling Together, Pulling Apart* (New York: Times Books, 2001).

25. Smith, *Civic Ideals*; Desmond King, *Making Americans: Immigration, Race, and the Origins of the Diverse Democracy* (Cambridge: Harvard University Press, 2000).

26. Gilens, *Why Americans Hate Welfare*; Bobo and Smith, "From Jim Crow Racism to Laissez-Faire Racism."

27. Sheri Berman, "Ideas, Norms, and Culture in Political Analysis," *Comparative Politics* 33 (2001): 233.

28. Institutional studies of policy-making are legion in political science. An exemplary, although by no means exhaustive, list might include Stephen Skowronek, *Building a New American State: The Expansion of National Administrative Capacities, 1877–1920* (Cambridge: Cambridge University Press, 1982); Theda Skocpol, *Protecting Soldiers and Mothers: The Political Origins of Social Policy in the United States* (Cambridge: Harvard University Press, 1992); Mathew D. McCubbins, Roger G. Noll, and Barry R. Weingast, "Administrative Procedures as Instruments of Political Control," *Journal of Law, Economics, and Organization* 3 (1987): 243–77; Keith Krehbiel, *Pivotal Politics: A Theory of U.S. Lawmaking* (Chicago: University of Chicago Press, 1998); Charles M. Cameron, *Veto Bargaining: Presidents and the Politics of Negative Power* (Cambridge: Cambridge University Press, 2000). These works represent a wide range of methodological approaches rooted in a variety of disciplinary backgrounds, from neoclassical microeconomics and the theory of games to macrohistorical sociology. But despite their differences, these varieties of institutionalism are united by a common set of concerns and assumptions about the role played by patterns of ordered regularity in social and political life. See Ellen M. Immergut, "The Theoretical Core of the New Institutionalism," *Politics and Society* 26 (1998): 5–34; Robert C. Lieberman, "Ideas, Institutions, and Political Order: Explaining Political Change," *American Political Science Review* 96 (2002): 697–712; Karen Orren and Stephen Skowronek, "Beyond the Iconography of Order: Notes for a 'New Institutionalism'," in *The Dynamics of American Politics: Approaches and Interpretations*, ed. Lawrence C. Dodd and Calvin Jillson (Boulder, Col.: Westview Press, 1994); Kathleen Thelen and Sven Steinmo, "Historical Institutionalism in Comparative Politics," in *Structuring Politics: Historical Institutionalism in Comparative Analysis*, ed. Sven Steinmo, Kathleen Thelen, and Frank Longstreth (Cambridge: Cambridge University Press, 1992).

29. V. O. Key, Jr., *Southern Politics in State and Nation* (New York: Alfred A. Knopf, 1949); William H. Riker, *Federalism: Origin, Operation, Significance* (Boston: Little, Brown, 1964); Ira Katznelson, *City Trenches: Urban Politics and*

the Patterning of Class in the United States (New York: Pantheon, 1981); Lieberman, *Shifting the Color Line*; Paul Frymer, *Uneasy Alliances: Race and Party Competition in America* (Princeton: Princeton University Press, 1999); Daniel Kryder, *Divided Arsenal: Race and the American State During World War II* (Cambridge: Cambridge University Press, 2000); Anthony W. Marx, *Making Race and Nation: A Comparison of the United States, South Africa, and Brazil* (Cambridge: Cambridge University Press, 1998).

30. Hochschild, "You Win Some, You Lose Some"; Philip A. Klinkner with Rogers M. Smith, *The Unsteady March: The Rise and Decline of Racial Equality in America* (Chicago: University of Chicago Press, 1999). Others note the importance of the international context in shaping American race policy, particularly during the Cold War, without going as far as Klinkner and Smith in proposing cataclysmic international (or worse, internal) conflict as a necessary condition for progress. See Mary L. Dudziak, *Cold War Civil Rights: Race and the Image of American Democracy* (Princeton: Princeton University Press, 2000); Thomas Borstelmann, *The Cold War and the Color Line: American Race Relations in the Global Arena* (Cambridge: Harvard University Press, 2001); John D. Skrentny, *The Minority Rights Revolution* (Cambridge: Harvard University Press, 2002), chaps. 2–3.

31. John David Skrentny, *The Ironies of Affirmative Action: Politics, Culture, and Justice in America* (Chicago: University of Chicago Press, 1996); Frank Dobbin and John R. Sutton, "The Strength of a Weak State: The Rights Revolution and the Rise of Human Resource Management Divisions," *American Journal of Sociology* 104 (1998): 441–76.

32. William H. Riker, *Liberalism Against Populism: A Confrontation Between the Theory of Democracy and the Theory of Social Choice* (San Francisco: W. H. Freeman, 1982); Ira Katznelson, Kim Geiger, and Daniel Kryder, "Limiting Liberalism: The Southern Veto in Congress, 1933–1950," *Political Science Quarterly* 108 (1993): 283–306; Keith T. Poole and Howard Rosenthal, *Congress: A Political-Economic History of Role Call Voting* (New York: Oxford University Press, 1997); Barry R. Weingast, "Political Stability and Civil War: Institutions, Commitment, and American Democracy," in Robert H. Bates, Avner Greif, Margaret Levi, Jean-Laurent Rosenthal, and Barry R. Weingast, *Analytic Narratives* (Princeton: Princeton University Press, 1998).

33. Michael Omi and Howard Winant, *Racial Formation in the United States: From the 1960s to the 1990s* (New York: Routledge, 1994); Lieberman, "Social Construction"; Tomás Almaguer, *Racial Fault Lines: The Historical Origins of White Supremacy in* California (Berkeley: University of California Press, 1994); Claire Jean Kim, "The Racial Triangulation of Asian Americans," *Politics and Society* 27 (1999): 105–38.

34. William H. Riker, *The Theory of Political Coalitions* (New Haven: Yale University Press, 1962), 9–12, 21; Barbara Hinckley, *Coalitions and Politics* (New York: Harcourt Brace Jovanovich, 1981), 4–7.

35. Walter W. Powell and Paul J. DiMaggio, eds., *The New Institutionalism in Organizational Analysis* (Chicago: University of Chicago Press, 1991); William H. Sewell, Jr., "A Theory of Structure: Duality, Agency, and Transformation," *American Journal of Sociology* 98 (1992): 1–29; Frank Dobbin, *Forging Industrial Pol-*

icy: The United States, Britain, and France in the Railway Age (Cambridge: Cambridge University Press, 1994); Skrentny, *The Minority Rights Revolution*; Peter A. Hall and Rosemary C. R. Taylor, "Political Science and the Three New Institutionalisms," *Political Studies* 44 (1996): 936–57; Smith, *Civic Ideals*; Adrian Favell, *Philosophies of Integration: Immigration and the Idea of Citizenship in France and Britain* (New York: St. Martin's, 1998); Erik Bleich, *Race Politics in Britain and France: Ideas and Policymaking since the 1960s* (Cambridge: Cambridge University Press, 2003); Michèle Lamont, ed., *The Cultural Territories of Race: Black and White Boundaries* (Chicago: University of Chicago Press; New York: Russell Sage Foundation, 1999); Michèle Lamont, *The Dignity of Working Men: Morality and the Boundaries of Race, Class, and Immigration* (New York: Russell Sage Foundation; Cambridge: Harvard University Press, 2000).

36. Charles E. Lindblom, "The Science of 'Muddling Through,' " *Public Administration Review* 19 (1959): 79–88; John W. Kingdon, *Agendas, Alternatives, and Public Policies* (Glenview, Ill.: Scott, Foresman, 1984); Deborah Stone, *Policy Paradox: The Art of Political Decision Making* (New York: Norton, 1997).

37. Hugh Heclo, *Modern Social Politics in Britain and Sweden: From Relief to Income Maintenance* (New Haven: Yale University Press, 1974), 305–6.

38. Arend Lijphart, "Comparative Politics and the Comparative Method," *American Political Science Review* 65 (1971): 682–98; Gary King, Robert O. Keohane, and Sidney Verba, *Designing Social Inquiry: Scientific Inference in Qualitative Research* (Princeton: Princeton University Press, 1994).

39. Klinkner with Smith, *The Unsteady March*; Doug McAdam, *Political Process and the Development of Black Insurgency, 1930–1970* (Chicago: University of Chicago Press, 1982).

40. See Orren and Skowronek, "Beyond the Iconography of Order"; Paul Pierson, "Increasing Returns, Path Dependence, and the Study of Politics," *American Political Science Review* 94 (2000): 251–67; Paul Pierson, "Not Just What, but *When*: Timing and Sequence in Political Processes," *Studies in American Political Development* 14 (2000): 72–92; Kathleen Thelen, "Historical Institutionalism in Comparative Politics," *Annual Review of Political Science* 2 (1999): 369–404; Hacker, *Divided Welfare State*, 303–11; Jacob S. Hacker, "The Historical Logic of National Health Insurance: Structure and Sequence in the Development of British, Canadian, and U.S. Medical Policy," *Studies in American Political Development* 12 (1998): 57–130; Daniel P. Carpenter, *The Forging of Bureaucratic Autonomy: Reputations, Networks, and Policy Innovation in Executive Agencies, 1862–1928* (Princeton: Princeton University Press, 2001), 35–36.

41. Randall Robinson, *The Debt: What America Owes to Blacks* (New York: Dutton, 2000); Lawrie Balfour, "Unreconstructed Democracy: W.E.B. Du Bois and the Case for Reparations," *American Political Science Review* 97 (2003): 33–44.

42. Hacker, *Two Nations*, 14. See also Bell, *Faces at the Bottom of the Well*, 3, 8; Roy L. Brooks, *Rethinking the American Race Problem* (Berkeley: University of California Press, 1990).

43. Myrdal, *An American Dilemma*; U.S. Department of Labor, Office of Policy Planning and Research, *The Negro Family: The Case for National Action* [the "Moynihan Report"] (Washington, D.C.: U.S. Government Printing Office,

1965); Dalton Conley, *Being Black, Living in the Red: Race, Wealth, and Social Policy in America* (Berkeley: University of California Press, 1999); Frederick Cooper, Thomas C. Holt, and Rebecca J. Scott, *Beyond Slavery: Explorations of Race, Labor, and Citizenship in Postemanicpation Societies* (Chapel Hill: University of North Carolina Press, 2000). For an elaboration and extended critique of these arguments, see Robert C. Lieberman, "Political Institutions and the Legacy of Slavery: The United States in Comparative Perspective," in *Living Memory: Slavery, Colonialism, and the Question of Integration in Europe and the Americas,* ed. Patrick Weil, Mickaëlla Périna, and Laurent Dubois (forthcoming). See also Stuart Hall, "Race, Articulation and Societies Structured in Dominance," in *Sociological Theories: Race and Colonialism* (Paris: Unesco, 1980).

44. These major precursors, to which I am deeply indebted, include principally Ira Katznelson, *Black Men, White Cities: Race, Politics, and Migration in the United States, 1900–30, and Britain, 1948–68* (Chicago: University of Chicago Press, 1976); and Marx, *Making Race and Nation.*

45. Theda Skocpol and Margaret Somers, "The Uses of Comparative History in Macrosocial Inquiry," *Comparative Studies in Society and History* 22 (1980): 174–97.

46. Marx, *Making Race and Nation*; George M. Fredrickson, *White Supremacy: A Comparative Study in American and South African History* (New York: Oxford University Press, 1981); George M. Fredrickson, *Black Liberation: A Comparative History of Black Ideologies in the United States and South Africa* (New York: Oxford University Press, 1995); Cooper, Holt, and Scott, *Beyond Slavery.*

47. Lieberman, *Shifting the Color Line*; Charles Noble, *Welfare as We Knew It: A Political History of the American Welfare State* (New York: Oxford University Press, 1997); Harold Wilensky, *The Welfare State and Equality: Structural and Ideological Roots of Public Expenditures* (Berkeley: University of California Press, 1975), 50–69. At least one study has found results consistent with Wilensky's heterogeneity hypothesis, but it has not been widely explored empirically. Alberto Alesina, Edward Glaeser, and Bruce Sacerdote, "Why Doesn't the United States Have a European-Style Welfare State?" *Brookings Papers on Economic Activity* 2 (2001): 187–254.

48. King, *Making Americans*; Matthew Frye Jacobson, *Whiteness of a Different Color: European Immigrants and the Alchemy of Race* (Cambridge: Harvard University Press, 1998). The foreign-born proportion of the United States population peaked around the turn of the twentieth century at nearly 15 percent. The foreign-born population was larger than the black population from the 1870s through the 1930s. By the 1920s, immigrants from Southern and Eastern Europe comprised two-fifths of the foreign-born population.

49. Language was the salient line of cleavage in Belgium and Switzerland and religion in the Netherlands (and, to some degree, in Switzerland as well). Both Britain and France had internal divisions along what might be called "ethno-national" lines, particularly concerning the Irish in Britain (although this was also partly a matter of religion) and a welter of provincial identities within France that were considered neither entirely French nor entirely alien. See Arend Lijphart, *Democracy in Plural Societies: A Comparative Exploration* (New Haven: Yale

University Press, 1977), 71–81; Mary J. Hickman, "Reconstructing Deconstructing 'Race': British Political Discourse about the Irish in Britain," *Ethnic and Racial Studies* 21 (1998): 288–307; Eugen Weber, *Peasants into Frenchmen: The Modernization of Rural France, 1870–1914* (Stanford: Stanford University Press, 1976).

50. Gøsta Esping-Andersen, *Politics Against Markets: The Social Democratic Road to Power* (Princeton: Princeton University Press, 1985); Seymour M. Lipset and Stein Rokkan, "Cleavage Structures, Party Systems, and Voter Alignments: An Introduction," in *Party Systems and Voter Alignments: Cross-National Perspectives*, ed. Seymour M. Lipset and Stein Rokkan (New York: Free Press, 1967); Hall, "Race, Articulation and Societies Structured in Dominance"; Anthony W. Marx, "The Nation-State and Its Exclusions," *Political Science Quarterly* 117 (2002): 103–26.

51. U.S. Social Security Board, *Social Security in America: The Factual Background of the Social Security Act as Summarized from Staff Reports to the Committee on Economic Security*, Social Security Publication No. 20 (Washington, D.C.: U.S. Government Printing Office, 1937), table opposite p. 184; Daniel T. Rodgers, *Atlantic Crossings: Social Politics in a Progressive Age* (Cambridge: Harvard University Press, 1998), 55–56, 228; Smith, *Civic Ideals*; Ian F. Haney López, *White by Law: The Legal Construction of Race* (New York: New York University Press, 1996).

52. The Netherlands probably also meets the criteria and might be a suitable comparative case, although I do not treat it here. See Jan Rath and Shamit Saggar, "Ethnicity as a Political Tool in Britain and the Netherlands," in *Ethnic and Racial Minorities in Advanced Industrial Democracies*, ed. Anthony M. Messina, Luis R. Fraga, Laurie A. Rhodebeck, and Frederick D. Wright (New York: Greenwood, 1992).

53. David Owen, "Size, Structure, and Growth of the Ethnic Minority Populations," in *Ethnicity in the 1991 Census, Volume 1: Demographic Characteristics of the Ethnic Minority Populations*, ed. David Coleman and John Salt (London: Her Majesty's Stationery Office, 1996), 88; Michèle Tribalat, "Les immigrés au recensement de 1990 et les populations liées à leur installation en France," *Population* 6 (Nov.-Dec. 1993): 1911–46. The American data are from the 2000 census and British data from the 2001 census. In the French case, this figure almost certainly understates the minority population because it is hard to identify and count French citizens who are of minority origin, especially those born in France. By comparison, the minority population, very roughly estimated, of the Netherlands is 9%, Germany 3%, Sweden 2%, and Spain less than 1%.

54. Winthrop D. Jordan, *White Over Black: American Attitudes Toward the Negro, 1550–1812* (Chapel Hill: University of North Carolina Press, 1968); George M. Fredrickson, *The Black Image in the White Mind: The Debate on Afro-American Character and Destiny, 1817–1914* (New York: Harper and Row, 1971); Reginald Horsman, *Race and Manifest Destiny: The Origins of American Anglo-Saxonism* (Cambridge: Harvard University Press, 1981); Philip D. Curtin, *The Image of Africa: British Ideas and Action, 1780–1850* (Madison: University of Wisconsin Press, 1964); William B. Cohen, *The French Encounter with Africans: White Response to Blacks, 1530–1880* (Bloomington: Indiana University

Press, 1980); Michael Hechter, *Internal Colonialism: The Celtic Fringe in British National Development, 1536–1966* (Berkeley: University of California Press, 1975); Richard Franklin Bensel, *Sectionalism and American Political Development: 1880–1980* (Madison: University of Wisconsin Press, 1984); Key, *Southern Politics*; Marx, *Making Race and Nation*; Linda Colley, *Britons: Forging the Nation, 1707–1837* (New Haven: Yale University Press, 1992); Maxim Silverman, *Deconstructing the Nation: Immigration, Racism and Citizenship in Modern France* (London: Routledge, 1992).

55. See Robert A. Dahl, *Polyarchy: Participation and Opposition* (New Haven: Yale University Press, 1971). On the fragility of the articulation of democracy and liberalism, see Fareed Zakaria, *The Future of Freedom: Illiberal Democracy at Home and Abroad* (New York: Norton, 2003).

56. See Rogers Brubaker, *Citizenship and Nationhood in France and Germany* (Cambridge: Harvard University Press, 1992).

57. I am indebted to Ira Katznelson for this formulation. See Katznelson, *Black Men, White Cities.*

58. Bleich, *Race Politics in Britain and France*; Favell, *Philosophies of Integration*; E.J.B. Rose, *Colour and Citizenship: A Report on British Race Relations* (London: Oxford University Press, 1969); Silverman, *Deconstructing the Nation*; Alec G. Hargreaves, *Immigration, "Race" and Ethnicity in Contemporary France* (London: Routledge, 1995); Jeremy Jennings, "Citizenship, Republicanism and Multiculturalism in Contemporary France," *British Journal of Political Science* 30 (2000): 575–98; Lamont, *The Dignity of Working Men*; Smith, *Civic Ideals*; Skrentny, *The Ironies of Affirmative Action*; Robert C. Lieberman, "Race, State, and Policy: The Development of Employment Discrimination Policy in the United States and Great Britain," in *Ethnicity, Social Mobility, and Public Policy in the United States and the United Kingdom*, ed. Glenn Loury, Tariq Modood, and Steven Teles (Cambridge: Cambridge University Press, 2005); Steven M. Teles, "Positive Action or Affirmative Action? The Persistence of Britain's Antidiscrimination Regime," in *Color Lines: Affirmative Action, Immigration, and Civil Rights Options for America* (Chicago: University of Chicago Press, 2001). By "multiculturalism," I refer simply to the idea that social groups, including racial and ethnic minorities, deserve recognition and legitimacy, and not more strident and controversial claims that "emphasize the oppression of minority cultures by the majority." See Nathan Glazer, *We Are All Multiculturalists Now* (Cambridge: Harvard University Press, 1997), 1–21.

59. Skowronek, *Building a New American State*; Skocpol, *Protecting Soldiers and Mothers*; Martin Shefter, "Party and Patronage: England, Germany, and Italy," *Politics and Society* 7 (1977): 403–51; Martin Shefter, "Party, Bureaucracy, and Political Change in the United States," in *Political Parties: Development and Decay*, ed. Louis Maisel and Joseph Cooper (Beverly Hills, Cal.: Sage, 1978); Sven Steinmo, *Taxation and Democracy: Swedish, British, and American Approaches to Financing the Modern State* (New Haven: Yale University Press, 1993); Key, *Southern Politics*; Grant McConnell, *Private Power and American Democracy* (New York: Alfred A. Knopf, 1966).

60. Steinmo, *Taxation and Democracy*; John D. Huber, *Rationalizing Parliament: Legislative Institutions and Party Politics in France* (Cambridge: Cam-

bridge University Press, 1996). Earlier French regimes, however, combined administrative centralization with highly fragmented policy-making in Parliament and the party system, and so it is important not to overstate the unchanging centralization of state power in French politics. See Ezra N. Suleiman, *Private Power and Centralization in France: The Notaires and the State* (Princeton: Princeton University Press, 1987); Douglas E. Ashford, *British Dogmatism and French Pragmatism: Central-Local Policymaking in the Welfare State* (London: George Allen and Unwin, 1982); Stanley Hoffmann, "Paradoxes of the French Political Community," in Stanley Hoffmann et al., *In Search of France* (Cambridge: Harvard University Press, 1963); Herrick Chapman, "French Democracy and the Welfare State," in *The Social Construction of Democracy, 1870–1990,* ed. George Reid Andrews and Herrick Chapman (New York: New York University Press, 1995).

61. Ellen M. Immergut, *Health Politics: Interests and Institutions in Western Europe* (Cambridge: Cambridge University Press, 1992).

62. Sylvia Dörr and Thomas Faist, "Institutional Conditions for the Integration of Immigrants in Welfare States: A Comparison of the Literature on Germany, France, Great Britain, and the Netherlands," *European Journal of Political Research* 31 (1997): 401–26; Brubaker, *Citizenship and Nationhood*; Tribalat, "Les immigrés au recensement de 1990"; Ceri Peach, Vaughan Robinson, Julia Maxted, and Judith Chance, "Immigration and Ethnicity," in *British Social Trends Since 1900: A Guide to the Changing Social Structure of Britain,* ed. A. H. Halsey (London: Macmillan, 1988), 565–70.

63. Brubaker, *Citizenship and Nationhood*; Weber, *Peasants Into Frenchmen*; Patrick Weil, *La France et ses étrangers: L'aventure d'une politique de l'immigration, 1938–1991* (Paris: Calmann-Lévy, 1991); Nathan Glazer and Daniel P. Moynihan, *Beyond the Melting Pot: The Negroes, Puerto Ricans, Jews, Italians, and Irish of New York City,* 2nd ed. (Cambridge: MIT Press, 1970); Gérard Noiriel, *The French Melting Pot: Immigration, Citizenship, and National Identity,* trans. Geoffroy de Laforcade (Minneapolis: University of Minnesota Press, 1996); Tribalat, "Les immigrés au recensement de 1990"; Omi and Winant, *Racial Formation in the United States,* 14–24; Yasemin Nuhoğlu Soysal, *Limits of Citizenship: Migrants and Postnational Membership in Europe* (Chicago: University of Chicago Press, 1994); David Jacobson, *Rights across Borders: Immigration and the Decline of Citizenship* (Baltimore: Johns Hopkins University Press, 1996); Christian Joppke, *Immigration and the Nation-State: The United States, Germany, and Great Britain* (Oxford: Oxford University Press, 1999); Christian Joppke and Ewa Morawska, eds., *Toward Assimilation and Citizenship: Immigrants in Liberal Nation-States* (Houndmills: Palgrave Macmillan, 2003).

64. In the 2000 Census, the first in which U.S. residents were allowed to check multiple racial categories, 12.9% of the population identified as black (12.3% as black alone, and the rest in combination with one or more other racial designations); 4.2% as Asian (3.6% alone); 1.5% as American Indian (0.9% alone); and 6.6% as "other" (5.5% alone). Latinos (who, under Census definitions, can be of any race) comprised 12.5%. Between 1990 and 2000, the Latino population grew by 57.9%.

65. Data from the 2001 UK Census; see also Tariq Modood, "Ethnicity and Political Mobilisation in Britain," in *Ethnicity, Social Mobility, and Public Policy*, ed. Loury, Modood, and Teles.

66. Weil, *La France et ses étrangers*; Fabienne Daguet and Suzanne Thave, *La population immigrée: Le résultat d'une longue histoire* (Paris: Institut Nationale de la Statistique et des Etudes Economiques, 1996); Tribalat, "Les immigrés au recensement de 1990," 1913, 1929; Michèle Tribalat, *Faire France: Une grande enquête sur les immigrés et leurs enfants* (Paris: La Découverte, 1995), 91–111; Catherine Borrel and Chloé Tavan, "La vie familiale des immigrés," in *France, portrait social 2003–2004* (Paris: Institut Nationale de la Statistique et des Etudes Economiques, 2004); David Stuart Blatt, "Immigration Politics and Immigrant Collective Action in France, 1968–1993" (Ph.D. diss., Cornell University, 1996); Aristide R. Zolberg and Long Litt Woon, "Why Islam Is Like Spanish: Cultural Incorporation in Europe and the United States," *Politics and Society* 27 (1999): 5–38.

67. Donald L. Horowitz, "Immigration and Group Relations in France and America," in *Immigrants in Two Democracies: French and American Experience*, ed. Donald L. Horowitz and Gérard Noiriel (New York: New York University Press, 1992), 13–16; Françoise Gaspard and Farhad Khosrokhavar, *Le foulard et la république* (Paris: La Découverte, 1995); Pierre Birnbaum, *The Idea of France*, trans. M. B. DeBevoise (New York: Hill and Wang, 2001), 224–34; Dilip Hiro, *Black British, White British: A History of Race Relations in Britain* (London: Grafton Books, 1991); Tariq Modood, *Not Easy Being British: Colour, Culture and Citizenship* (Stoke-on-Trent: Runnymede Trust and Trentham Books, 1992); Key, *Southern Politics*; Blatt, "Immigration Politics and Immigrant Collective Action"; Modood, "Ethnicity and Political Mobilisation."

68. On the disjuncture between the origins and sustenance of ethnic (and, by extension, racial) conflicts, see Ashutosh Varshney, "Nationalism, Ethnic Conflict, and Rationality," *Perspectives on Politics* 1 (2003): 85–99.

69. Ira Katznelson, "Structure and Configuration in Comparative Politics," in *Comparative Politics: Rationality, Culture, and Structure*, ed. Mark Irving Lichbach and Alan S. Zuckerman (Cambridge: Cambridge University Press, 1997).

70. Lieberman, "Ideas, Institutions, and Political Order." See also Peter A. Hall, "Policy Paradigms, Social Learning, and the State: The Case of Economic Policymaking in Britain," *Comparative Politics* 25 (1993): 275–96.

CHAPTER TWO

1. T. H. Marshall, "Citizenship and Social Class," in *Class, Citizenship, and Social Development* (Garden City, N.Y.: Doubleday, 1964); Peter Baldwin, *The Politics of Social Solidarity: Class Bases of the European Welfare State, 1875–1975* (Cambridge: Cambridge University press, 1990); Bo Rothstein, *Just Institutions Matter: The Moral and Political Logic of the Universal Welfare State* (Cambridge: Cambridge University Press, 1998); Gøsta Esping-Andersen, *The Three Worlds of Welfare Capitalism* (Princeton: Princeton University Press, 1990); Gary P. Freeman, "Migration and the Political Economy of the Welfare State," *Annals of the*

American Academy of Political and Social Science 485 (1986): 51–63; Ann Shola Orloff, "Gender and the Social Rights of Citizenship: The Comparative Analysis of Gender Relations and Welfare States," *American Sociological Review* 58 (1993): 303–28; Robert C. Lieberman, *Shifting the Color Line: Race and the American Welfare State* (Cambridge: Harvard University Press, 1998); Bill Jordan, *The New Politics of Welfare: Social Justice in a Global Context* (London: Sage, 1998), 207–11.

2. Anthony W. Marx, *Making Race and Nation: A Comparison of the United States, South Africa, and Brazil* (Cambridge: Cambridge University Press, 1998); Marx, "The Nation State and Its Exclusions," *Political Science Quarterly* 117 (2002): 103–26; Baldwin, *Politics of Social Solidarity.*

3. E. E. Schattschneider, *The Semisovereign People: A Realist's View of Democracy in America* (New York: Holt, Rinehart and Winston, 1960), 69.

4. Paul Pierson, *Dismantling the Welfare State? Reagan, Thatcher, and the Politics of Retrenchment* (Cambridge: Cambridge University Press, 1994); Paul Pierson, ed., *The New Politics of the Welfare State* (Oxford: Oxford University Press, 2001); Jacob S. Hacker, *The Divided Welfare State: The Battle over Public and Private Social Benefits in the United States* (Cambridge: Cambridge University Press, 2002).

5. George M. Fredrickson, *Racism: A Short History* (Princeton: Princeton University Press, 2002), 9.

6. On the concept of racial rule as a category that encompasses both slavery and colonialism, among a variety of other forms of power based in racial distinctions, see David Theo Goldberg, *The Racial State* (Malden, Mass.: Blackwell, 2002). Goldberg's essay usefully parses patterns of racialist thought and their articulation with state building and state power. He contrasts "naturalist" and "historicist" presumptions about racial difference—the former encompassing the belief in biological inferiority and the latter historical underdevelopment—and argues that these two formulations of race produce different forms of racial rule, "slavery, segregation, and forced labor in the former mode; assimilationism, indirect rule, and developmentalism in the latter." But his analysis remains at such a high level of abstraction, particularly his conceptualization of the state, that it offers few hooks on which to hang concrete analyses of the causal propositions that are embedded in his verbose and often impenetrable prose. The comparative history I offer in this chapter suggests that Goldberg's principal distinction is too facile to stand up to rigorous empirical analysis, although it is not set up as a direct test of his hypotheses. (Oddly, he criticizes Anthony Marx's *Making Race and Nation* for similar lapses even though Marx attempts—successfully, in my view—to develop and test similar theoretical propositions.)

7. W.E.B. Du Bois, *The Souls of Black Folk* (1903; reprint, New York: Library of America, 1986), 16; W. E. Burghardt Du Bois, "The Freedmen's Bureau," *Atlantic Monthly* 87 (March 1901): 354.

8. David Levering Lewis, *W.E.B. Du Bois: Biography of a Race, 1868–1919* (New York: Henry Holt, 1993); David Levering Lewis, *W.E.B. Du Bois: The Fight for Equality and the American Century, 1919–1963* (New York: Henry Holt, 2000); Carol Anderson, *Eyes Off the Prize: The United Nations and the African American Struggle for Human Rights, 1944–1955* (Cambridge: Cambridge Uni-

versity Press, 2003); Ira Katznelson, "Du Bois's Century," *Social Science History* 23 (1999): 459–74; Lawrie Balfour, "Unreconstructed Democracy: W.E.B. Du Bois and the Case for Reparations," *American Political Science Review* 97 (2003): 33–44.

9. Hannah Arendt, *The Origins of Totalitarianism* (New York: Harcourt, Brace Jovanovich, 1968), 185.

10. Du Bois, *Souls of Black Folk*, 16.

11. For a useful summary and synthesis, see Winfried Baumgart, *Imperialism: The Idea and Reality of British and French Colonial Expansion, 1880–1914* (New York: Oxford University Press, 1982); see also Rudolf von Albertini, *Decolonization: The Administration and Future of the Colonies, 1919–1960*, trans. Francisca Garvie (Garden City, N.Y.: Doubleday, 1971); Albert Memmi, *The Colonizer and the Colonized*, trans. Howard Greenfeld (New York: Orion Press, 1965); Stuart Hall, "Race, Articulation and Societies Structured in Dominance," in *Sociological Theories: Race and Colonialism* (Paris: Unesco, 1980); Fredrickson, *Racism*, 107–10.

12. Richard Franklin Bensel, *Sectionalism and American Political Development: 1880–1980* (Madison: University of Wisconsin Press, 1984), 73–83; Ira Katznelson, *City Trenches: Urban Politics and the Patterning of Class in the United States* (New York: Pantheon, 1981); Lawrence Goodwyn, *Democratic Promise: The Populist Moment in America* (New York: Oxford University Press, 1976); C. Vann Woodward, *The Strange Career of Jim Crow*, 3rd rev. ed. (New York: Oxford University Press, 1974); Theda Skocpol, *Protecting Soldiers and Mothers: The Political Origins of Social Policy in the United States* (Cambridge: Harvard University Press, 1992).

13. E. J. Hobsbawm, *The Age of Empire, 1875–1914* (New York: Pantheon, 1987); Benedict Anderson, *Imagined Communities: Reflections on the Origin and Spread of Nationalism*, rev. ed. (London: Verso, 1991).

14. Hobsbawm, *Age of Empire*, 102; Abram de Swaan, *In Care of the State: Health Care, Education and Welfare in Europe and the USA in the Modern Era* (New York: Oxford University Press, 1988).

15. Franklin D. Roosevelt, "Message to the Congress Reviewing the Broad Objectives and Accomplishments of the Administration, June 8, 1934," in *The Public Papers and Addresses of Franklin D. Roosevelt*, ed. Samuel I. Rosenman (New York: Random House, 1938), 3:291; see also Marshall, "Citizenship and Social Class."

16. Marx, *Making Race and Nation*.

17. The boundary between "white" and "nonwhite" has always been somewhat fluid, a matter of more than just genes and skin color. In interwar Britain, for example, natives of Malta, Cyprus, the Seychelles, Gibraltar, and Mauritius were exempted from registration requirements that were otherwise imposed on all "coloured" seamen, but only after a political battle. For the purposes of this discussion, I have simply used the common distinction made in contemporaneous documents between "European" and "indigenous" or "native" inhabitants. These data should not be taken as precise measures but rather as a broad-brush picture of nonwhite populations of the French and British empires. See Laura

Tabili, *"We Ask for British Justice"*: *Workers and Racial Difference in Late Imperial Britain* (Ithaca: Cornell University Press, 1994).

18. J. R. McCulloch, *A Statistical Account of the British Empire* (London: Charles Knight, 1837), 1:600; McCulloch, *A Descriptive and Statistical Account of the British Empire*, 4th ed. (London: Longmans, Brown, Green and Longman, 1854), 1:448; J. Milleret, *La France depuis 1830: Aperçus sur sa situation politique, militaire, coloniale, et financière* (Paris: Librairie Perrotin, 1838), vii, 547; U.S. Bureau of the Census, *Historical Statistics of the United States: Colonial Times to 1970* (Washington, D.C.: U.S. Government Printing Office, 1975), 1: 22.

19. *Fabianism and the Empire: A Manifesto by the Fabian Society* (London: Grant Richards, 1900), 15.

20. Raymond F. Betts, *France and Decolonisation, 1900–1960* (London: Macmillan, 1991), 15; James R. Grossman, *Land of Hope: Chicago, Black Southerners, and the Great Migration* (Chicago: University of Chicago Press, 1989); *The British Empire: A Report on its Structure and Problems by a Study Group of Members of the Royal Institute of International Affairs* (London: Oxford University Press, 1937); Charles W. Domville-Fife, *The Encyclopedia of the British Empire*, 3rd ed. (London: Virtue, n.d.); Maurice Allain, *L'Empire français d'outre mer: Le domain français par le texte et par l'image* (Montpellier: Editorial Argentor, 1939); Colin Dyer, *Population and Society in Twentieth Century France* (New York: Holmes and Meier, 1978), 64; Robert Delerm, *Cent millions de français* (Paris: Presses Universitaires de France, 1967); U.S. Bureau of the Census, *Historical Statistics*, 1:22; V. O. Key, Jr., *Southern Politics in State and Nation* (New York: Alfred A. Knopf, 1949).

21. Seymour M. Lipset and Stein Rokkan, "Cleavage Structures, Party Systems, and Voter Alignments: An Introduction," in *Party Systems and Voter Alignments: Cross-National Perspectives*, ed. Seymour M. Lipset and Stein Rokkan (New York: Free Press, 1967).

22. Because the impact of race on the American welfare state is a relatively common theme, the American case receives less weight in this chapter than in the rest of the book. The effect of colonialism and race on European political development, however, is less familiar and the British and French cases receive greater emphasis here. See Jill Quadagno, *The Color of Welfare: How Racism Undermined the War on Poverty* (New York: Oxford University Press, 1994); Charles Noble, *Welfare as We Knew It: A Political History of the American Welfare State* (New York: Oxford University Press, 1997); Lieberman, *Shifting the Color Line*; Michael K. Brown, *Race, Money, and the American Welfare State* (Ithaca: Cornell University Press, 1999); Martin Gilens, *Why Americans Hate Welfare: Race, Media, and the Politics of Antipoverty Policy* (Chicago: University of Chicago Press, 1999); Deborah Elizabeth Ward, "Mothers' Pensions: The Institutional Legacy of the American Welfare State" (Ph.D. diss., Columbia University, 2000); Sanford F. Schram, Joe Soss, and Richard C. Fording, eds., *Race and the Politics of Welfare Reform* (Ann Arbor: University of Michigan Press, 2003); George Steinmetz, "The Implications of Colonial and Postcolonial Studies for the Study of Europe," *European Studies Newsletter* 32, nos. 3–4 (January 2003): 1–3.

23. Gareth Davies and Martha Derthick, "Race and Social Welfare Policy: The Social Security Act of 1935," *Political Science Quarterly* 112 (1997): 217–35.

24. Rebecca J. Scott, "Fault Lines, Color Lines, and Party Lines: Race, Labor, and Collective Action in Louisiana and Cuba, 1862–1912," in Frederick Cooper, Thomas C. Holt, and Rebecca J. Scott, *Beyond Slavery: Explorations of Race, Labor, and Citizenship in Postemancipation Societies* (Chapel Hill: University of North Carolina Press, 2000); Marx, *Making Race and Nation*.

25. Skocpol, *Protecting Soldiers and Mothers*; Ann Shola Orloff, *The Politics of Pensions: A Comparative Analysis of Britain, Canada, and the United States, 1880–1940* (Madison: University of Wisconsin Press, 1993).

26. *Plessy v. Ferguson*, 163 U.S. 537 (1896), 544, 559.

27. Rogers M. Smith, *Civic Ideals: Conflicting Visions of Citizenship in U.S. History* (New Haven: Yale University Press, 1997); Desmond King, *Making Americans: Immigration, Race, and the Origins of the Diverse Democracy* (Cambridge: Harvard University Press, 2000); Matthew Frye Jacobson, *Whiteness of a Different Color: European Immigrants and the Alchemy of Race* (Cambridge: Harvard University Press, 1998); Gary Gerstle, *American Crucible: Race and Nation in the Twentieth Century* (Princeton: Princeton University Press, 2001); George M. Fredrickson, *The Black Image in the White Mind: The Debate on Afro-American Character and Destiny, 1817–1914* (New York: Harper and Row, 1971).

28. Richard M. Valelly, "National Parties and Racial Disenfranchisement," in *Classifying by Race*, ed. Paul E. Peterson (Princeton: Princeton University Press, 1995).

29. Key, *Southern Politics*; Ira Katznelson, Kim Geiger, and Daniel Kryder, "Limiting Liberalism: The Southern Veto in Congress, 1933–1950," *Political Science Quarterly* 108 (1993): 283–306.

30. Keith Krehbiel, *Pivotal Politics: A Theory of U.S. Lawmaking* (Chicago: University of Chicago Press, 1998); Skocpol, *Protecting Soldiers and Mothers*; Christopher Howard, "Sowing the Seeds of 'Welfare': The Transformation of Mother's Pensions, 1900–1940," *Journal of Policy History* 4 (1992): 188–227; Ward, "Mothers' Pensions."

31. Baldwin, *Politics of Social Solidarity*.

32. The remainder of this paragraph and the next rely on Lieberman, *Shifting the Color Line*.

33. Theda Skocpol, "The Limits of the New Deal System and the Roots of Contemporary Welfare Dilemmas," in *The Politics of Social Policy in the United States*, ed. Margaret Weir, Ann Shola Orloff, and Theda Skocpol (Princeton: Princeton University Press, 1988); Nancy J. Weiss, *Farewell to the Party of Lincoln: Black Politics in the Age of FDR* (Princeton: Princeton University Press, 1983); Edward G. Carmines and James A. Stimson, *Issue Evolution: Race and the Transformation of American Politics* (Princeton: Princeton University Press, 1989); Katznelson, *City Trenches*.

34. Martha Derthick, *Policymaking for Social Security* (Washington, D.C.: Brookings Institution, 1979).

35. Robert C. Lieberman and John S. Lapinski, "American Federalism, Race, and the Administration of Welfare," *British Journal of Political Science* 31 (2001): 303–29; Ira Katznelson, *Black Men, White Cities: Race, Politics, and Migration*

in the United States, 1900–30, and Britain, 1948–68 (Chicago: University of Chicago Press, 1976).

36. Sir Halford Mackinder, *The World War and After* (London: G. Philip, 1924), 266. Cited in Bernard Semmel, *Imperialism and Social Reform: English Social-Imperial Thought, 1895–1914* (London: George Allen and Unwin, 1960), 176.

37. There were, of course, whites living in the colonies, especially in Australia, Canada, and New Zealand, and South Africa, and also elsewhere in Africa, Asia and the Caribbean, although in these colonies white populations were quite sparse. One estimate in the 1920s put the white population of British territories in Africa (excluding South Africa) at twenty thousand out of forty-two million. *Labour and the Empire* (London: Trades Union Congress and the Labour Party, 1926), 8. There is something of a history of nonwhites in Britain, but theirs was a limited presence until the twentieth century. See Peter Fryer, *Staying Power: The History of Black People in Britain* (London: Pluto, 1984); Gretchen Gerzina, *Black London: Life Before Emancipation* (New Brunswick, N.J.: Rutgers University Press, 1995).

38. David Armitage, *The Ideological Origins of the British Empire* (Cambridge: Cambridge University Press, 2000); Uday Singh Mehta, *Liberalism and Empire: A Study in Nineteenth-Century British Liberal Thought* (Chicago: University of Chicago Press, 1999), 146–47; William Shakespeare, *Richard II*, 2.1.40–49.

39. Linda Colley, *Britons: Forging the Nation: 1707–1837* (New Haven: Yale University Press, 1992), esp. pp. 130–31.

40. Colley, *Britons*, 102–3; see also John Brewer, *The Sinews of Power: War, Money, and the English State, 1688–1783* (New York: Alfred A. Knopf, 1989).

41. Mehta, *Liberalism and Empire*. This school of thought is most closely associated with the Mills, James and his son John Stuart, both of whom made their careers with the East India Company, which governed India until 1858 when it passed to the responsibility of the Crown. See, especially, John Stuart Mill, *On Liberty* and *Considerations on Representative Government*.

42. Robert A. Huttenback, *Racism and Empire: White Settlers and Colored Immigrants in the British Self-Governing Colonies, 1830–1910* (Ithaca: Cornell University Press, 1976), 17–18.

43. Fryer, *Staying Power*, 14–15, 43–47.

44. Hobsbawm, *Age of Empire*, 85; Peter T. Marsh, *Joseph Chamberlain: Entrepreneur in Politics* (New Haven: Yale University Press, 1994); Peter Clarke, *Hope and Glory: Britain, 1900–1990* (London: Penguin, 1996), 20.

45. Douglas A. Lorimer, *Colour, Class and the Victorians: English Attitudes to the Negro in the Mid-Nineteenth Century* (Leicester: Leicester University Press, 1978), 157, 169; Partha Sarathi Gupta, *Imperialism and the British Labour Movement, 1914–1964* (New York: Holmes and Meier, 1975), 10; Bentley B. Gilbert, *The Evolution of National Insurance in Great Britain: The Origins of the Welfare State* (London: Michael Joseph, 1966), 202.

46. *Labour and the Empire*; *Labour's Colonial Policy, 1. The Plural Society* (London: Labour Party, 1956); Gupta, *Imperialism and the British Labour Movement*.

47. *Fabianism and the Empire*, 22.

48. Gupta, *Imperialism and the British Labour Movement*, 11–12.

49. Huttenback, *Racism and Empire*; Semmel, *Imperialism and Social Reform*; Marsh, *Joseph Chamberlain*, 406–47.

50. Alfred Milner, "The Two Nations," in *The Nation and the Empire* (London: Constable, 1913), 496; cited in Semmel, *Imperialism and Social Reform*, 180. On Jowett, Balliol, and their influence on Milner, see Frank M. Turner, *The Greek Heritage in Victorian Britain* (New Haven: Yale University Press, 1981), 414–32; Thomas Pakenham, *The Boer War* (New York: Random House, 1979), 5–6, 12–13.

51. Marsh, *Joseph Chamberlain*, 330, 341, 370–72, 563–75; John Macnicol, *The Politics of Retirement in Britain, 1878–1948* (Cambridge: Cambridge University Press, 1998), 65–75; Gilbert, *Evolution of National Insurance*, 198–99; Derek Fraser, *The Evolution of the British Welfare State: A History of Social Policy since the Industrial Revolution* (London: Macmillan, 1973), 130–31; Thomas C. Holt, *The Problem of Freedom: Race, Labor, and Politics in Jamaica and Britain, 1832–1938* (Baltimore: Johns Hopkins University Press, 1992), 317–18, 331–32.

52. Gilbert, *Evolution of National Insurance*, 60; Macnicol, *Politics of Retirement*, 142.

53. *Report of the Inter-Departmental Committee on Physical Deterioration*, Cd. 2175 (1904). The statistics on recruitment are on pp. 95–97. Desmond King, *In the Name of Liberalism: Illiberal Social Policy in the United States and Britain* (Oxford: Oxford University Press, 1999), 67; Gilbert, *Evolution of National Insurance*, 59–101.

54. Semmel, *Imperialism and Social Reform*; Gupta, *Imperialism and the British Labour Movement*.

55. Karl Polanyi, *The Great Transformation: The Political and Economic Origins of Our Time* (New York: Rinehart, 1944); Fraser, *Evolution of the British Welfare State*, 133–43. The quotation is on p. 143.

56. Gilbert, *Evolution of National Insurance*, 95–97; Macnicol, *Politics of Retirement*, 153; Paul M. Kennedy, *The Rise and Fall of British Naval Mastery* (New York: Scribner's, 1976), 205–37; Clarke, *Hope and Glory*, 53–56; Sven Steinmo, *Taxation and Democracy: Swedish, British, and American Approaches to Financing the Modern State* (New Haven: Yale University Press, 1993); Ann Shola Orloff and Theda Skocpol, "Why Not Equal Protection? Explaining the Politics of Public Social Spending in Britain, 1900–1911, and the United States, 1880–1920," *American Sociological Review* 49 (1984): 726–50.

57. Catherine Jones, *Immigration and Social Policy in Britain* (London: Tavistock, 1977), 14; David Roberts, *Victorian Origins of the British Welfare State* (New Haven: Yale University Press, 1960); José Harris, *Unemployment and Politics: A Study in English Social Policy, 1886–1914* (Oxford: Oxford University Press, 1972), 363–66. See also de Swaan, *In Care of the State*.

58. Baldwin, *Politics of Social Solidarity*, 99–102; A. I. Ogus, "Britain," in *The Evolution of Social Insurance, 1881–1981: Studies of Germany, France, Great Britain, Austria and Switzerland*, ed. Peter A. Köhler and Hans F. Zacher (London: Frances Pinter, 1982), 173–87; Desmond King, *Actively Seeking Work? The Politics of Unemployment and Welfare Policy in the United States and Great Britain* (Chicago: University of Chicago Press, 1995).

59. On the details of the pension plan, see Gilbert, *Evolution of National Insurance*, 222–24; Macnicol, *Politics of Retirement*, 155–62.

60. *Parliamentary Debates*, 4th ser., vol. 190 (1908), cols. 661–62 (Haldane), 672–76, 1567, 1569–70, 1742–43 (Asquith); Macnicol, *Politics of Retirement*, 158–61.

61. *Parliamentary Debates*, 4th ser., vol. 190 (1908), cols. 1570–71.

62. Jewish immigrants were, however, considerably less likely to be paupers than were members of the native British population. Jones, *Immigration and Social Policy*, 88–89.

63. *Parliamentary Debates*, 4th ser., vol. 190 (1908), cols. 1567–68, 1575 (Rawlinson), 1578–84.

64. Gilbert, *Evolution of National Insurance*.

65. *Parliamentary Debates* (Commons), 5th ser., vol. 25 (1911), col. 609.

66. Gilbert, *Evolution of National Insurance*, 287–88.

67. Marshall, "Citizenship and Social Class"; Semmel, *Imperialism and Social Reform*; Hobsbawm, *Age of Empire*, 101–4; Orloff and Skocpol, "Why Not Equal Protection?"

68. Sanford Elwitt, *The Third Republic Defended: Bourgeois Reform in France, 1880–1914* (Baton Rouge: Louisiana State University Press, 1986), 82–84.

69. Alice L. Conklin, *A Mission to Civilize: The Republican Idea of Empire in France and West Africa, 1895–1930* (Stanford: Stanford University Press, 1997); Raoul Girardet, *L'Idée coloniale en France de 1871 à 1962* (Paris: La Table Ronde, 1972), 47–48, 54.

70. D. Bruce Marshall, *The French Colonial Myth and Constitution-Making in the Fourth Republic* (New Haven: Yale University Press, 1973), 5–6.

71. Gary Wilder, "Framing Greater France Between the Wars," *Journal of Historical Sociology* 14 (2001): 198–220; Jean Rivero, "The Jacobin and Liberal Traditions," in *Liberty/Liberté: The American and French Experiences*, ed. Joseph Klaits and Michael H. Haltzel (Washington, D.C.: Woodrow Wilson Center Press; Baltimore: Johns Hopkins University Press, 1991); Dyer, *Population and Society in Twentieth Century France*, 5; Patrick Weil, *La France et ses étrangers: L'aventure d'une politique de l'immigration, 1938–1991* (Paris: Calmann-Lévy, 1991), 372–73; Girardet, *L'Idée coloniale*, 45; Marshall, *The French Colonial Myth*, 31–32; Alfred Cobban, *A History of Modern France* (New York: Braziller, 1965), 3: 91.

72. Eugen Weber, *Peasants into Frenchmen: The Modernization of Rural France, 1870–1914* (Stanford: Stanford University Press, 1976), esp. 3–22, 485–93. The quotation is on p. 485.

73. Zeev Sternhell, *Neither Right Nor Left: Fascist Ideology in France*, trans. David Maisel (Berkeley: University of California Press, 1986), 44–48; Pierre Birnbaum, *Jewish Destinies: Citizenship, State, and Community in Modern France*, trans. Arthur Goldhammer (New York: Hill and Wang, 2000). See also Cobban, *History of Modern France*, 3:90.

74. Gérard Noiriel, *The French Melting Pot: Immigration, Citizenship, and National Identity*, trans. Geoffroy de Laforcade (Minneapolis: University of Minnesota Press, 1996), 189–218; Catherine Wihtol de Wenden, *Les immigrés et la politique: Cent cinquante ans d'évolution* (Paris: Presses de la Fondation Natio-

nale des Sciences Politiques, 1988), 24–29; Rogers Brubaker, *Citizenship and Nationhood in France and Germany* (Cambridge: Harvard University Press, 1992), 98–102.

75. Albert Sarraut, *La mise en valeur des colonies françaises* (Paris: Payot, 1923), 113; quoted in Wilder, "Framing Greater France," 210. See also Marshall, *The French Colonial Myth*; Girardet, *L'Idée coloniale*, 24–25, 44; Herman Lebovics, *True France: The Wars over Cultural Identity, 1900–1945* (Ithaca: Cornell University Press, 1992); Eric Savarese, *L'ordre colonial et sa légitimation en France métropolitaine: Oublier l'autre* (Paris: L'Harmattan, 1998).

76. Wilder, "Framing Greater France," 210.

77. Sternhell, *Neither Right Nor Left*; Lebovics, *True France* Jacques Barzun, *Race: A Study in Superstition*, rev. ed. (New York: Harper and Row, 1965); Michael R. Marrus and Robert O. Paxton, *Vichy France and the Jews* (New York: Basic, 1981); Pierre Birnbaum, *The Idea of France*, trans. M. B. DeBevoise (New York: Hill and Wang, 2001), 228–41; Régis Debray, *La République expliquée à ma fille* (Paris: Seuil, 1998).

78. Semmel, *Imperialism and Social Reform*, 237–38; Baumgart, *Imperialism*; Bertrand Renouvin, *Charles Maurras, L'Action Française et la question sociale* (Paris: Ars Magna, 1983); Philip Nord, *The Republican Moment: Struggles for Democracy in Nineteenth-Century France* (Cambridge: Harvard University Press, 1995), 3, 59–61, 134–35; Cobban, *History of Modern France*, 3:21–24, 91–93; Elwitt, *Third Republic Defended*, 83–84. See also Frederick Cooper, *Decolonization and African Society: The Labor Question in French and British Africa* (Cambridge: Cambridge University Press, 1996); Girardet, *L'Idée coloniale*, 58–59, 146–47.

79. Stanley Hoffmann, "Paradoxes of the French Political Community," in Stanley Hoffmann et al., *In Search of France* (Cambridge: Harvard University Press, 1963), 5–8; Nord, *The Republican Moment*, 48–49. See also Vivien A. Schmidt, *Democratizing France: The Political and Administrative History of Decentralization* (Cambridge: Cambridge University Press, 1990), 43–45; Elwitt, *Third Republic Defended*, 67–68.

80. Hoffmann, "Paradoxes of the French Political Community," 15–16. For a contrasting view but one that also emphasizes the Third Republic's essentially narrow bourgeois character, see Nord, *The Republican Moment*. See also Ellen Immergut, *Health Politics: Interests and Institutions in Western Europe* (Cambridge: Cambridge University Press, 1992), 80–85.

81. Hobsbawm, *Age of Empire*, 102; Elwitt, *Third Republic Defended*, 293–95; Cobban, *History of Modern France*, 3:56–60.

82. Henri Hatzfeld, *Du paupérisme à la sécurité sociale: Essai sur les origines de la sécurité sociale en France, 1850–1940* (Paris: Armand Colin, 1971), 263–320.

83. Lebovics, *True France*, 62; Girardet, *L'Idée coloniale*, 118–19; Albertini, *Decolonization*, 265–68.

84. Skocpol, *Protecting Soldiers and Mothers*; Theda Skocpol, "African Americans in U.S. Social Policy," in *Classifying by Race*, ed. Peterson. For a contrasting view of Civil War pensions in the United States, see Linda Faye Williams, *The Constraint of Race: Legacies of White Skin Privilege in America* (University Park: Pennsylvania State University Press, 2003).

85. Schmidt, *Democratizing France*, 43–45, 52; Renouvin, *Charles Maurras*, 46–56.

86. Hatzfeld, *Du paupérisme à la sécurité sociale*; Herrick Chapman, "French Democracy and the Welfare State," in *The Social Construction of Democracy, 1870–1990*, ed. George Reid Andrews and Herrick Chapman (New York: New York University Press, 1995), 293–95; Baldwin, *Politics of Social Solidarity*, 102–5; de Swaan, *In Care of the State*, 146–48, 198–204; Elwitt, *Third Republic Defended*, 170–216; Douglas E. Ashford, "Advantages of Complexity: Social Insurance in France," in *The French Welfare State: Surviving Social and Ideological Change*, ed. John S. Ambler (New York: New York University Press, 1991); Yves Saint-Jours, "France," in *Evolution of Social Insurance*, ed. Köhler and Zacher, 107–119; Susan Pedersen, *Family, Dependence, and the Origins of the Welfare State: Britain and France, 1914–1945* (Cambridge: Cambridge University Press, 1993), 224–91; Lori Robin Weintrob, "From Fraternity to Solidarity: Mutual Aid, Popular Sociability, and Social Reform in France, 1880–1914" (Ph.D. diss., University of California, Los Angeles, 1996).

CHAPTER THREE

1. Gøsta Esping-Andersen, *The Three Worlds of Welfare Capitalism* (Princeton: Princeton University Press, 1990); Hilary Silver, "National Consequences of the New Urban Poverty: Social Structural Change in Britain, France and the United States," *International Journal of Urban and Regional Research* 17 (1993): 336–54; Giuliano Bonoli, "Classifying Welfare States: A Two Dimension Approach," *Journal of Social Policy* 26 (1997): 351–72; Paul Pierson, "Coping with Permanent Austerity: Welfare State Restructuring in Affluent Democracies," in *The New Politics of the Welfare State*, ed. Paul Pierson (Oxford: Oxford University Press, 2001), 428–31.

2. Pierson, "Coping with Permanent Austerity," 432; Paul Pierson, *Dismantling the Welfare State? Reagan, Thatcher, and the Politics of Retrenchment* (Cambridge: Cambridge University Press, 1994); Martin Gilens, *Why Americans Hate Welfare: Race, Media, and the Politics of Antipoverty Policy* (Chicago: University of Chicago Press, 1999).

3. Esping-Andersen, *Three Worlds of Welfare Capitalism*; Jonah D. Levy, "Vice into Virtue? Progressive Politics and Welfare Reform in Continental Europe," *Politics and Society* 27 (1999): 239–73; Bonoli, "Classifying Welfare States"; Mark Kesselman, "The Triple Exceptionalism of the French Welfare State," in *Diminishing Welfare: A Cross-National Study of Social Provision*, ed. Gertrude Schaffner Goldberg and Marguerite G. Rosenthal (Westport, Conn.: Auburn House, 2002); Gøsta Esping-Andersen, "Welfare States without Work: The Impasse of Labour Shedding and Familialism in Continental European Social Policy," in *Welfare States in Transition: National Adaptations in Global Economies*, ed. Gøsta Esping-Andersen (London: Sage, 1996).

4. Ann Shola Orloff, "Gender and the Social Rights of Citizenship: The Comparative Analysis of Gender Relations and Welfare States," *American Sociological Review* 58 (1993): 303–28; Julia S. O'Connor, Ann Shola Orloff, and Sheila

Shaver, *States, Markets, Families: Gender, Liberalism and Social Policy in Australia, Canada, Great Britain, and the United States* (Cambridge: Cambridge University Press, 1999).

5. On varieties of federalism, see Alfred C. Stepan, "Federalism and Democracy: Beyond the U.S. Model," *Journal of Democracy* 10, no. 4 (October 1999): 19–34.

6. Robert C. Lieberman, *Shifting the Color Line: Race and the American Welfare State* (Cambridge: Harvard University Press, 1998).

7. V. O. Key, Jr., *Southern Politics in State and Nation* (New York: Knopf, 1949); Grant McConnell, *Private Power and American Democracy* (New York: Knopf, 1966); Theodore J. Lowi, *The End of Liberalism: The Second Republic of the United States*, 2nd ed. (New York: Norton, 1979); Paul E. Peterson, *City Limits* (Chicago: University of Chicago Press, 1981); Paul E. Peterson, *The Price of Federalism* (Washington, D.C.: Brookings Institution, 1995); R. Kent Weaver, "The Politics of Blame Avoidance," *Journal of Public Policy* 6 (1986): 371–98.

8. Stephan and Abigail Thernstrom, *America in Black and White: One Nation, Indivisible* (New York: Simon and Schuster, 1997); Orlando Patterson, *The Ordeal of Integration: Progress and Resentment in America's "Racial" Crisis* (New York: Civitas/Counterpoint, 1997); Will Kymlicka, *Multicultural Citizenship: A Liberal Theory of Minority Rights* (Oxford: Oxford University Press, 1995).

9. Lieberman, *Shifting the Color Line*.

10. Senate Committee on Finance, *Economic Security Act*, 74th Cong., 1st sess., 1935, 641. See also Lieberman, *Shifting the Color Line*, chap. 2; Dona Cooper Hamilton and Charles V. Hamilton, *The Dual Agenda: The African-American Struggle for Civil Rights and Economic Equality* (New York: Columbia University Press, 1997), 27–32.

11. House Committee on Ways and Means, *Economic Security Act*, 74th Cong., 1st sess., 1935, 597–609. See also Regina Werum, "Sectionalism and Racial Politics: Federal Vocational Policies and Programs in the Predesegregation South," *Social Science History* 21 (1997): 399–453. The mention of "Judge Wharton" in the hearing transcript is a stenographer's error. Houston was referring to James Edwin Horton, the Alabama judge who presided over the 1933 retrial of Haywood Patterson, one of the nine black men accused of raping two white women on a train in 1931—known as the Scottsboro boys after the town in which they were initially jailed after their arrest. (The United States Supreme Court, in *Powell v. Alabama* [287 U.S. 45 (1932)], had overturned their initial convictions because they were denied the right to counsel.) Horton won praise for his fair conduct of the trial but was widely vilified in the South after he set aside the jury's guilty verdict and death sentence and ordered a new trial on grounds of insufficient evidence. The cases were subsequently transferred to another judge's court and Horton was defeated for reelection as a judge in 1934, ending a promising judicial and political career. See Dan T. Carter, *Scottsboro: A Tragedy of the American South*, rev. ed. (Baton Rouge: Louisiana State University Press, 1979), 192–273.

12. Senate Committee on Finance, *Economic Security Act*, 640–47; House Committee on Ways and Means, *Economic Security Act*, 796–98.

13. Edwin Amenta, *Bold Relief: Institutional Politics and the Origins of Modern American Social Policy* (Princeton: Princeton University Press, 1998). On race and the Works Progress Administration, see pp. 157–59. Alan Brinkley, *The End of Reform: New Deal Liberalism in Recession and War* (New York: Knopf, 1995).

14. This was less true of Unemployment Insurance, which is something of a federal-state hybrid than Old-Age Insurance, which is strictly a national policy. The structure of American public health insurance also mirrors that of income-support policy in that it is divided between a national social insurance program (Medicare) for the elderly and a decentralized means-tested program (Medicaid) for the poor. Lieberman, *Shifting the Color Line*, chap. 5; Theodore R. Marmor, *The Politics of Medicare* (Chicago: Aldine, 1973), 85; Lawrence R. Jacobs, *The Health of Nations: Public Opinion and the Making of American and British Health Policy* (Ithaca: Cornell University Press, 1993), 161–62.

15. Michael B. Katz, *In the Shadow of the Poorhouse: A Social History of Welfare in America* (New York: Basic, 1986); Katz, *The Undeserving Poor: From the War on Poverty to the War on Welfare* (New York: Pantheon, 1989); Frances Fox Piven and Richard A. Cloward, *Regulating the Poor: The Functions of Public Welfare* (New York: Pantheon, 1971); Karl Polanyi, *The Great Transformation: The Political and Economic Origins of Our Time* (New York: Rinehart, 1944); Theda Skocpol, *Protecting Soldiers and Mothers: The Political Origins of Social Policy in the United States* (Cambridge: Harvard University Press, 1992); Christopher Howard, "Sowing the Seeds of 'Welfare': The Transformation of Mother's Pensions, 1900–1940," *Journal of Policy History* 4 (1992): 188–227; Deborah Elizabeth Ward, "Mothers' Pensions: The Institutional Legacy of the American Welfare State" (Ph.D. diss., Columbia University, 2000); Christopher Howard, "The American Welfare State, or States?" *Political Research Quarterly* 52 (1999): 421–42; Lieberman, *Shifting the Color Line*.

16. Rogers M. Smith, *Civic Ideals: Conflicting Visions of Citizenship in U.S. History* (New Haven: Yale University Press, 1997); U.S. Social Security Board, *Social Security in America: The Factual Background of the Social Security Act as Summarized from Staff Reports to the Committee on Economic Security*, Social Security Board Publication No. 20 (Washington, D.C.: U.S. Government Printing Office, 1937), 184; W. Andrew Achenbaum, *Social Security: Visions and Revisions* (Cambridge: Cambridge University Press, 1986), 32–34.

17. In addition to Houston of the NAACP, leaders of the National Urban League, among others, expressed their disapproval of the Social Security Act's structure, and their positions were widely reported and applauded in the black press. Senate Committee on Finance, *Economic Security Act*, 487–89; "Interest in Negro Lacking, Says Wile," *New York Times*, 20 February 1935; "Exempted," editorial, *Pittsburgh Courier*, 9 March 1935; "Word of Warning," editorial, *Amsterdam News*, 28 January 1935, 8. See also Hamilton and Hamilton, *The Dual Agenda*.

18. Smith, *Civic Ideals*; Ira Katznelson and Sean Farhang, "The Southern Imposition: Congress and Labor in the New Deal and Fair Deal," *Studies in American Political Development* 19 (2005); Desmond King, *Making Americans: Immigration, Race, and the Origins of the Diverse Democracy* (Cambridge: Harvard University Press, 2000); Mae M. Ngai, "The Architecture of Race in American

Immigration Law: A Reexamination of the Immigration Act of 1924," *Journal of American History* 86 (1999): 67–92; Gary Gerstle, *American Crucible: Race and Nation in the Twentieth Century* (Princeton: Princeton University Press, 2001); Ira Katznelson, *City Trenches: Urban Politics and the Patterning of Class in the United States* (New York: Pantheon, 1981); Thomas J. Sugrue, "Crabgrass-Roots Politics: Race, Rights, and the Reaction against Liberalism in the Urban North, 1940–1964," *Journal of American History* 82 (1995): 551–78; Thomas J. Sugrue, *The Origins of the Urban Crisis: Race and Inequality in Postwar Detroit* (Princeton: Princeton University Press, 1996).

19. Pierson, *Dismantling the Welfare State?*; David R. James, "The Transformation of the Southern Racial State: Class and Race Determinants of Local-State Structures," *American Sociological Review* 53 (1988): 191–208; Robert C. Lieberman and John S. Lapinski, "American Federalism, Race and the Administration of Welfare," *British Journal of Political Science* 31 (2001): 303–29; Ira Katznelson, *Black Men, White Cities: Race, Politics, and Migration in the United States, 1900–1930, and Britain, 1948–1968* (Chicago: University of Chicago Press, 1976); Martin Shefter, *Political Parties and the State: The American Historical Experience* (Princeton: Princeton University Press, 1994); David Levering Lewis, *W.E.B. Du Bois: Biography of a Race, 1868–1919* (New York: Holt, 1993); David Levering Lewis, *W.E.B. Du Bois: The Fight for Equality and the American Century, 1919–1963* (New York: Holt, 2000); Nancy J. Weiss *The National Urban League, 1910–1940* (New York: Oxford University Press, 1974); Dean Robinson, *Black Nationalism in American Politics and Thought* (Cambridge: Cambridge University Press, 2001), 24–33; Eric Arnesen, *Brotherhoods of Color: Black Railroad Workers and the Struggle for Equality* (Cambridge: Harvard University Press, 2001); Beth Tompkins Bates, *Pullman Porters and the Rise of Protest Politics in Black America, 1925–1945* (Chapel Hill: University of North Carolina Press, 2001); Richard Kluger, *Simple Justice: The History of Brown v. Board of Education and Black America's Struggle for Equality* (New York: Knopf, 1975); Mark V. Tushnet, *The NAACP's Legal Strategy against Segregated Education, 1925–1950* (Chapel Hill: University of North Carolina Press, 1987); Daniel Kryder, *Divided Arsenal: Race and the American State During World War II* (Cambridge: Cambridge University Press, 2000); Philip A. Klinkner with Rogers M. Smith, *The Unsteady March: The Rise and Decline of Racial Equality in America* (Chicago: University of Chicago Press, 1999).

20. E.J.B. Rose, *Colour and Citizenship: A Report on British Race Relations* (London: Oxford University Press, 1969), 3.

21. Michel Wieviorka, *La France raciste* (Paris: Seuil, 1992), 25–26, 34–35; Pierre Rosanvallon, *The New Social Question: Rethinking the Welfare State*, trans. Barbara Harshav (Princeton: Princeton University Press, 2000), 13–16.

22. U.S. Social Security Board, *Social Security in America*, 17–27; Daniel T. Rodgers, *Atlantic Crossings: Social Politics in a Progressive Age* (Cambridge: Harvard University Press, 1998); A. I. Ogus, "Britain," in *The Evolution of Social Insurance, 1881–1981: Studies of Germany, France, Great Britain, Austria and Switzerland*, ed. Peter A. Köhler and Hans F. Zacher (London: Frances Pinter, 1982), 153–54, 189–90.

23. *Report of the Royal Commission on the Poor Laws and Relief of Distress*, Cd. 4499 (1909); Sidney and Beatrice Webb, *The Break-up of the Poor Law: Being Part One of the Minority Report of the Poor Law Commission* (London: Longmans, Green, 1909); Derek Fraser, *The Evolution of the British Welfare State: A History of Social Policy since the Industrial Revolution* (London: Macmillan, 1973), 146–49.

24. Board of Guardians (Default) Act 1926; Poor Law Act 1927; Local Government Act 1929.

25. Ann Shola Orloff and Theda Skocpol, "Why Not Equal Protection? Explaining the Politics of Public Social Spending in Britain, 1900–1911, and the United States, 1880–1920," *American Sociological Review* 49 (1984): 726–50.

26. Britain would resist imposing tariffs until 1931. E. J. Hobsbawm, *Industry and Empire: From 1750 to the Present Day* (London: Weidenfeld and Nicholson, 1968), 225–48; Peter Gourevitch, *Politics in Hard Times: Comparative Responses to International Economic Crises* (Ithaca: Cornell University Press, 1986), 76–83, 135–40.

27. Uday Singh Mehta, *Liberalism and Empire: A Study in Nineteenth-Century British Liberal Thought* (Chicago: University of Chicago Press, 1999); Desmond King, *In the Name of Liberalism: Illiberal Social Policy in the United States and Britain* (Oxford: Oxford University Press, 1999).

28. Smith, *Civic Ideals*; Ira Katznelson, "Liberal Maps for Technology's Powers: Six Questions," *Social Research* 64 (1997): 1333–37; Carol Horton, "Liberal Equality and the Civic Subject: Identity and Citizenship in Reconstruction America," and Rogers M. Smith, "Liberalism and Racism: The Problem of Analyzing Traditions," in *The Liberal Tradition in American Politics: Reassessing the Legacy of American Liberalism*, ed. David F. Ericson and Louisa Bertch Green (New York: Routledge, 1999).

29. Robert A. Huttenback, *Racism and Empire: White Settlers and Colored Immigrants in the British Self-Governing Colonies, 1830–1910* (Ithaca: Cornell University Press, 1976), 17–18; Lynn Hollen Lees, *Exiles of Erin: Irish Migrants in Victorian London* (Ithaca: Cornell University Press, 1979); Mary J. Hickman and Bronwen Walter, "Deconstructing Whiteness: Irish Women in Britain," *Feminist Review* 50 (1995): 5–19; Mary J. Hickman, "Reconstructing Deconstructing 'Race': British Political Discourses about the Irish in Britain," *Ethnic and Racial Studies* 21 (1998): 288–307; Mary Hickman, "'Binary Opposites' or 'Unique Neighbours'? The Irish in Multi-Ethnic Britain," *Political Quarterly* 71 (2000): 50–58; Randall Hansen, *Citizenship and Immigration in Post-War Britain: The Institutional Origins of a Multicultural Nation* (Oxford: Oxford University Press, 2000), 45–48, 109–119.

30. Catherine Jones, *Immigration and Social Policy in Britain* (London: Tavistock, 1977).

31. Hickman, "Reconstructing Deconstructing 'Race,' " 291–92.

32. T. H. Marshall, "Citizenship and Social Class," in *Class, Citizenship, and Social Development* (Garden City, N.Y.: Doubleday, 1964).

33. Bentley B. Gilbert, *The Evolution of National Insurance in Great Britain: The Origins of the Welfare State* (London: Michael Joseph, 1966), 165–67.

34. Laura Tabili, *"We Ask for British Justice": Workers and Racial Difference in Late Imperial Britain* (Ithaca: Cornell University Press, 1994); Anthony H. Richmond, *The Colour Problem: A Study of Racial Relations* (Harmondsworth: Penguin, 1955), 234–36.

35. Hansen, *Citizenship and Immigration*; Kathleen Paul, *Whitewashing Britain: Race and Citizenship in the Postwar Era* (Ithaca: Cornell University Press, 1997).

36. Peter Baldwin, *The Politics of Social Solidarity: Class Bases of the European Welfare State, 1875–1975* (Cambridge: Cambridge University Press, 1990); Douglas E. Ashford, "Advantages of Complexity: Social Insurance in France," in *The French Welfare State: Surviving Social and Ideological Change*, ed. John S. Ambler (New York: New York University Press, 1991); Pierre Laroque, ed., *The Social Institutions of France* (New York: Gordon and Breach, 1983), 113–50; Louis-Charles Viossat, "Protection et institutions sociales," in *La protection sociale en France*, ed. Marc de Montalembert (Paris: Documentation Française, 1995); Yves Saint-Jours, "France," in *The Evolution of Social Insurance*, ed. Köhler and Zacher; Henri Hatzfeld, *Du paupérisme à la sécurité sociale: Essai sur les origines de la sécurité sociale en France, 1850–1940* (Paris: Armand Colin, 1971); Bruno Palier, "'Defrosting' the French Welfare State," in *Recasting European Welfare States*, ed. Maurizio Ferrera and Martin Rhodes (London: Frank Cass, 2000), 116–17; Daniel Béland and Randall Hansen, "Reforming the French Welfare State: Solidarity, Social Exclusion and the Three Crises of Citizenship," *West European Politics* 23 (2000): 51–53; Stanley Hoffmann, "Paradoxes of the French Political Community," in Stanley Hoffmann et al., *In Search of France* (Cambridge: Harvard University Press, 1963); Herrick Chapman, "French Democracy and the Welfare State," in *The Social Construction of Democracy, 1870–1990*, ed. George Reid Andrews and Herrick Chapman (New York: New York University Press, 1995).

37. Susan Pedersen, *Family, Dependence, and the Origins of the Welfare State: Britain and France, 1914–1945* (Cambridge: Cambridge University Press, 1993); Saint-Jours, "France," 106–7, 118–19; Rémi Lenoir, "Family Policy in France Since 1938," in *The French Welfare State*, ed. Ambler; Barbara R. Bergmann, *Saving Our Children from Poverty: What the United States Can Learn from France* (New York: Russell Sage Foundation, 1996), 53–59.

38. Herman Lebovics, *True France: The Wars over Cultural Identity, 1900–1945* (Ithaca: Cornell University Press, 1992), 80–81; Charles-Robert Ageron, *France coloniale ou parti colonial* (Paris: Presses Universitaires de France, 1978); Pierre Birnbaum, *L'affaire Dreyfus: La république en péril* (Paris: Gallimard, 1994); Zeev Sternhell, *Neither Right Nor Left: Fascist Ideology in France*, trans. David Maisel (Berkeley: University of California Press, 1986); Pierre Birnbaum, *The Idea of France*, trans. M. B. DeBevoise (New York: Hill and Wang, 2001).

39. Alexis de Tocqueville, *Democracy in America*, trans. Harvey C. Mansfield and Delba Winthrop (Chicago: University of Chicago Press, 2000), 184.

40. Philip Nord, *The Republican Moment: Struggles for Democracy in Nineteenth-Century France* (Cambridge: Harvard University Press, 1995), 52; Gérard Noiriel, *The French Melting Pot: Immigration, Citizenship, and National Identity*, trans. Geoffroy de Laforcade (Minneapolis: University of Minnesota Press, 1996).

CHAPTER FOUR

1. Philip A. Klinkner with Rogers M. Smith, *The Unsteady March: The Rise and Decline of Racial Equality in America* (Chicago: University of Chicago Press, 1999); Daniel Kryder, *Divided Arsenal: Race and the American State During World War II* (Cambridge: Cambridge University Press, 2000); Mary L. Dudziak, *Cold War Civil Rights: Race and the Image of American Democracy* (Princeton: Princeton University Press, 2000); Thomas Borstelmann, *The Cold War and the Color Line: American Race Relations in the Global Arena* (Cambridge: Harvard University Press, 2001); John D. Skrentny, *The Minority Rights Revolution* (Cambridge: Harvard University Press, 2002); *Smith v. Allwright,* 321 U.S. 649 (1944); *Shelley v. Kraemer,* 334 U.S. 1 (1948); Michael R. Marrus and Robert O. Paxton, *Vichy France and the Jews* (New York: Basic, 1981).

2. "The Atlantic Charter. Official Statement on Meeting Between the President and Prime Minister Churchill. August 14, 1941." In *The Public Papers and Addresses of Franklin D. Roosevelt,* ed. Samuel I. Rosenman (New York: Harper and Brothers, 1950), 10: 315.

3. T. H. Marshall, "Citizenship and Social Class," in *Class, Citizenship, and Social Development* (Garden City, N.Y.: Doubleday, 1964).

4. Franklin D. Roosevelt, "'Unless There Is Security Here at Home, There Cannot Be Lasting Peace in the World'—Message to Congress on the State of the Union. January 11, 1944," in *Public Papers and Addresses,* 13: 41.

5. Edwin Amenta, *Bold Relief: Institutional Politics and the Origins of Modern American Social Policy* (Princeton: Princeton University Press, 1999); Margaret Weir, *Politics and Jobs: The Boundaries of Employment Policy in the United States* (Princeton: Princeton University Press, 1992); Alan Brinkley, *The End of Reform: New Deal Liberalism in Recession and War* (New York: Knopf, 1995); Ira Katznelson and Bruce Pietrykowski, "Rebuilding the American State: Evidence from the 1940s," *Studies in American Political Development* 5 (1991): 301–39. For an alternative periodization that perceives more continuity in this era of American liberalism, see David Plotke, *Building a Democratic Political Order: Reshaping American Liberalism in the 1930s and 1940s* (Cambridge: Cambridge University Press, 1996). See also Karen Orren and Stephen Skowronek, "Regimes and Regime Building in American Government: A Review of Literature on the 1940s," *Political Science Quarterly* 113 (1998–99): 689–702.

6. Edwin E. Witte, *The Development of the Social Security Act* (Madison: University of Wisconsin Press, 1962), 173–89, 208–10; Jacob S. Hacker, "The Historical Logic of National Health Insurance: Structure and Sequence in the Development of British, Canadian, and U.S. Medical Policy," *Studies in American Political Development* 12 (1998): 113–17; James A. Morone, *The Democratic Wish: Popular Participation and the Limits of American Government* (New York: Basic, 1990), 257–59; Martha Derthick, *Policymaking for Social Security* (Washington, D.C.: Brookings Institution, 1979); Jerry R. Cates, *Insuring Inequality: Administrative Leadership in Social Security, 1935–54* (Ann Arbor: University of Michigan Press, 1983); Robert C. Lieberman, *Shifting the Color Line: Race and the American Welfare State* (Cambridge: Harvard University Press, 1998).

7. Gøsta Esping-Andersen, *The Three Worlds of Welfare Capitalism* (Princeton: Princeton University Press, 1990), 70–71.

8. Christopher Howard, *The Hidden Welfare State: Tax Expenditures and Social Policy in the United States* (Princeton: Princeton University Press, 1997); Jacob S. Hacker, *The Divided Welfare State: The Battle over Public and Private Social Benefits in the United States* (Cambridge: Cambridge University Press, 2002); Weir, *Politics and Jobs*; Paul E. Peterson, *City Limits* (Chicago: University of Chicago Press, 1981); Robert C. Lieberman and Greg M. Shaw, "Looking Inward, Looking Outward: The Politics of State Welfare Innovation under Devolution," *Political Research Quarterly* 53 (2000): 215–40.

9. OECD, *New Orientations for Social Policy*, Social Policy Studies No. 12 (Paris: OECD, 1994); OECD Social Expenditures Database.

10. The OECD Social Expenditures Database, from which these figures were derived, divides public expenditures into thirteen major categories. The data for figure 4.1 are the totals of all categories; the data for figure 4.2 exclude the category "Health."

11. This figure is based on data collected and categorized by the International Labour Organization, and so it may not be strictly comparable with the OECD data reported in figures 4.1 and 4.2. Beginning in 1978, the ILO stopped reporting "Public Health" as a separate spending category and began folding it into the other categories as appropriate. International Labour Organization, *The Cost of Social Security* (Geneva: International Labour Organization, various years).

12. Edwin Amenta and Theda Skocpol, "Redefining the New Deal: World War II and the Development of Social Provision in the United States," in *The Politics of Social Policy in the United States*, ed. Margaret Weir, Ann Shola Orloff, and Theda Skocpol (Princeton: Princeton University Press, 1988); Peter Baldwin, *The Politics of Social Solidarity: Class Bases of the European Welfare State, 1875–1975* (Cambridge: Cambridge University Press, 1990).

13. *Social Insurance and Allied Services*, Cmd. 6404 (1942); John Macnicol, *The Politics of Retirement in Britain, 1878–1948* (Cambridge: Cambridge University Press, 1998), 347–84, 386; A. I. Ogus, "Britain," in *The Evolution of Social Insurance, 1881–1981: Studies of Germany, France, Great Britain, Austria and Switzerland*, ed. Peter A. Köhler and Hans F. Zacher (London: Frances Pinter, 1982), 190–95; Peter Clarke, *Hope and Glory: Britain, 1900–1990* (London: Penguin, 1996), 213–14; José Harris, "Some Aspects of Social Policy in Britain During the Second World War," in *The Emergence of the Welfare State in Britain and Germany, 1850–1950*, ed. W. J. Mommsen with Wolfgang Mock (London: Croom Helm, 1981), 258–59.

14. Macnicol, *Politics of Retirement*, 371–81.

15. Lawrence R. Jacobs, *The Health of Nations: Public Opinion and the Making of American and British Health Policy* (Ithaca: Cornell University Press, 1993), 167–89; J. Heß, "The Social Policy of the Attlee Government," in *The Emergence of the Welfare State*, ed. Mommsen and Mock; Derek Fraser, *The Evolution of the British Welfare State: A History of Social Policy since the Industrial Revolution* (London: Macmillan, 1973), 213–14.

16. Esping-Andersen, *The Three Worlds of Welfare Capitalism*, 70–71; Giuliano Bonoli, "Classifying Welfare States: A Two-Dimension Approach," *Journal*

of Social Policy 26 (1997): 351–72; OECD, *Social Expenditure, 1960–1990: Problems of Growth and Control* (Paris: OECD, 1985). Estimates of means-tested benefit spending in Britain were calculated from data reported by the UK Department for Work and Pensions, "Benefit Expenditure in Great Britain 1991/92 to 2003/04," available at www. dwp.gov.uk/asd/index.htm.

17. Peter A. Hall, *Governing the Economy: The Politics of State Intervention in Britain and France* (New York: Oxford University Press, 1986); Peter A. Hall and David Soskice, eds., *Varieties of Capitalism: The Institutional Foundations of Comparative Advantage* (Oxford: Oxford University Press, 2001); Paul Pierson, *Dismantling the Welfare State? Reagan, Thatcher, and the Politics of Retrenchment* (Cambridge: Cambridge University Press, 1994).

18. Baldwin, *Politics of Social Solidarity*, 116–34; Catherine Jones, *Immigration and Social Policy in Britain* (London: Tavistock, 1977), 185; Fraser, *Evolution of the British Welfare State*, 217.

19. OECD, *New Orientations for Social Policy*, Social Policy Studies No. 12 (Paris: OECD, 1994); OECD Social Expenditures Database; see also Pierson, *Dismantling the Welfare State?* 144–45.

20. Herrick Chapman, "French Democracy and the Welfare State," in *The Social Construction of Democracy, 1870–1990*, ed. George Reid Andrews and Herrick Chapman (New York: New York University Press, 1995), 295; Yves Saint-Jours, "France," in *The Evolution of Social Insurance*, ed. Köhler and Zacher, 122–24; Henry C. Galant, "The French Social Security System: The Politics of Administration" (Ph.D. diss., Harvard University, 1953), 39–42; Pierre Laroque, "From Social Insurance to Social Security: Evolution in France," *International Labour Review* 57 (1948): 565–90.

21. Saint-Jours, "France," 125–26; Galant, "The French Social Security System," 91–97; Chapman, "French Democracy and the Welfare State," 296; Douglas E. Ashford, "The Advantages of Complexity: Social Insurance in France," in *The French Welfare State: Surviving Social and Ideological Change*, ed. John S. Ambler (New York: New York University Press, 1991), 38–40. On the powers and limits of the French executive, see Ellen M. Immergut, *Health Politics: Interests and Institutions in Western Europe* (Cambridge: Cambridge University Press, 1992).

22. Ashford, "Advantages of Complexity," 41; Saint-Jours, "France," 129; Pierre Laroque, ed., *The Social Institutions of France* (New York: Gordon and Breach, 1983), 60, 113–20, 125–34; Baldwin, *Politics of Social Solidarity*, 163–86; Chapman, "French Democracy and the Welfare State," 297, 310–11.

23. Giuliano Bonoli and Bruno Palier, "From Work to Citizenship? Current Transformations in the French Welfare State," in *Citizenship and Welfare State Reform in Europe*, ed. Jet Bussemaker (London: Routledge, 1999), 47–49.

24. Susan Pedersen, *Family, Dependence, and the Origins of the Welfare State: Britain and France, 1914–1945* (Cambridge: Cambridge University Press, 1993); Gøsta Esping-Andersen, "Welfare States without Work: The Impasses of Labour Shedding and Familialism in Continental European Social Policy," in *Welfare States in Transition: National Adaptations in Global Economies*, ed. Gøsta Esping-Andersen (London: Sage, 1996); Paul Pierson, "Coping with Permanent Austerity: Welfare State Restructuring in Affluent Democracies," in *The New Politics*

of the Welfare State, ed. Paul Pierson (Oxford: Oxford University Press, 2001), 445–52; Laroque, *Social Institutions of France*, 323–48; Barbara R. Bergmann, *Saving Our Children From Poverty: What the United States Can Learn from France* (New York: Russell Sage Foundation, 1996); Jonah D. Levy, "Vice Into Virtue? Progressive Politics and Welfare Reform in Continental Europe," *Politics and Society* 27 (1999): 239–73; Daniel Béland and Randall Hansen, "Reforming the French Welfare State: Solidarity, Social Exclusion, and the Three Crises of Citizenship," *West European Politics* 23 (2000): 47–64.

25. Laroque, *Social Institutions of France*, 70, 103–5; Vivien A. Schmidt, *Democratizing France: The Political and Administrative History of Decentralization* (Cambridge: Cambridge University Press, 1990), 107; Mark Kesselman, "The Tranquil Revolution at Clochemerle: Socialist Decentralization in France," in *Socialism, the State, and Public Policy in France*, ed. Philip G. Cerny and Martin A. Schain (New York: Methuen, 1985); Douglas E. Ashford, "Decentralizing France," in *The French Socialist Experiment*, ed. John S. Ambler (Philadelphia: Institute for the Study of Human Issues, 1985).

26. Esping-Andersen, *Three Worlds of Welfare Capitalism*; Levy, "Vice into Virtue?"; Bonoli, "Classifying Welfare States." On the difficulties of characterizing France's welfare state, see Mark Kesselman, "The Triple Exceptionalism of the French Welfare State," in *Diminishing Welfare: A Cross-National Study of Social Provision*, ed. Gertrude Schaffner Goldberg and Marguerite G. Rosenthal (Westport, Conn.: Auburn House, 2002).

27. David R. Cameron, "Continuity and Change in French Social Policy: The Welfare State Under Gaullism, Liberalism, and Socialism," in *The French Welfare State*, ed. Ambler; Pierson, "Coping with Permanent Austerity," 445–48.

28. There is a gap in the middle of figure 4.5 because for the five-year period 1967–1971, there are no data for France reported in the International Labour Office Publication, *The Costs of Social Security*, from which this figure and the comparable figures for the United States and Britain (figures 4.3 and 4.4) were compiled. Also, health spending is not reported separately from other categories for France at any point in the time series.

29. Saint-Jours, "France," 142. By contrast, civil servants are less privileged compared to other workers in the American and British welfare states. In any event, combined public employee and social insurance expenditures are higher in France than in either the United States or Britain.

30. Esping-Andersen, "Welfare States Without Work."

31. Nicholas Lemann, *The Promised Land: The Great Black Migration and How It Changed America* (New York: Knopf, 1991), 6. On the earlier wave of black migration, see James R. Grossman, *Land of Hope: Chicago, Black Southerners, and the Great Migration* (Chicago: University of Chicago Press, 1989).

32. U.S. Bureau of the Census, *Historical Statistics of the United States, Colonial Times to 1957* (Washington, D.C.: U.S. Government Printing Office, 1960), 89–94; U.S. Bureau of the Census, *The Social and Economic Status of the Black Population in the United States: An Historical View, 1790–1978*. Current Population Reports, Special Studies Series P-23, No. 80 (Washington, D.C.: U.S. Government Printing Office, 1979).

33. The share of employed blacks working in agriculture declined from 62% in 1910 to 33% in 1940, 9% in 1960, and 3% in 1970. The share working in manufacturing and construction went from 9% in 1910 to 15% in 1940, 24% in 1960, and 26% in 1970. U.S. Bureau of the Census, *Social and Economic Status of the Black Population*, 73, 77.

34. Paul Frymer, *Uneasy Alliances: Race and Party Competition in America* (Princeton: Princeton University Press, 1999), 95–96.

35. Thomas J. Sugrue, *The Origins of the Urban Crisis: Race and Inequality in Postwar Detroit* (Princeton: Princeton University Press, 1996); Kenneth T. Jackson, *Crabgrass Frontier: The Suburbanization of the United States* (New York: Oxford University Press, 1985); Arnold R. Hirsch, *Making the Second Ghetto: Race and Housing in Chicago, 1940–1960* (Chicago: University of Chicago Press, 1998); Douglas S. Massey and Nancy A. Denton, *American Apartheid: Segregation and the Making of the Underclass* (Cambridge: Harvard University Press, 1993); Ira Katznelson, *Black Men, White Cities: Race, Politics, and Migration in the United States, 1900–1930, and Britain, 1948–1968* (Chicago: University of Chicago Press, 1976); David R. Mayhew, *Placing Parties in American Politics: Organization, Electoral Settings, and Government Activity in the Twentieth Century* (Princeton: Princeton University Press, 1986); Steven P. Erie, *Rainbow's End: Irish-Americans and the Dilemmas of Urban Machine Politics, 1840–1985* (Berkeley: University of California Press, 1988); Frymer, *Uneasy Alliances*.

36. Richard Franklin Bensel, *Sectionalism and American Political Development: 1880–1980* (Madison: University of Wisconsin Press, 1984); Barrington Moore, Jr., *Social Origins of Dictatorship and Democracy: Lord and Peasant in the Making of the Modern World* (Boston: Beacon, 1966); Richard Franklin Bensel, *The Political Economy of American Industrialization, 1877–1900* (Cambridge: Cambridge University Press, 2000); Katznelson, *Black Men, White Cities*, 36–42.

37. Zig Layton-Henry, "Britain: The Would-Be Zero Immigration Country," in *Controlling Immigration: A Global Perspective*, ed. Wayne A. Cornelius, Philip L. Martin, and James F. Hollifield (Stanford: Stanford University Press, 1994), 281; Gary P. Freeman, *Immigrant Labor and Racial Conflict in Industrial Societies: The French and British Experience, 1945–1975* (Princeton: Princeton University Press, 1979); Kathleen Paul, *Whitewashing Britain: Race and Citizenship in the Postwar Era* (Ithaca: Cornell University Press, 1997), 111–18; Rose, *Colour and Citizenship*, 66; Randall Hansen, *Citizenship and Immigration in Post-War Britain: The Institutional Origins of a Multicultural Nation* (Oxford: Oxford University Press, 2000), 35–61.

38. Ceri Peach, *West Indian Migration to Britain: A Social Geography* (London: Oxford University Press, 1968), 11–15; Katznelson, *Black Men, White Cities*, 33–34; Rose, *Colour and Citizenship*, 69; Freeman, *Immigrant Labor and Racial Conflict*, 23–34; Layton-Henry, "Britain," 275. The New Commonwealth comprises the West Indies, India, and Pakistan, as well as Cyprus, East and West Africa, and Hong Kong and excludes Australia, New Zealand, Canada, Rhodesia, and South Africa.

39. Hansen, *Citizenship and Immigration*, 62–79, 100–24, 169–76; Katznelson, *Black Men, White Cities*; Anthony M. Messina, *Race and Party Competition*

in Britain (Oxford: Oxford University Press, 1989); Freeman, *Immigrant Labor and Racial Conflict*, 24–25.

40. Anthony H. Richmond, *The Colour Problem: A Study of Racial Relations* (Harmondsworth: Penguin, 1955), 231; K. Jones and A. D. Smith, *The Economic Impact of Commonwealth Immigration*, National Institute of Economic and Social Research Occasional Paper 24 (Cambridge: Cambridge University Press, 1970), 5–13; Rose, *Colour and Citizenship*, 96–99; Ceri Peach, Vaughan Robinson, Julia Maxted, and Judith Chance, "Immigration and Ethnicity," in *British Social Trends since 1900: A Guide to the Changing Social Structure of Britain*, ed. A. H. Halsey (Houndmills: Macmillan, 1988), 564.

41. Peach, *West Indian Migration to Britain*, 62–68; Jones and Smith, *Economic Impact of Commonwealth Immigration*, 52–54; Peach et al., "Immigration and Ethnicity," 564; Richmond, *The Colour Problem*, 254; Crispin Cross, *Ethnic Minorities in the Inner City: The Ethnic Dimension in Urban Deprivation in England* (London: Commission for Racial Equality, 1978); J. A. G. Griffin, Judith Henderson, Margaret Usborne, and Donald Wood, *Coloured Immigrants in Britain* (London: Oxford University Press, 1960), 57, 216–17; Michael P. Banton, *The Coloured Quarter: Negro Immigrants in an English City* (London: Jonathan Cape, 1955).

42. Paul Foot, *Immigration and Race in British Politics* (Harmondsworth: Penguin, 1965).

43. Paul Foot, *The Rise of Enoch Powell: An Examination of Enoch Powell's Attitude to Immigration and Race* (Harmondsworth: Penguin, 1969); Hansen, *Citizenship and Immigration*, 182–90; Rose, *Colour and Citizenship*, 535–36, 545, 616–18.

44. On Goldwater's impact on the American party system, see Edward G. Carmines and James A. Stimson, *Issue Evolution: Race and the Transformation of American Politics* (Princeton: Princeton University Press, 1989); on Wallace's, see Dan T. Carter, *The Politics of Race: George Wallace, the Origins of the New Conservatism, and the Transformation of American Politics* (New York: Simon and Schuster, 1995). See also Thomas J. Sugrue, "Crabgrass-Roots Politics: Race, Rights, and the Reaction Against Liberalism in the Urban North," *Journal of American History* 82 (1995): 551–78.

45. Dilip Hiro, *Black British, White British: A History of Race Relations in Britain* (London: Grafton Books, 1991); Paul Gilroy, *"There Ain't No Black in the Union Jack": The Cultural Politics of Race and Nation* (London: Hutchinson, 1987), 236–40; Tariq Modood, "Ethnicity and Political Mobilisation in Britain," in *Ethnicity, Social Mobility, and Public Policy in the United States and the United Kingdom*, ed. Glenn Loury, Tariq Modood, and Steven Teles (Cambridge: Cambridge University Press, 2005); Charles Murray, "Underclass," *Sunday Times Magazine*, 26 November 1989; Messina, *Race and Party Competition*.

46. Immanuel Wallerstein, "Three Paths of National Development in Sixteenth-Century Europe," *Studies in Comparative International Development* 7 (1972): 95–101; Immanuel Wallerstein, *The Modern World-System: Capitalist Agriculture and the Origins of the European World-Economy in the Sixteenth Century* (New York: Academic Press, 1974); E. J. Hobsbawm, *Industry and Empire: From 1750 to the Present Day* (London: Weidenfeld and Nicholson, 1968);

Peter Fryer, *Staying Power: The History of Black People in Britain* (London: Pluto, 1984), 14–66.

47. Thomas C. Holt, *The Problem of Freedom: Race, Labor, and Politics in Jamaica and Britain, 1832–1938* (Baltimore: Johns Hopkins University Press, 1992); Frederick Cooper, Thomas C. Holt, and Rebecca J. Scott, *Beyond Slavery: Explorations of Race, Labor, and Citizenship in Postemancipation Societies* (Chapel Hill: University of North Carolina Press, 2000); Douglas Manley, Ivo de Souza, Albert Hyndman, et al., *The West Indian Comes to England: A Report Prepared for the Trustees of the London Parochial Charities by the Family Welfare Association* (London: Routledge and Kegan Paul, 1960), 15.

48. Rose, *Colour and Citizenship*, 22.

49. Gérard Noiriel, *The French Melting Pot: Immigration, Citizenship, and National Identity*, ed. Geoffroy de Laforcade (Minneapolis: University of Minnesota Press, 1996); Catherine Wihtol de Wenden, *Les immigrés et la politique: Cent cinquante ans d'évolution* (Paris: Presses de la Fondation National des Sciences Politiques, 1988), 18, 19–53; Patrick Weil, *La France et ses étrangers: L'aventure d'une politique de l'immigration, 1938–1991* (Paris: Calmann-Lévy, 1991), 370–73; Noiriel, *The French Melting Pot*, 100–105; Rogers Brubaker, *Citizenship and Nationhood in France and Germany* (Cambridge: Harvard University Press, 1992), 105–6. This is not an exhaustive list of countries sending immigrants to France, but it captures the main trends.

50. Weil, *La France et ses étrangers*, 54–62.

51. Ibid., 64.

52. Freeman, *Immigrant Labor and Racial Conflict*, 68–85; Patrick Ireland, *The Policy Challenge of Ethnic Diversity: Immigrant Politics in France and Switzerland* (Cambridge: Harvard University Press, 1994); Noiriel, *French Melting Pot*; Weil, *La France et ses étrangers*, 65–67; James F. Hollifield, "Immigration and Republicanism in France: The Hidden Consensus," in *Controlling Immigration*, ed. Cornelius, Martin, and Hollifield, 152–56; Weil, *La France et ses étrangers*, 68–87.

53. Michèle Tribalat, *Faire France: Une enquête sur les immigrés et leurs enfants* (Paris: La Découverte, 1995); Gérard Noiriel, "Difficulties in French Historical Research on Immigration," and Roxane Silberman, "French Immigration Statistics," in *Immigrants in Two Democracies: French and American Experience*, ed. Donald L. Horowitz and Gérard Noiriel (New York: New York University Press, 1992).

54. Freeman, *Immigrant Labor and Racial Conflict*, 21–23; Weil, *La France et ses étrangers*, 62, 64, 66, 369, 375, 384; Youssef Alouane, *L'Emigration maghrébine en France* (Tunis: Cérès Productions, 1979), 9–22; André Lebon, "Immigrés et étrangers en France: Tendances 1988 / mi-1989" (Paris: Documentation Française, 1989), 30–31, 41; Michèle Tribalat, *Faire France*, 183–214; Michèle Tribalat, "Les immigrés au recensement de 1990 et les populations liées à leur installation en France," *Population* 6 (1993): 1920; Nonna Mayer, *Ces français qui votent FN* (Paris: Flammarion, 1999), 248–50; Romain Garbaye, "Ethnic Minorities, Cities, and Institutions: A Comparison of the Models of Management of Ethnic Diversity of a French and a British City," EU Working Papers, RSC No. 2000/13 (San Domenico: European University Institute, 2000).

55. Robert C. Lieberman, "A Tale of Two Countries: The Politics of Color-Blindness in France and the United States," *French Politics, Culture and Society* 19, no. 3 (Fall 2001): 32–59; Michèle Lamont, *The Dignity of Working Men: Morality and the Boundaries of Race, Class, and Immigration* (New York: Russell Sage Foundation; Cambridge: Harvard University Press, 2000); Pierre Birnbaum, *The Idea of France*, trans. M. B. DeBevoise (New York: Hill and Wang, 2001); Eric Fassin, "'Good to Think': The American Reference in French Discourses of Immigration and Ethnicity," in *Multicultural Questions*, ed. Christian Joppke and Steven Lukes (Oxford: Oxford University Press, 1999); David Stuart Blatt, "Immigration Politics and Immigrant Collective Action in France, 1968–1993" (Ph.D. diss., Cornell University, 1996).

56. Geneviève Koubi, "Droit et minorités dans la république française," in *Le droit et les minorités: Analyses et textes*, ed. Alain Fenet (Brussels: Emile Bruylant, 1995), 213–14; Patrick R. Ireland, "Race, Immigration, and the Politics of Hate," in *The Mitterrand Era: Policy Alternatives and Political Mobilization in France*, ed. Anthony Daley (New York: New York University Press, 1996), 262–63; Schmidt, *Democratizing France*; Mayer, *Ces français qui votent FN*; Vaughan Rogers, "The Front National in Provence-Alpes-Côtes d'Azur: A Case of Institutionalized Racism?," in *Race, Discourse and Power in France*, ed. Maxim Silverman (Aldershot: Avebury, 1991); Françoise Gaspard, *A Small City in France*, trans. Arthur Goldhammer (Cambridge: Harvard University Press, 1995); Jonathan Marcus, *The National Front and French Politics: The Resistible Rise of Jean-Marie Le Pen* (New York: New York University Press, 1995); Garbaye, "Ethnic Minorities, Cities, and Institutions."

57. Rudolf von Albertini, *Decolonization: The Administration and Future of the Colonies, 1919–1960*, trans. Francisca Garvie (Garden City, N.Y.: Doubleday, 1971), 265–78.

58. There were an estimated 300,000 harkis, tens of thousands of whom were tortured and killed by the Algerian National Liberation Front for collaborating with the French, before approximately 75,000 of them were able to settle in France. Yvan Gastaut, *L'immigration et l'opinion en France sous la Ve République* (Paris: Seuil, 2000), 35–36; Sophie Body-Gendrot, "Immigration, Marginality, and French Social Policy," in *Poverty, Inequality, and the Future of Social Policy: Western States in the New World Order*, ed. Katherine McFate, Roger Lawson, and William Julius Wilson (New York: Russell Sage Foundation, 1995), 573–74.

59. Brubaker, *Citizenship and Nationhood*; Patrick Weil, *Mission d'étude des législations de la nationalité et de l'immigration* (Paris: Documentation Française, 1997); Miriam Feldblum, *Reconstructing Citizenship: The Politics of Nationality Reform and Immigration in Contemporary France* (Albany: State University of New York Press, 1999).

CHAPTER FIVE

1. Aldon D. Morris, *The Origins of the Civil Rights Movement: Black Communities Organizing for Change* (New York: Free Press, 1984); Fredrick C. Harris,

Something Within: Religion in African-American Political Activism (New York: Oxford University Press, 1999).

2. Although explicitly discriminatory arrangements, such as restrictive racial covenants on property deeds, were frequently upheld by the courts. See Michael Jones-Correa, "The Origins and Diffusion of Restrictive Racial Covenants," *Political Science Quarterly* 115 (2000–1): 541–68.

3. David J. Garrow, *Bearing the Cross: Martin Luther King, Jr., and the Southern Christian Leadership Conference* (New York: William Morrow, 1986), 266. Garrow is quoting from a January 1963 memo from Bayard Rustin and two colleagues to A. Philip Randolph proposing what became the March on Washington.

4. Mark H. Leff, "Taxing the 'Forgotten Man': The Politics of Social Security Finance in the New Deal," *Journal of American History* 70 (1983): 359–81; Edward D. Berkowitz, "The First Advisory Council and the 1939 Amendments," in *Social Security After Fifty: Successes and Failures,* ed. Edward D. Berkowitz (Westport, Conn.: Greenwood, 1987); Eric M. Patashnik, *Putting Trust in the U.S. Budget: Federal Trust Funds and the Politics of Commitment* (Cambridge: Cambridge University Press, 2000), 64–69.

5. Edwin Amenta, Bruce G. Carruthers, and Yvonne Zylan, "A Hero for the Aged? The Townsend Movement, the Political Mediation Model, and U.S. Old-Age Policy, 1934–1950," *American Journal of Sociology* 98 (1992): 308–39; Arthur J. Altmeyer, *The Formative Years of Social Security* (Madison: University of Wisconsin Press, 1966), 221–35, 298–301; Robert C. Lieberman, *Shifting the Color Line: Race and the American Welfare State* (Cambridge: Harvard University Press, 1998), 69–70; Julian E. Zelizer, *Taxing America: Wilbur D. Mills, Congress, and the State, 1945–1975* (Cambridge: Cambridge University Press, 1998), 79–80; Martha Derthick, *Policymaking for Social Security* (Washington, D.C.: Brookings Institution, 1979), 144–56; Edward D. Berkowitz, *Mr. Social Security: The Life of Wilbur J. Cohen* (Lawrence: University Press of Kansas, 1995), 81–85.

6. Robert C. Lieberman, "Race and the Organization of Welfare Policy," in *Classifying by Race,* ed. Paul E. Peterson (Princeton: Princeton University Press, 1995), 171–76; Michael K. Brown, *Race, Money, and the American Welfare State* (Ithaca: Cornell University Press, 1999), 129–31; Lieberman, *Shifting the Color Line,* 113–17.

7. Derthick, *Policymaking for Social Security,* 272–74; Zelizer, *Taxing America,* 66–81; Cates, *Insuring Inequality,* 104–35.

8. Zelizer, *Taxing America,* 317–43; Derthick, *Policymaking for Social Security,* 349–57; Joan Hoff, *Nixon Reconsidered* (New York: Basic, 1994), 135–36.

9. Derthick, *Policymaking for Social Security,* 345–46; David R. Mayhew, *Divided We Govern: Party Control, Lawmaking, and Investigations, 1946–1990* (New Haven: Yale University Press, 1991), 93, 107; Zelizer, *Taxing America,* 333–37; Herbert Stein, *Presidential Economics: The Making of Economic Policy from Roosevelt to Reagan and Beyond,* 2nd rev. ed. (Washington, D.C.: American Enterprise Institute, 1988), 188.

10. In fact, some economists believe, benefits since the 1970s may have grown faster than inflation, because indexing is based on the Consumer Price Index, which appears to overstate inflation. See R. Kent Weaver, "Controlling Entitlements," in

The New Direction in American Politics, ed. John E. Chubb and Paul E. Peterson (Washington, D.C.: Brookings Institution, 1985), 312; Advisory Commission to Study the Consumer Price Index [Boskin Commission], "Toward a More Accurate Measure of the Cost of Living," Final Report to the Senate Finance Committee, 4 December 1996.

11. Lieberman, *Shifting the Color Line*, 72; Melissa Nobles, *Shades of Citizenship: Race and the Census in Modern Politics* (Stanford: Stanford University Press, 2000), 79–84.

12. In 1999, life expectancies at birth in the United States were as follows: white men, 74.6 years; black men, 67.8 years; white women, 79.9 years; black women, 74.7 years. At age 65, life expectancies were as follows: white men, 16.1 years; black men, 14.3 years; white women, 19.2 years; black women, 17.3 years. Data are from the Centers for Disease Control, National Center for Health Statistics.

13. David Ellwood calls this dilemma, which is not unique to France, the "targeting-isolation" conundrum; see his *Poor Support: Poverty in the American Family* (New York: Basic, 1988), 23–25. On a parallel dilemma in the United States, see Theda Skocpol, "Targeting Within Universalism: Politically Viable Policies to Combat Poverty in the United States," and Robert Greenstein, "Universal and Targeted Approaches to Relieving Poverty: An Alternative View," in *The Urban Underclass*, ed. Christopher Jencks and Paul E. Peterson (Washington, D.C.: Brookings Institution, 1991).

14. Gary P. Freeman, *Immigrant Labor and Racial Conflict in Industrial Societies: The French and British Experience, 1945–1975* (Princeton: Princeton University Press, 1979), 77–79.

15. The FAS's full name was originally the Fond d'Action Sociale pour les Travailleurs Migrants (Social Action Fund for Migrant Workers). In 2001 it became the Fond d'Action et de Soutien pour l'Intégration et la Lutte contre les Discriminations (Fund for Action and Support for Integration and the Fight Against Discrimination), or FASID. On the Fourth Republic and the transition to the Fifth, see Philip M. Williams, *Crisis and Compromise: Politics in the Fourth Republic* (London: Longmans, Green, 1964); John D. Huber, *Rationalizing Parliament: Legislative Institutions and Party Politics in France* (Cambridge: Cambridge University Press, 1996), 1–2.

16. Stephen Castles and Godula Kosack, *Immigrant Workers and Class Structure in Western Europe* (London: Oxford University Press, 1973), 255–56; Robin S. Silver, "Conditions of Autonomous Action and Performance: A Study of the Fonds d'Action Sociale," *Administration and Society* 24 (1993): 494–95; Fonds d'Action Social pour les Travailleurs Migrants, *Dix ans au service des étrangers et des migrants* (Paris: Ministére du Travail, de l'Emploi, et de la Population, 1969); Pierre Laroque, ed., *The Social Institutions of France* (New York: Gordon and Breach, 1983), 741; Castles and Kosack, *Immigrant Workers and Class Structure*, 256.

17. Martin A. Schain, "Minorities and Immigrant Incorporation in France: The State and the Dynamics of Multiculturalism," in *Multicultural Questions*, ed Christian Joppke and Steven Lukes (Oxford: Oxford University Press, 1999), 211–14; Freeman, *Immigrant Labor and Racial Conflict*, 83; Yasemin Nuhoğlu Soysal, *Limits of Citizenship: Migrants and Postnational Membership in Europe*

(Chicago: University of Chicago Press, 1994), 59–61; Silver, "Autonomous Action and Performance," 505.

18. Margaret Weir, "The Politics of Racial Isolation in Europe and America," in *Classifying by Race*, ed. Paul E. Peterson (Princeton: Princeton University Press, 1995); Françoise Gaspard, *A Small City in France*, trans. Arthur Goldhammer (Cambridge: Harvard University Press, 1995); see also Paul E. Peterson, *City Limits* (Chicago: University of Chicago Press, 1981); Sophie Body-Gendrot, "Immigration, Marginality, and French Social Policy," in *Poverty, Inequality, and the Future of Social Policy: Western States in the New World Order*, ed. Katherine McFate, Roger Lawson, and William Julius Wilson (New York: Russell Sage Foundation, 1995), 577; Claude Taffin, "Le logement des étrangers en France," *Economie et Statistique* 242 (April 1991): 63–67; Sophie Body-Gendrot, *Ville et violence* (Paris: Presses Universitaires de France, 1993).

19. Romain Garbaye, "Ethnic Minorities, Cities, and Institutions: A Comparison of the Models of Management of Ethnic Diversity of a French and a British City," EU Working Papers, RSC No. 2000/13 (San Domenico: European University Institute, 2000); Damian Moore, "Marseille: Institutional Links with Ethnic Minorities and the French Republican Model," in *Multicultural Policies and Modes of Citizenship in European Cities*, ed. Alisdair Rogers and Jean Tillie (Aldershot: Ashgate, 2001).

20. Circulaire No. 90–028, 1 February 1990, in Bruno Liensol and Françoise Oeuvrard, "Le fonctionnement des Zones d'Education Prioritaires et les activités pédagogiques des établissements," *Education et Formations* 32 (November 1992): 45.

21. Christine Garin, "ZEP: La grande désillusion," *Autrement* 136 (March 1993): 97; Claude Mesliand, "Les zones d'éducation prioritaires: Evolution et perspectives," *Savoir* 8 (April–June 1996): 135; Hervé Deguin, *Un exemple d'élargissement des politiques sociales: Les zones d'éducation prioritaires de 1981 à 1986* (Paris: Institut d'études politiques de Paris, Section service public, 1987), 26B-27A.

22. Circulaire No. 81–536, 28 December 1981, in Deguin, *Un exemple d'élargissement*, 10.

23. Freeman, *Immigrant Labor and Racial Conflict*, 171–72; Weir, "The Politics of Racial Isolation," 236–39; Françoise Lorcerie, *Le partenariat et la "relance" du ZEP, Marseille, 1991–1992*, Rapport à la DPM et au FAS Septembre 1992 (Aix-en-Provence: Institut de recherches sur le monde arabe et musulman, 1993); Soysal, *Limits of Citizenship*, 60–61; Schain, "Minorities and Immigrant in France"; Michel Wieviorka, *La France raciste* (Paris: Seuil, 1992), 37–39.

24. Barbara R. Bergmann, *Saving Our Children from Poverty: What the United States Can Learn from France* (New York: Russell Sage Foundation, 1996), 34; "Deux maternelles de Montfermeil privées de cantine," *Le Monde*, 12 January 1990; "L'acceuil des enfants dans les maternelles," *Le Monde*, 13 January 1990; "Les deux écoles maternelles de Montfermeil fonctionnent normalement," *Le Monde*, 15 January 1990; Steven Greenhouse, "For Emigres, a Lesson that Begins in the Nursery," *New York Times*, 3 March 1990, 4; Haut Conseil à l'Intégration, *Lutte contre les discriminations: Faire respecter le principe de l'égalité* (Paris: Documentation Française, 1998), 16; Commission Nationale Consultative des Droits de l'Homme, *La lutte contre les discriminations et la xénophobie* (Paris:

Documentation Française, 1999), 176; François Vourc'h, Véronique de Rudder, and Maryse Tripier, "Racisme et discriminations dans le travail: Une réalité occultée," *L'Homme et la Société* 121–22 (July–December 1996): 157. One of these instances, the family leave case, was a decision of the Conseil d'Etat, the supreme authoritative appellate administrative body of the French state.

25. Michèle Tribalat, *Faire France: Une enquête sur les immigrés et leurs enfants* (Paris: La Découverte, 1995); Gérard Noiriel, "Difficulties in French Historical Research on Immigration," and Roxane Silberman, "French Immigration Statistics," in *Immigrants in Two Democracies: French and American Experience*, ed. Donald L. Horowitz and Gérard Noiriel (New York: New York University Press, 1992).

26. Jeroen Doomernik, "The Effectiveness of Integration Policies Toward Immigrants and Their Descendants in France, Germany, and the Netherlands," International Migration Paper No. 27 (Geneva: International Labour Organisation, Conditions of Work Branch, 1998), 27–29, 33–34; Michèle Tribalat, "Jeunes d'origine étrangère en France," *Futuribles* 215 (December 1996): 73–76.

27. Danièle Lochak, "Les discriminations frappant les étrangers sont-elles licites?" *Droit Social* (January 1990): 79–82; Zegers de Beijl, "International Migration for Employment," 12; Philippe Bataille, *Le racisme au travail* (Paris: La Découverte, 1997); Vourc'h, de Rudder, and Tripier, "Racisme et discriminations." See Roger Waldinger and Thomas Bailey, "The Continuing Significance of Race: Racial Conflict and Racial Discrimination in Construction," *Politics and Society* 19 (1991): 291–323.

28. Catherine Wihtol de Wenden, *Les immigrés et la politique: Cent cinquante ans d'évolution* (Paris: Presses de la Fondation National des Sciences Politiques, 1988); Tribalat, *Faire France*; Gérard Noiriel, *The French Melting Pot: Immigration, Citizenship, and National Identity*, trans. Geoffroy de Laforcade (Minneapolis: University of Minnesota Press, 1996); Rogers Brubaker, *Citizenship and Nationhood in France and Germany* (Cambridge: Harvard University Press, 1992); Alec G. Hargreaves, *Immigration, "Race" and Ethnicity in Contemporary France* (London: Routledge, 1995); Miriam Feldblum, *Reconstructing Citizenship: The Politics of Nationality Reform and Immigration in Contemporary France* (Albany: State University of New York Press, 1999); Vincent Geisser, *Ethnicité républicaine: Les elites d'origine maghrébine dans le système politique français* (Paris: Presses de la Fondation Nationale des Sciences Politiques, 1997).

29. Sylvia Dörr and Thomas Faist, "Institutional Conditions for the Integration of Immigrants in Welfare States: A Comparison of the Literature on Germany, France, Great Britain, and the Netherlands," *European Journal of Political Research* 31 (1997): 409; Laroque, *Social Institutions of France*, 107; Ian Gordon, "The Impact of Economic Change on Minorities and Migrants in Western Europe," in *Poverty, Inequality, and the Future of Social Policy*, ed. McFate, Lawson, and Wilson, 534–37.

30. Haut Conseil à l'Intégration, *Lutte contre les discriminations*, 15–19; ILO Convention No. 118, Convention Concerning Equality of Treatment of Nationals and Non-Nationals in Social Security. Neither the United Kingdom nor the United States has ratified the convention.

31. Bergmann, *Saving Our Children From Poverty*, 50–51, 66.

32. Dörr and Faist, "Institutional Conditions"; René Lenoir, *Les Exclus: Un français sur dix* (Paris: Seuil, 1993); Hilary Silver, "Social Exclusion and Social Solidarity: Three Paradigms," *International Labour Review* 133 (1994): 531–78; Martin Evans, "Beyond the Rhetoric: The Institutional Basis of Social Exclusion," *IDS Bulletin* 29 (1998): 42–49.

33. Paul Spicker, "Concepts of Welfare and Solidarity in Britain and France," in *Discourse on Inequality*, ed. Edwards and Révauger; Serge Paugam, *La société française et ses pauvres: L'expérience du revenu minimum d'insertion* (Paris: Presses Universitaires de France, 1993), 87–106, 158.

34. Patrick Ireland, *The Policy Challenge of Ethnic Diversity: Immigrant Politics in France and Switzerland* (Cambridge: Harvard University Press, 1994); David Stuart Blatt, "Immigration Politics and Immigrant Collective Action in France, 1968–1993" (Ph.D. diss., Cornell University, 1996); Juliette Minces, "Inequalities in France: The Case of Immigration," trans. Paul Hartley, in *Equality and Inequality in France*, ed. Peter Morris (Proceedings of the Fourth Annual Conference of the Association for the Study of Modern and Contemporary France, 1983); Dörr and Faist, "Institutional Conditions," 410–14; Bataille, *Le racisme au travail*, 75–103.

35. Laroque, *Social Institutions of France*, 730; Loïc J. D. Wacquant, "The Comparative Structure and Experience of Urban Exclusion: 'Race,' Class, and Space in Chicago and Paris," in *Poverty, Inequality, and the Future of Social Policy*, ed. McFate, Lawson, and Wilson, 553, 561; Abdelkader Balbahri, *Immigrations et situations postcoloniales: Le cas des maghrébins en France* (Paris: L'Harmattan, 1982); Michel Forsé, Jean-Pierre Jaslin, Yannick Lemel, Henri Mendras, Denis Stoclet, and Jean-Hugues Déchaux, *Recent Social Trends in France: 1960–1990*, trans. Liam Gavin (Frankfurt am Main: Campus Verlag; Montreal: McGill-Queens University Press, 1993), 329–30, 332; Doomernik, "The Effectiveness of Integration Policies,"; Ashford, "Advantages of Complexity"; Loïc J. D. Wacquant, "Urban Outcasts: Stigma and Division in the Black American Ghetto and the French Urban Periphery," *International Journal of Urban and Regional Research* 17 (1993): 366–83; Weir, "The Politics of Racial Isolation"; Roger Lawson and William Julius Wilson, "Poverty, Social Rights, and the Quality of Citizenship," in *Poverty, Inequality, and the Future of Social Policy*, ed. McFate, Lawson, and Wilson; William Julius Wilson, *When Work Disappears: The World of the New Urban Poor* (New York: Knopf, 1996).

CHAPTER SIX

1. Frances Fox Piven and Richard A. Cloward, *Poor People's Movements: Why They Succeed, How They Fail* (New York: Pantheon, 1977).

2. Robert C. Lieberman, *Shifting the Color Line: Race and the American Welfare State* (Cambridge: Harvard University Press, 1998), 150–51; Robert C. Lieberman and John S. Lapinski, "American Federalism, Race, and the Administration of Welfare," *British Journal of Political Science* 31 (2001): 303–29; Robert C. Lieberman, "Political Time and Policy Coalitions: Structure and Agency in Presidential Power," in *Presidential Power: Forging the Presidency for the Twenty-*

First Century, ed. Robert Y. Shapiro, Martha Joynt Kumar, and Lawrence R. Jacobs (New York: Columbia University Press, 2000), 286–87.

3. Frances Fox Piven and Richard A. Cloward, *Regulating the Poor: The Functions of Public Welfare* (New York: Pantheon, 1971), 139–40, 192, 354–65; Jacob Fisher, "The Comparability of Public Assistance Payments and Social Insurance Benefits," *Social Security Bulletin* 7 (December 1944): 9; Steven M. Teles, *Whose Welfare? AFDC and Elite Politics* (Lawrence: University Press of Kansas, 1996), 24–26; Winifred Bell, *Aid to Dependent Children* (New York: Columbia University Press, 1965), 137–51; "Suffer Little Children," *Nation* 191 (24 September 1960): 171; Joseph P. Ritz, *The Despised Poor: Newburgh's War on Welfare* (Boston: Beacon, 1966); see Lieberman, *Shifting the Color Line,* 155–61.

4. See Stephen Skowronek, *The Politics Presidents Make: Leadership from John Adams to George Bush* (Cambridge: Harvard University Press, 1993), 332–41; Robert Dallek, *Flawed Giant: Lyndon Johnson and His Times* (New York: Oxford University Press, 1998), 60–61, 75–77, 83.

5. White House Conference "To Fulfill These Rights," Council's Report and Recommendations to the Conferences, 1–2 June 1966, in *Civil Rights During the Johnson Administration,* part 1, reel 6, 30–31. This report language was drafted by the staff members organizing the conference and submitted to the White House for approval in advance of the conference, which was held in early June 1966. On the links between the civil rights and social welfare agendas, see Dona Cooper Hamilton and Charles V. Hamilton, *The Dual Agenda: The African-American Struggle for Civil Rights and Economic Equality* (New York: Columbia University Press, 1997).

6. Ira Katznelson, "Was the Great Society a Lost Opportunity?," in *The Rise and Fall of the New Deal Order, 1930–1980,* ed. Steve Fraser and Gary Gerstle (Princeton: Princeton University Press, 1989).

7. *Social Security Bulletin,* Annual Statistical Supplement, 1967, 124; Piven and Cloward, *Regulating the Poor,* 354–65; Lieberman, "Political Time and Policy Coalitions."

8. On the assembly and adoption of the Economic Opportunity Act, see James L. Sundquist, *Politics and Policy: The Eisenhower, Kennedy, and Johnson Years* (Washington, D.C.: Brookings Institution, 1968), 134–49; Daniel P. Moynihan, *Maximum Feasible Misunderstanding: Community Action in the War on Poverty* (New York: Free Press, 1969); Allen J. Matusow, *The Unraveling of America: A History of Liberalism in the 1960s* (New York: Harper and Row, 1984), 244–47; Gareth Davies, *From Opportunity to Entitlement: The Transformation and Decline of Great Society Liberalism* (Lawrence: University Press of Kansas, 1996), 30–53.

9. Ira Katznelson, Kim Geiger, and Daniel Kryder, "Limiting Liberalism: The Southern Veto in Congress, 1933–1950," *Political Science Quarterly* 108 (1993): 283–306; Keith T. Poole and Howard Rosenthal, *Congress: A Political-Economic History of Roll Call Voting* (New York: Oxford University Press, 1997), 44; telephone conversation between John F. Kennedy and Carl Albert, 12 June 1963, quoted in Taylor Branch, *Parting the Waters: America in the King Years, 1954–1963* (New York: Simon and Schuster, 1988), 827–28.

10. J. David Greenstone, *Labor in American Politics* (New York: Knopf, 1969); Nelson Lichtenstein, "From Corporatism to Collective Bargaining: Organized Labor and the Eclipse of Social Democracy in the Postwar Era," in *The Rise and Fall of the New Deal Order*, ed. Fraser and Gerstle; David R. Mayhew, *Placing Parties in American Politics: Organization, Electoral Settings, and Government Activity in the Twentieth Century* (Princeton: Princeton University Press, 1986), 318–27; Thomas J. Sugrue, "Crabgrass-Roots Politics: Race, Rights, and the Reaction against Liberalism in the Urban North, 1940–1964," *Journal of American History* 82 (1995): 551–78; John David Skrentny, *The Ironies of Affirmative Action: Politics, Culture, and Justice in America* (Chicago: University of Chicago Press, 1996); Hugh Davis Graham, *The Civil Rights Era: Origins and Development of National Policy, 1960–1972* (New York: Oxford University Press, 1990).

11. Robert A. Caro, *Master of the Senate* (New York: Knopf, 2002).

12. Expanding the committee was Rayburn's (and Kennedy's) original intention during the months after the 1960 election. As the Eighty-Seventh Congress opened in January 1961, it appeared that Rayburn would not be able to marshal enough votes in the House to carry the proposal, and so he switched his focus to purging Colmer, who had openly opposed the Kennedy-Johnson ticket, from the committee and replacing him with a "party regular." When this option ran into obstacles, Rayburn returned to the original plan of committee expansion and muscled it through the House. John D. Morris, "Congress Likely to Give Kennedy Most of Program," *New York Times*, 1 January 1961, 1, 26; John D. Morris, "Congress to Open Today; Rayburn Moving to Curb Conservative Rules Bloc," *New York Times*, 3 January 1961, 1, 18; John D. Morris, "Kennedy Wins in House, 217 to 212, on Rules Committee Expansion; Drafts New Plans for Congress," *New York Times*, 1 February 1961, 1, 24.

13. Edward G. Carmines and James A. Stimson, *Issue Evolution: Race and the Transformation of American Politics* (Princeton: Princeton University Press, 1989).

14. A diminution of local control over AFDC did occur after about 1969, as a result of action by the federal courts rather than Congress. See R. Shep Melnick, *Between the Lines: Interpreting Welfare Rights* (Washington, D.C.: Brookings Institution, 1994), and Teles, *Whose Welfare?*

15. James A. Morone, *The Democratic Wish: Popular Participation and the Limits of American Government* (New York: Basic, 1990), 218–52; J. David Greenstone and Paul E. Peterson, *Race and Authority in Urban Politics: Community Participation and the War on Poverty* (New York: Russell Sage Foundation, 1973); Sundquist, *Politics and Policy*, 141–45, 151–54; Matusow, *Unraveling of America*, 111–12, 113–14, 125–26.

16. House Committee on Ways and Means, *Economic Security Act*, 974–77; *Congressional Record*, 88th Cong., 2nd sess., 1964, 110, pt. 14: 18198–99; Lieberman, *Shifting the Color Line*, 52–53.

17. House Committee on Education and Labor, Subcommittee on the War on Poverty Program, *Economic Opportunity Act of 1964*, 88th Cong., 2d sess., 1964, 322; Carmines and Stimson, *Issue Evolution*; Sundquist, *Politics and Policy*, 147, 149.

18. Lyndon Baines Johnson, *The Vantage Point: Perspectives of the Presidency, 1963–1969* (New York: Holt, Rinehart and Winston, 1971), 77–78; Charles V. Hamilton, *Adam Clayton Powell, Jr.: The Political Biography of an American Dilemma* (New York: Atheneum, 1991), 369–74; Sundquist, *Politics and Policy,* 148. See also Moynihan, *Maximum Feasible Misunderstanding.*

19. "Antipoverty Aide Says Wallace Sought Ouster," *New York Times,* 12 March 1965, 19; Marjorie Hunter, "Wallace Defied on Poverty Funds," *New York Times,* 14 April 1965; Roy Reed, "Wallace Vetoes a Poverty Grant," *New York Times,* 12 May 1965; Marjorie Hunter, "House Group Votes Poverty Veto Curb," *New York Times,* 14 May 1965, 1, 18; Marjorie Hunter, "Poverty Program May Restore Veto," *New York Times,* 18 May 1965, 39; Marjorie Hunter, "Governors to Get Antipoverty Veto," *New York Times,* 21 May 1965, 16; *Congressional Quarterly Almanac* 21 (1965): 406; Sundquist, *Politics and Policy,* 149–50.

20. Richard P. Young and Jerome S. Burstein, "Federalism and the Demise of Prescriptive Racism in the United States," *Studies in American Political Development* 9 (1995): 1–54.

21. Contrast this interpretation with the claim that in 1964, Southern Democrats no longer had an incentive to block national welfare legislation because of the demise of manual cotton agriculture and the accompanying disappearance of paternalism in the Southern political economy. See Lee J. Alston and Joseph P. Ferrie, *Southern Paternalism and the American Welfare State: Economics, Politics, and Institutions in the South, 1865–1965* (Cambridge: Cambridge University Press, 1999).

22. Morone, *Democratic Wish,* 233–42; Moynihan, *Maximum Feasible Misunderstanding,* 150; Matusow, *Unraveling of American Liberalism,* 253–54.

23. Memorandum, Carl Holman to Lee White, 16 December 1967, Office Files of Lee C. White, Box 5, Lyndon B. Johnson Library (hereafter cited as LBJL); Lieberman and Lapinski, "American Federalism"; Greenstone and Peterson, *Race and Authority in Urban Politics;* Matusow, *Unraveling of American Liberalism,* 245–52.

24. Katznelson, Geiger, and Kryder, "Limiting Liberalism."

25. See Matusow, *Unraveling of American Liberalism,* 269–70; Davies, *From Opportunity to Entitlement,* 196–97; Scott J. Spitzer, "The Liberal Dilemma: Welfare and Race, 1960–1975" (Ph.D. diss., Columbia University, 2000), 237–38.

26. *Congressional Record,* 90th Cong., 1st sess., 1967, 113, pt. 23: 31411, 31414–15.

27. *Congressional Quarterly Weekly Report* 22 (1967): 2319.

28. Lyndon B. Johnson, "Special Message to the Congress Recommending a 12-Point Program for America's Children and Youth, February 8, 1967," in *Public Papers of the Presidents of the United States: Lyndon B. Johnson, 1967* (Washington, D.C.: U.S. Government Printing Office, 1968), 155; Davies, *From Opportunity to Entitlement,* 160–61; Lieberman, *Shifting the Color Line,* 51–52.

29. Lyndon B. Johnson, "Commencement Address at Howard University: 'To Fulfill These Rights,' June 4, 1965," in *Public Papers of the Presidents of the United States: Lyndon B. Johnson, 1965* (Washington, D.C.: U.S. Government Printing Office 1966), 636.

30. Thomas J. Sugrue, *The Origins of the Urban Crisis: Race and Inequality in Postwar Detroit* (Princeton: Princeton University Press, 1996), 259–60; National Advisory Commission on Civil Disorders [Kerner Commission], *Report* (New York: Bantam, 1968), 35–108, and charts (unpaginated).

31. Memorandum, Carl Holman to Lee White, 16 December 1965, Office Files of Lee C. White, Box 5, LBJL; Memorandum, Humphrey to Johnson, 27 July 1967, HU, White House Central File (hereafter cited as WHCF), Box 5, LBJL.

32. Memorandum, Califano to Johnson, 25 July 1967, WE, WHCF, Box 30, LBJL.

33. Memorandum, Fred Panzer to Johnson, 18 September 1967, Confidential File, Box 82, LBJL.

34. Memorandum, Loyd Hackler to Johnson, 2 August 1967, HU, WHCF, Box 6, LBJL.

35. "Myths and Facts about OEO," September 1967, WE, WHCF, Box 30, LBJL.

36. Julian E. Zelizer, *Taxing America: Wilbur D. Mills, Congress, and the State, 1945–1975* (Cambridge: Cambridge University Press, 1998); Gilbert Y. Steiner, *The State of Welfare* (Washington, D.C.: Brookings Institution, 1971), 44–46.

37. Lieberman, *Shifting the Color Line*, 170–73; *Congressional Record*, 90th Cong., 2nd sess., 113, pt. 17: 22783, 23058–59, pt. 27, 36679–82; Senate Committee on Finance, *Social Security Amendments of 1967*, 1260–61, 1263; Piven and Cloward, *Poor People's Movements*, chap. 5; John W. Finley, "Senate Liberals Caught Napping," *New York Times*, 15 December 1967, 1, 20.

38. *King v. Smith* [392 U.S. 309 (1968)] limited states' discretion in setting eligibility rules; *Shapiro v. Thompson* [394 U.S. 618 (1969)] struck down state residency requirements for AFDC; *Goldberg v. Kelly* [397 U.S. 254 (1970)] required a hearing before a state could cut off an individual recipient's benefits. See Melnick, *Between the Lines*, 65–132; Teles, *Whose Welfare?* 107–16.

39. Paul E. Peterson, *City Limits* (Chicago: University of Chicago Press, 1981); Paul E. Peterson, *The Price of Federalism* (Washington, D.C.: Brookings Institution, 1995); Lieberman, *Shifting the Color Line*; Lieberman and Lapinski, "American Federalism."

40. Teles, *Whose Welfare?*, 19–24; Richard C. Fording, "The Political Response to Black Insurgency: A Critical Test of Competing Theories of the State," *American Political Science Review* 95 (2001): 115–30.

41. Before the 1980s, AFDC data were not reported separately for Hispanics. For later data, the categories "White" and "Black" refer only to non-Hispanics. ADC/AFDC/TANF data are from Fisher, "Comparability of Public Assistance Payments"; Elizabeth Alling and Agnes Leisy, "Aid to Dependent Children in a Postwar Year," *Social Security Bulletin* 13 (August 1950): 5; and the publication that was variously called "Characteristics and Incomes of Families Assisted by Aid to Dependent Children," "Characteristics and Financial Circumstances of AFDC Recipients," and currently the TANF "Annual Report to Congress."

42. Kathryn Edin and Laura Lein, *Making Ends Meet: How Single Mothers Survive Welfare and Low-Wage Work* (New York: Russell Sage Foundation, 1997); Larry L. Orr, "Income Transfers as a Public Good: An Application to AFDC," *American Economic Review* 66 (1976): 359–71; Gerald C. Wright, Jr.,

"Racism and Welfare Policy in America," *Social Science Quarterly* 57 (1976): 718–30; Christopher Howard, "The American Welfare State, or States?," *Political Research Quarterly* 51 (1999): 421–42; William Julius Wilson, *The Truly Disadvantaged: The Inner City, the Underclass, and Public Policy* (Chicago: University of Chicago Press, 1987); Martin Gilens, *Why Americans Hate Welfare: Race, Media, and the Politics of Antipoverty Policy* (Chicago: University of Chicago Press, 1999); David T. Ellwood, *Poor Support: Poverty in the American Family* (New York: Basic, 1988), 190–215; Margaret Weir, ed., *The Social Divide: Political Parties and the Future of Activist Government* (Washington, D.C.: Brookings Institution; New York: Russell Sage Foundation, 1998); Teles, *Whose Welfare?*.

43. R. Kent Weaver, *Ending Welfare as We Know It* (Washington, D.C.: Brookings Institution, 2000); Charles M. Cameron, *Veto Bargaining: Presidents and the Politics of Negative Power* (Cambridge: Cambridge University Press, 2000), 20–22; Joe Soss, Sanford F. Schram, Thomas P. Vartanian, and Erin O'Brien, "Setting the Terms of Relief: Explaining State Policy Choices in the Devolution Revolution," *American Journal of Political Science* 45 (2001): 378–95; Kenneth Finegold and Sarah Staveteig, "Race, Ethnicity, and Welfare Reform," in *Welfare Reform: The Next Act*, ed. Alan Weil and Kenneth Finegold (Washington, D.C.: Urban Institute Press, 2002); Lael R. Keiser, Peter R. Mueser, and Seung-Whan Choi "Race, Bureaucratic Discretion, and the Implementation of Welfare Reform," *American Journal of Political Science* 48 (2004): 314–27; Sanford F. Schram, "Contextualizing Racial Disparities in Welfare Reform: Toward a New Poverty Research," *Perspectives on Politics* (forthcoming).

44. Laura Tabili, *"We Ask for British Justice": Workers and Racial Difference in Late Imperial Britain* (Ithaca: Cornell University Press, 1994); Sheila Patterson, *Dark Strangers: A Sociological Study of the Absorption of a Recent West Indian Migrant Group in Brixton, South London* (Bloomington: Indiana University Press, 1964), 408; Sheila Patterson, *Immigration and Race Relations in Britain, 1960–1967* (Oxford: Oxford University Press, 1969), 114; Douglas Manley, Ivo de Souza, Albert Hyndman, et al., *The West Indian Comes to England: A Report Prepared for the Trustees of the London Parochial Charities by the Family Welfare Association* (London: Routledge and Kegan Paul, 1960), 54; Anthony H. Richmond, *The Colour Problem: A Study of Racial Relations* (Harmondsworth: Penguin, 1955), 267; Catherine Jones, *Immigration and Social Policy in Britain* (London: Tavistock, 1977), 147–48; E.J.B. Rose, *Colour and Citizenship: A Report on British Race Relations* (London: Oxford University Press, 1969), 21–22; "The Dark Million," *Times*, 18 January 1965, 6; Hannan Rose and Margot Levy, "The Local Committees," in *The Prevention of Racial Discrimination in Britain*, ed. Simon Abbott (London: Oxford University Press, 1971), 333–34; Paul Foot, *Immigration and Race in British Politics* (Harmondsworth: Penguin, 1965), 129–33; Randall Hansen, *Citizenship and Immigration in Post-War Britain: The Institutional Origins of a Multicultural Nation* (Oxford: Oxford University Press, 2000), 62–79; Nicholas Deakin and Brian Cohen, "Other Measures Against Racial Discrimination," in *The Prevention of Racial Discrimination*, ed. Abbott, 385–87.

45. Richmond, *The Colour Problem*, 236–37.

46. Rose and Levy, "The Local Committees," 335–36; Manley et al., *The West Indian Comes to England*, 155, 161–62, 180–81; Patterson, *Immigration and Race Relations*, 294–309; J.A.G. Griffin, Judith Henderson, Margaret Usborne, and Donald Wood, *Coloured Immigrants in Britain* (London: Oxford University Press, 1960), 36–37; Patterson, *Dark Strangers*, 262–64.

47. Patterson, *Immigration and Race Relations*, 114–18, 293–94; Deakin and Cohen, "Other Measures," 386–87; Manley et al., *The West Indian Comes to England*, 54–57; Rose, *Colour and Citizenship*, 211, 221, 522–25; Patterson, *Dark Strangers*, 408–9; Foot, *Immigration and Race in British Politics*, 221–24.

48. Hansen, *Citizenship and Immigration*, 136–46, 150–52; Patterson, *Immigration and Race Relations*, 118–28; *Immigration from the Commonwealth*, Cmd. 2739 (1965); Ira Katznelson, *Black Men, White Cities: Race, Politics, and Migration in the United States, 1900–1930, and Britain, 1948–1968* (Chicago: University of Chicago Press, 1976), 139–51.

49. Manley et al., *The West Indian Comes to England*, 109–12; Jones, *Immigration and Social Policy*, 195–96. See also Richmond, *The Colour Problem*, 283, 290–91; Ian Law, *Racism, Ethnicity and Social Policy* (London: Prentice Hall, 1996), 58–60.

50. K. Jones, "Immigrants and the Social Services," *National Institute Economic Review* 41 (August 1967): 33–35; Ernest Krausz, *Ethnic Minorities in Britain* (London: MacGibbon and Kee, 1971), 106–7.

51. Results and analyses of the four surveys were published as W. W. Daniel, *Racal Discrimination in England* (Harmondsworth: Penguin, 1968); David J. Smith, *Racial Disadvantage in Britain* (Harmondsworth: Penguin, 1977); Colin Brown, *Black and White in Britain* (Aldershot: Gower, 1984); and Tariq Modood, Richard Berthoud, et al., *Ethnic Minorities in Britain: Diversity and Disadvantage* (London: Policy Studies Institute, 1997) See Richard Berthoud, Tariq Modood, and Patten Smith's introduction to Modood et al., *Ethnic Minorities in Britain*, 1–3; Rose, *Colour and Citizenship*, 525–32.

52. Brown, *Black and White in Britain*, 233–35, 242.

53. Sylvia Dörr and Thomas Faist, "Institutional Conditions for the Integration of Immigrants in Welfare States: A Comparison of the Literature on Germany, France, Great Britain, and the Netherlands," *European Journal of Political Research* 31 (1997): 411, 414; Roger Zegers de Beijl, "International Migration for Employment: Discrimination of Migrant Workers in Western Europe," World Employment Programme Working Paper (Geneva: International Labour Organisation, 1991), 36–41.

54. Modood et al., *Ethnic Minorities in Britain*, 153–56.

55. Juliet Cook and Shantu Watt, "Racism, Women and Poverty," in *Women and Poverty in Britain in the 1990s*, ed. Caroline Glendinning and Jane Millar (New York: Harvester Wheatsheaf, 1992), 19–20.

56. Law, *Racism, Ethnicity and Social Policy*, 61–75.

57. Alan Marsh and Stephen McKay, *Families, Work, and Benefits* (London: Policy Studies Institute, 1993), 16, 37–38, 42; Alice Bloch, *Access to Benefits: The Information Needs of Minority Ethnic Groups* (London: Policy Studies Institute, 1993), 17–18, 35, 41.

58. Trevor Jones, *Britain's Ethnic Minorities: An Analysis of the Labour Force Survey* (London: Policy Studies Institute, 1993), 123–36; Modood et al., *Ethnic Minorities in Britain*, 161, 252–56.

59. Tariq Modood, "Ethnic Equality in Britain: Progress and Its Limits," in *Discourse on Inequality in France and Britain*, ed. John Edwards and Jean-Paul Révauger (Aldershot: Ashgate, 1998). See also Office of Population Censuses and Surveys, Social Survey Division, *The General Household Survey: Introductory Report* (London: Her Majesty's Stationery Office, 1973), 81–83; Daniel, *Racial Discrimination in England*, 61–63; Smith, *Racial Disadvantage in Britain*; Brown, *Black and White in Britain*, 150–227; Modood, *Ethnic Minorities in Britain*, 88–99. Once again, there are significant differences among nonwhite groups in unemployment, job status relative to qualifications, and earnings. Generally speaking, Indians (especially men) are most similar to whites in their employment profile, while Pakistani and Bangladeshi workers (especially women) are most disadvantaged, with Caribbean blacks and other groups falling somewhere in between.

60. Daniel, *Racial Discrimination in England*, 177–80; Jones, *Britain's Ethnic Minorities*, 144–45; Office of Population Censuses and Surveys, *General Household Survey*, 143. Again, nonwhite groups differ in their levels of council tenancy: Caribbeans and Pakistanis are much more likely than Indians to live in council housing, a disparity that has expanded since the large-scale privatization of council housing under Thatcher.

61. Modood et al., *Ethnic Minorities in Britain*, 159–62; Office of Population Censuses and Surveys, *General Household Survey*, 144–46; Modood, "Ethnic Equality in Britain"; Zegers de Beijl, "International Migration for Employment," 36–39; Joseph Rowntree Foundation, *Inquiry into Income and Wealth* (York: Joseph Rowntree Foundation, 1995), 1:28. Incomes differ across nonwhite groups. Indians are more likely to be in the middle-income ranges, while more than 40 percent of West Indians and more than half of Pakistanis and Bangladeshis are in the lowest quintile.

62. Brian Cathcart, *The Case of Stephen Lawrence* (London: Viking, 1999); *The Stephen Lawrence Inquiry: Report of an Inquiry by Sir William Macpherson of Cluny*, Cmnd. 4262-I (1999), chap. 6.

63. *Community Cohesion: A Report of the Independent Review Team* (London: Home Office, 2001), 9–10.

64. Jennifer L. Hochschild, "You Win Some, You Lose Some: Explaining the Pattern of Success and Failure in the Second Reconstruction," in *Taking Stock: American Government in the Twentieth Century*, ed. Morton Keller and R. Shep Melnick (Washington, D.C.: Woodrow Wilson Center Press; Cambridge: Cambridge University Press, 1999).

65. Howard Schuman, Charlotte Steeh, Lawrence Bobo, and Maria Krysan, *Racial Attitudes in America: Trends and Interpretations*, rev. ed. (Cambridge: Harvard University Press, 1997); Lawrence D. Bobo and Ryan A. Smith, "From Jim Crow Racism to Laissez-Faire Racism: The Transformation of Racial Attitudes," in *Beyond Pluralism: The Conception of Groups and Group Identities in America*, ed. Wendy F. Katkin, Ned Landsman, and Andrea Tyree (Urbana: University of Illinois Press, 1998); U. S. Bureau of Labor Statistics, *Current Population Survey*, Series P-60; Bureau of Labor Statistics, *Employment and Earnings*.

CHAPTER SEVEN

1. T. H. Marshall, "Citizenship and Social Class," in *Class, Citizenship, and Social Development* (Garden City, N.Y.: Doubleday, 1964), 75, 80. See also Karl Polanyi, *The Great Transformation: The Political and Economic Origins of Our Time* (New York: Rinehart, 1944).

2. Judith N. Shklar, *American Citizenship: The Quest for Inclusion* (Cambridge: Harvard University Press, 1991); Eric Foner, *Free Soil, Free Labor, Free Men: The Ideology of the Republic Party Before the Civil War* (New York: Oxford University Press, 1970); First Debate with Stephen A. Douglas at Ottawa, Illinois, 21 August 1858, in *The Collected Works of Abraham Lincoln*, ed. Roy P. Basler (New Brunswick, N.J.: Rutgers University Press, 1953), 3:16.

3. Ian Gordon, "The Impact of Economic Change on Minorities in Western Europe," in *Poverty, Inequality, and the Future of Social Policy: Western States in the New World Order*, ed. Katherine McFate, Roger Lawson, and William Julius Wilson (New York: Russell Sage Foundation, 1995); R. Zegers de Beijl and W. R. Böhning, "Labour Market Integration of Migrants and Legislative Measures to Combat Discrimination," International Migration Paper No. 8 (Geneva: International Labour Organization, Employment Department, 1995); Mark Levitan, "A Crisis of Black Male Unemployment: Unemployment and Joblessness in New York City, 2003" (New York: Community Service Society, 2004); Bruce Western and Katherine Beckett, "How Unregulated Is the U.S. Labor Market? The Penal System as a Labor Market Institution," *American Journal of Sociology* 104 (1999): 1030–60; Christopher Uggen and Jeff Manza, "Democratic Contraction? Political Consequences of Felon Disenfranchisement in the United States," *American Sociological Review* 67 (2002): 777–803.

4. Erik Bleich, "The French Model: Color-Blind Integration," in *Color Lines: Affirmative Action, Immigration, and Civil Rights Options for America*, ed. John David Skrentny (Chicago: University of Chicago Press, 2001); E.J.B. Rose, *Colour and Citizenship: A Report on British Race Relations* (London: Oxford University Press, 1969); Commission on the Future of Multi-Ethnic Britain, *The Future of Multi-Ethnic Britain* (London: Profile Books, 2000).

5. C. Vann Woodward, *The Strange Career of Jim Crow*, 3rd rev. ed. (New York: Oxford University Press, 1974); William Julius Wilson, *The Declining Significance of Race: Blacks and Changing American Institutions* (Chicago: University of Chicago Press, 1978); Thomas J. Sugrue, *The Origins of the Urban Crisis: Race and Inequality in Postwar Detroit* (Princeton: Princeton University Press, 1996); Eric Arnesen, *Brotherhoods of Color: Black Railroad Workers and the Struggle for Equality* (Cambridge: Harvard University Press, 2001); Bruce Nelson, *Divided We Stand: American Workers and the Struggle for Black Equality* (Princeton: Princeton University Press, 2001); David R. Roediger, *The Wages of Whiteness: Race and the Making of the American Working Class* (London: Verso, 1991); Desmond King, *Separate and Unequal: Black Americans and the U.S. Federal Government* (Oxford: Oxford University Press, 1995).

6. David Levering Louis, *W.E.B. Du Bois: Biography of a Race, 1868–1919* (New York: Henry Holt, 1993); Louis R. Harlan, *Booker T. Washington: The Wizard of Tuskegee, 1901–1915* (New York: Oxford University Press, 1983);

W.E.B. Du Bois, *The Souls of Black Folk* (1903; reprint, New York: Library of America, 1986), chap. 3; Ramón G. Vela, "The Washington-Du Bois Controversy and African-American Protest: Ideological Conflict and Its Consequences," *Studies in American Political Development* 16 (2002): 88–109.

7. William J. Wilson, *Power, Racism, and Privilege: Race Relations in Theoretical and Sociohistorical Perspective* (New York: Free Press, 1973), 121–27; Franklin D. Roosevelt, "Executive Order No. 8802. June 25, 1941," in *The Public Papers and Addresses of Franklin D. Roosevelt*, ed. Samuel I. Rosenman (New York: Harper and Brothers, 1950), 10:233–37; Daniel Kryder, *Divided Arsenal: Race and the American State During World War II* (Cambridge: Cambridge University Press, 2000), 53–66, 88–132; King, *Separate and Unequal*, 74–78, 208–9; Russell L. Riley, *The Presidency and the Politics of Racial Inequality: Nation-Keeping from 1831 to 1965* (New York: Columbia University Press, 1999), 145–52; John David Skrentny, *The Ironies of Affirmative Action: Politics, Culture, and Justice in America* (Chicago: University of Chicago Press, 1996), 114–17; Paul Burstein, *Discrimination, Jobs, and Politics: The Struggle for Equal Employment Opportunity in the United States since the New Deal* (Chicago: University of Chicago Press, 1985); *Congressional Record*, 88th Cong., 2nd sess., 1964, 110, pt. 5: 6548; Joseph P. Witherspoon, "Civil Rights Policy in the Federal System: Proposals for a Better Use of Administrative Process," *Yale Law Journal* 74 (1965): 1171–72, 1239–42.

8. Gunnar Myrdal, *An American Dilemma: The Negro Problem and Modern Democracy* (New York: Harper and Brothers, 1944), 416.

9. Riley, *The Presidency and the Politics of Racial Inequality*, 158–64; President's Committee on Civil Rights, *To Secure These Rights* (Washington, D.C.: U.S. Government Printing Office, 1947); V. O. Key, Jr., *Southern Politics in State and Nation* (New York: Knopf, 1949), 329–35.

10. Burstein, *Discrimination, Jobs, and Politics*, 13–39; Myrdal, *An American Dilemma*; Rogers M. Smith, "Beyond Tocqueville, Myrdal, and Hartz: The Multiple Traditions in America," *American Political Science Review* 87 (1993): 549–66; Mary L. Dudziak, *Cold War Civil Rights: Race and the Image of Democracy* (Princeton: Princeton University Press, 2000); Thomas Borstelmann, *The Cold War and the Color Line: American Race Relations in the Global Arena* (Cambridge: Harvard University Press, 2001); John D. Skrentny, *The Minority Rights Revolution* (Cambridge: Harvard University Press, 2002).

11. Burstein, *Discrimination, Jobs, and Politics*, 13–39; *Congressional Record*, 84th Cong., 2nd sess., 1956, 102, pt. 4, 4515–16; *Brown v. Board of Education*, 347 U.S. 483 (1954); *Brown v. Board of Education*, 349 U.S. 294 (1955). Nineteen senators and eighty-one representatives signed the manifesto; the only senators from the eleven former confederate states who did not sign were Lyndon Johnson of Texas and Albert Gore, Sr., and Estes Kefauver of Tennessee.

12. Brian K. Landsberg, *Enforcing Civil Rights: Race Discrimination and the Department of Justice* (Lawrence: University Press of Kansas, 1997), 8–10; Dwight D. Eisenhower, *Waging Peace, 1956–1961* (Garden City, N.Y.: Doubleday, 1965), 154–75.

13. Skrentny, *Ironies of Affirmative Action*, 28–35.

14. Ira Katznelson, *Black Men, White Cities: Race, Politics, and Migration in the United States, 1900–1930, and Britain, 1948–1968* (Chicago: University of Chicago Press, 1976). The quotation is on p. 125.

15. Katznelson, *Black Men, White Cities*, 127–28; quoting Anthony Adair, "Immigration Control and Integration," *Contemporary Review* (April 1966), 177. Randall Hansen's research has revealed substantial conflict and debate within the parties on immigration and race during this period, somewhat softening both the "pre-political" and "consensus" parts of Katznelson's formulation. The consequences, however, amount to the same thing — national policy stasis between 1948 and 1962. See Randall Hansen, *Citizenship and Immigration in Post-War Britain: The Institutional Origins of a Multicultural Nation* (Oxford: Oxford University Press, 2000).

16. Hannan Rose and Margot Levy, "The Local Committees," in *The Prevention of Racial Discrimination in Britain*, ed. Simon Abbott (London: Oxford University Press, 1971), 345.

17. Tariq Modood, "Ethnicity and Political Mobilisation in Britain," in *Ethnicity, Social Mobility, and Public Policy in the United States and the United Kingdom*, ed. Glenn Loury, Tariq Modood, and Steven Teles (Cambridge: Cambridge University Press, 2005); Rose, *Colour and Citizenship*, 380–93.

18. Katznelson, *Black Men, White Cities*, 154–56; Modood, "Ethnicity and Political Mobilisation"; Erik Bleich, *Race Politics in Britain and France: Ideas and Policymaking since the 1960s* (Cambridge: Cambridge University Press, 2003).

19. Hansen, *Citizenship and Immigration*, 87–88, 132, 138; Anthony Lester and Geoffrey Bindman, *Race and Law in Great Britain* (Cambridge: Harvard University Press, 1972), 107–9; Bleich, *Race Politics in Britain and France*, 41–42; Colin Brown, "Ethnic Pluralism in Britain: The Demographic and Legal Background," in *Ethnic Pluralism and Public Policy: Achieving Equality in the United States and Britain*, ed. Nathan Glazer and Ken Young (Lexington, Mass.: D. C. Heath, 1983), 51.

20. Brian Lapping, *The Labour Government, 1964–70* (Harmondsworth: Penguin, 1970), 111; Lester and Bindman, *Race and Law*, 108–12; Jeffrey Jowell, "The Administrative Enforcement of Laws Against Discrimination," *Public Law* (Summer 1965): 119–86; Bleich, *Race Politics in Britain and France*, 49–59.

21. Katznelson, *Black Men, White Cities*, 149.

22. Mark Abrams, "Introduction," to W. W. Daniel, *Racial Discrimination in Britain* (Harmondsworth: Penguin, 1968), 12; Rose, *Colour and Citizenship*, 525–33.

23. Daniel, *Racial Discrimination in Britain*; David J. Smith, *Racial Disadvantage in Employment* (London: Political and Economic Planning, 1974); Roger Jowell and Patricia Prescott Clarke, "Racial Discrimination and White-collar Workers in Britain," *Race* 11 (1970): 397–417; Rose, *Colour and Citizenship*, 407–15, 534–36, 686–87; Bleich, *Race Politics in Britain and France*, 70–84; Brown, "Ethnic Pluralism in Britain," 51–52.

24. Bleich, *Race Politics in Britain and France*, 101–7; Rose, *Colour and Citizenship*, 2, 15–17.

25. Pierre Birnbaum, *The Idea of France*, trans. M. B. DeBevoise (New York: Hill and Wang, 2001), 162.

26. Birnbaum, *The Idea of France*, 144–62; Alexander Werth, *France, 1940–1955* (New York: Henry Holt, 1956), 284–90; Pierre Birnbaum, *"La France aux Français": Histoire des haines nationalistes* (Paris: Seuil, 1993); Michael R. Marrus and Robert O. Paxton, *Vichy France and the Jews* (New York: Basic, 1981); Zeev Sternhell, *Neither Right nor Left: Fascist Ideology in France*, trans. David Maisel (Berkeley: University of California Press, 1986); Danièle Lochak, "La race: Une catégorie juridique," *Mots* 33 (Dec. 1992): 291–303; Francis Jacob, "Les lois françaises contre le racisme," *Les Dossiers d'Hommes et Libertés* 2 (January–February 2001): 8; Nonna Mayer, "L'antisémitisme français à l'aune des sondages," in *Racisme et modernité*, ed. Michel Wieviorka (Paris: La Découverte, 1993), 278–81.

27. Mouvement contre le racisme et pour l'amitié entre les peuples [hereafter MRAP], *Chronique du flagrant racisme* (Paris: La Découverte, 1984), 9–12; Bleich, *Race Politics in Britain and France*, 118–20.

28. Yasemin Nuhoğlu Soysal, *Limits of Citizenship: Migrants and Postnational Membership in Europe* (Chicago: University of Chicago Press, 1994); Pierre-André Taguieff, *La force du préjugé: Essai sur le racisme et ses doubles* (Paris: La Découverte, 1987).

29. Bleich, *Race Politics in Britain and France*, 123–29.

30. Ian Forbes and Geoffrey Mead, *Measure for Measure: A Comparative Analysis of Measures to Combat Racial Discrimination in the Member Countries of the European Community* (Southampton: Equal Opportunities Study Group, University of Southampton, 1992); United Nations, *Committee on the Elimination of Racial Discrimination and the Progress Made Towards the Achievement of the Objectives of the International Convention on the Elimination of All Forms of Racial Discrimination* (New York: United Nations, 1979); see also Patrick R. Ireland, "Migration, Free Movement, and Immigrant Integration in the EU: A Bifurcated Policy Response," in *European Social Policy: Between Fragmentation and Integration*, ed. Stephan Leibfried and Paul Pierson (Washington, D.C.: Brookings Institution, 1995). Great Britain ratified the racial discrimination convention in 1969; the United States did not ratify it until 1994.

31. Doug McAdam, *Political Process and the Development of Black Insurgency, 1930–1970* (Chicago: University of Chicago Press, 1982); Edward G. Carmines and James A. Stimson, *Issue Evolution: Race and the Transformation of American Politics* (Princeton: Princeton University Press, 1989); Paul Frymer, *Uneasy Alliances: Race and Party Competition in America* (Princeton: Princeton University Press, 1999); Thomas J. Sugrue, "Crabgrass-Roots Politics: Race, Rights, and the Reaction Against Liberalism in the Urban North, 1940–1964," *Journal of American History* 82 (1995): 551–78; Robert Dallek, *An Unfinished Life: John F. Kennedy, 1917–1963* (Boston: Little, Brown, 2003), 599–606, 640–42.

32. Ira Katznelson, Kim Geiger, and Daniel Kryder, "Limiting Liberalism: The Southern Veto in Congress, 1933–1950," *Political Science Quarterly* 108 (1993): 191–208.

33. Landsberg, *Enforcing Civil Rights*, 10–13, 69, 73.

34. Hugh Davis Graham, *The Civil Rights Era: Origins and Development of National Policy, 1960–1972* (New York: Oxford University Press, 1990), 131–34; Dallek, *An Unfinished Life*, 642–48; Robert D. Loevy, *To End All Segregation: The Politics of the Passage of the Civil Rights Act of 1964* (Lanham, Md.: Univer-

sity Press of America, 1990), 52–54; Irving Bernstein, *Promises Kept: John F. Kennedy's New Frontier* (New York: Oxford University Press, 1991), 102–13. For an exhaustive account of the congressional debate, negotiations, and machinations, see Charles and Barbara Whalen, *The Longest Debate: A Legislative History of the 1964 Civil Rights Act* (Cabin John, Md.: Seven Locks, 1985).

35. House Worksheet, 20 January 1964, LE/HU, White House Central File (hereafter cited as WHCF), Box 65, Lyndon B. Johnson Library (hereafter cited as LBJL); Sarah A. Binder and Steven S. Smith, *Politics or Principle? Filibustering in the United States Senate* (Washington, D.C.: Brookings Institution, 1997), 95–96, 101–11, 136–41; Bernstein, *Promises Kept*, 104–7, 109; Whalen and Whalen, *The Longest Debate*; Graham, *Civil Rights Era*, 141–52.

36. Carmines and Stimson, *Issue Evolution*; Philip A. Klinkner, *The Losing Parties: Out-Party National Committees, 1956–1993* (New Haven: Yale University Press, 1994), 49–60. See also Rick Perlstein, *Before the Storm: Barry Goldwater and the Unmaking of the American Consensus* (New York: Hill and Wang, 2001).

37. Keith T. Poole and Howard Rosenthal, *Congress: A Political-Economic History of Roll Call Voting* (New York: Oxford University Press, 1997); Robert C. Lieberman, "Weak State, Strong Policy: Paradoxes of Race Policy in the United States, Great Britain, and France," *Studies in American Political Development* 16 (2002): 142; Daniel B. Rodriguez and Barry R. Weingast, "The Positive Political Theory of Legislative History: New Perspectives on the 1964 Civil Rights Act and Its Interpretation," *University of Pennsylvania Law Review* 151 (2003): 1417–1542. NOMINATE data and Voteview software to view and analyze them are available from Poole's home page on the World Wide Web at http://voteview .uh.edu. Only one Democrat, Frank Lausche of Ohio, was to the Right of the most liberal Republican, Jacob Javits of New York.

38. *Congressional Record*, 88th Cong., 2d sess., 1964, 110, pt. 11: 14319; Perlstein, *Before the Storm*, 18, 21, 363–64; Whalen and Whalen, *The Longest Debate*, 212–13.

39. Keith Krehbiel, *Pivotal Politics: A Theory of U.S. Lawmaking* (Chicago: University of Chicago Press, 1998). Parties are notably absent from Krehbiel's account of policy-making pivots. Nevertheless, given the distribution of civil rights views among Democratic and Republican senators, it is clear that the filibuster pivot was a Republican. Thus my approach, which emphasizes Dirksen's role both as Republican leader and as a senator near the pivotal point for cloture, is broadly consistent with Krehbiel's analysis of pivots in policy-making.

40. "Memorandum Describing Changes in H.R. 7152 Embodied in Amendment No. 656 Offered by Senators Dirksen, Mansfield, Humphrey, and Kuchel," 1964 Justice Department Preparation of Bill Material, Box 1, Legislative Background, Civil Rights Act of 1964, p. 8, LBJL.

41. *Civil Rights Act of 1964*, Public Law 88–352, sec. 703 (j); "Memorandum Describing Changes in H.R. 7152," p. 10.

42. *Congressional Record*, 88th Cong., 2d sess., 1964, 110, pt. 6: 7240. See also *Congressional Record*, 88th Cong., 2d sess., 1964, 110, pt. 5: 6549; Skrentny, *Ironies of Affirmative Action*, 3; see also pp. 120–21, 268–69.

43. Skrentny, *Ironies of Affirmative Action*, 2–4, 34, 120–21, 244.

44. Graham, *Civil Rights Era*, 145–49; "Memorandum Describing Changes in H.R. 7152," pp. 1–2, 9; Memorandum, Burke Marshall to Katzenbach, 12 March 1964, 1964 Justice Department Preparation of Bill Material, Box 1, Legislative Background, Civil Rights Act of 1964, LBJL.

45. I am indebted to Frank Dobbin for this point. See Michael I. Sovern, *Legal Restraints on Racial Discrimination in Employment* (New York: Twentieth Century Fund, 1966). On segregation and discrimination in federal employment, see King, *Separate and Unequal*.

46. Burstein, *Discrimination, Jobs, and Politics*.

47. Katznelson, *Black Men, White Cities*, 197. See also Simon Abbott, "The National Committee for Commonwealth Immigrants, the Community Relations Commission," in *Prevention of Racial Discrimination*, ed. Abbott, 312–17.

48. Anthony M. Messina, "Ethnic Minorities and the British Party System in the 1990s and Beyond," in *Race and British Electoral Politics*, ed. Shamit Saggar (London: UCL Press, 1998); Douglas S. Massey and Nancy A. Denton, *American Apartheid: Segregation and the Making of the Underclass* (Cambridge: Harvard University Press, 1993); Ceri Peach, "London and New York: Contrasts in British and American Models of Segregation," *International Journal of Population Geography* 5 (1999): 319–46; Anthony M. Messina, *Race and Party Competition in Britain* (Oxford: Oxford University Press, 1989), 160–77; Ivor Crewe, "Representation and the Ethnic Minorities in Britain," in *Ethnic Pluralism and Public Policy*, ed. Glazer and Young; Richard Skellington, *"Race" in Britain Today*, 2d ed. (London: Sage, 1996), 235–41; Steven M. Teles, "Positive Action or Affirmative Action? The Persistence of Britain's Antidiscrimination Regime," in *Color Lines*, ed. Skrentny, 260–61; Shamit Saggar and Anthony Heath, "Race: Towards a Multicultural Electorate," in *Critical Elections: British Parties and Voters in Long-Term Perspective*, ed. Geoffrey Evans and Pippa Norris (London: Sage, 1999).

49. Messina, *Race and Party Competition*, 143–49; Hansen, *Citizenship and Immigration*, 225–28.

50. *Parliamentary Debates* (Commons), 5th ser., vol. 906, cols. 1547–48.

51. Quoted in Sheila Patterson, *Immigration and Race Relations in Britain, 1960–1967* (London: Oxford University Press, 1969), 112–13. See also Rose, *Colour and Citizenship*, 23–25, 662–65.

52. *Parliamentary Debates* (Commons), 5th ser., vol. 906, cols. 1548, 1552. See also Christopher McCrudden, "Anti-Discrimination Goals and the Legal Process," in *Ethnic Pluralism and Public Policy*, ed. Glazer and Young.

53. *Parliamentary Debates* (Commons), 5th Series, vol. 906, cols. 1574, 1588–89, 1591, 1607–8.

54. *Parliamentary Debates* (Commons), 5th Series, vol. 906, cols. 1663–64.

55. Forbes and Mead, *Measure for Measure*; Martin MacEwen, "Anti-Discrimination Law in Great Britain," *New Community* 40 (1994): 353–70; Chris Boothman and Martin MacEwen, "The British Commission for Racial Equality as an Enforcement Agency," in *Anti-Discrimination Law Enforcement: A Comparative Perspective*, ed. Martin MacEwen (Aldershot: Avebury, 1997).

56. On the Fourth Republic, see Philip M. Williams, *Crisis and Compromise: Politics in the Fourth Republic* (London: Longmans, Green, 1964). See also John D.

Huber, *Rationalizing Parliament: Legislative Institutions and Party Politics in France* (Cambridge: Cambridge University Press, 1996), 1–2.

57. None actually voted against it, although nearly one-third of the Socialists in the Assembly abstained. Williams, *Crisis and Compromise*, 93, 100–101, 400, 501.

58. Williams, *Crisis and Compromise*, 330; Anthony Daley, "François Mitterrand, the Left and Political Mobilization in France," and Patrick R. Ireland, "Race, Immigration and the Politics of Hate," in *The Mitterrand Era: Policy Alternatives and Political Mobilization in France*, ed. Anthony Daley (New York: New York University Press, 1996); Patrick R. Ireland, *The Policy Challenge of Ethnic Diversity: Immigrant Politics in France and Switzerland* (Cambridge: Harvard University Press, 1994); Catherine Wihtol de Wenden, *Les immigrés et la politique: Cent cinquante ans d'évolution* (Paris: Presses de la Fondation Nationale des Sciences Politiques, 1988), 128–30.

59. Huber, *Rationalizing Parliament*; Douglas E. Ashford, *Politics and Policy in France: Living with Uncertainty* (Philadelphia: Temple University Press, 1982), 18–25; Alexis de Tocqueville, *The Old Régime and the French Revolution*, trans. Stuart Gilbert (New York: Anchor Books, 1955); Williams, *Crisis and Compromise*, 2. See also Jonah D. Levy, *Tocqueville's Revenge: State, Society, and Economy in Contemporary France* (Cambridge: Harvard University Press, 1999).

60. Ezra N. Suleiman, *Private Power and Centralization in France: The Notaires and the State* (Princeton: Princeton University Press, 1987); Pierre Rosanvallon, *L'Etat en France de 1789 à nos jours* (Paris: Seuil, 1990); Douglas E. Ashford, *British Dogmatism and French Pragmatism: Central-Local Policymaking in the Welfare State* (London: George Allen and Unwin, 1982); Ellen M. Immergut, *Health Politics: Interests and Institutions in Western Europe* (Cambridge: Cambridge University Press, 1992); Williams, *Crisis and Compromise*, 163–69, 456–58; Nonna Mayer, *Ces Français qui votent FN* (Paris: Flammarion, 1999), 247–67.

61. Bleich, *Race Politics in Britain and France*, chap. 5; Assemblée Nationale, Proposition de loi no. 38, 15 April 1959; Freeman, *Immigrant Labor and Racial Conflict*, 85–94; Michel Wieviorka, *Violence en France* (Paris: Seuil, 1999), 26; Maxim Silverman, *Deconstructing the Nation: Immigration, Racism and Citizenship in Modern France* (London: Routledge, 1992), 48–50; Wihtol de Wenden, *Les immigrés et la politique*, 165–69; MRAP, *Chronique du flagrant racisme*, 22–28, 30.

62. MRAP, *Chronique du flagrant racisme*, 13. In 1979, LICA became LICRA, the International League Against Racism and Antisemitism.

63. *Journal Officiel de la République Française, Débats Parlementaires, Assemblée Nationale*, 1972, no. 41 (8 June), 2290–91, 2295; MRAP, *Chronique du flagrant racisme*, 30–31. This provision was intended to allow two organizations in particular to pursue antidiscrimination cases: MRAP and LICA, although other groups have since used this power to bring suits. Jacqueline Costa-Lascoux, "Des lois contre le racisme," in *Face au racisme*, ed. Pierre-André Taguieff (Paris: La Découverte, 1991), 2:114; Jacqueline Costa-Lascoux, "French Legislation Against Racism and Discrimination," *New Community* 20 (1994): 373.

64. Forbes and Mead, *Measure for Measure*, 35. See also Costa-Lascoux, "French Legislation Against Racism."

65. *Journal Officiel de la République Française, Débats Parlementaires, Assemblée Nationale*, 1972, no. 41 (8 June), 2281, 2287–88.

66. Léon Lyon-Caen, "Deux propositions de loi contre le racisme," *Droits et Libertés*, 31 March 1959, reprinted in MRAP, *Chronique du flagrant racisme*, 117–22; Bleich, *Race Politics in Britain and France*, 121–22; Michel Hannoun, *L'homme est l'éspérance de l'homme: Rapport sur le racisme et les discriminations en France au secrétaire d'état auprès du premier ministre chargé des droits de l'homme* (Paris: Documentation Française, 1987), 96, 104, 106; Costa-Lascoux, "French Legislation Against Racism," 375; Forbes and Mead, *Measure for Measure*, 35; MacEwen, "Anti-Discrimination Law in Great Britain," 367.

67. R. Kent Weaver and Bert A. Rockman, "Assessing the Effects of Institutions," in *Do Institutions Matter? Government Capabilities in the United States and Abroad*, ed. R. Kent Weaver and Bert A. Rockman (Washington, D.C.: Brookings Institution, 1993).

68. Eric Fassin, "'Good to Think': The American Reference in French Discourses of Immigration and Ethnicity," and Martin Schain, "Minorities and Immigrant Incorporation in France: The State and the Dynamics of Multiculturalism," in *Multicultural Questions*, ed. Christian Joppke and Steven Lukes (Oxford: Oxford University Press, 1999); Peter A. Hall, "Policy Paradigms, Social Learning, and the State: The Case of Economic Policymaking in Britain," *Comparative Politics* 25 (1993): 275–96; Birnbaum, *The Idea of France*.

CHAPTER EIGHT

1. *Grutter v. Bollinger*, 539 U.S. 306 (2003), 331, 334, 339.

2. David R. Mayhew, *America's Congress: Actions in the Public Sphere, James Madison Through Newt Gingrich* (New Haven: Yale University Press, 2000), 167.

3. On the importance of institutional venues, see Frank R. Baumgartner and Bryan D. Jones, *Agendas and Instability in American Politics* (Chicago: University of Chicago Press, 1993).

4. Terry M. Moe, "The Politicized Presidency," in *The New Direction in American Politics*, ed. John E. Chubb and Paul E. Peterson (Washington, D.C.: Brookings Institution, 1985); Bruce Miroff, "Presidential Leverage over Social Movements: The Johnson White House and Civil Rights," *Journal of Politics* 43 (1981): 2–23; Rusell L. Riley, *The Presidency and the Politics of Racial Equality: Nation-Keeping from 1831 to 1965* (New York: Columbia University Press, 1999).

5. Memorandum, Hobart Taylor to Johnson, 7 May 1964, HU 2, White House Central File (hereafter cited as WHCF), Lyndon B. Johnson Library (hereafter cited as LBJL).

6. Memorandum, William L. Taylor to Lee White, 17 June 1964, Office Files of Lee C. White, Box 2, LBJL.

7. Memorandum, Lee C. White to Johnson, 28 September 1964, LE, WHCF, Box 167, LBJL; Hugh Davis Graham, *The Civil Rights Era: Origins and Develop-*

ment of National Policy, 1960–1972 (New York: Oxford University Press, 1990), 177–79.

8. A. Philip Randolph Institute, *The Reluctant Guardians: A Survey of the Enforcement of Federal Civil Rights Laws* (Washington, D.C., 1969).

9. Graham, *Civil Rights Era*, 146; Memorandum, Labor-Welfare Division to Kermit Gordon, 26 June 1964, Office Files of Lee C. White, Box 2, LBJL; Memorandum, Kermit Gordon to Lee White, 22 August 1964, *Civil Rights During the Johnson Administration, 1963–1969: A Collection from the Holdings of the Lyndon Baines Johnson Library*, part 1, reel 13; Department of Labor Suggestions for Preliminary Implementation of Title VII, *Civil Rights During Johnson*, part 1, reel 13; Memorandum, George E. Reedy to Hobart Taylor, Jr., undated [before 7 July 1964], FG, WHCF, Box 403, LBJL.

10. Memorandum, Nicholas deB. Katzenbach to Humphrey, 23 November 1964, *Civil Rights During Johnson*, part 1, reel 2; Johnson to Humphrey, 2 December 1964, *Civil Rights During Johnson*, part 1, reel 2.

11. Graham, *Civil Rights Era*, 161–62.

12. LeRoy Collins, "Analysis of Civil Rights Functions of the Federal Government and Recommendations for their Consolidation in a Single Agency," July 1965, HU 2, Confidential File, WHCF, Box 56, LBJL; Memorandum, Joe Califano to Harry McPherson, 20 August 1965, HU, WHCF, Box 3, LBJL.

13. Memorandum, Humphrey to Johnson, 17 September 1965, *Civil Rights During Johnson*, part 1, reel 7.

14. Memorandum, Humphrey to Johnson, 24 September 1965, HU 2, WHCF, Box 3, LBJL; Executive Order 11246, *Federal Register* 30 (1965): 12319; John Herbers, "Rights Bloc Fear Easing of Enforcement by U.S.," *New York Times*, 17 October 1965, pp. 1, 78; Graham, *Civil Rights Era*, 180–87; John David Skrentny, *The Ironies of Affirmative Action: Politics, Culture, and Justice in America* (Chicago: University of Chicago Press, 1996), 133–34.

15. On administrative pragmatism in both the EEOC and the OFCC, see Skrentny, *Ironies of Affirmative Action*, 111–44. Although the OFCC never actually canceled a contract during the Johnson administration, it did not actually need to do so in order to be powerful. Merely the threat of cancellation gave it substantial leverage *before* contracts were awarded. See Skrentny, *Ironies of Affirmative Action*, 134; Graham, *Civil Rights Era*, 282–87.

16. Memorandum, Louis Martin to James R. Jones, 16 December 1967, HU 2, WHCF, Box 7, LBJL.

17. Memorandum, Loyd Hackler to Johnson, 2 August 1967, HU 2, WHCF, Box 6, LBJL; Memorandum, Harry McPherson to J. Willard Wirtz, 10 August 1967, Office Files of Harry McPherson, Box 7, LBJL; Memorandum, J. Willard Wirtz to Clifford Alexander, 5 September 1967, Office Files of Harry McPherson, Box 7, LBJL; Memorandum, Clifford Alexander to J. Willard Wirtz, 14 September 1967, Office Files of Harry McPherson, Box 7, LBJL.

18. Memorandum, Robert J. Brown to Nixon, 21 April 1969, HU 2, WHCF, Box 1, Nixon Presidential Materials, National Archives (hereafter cited as NPM); Memorandum, Robert J. Brown to Nixon, 16 April 1969, Ex HU 2, WHCF, Box 1, NPM. Brown had raised a similar point in a letter to Johnson in 1967. Robert J. Brown to Johnson, 11 December 1967, HU 2, WHCF, Box 7, LBJL.

19. White House aide Daniel Patrick Moynihan asserted the existence of a working-class, moderate "silent black majority" in his famous "benign neglect" memo to Nixon of January 1970, which was leaked to the *New York Times* (and acknowledged by Moynihan) in February. *New York Times*, 1 March 1970, pp. 1, 69. Columbia political scientist Charles Hamilton more or less corroborated Moynihan's claim in the *New York Times Magazine* later that spring. Charles V. Hamilton, "The Silent Black Majority," *New York Times Magazine*, 10 May 1970, 25 ff. Memorandum, Stephen Bull to John Ehrlichman, 15 May 1969, HU 2, WHCF, Box 1, NPM; Memorandum, Ken Cole to Bryce Harlow, 3 June 1969, HU 2, WHCF, Box 1, NPM; Memorandum, John R. Brown III to Jeb Magruder, 3 February 1970, Ex HU 2, WHCF, Box 2, NPM; Memorandum, Donald Rumsfeld to Nixon, 28 May 1970, Ex HU 2, Box 2, NPM; Memorandum, Lamar Alexander to Bryce Harlow, Ex HU 2, WHCF, Box 2, NPM. See generally Paul Frymer and John David Skrentny, "Coalition-Building and the Politics of Electoral Capture During the Nixon Administration: African Americans, Labor, Latinos," *Studies in American Political Development* 12 (1998): 131–61.

20. A. Philip Randolph Institute, *Reluctant Guardians*, 4, 26–29, 31–32, II-1–21; Civil Rights and OMB, Bradley H. Patterson, Jr. Office Files, WHCF, Box 21, NPM.

21. John Herbers, "Problems Face Job Rights Unit As Roosevelt Assumes Office," *New York Times*, 3 June 1965, p. 23.

22. *Congressional Record*, 88th Cong., 2d sess., 1964, 110, pt. 4: 5439; "Attacks on the Civil Rights Bill Made by Senator Thurmond in Debate on March 17, 1964, and Answers Thereto," 1964 Justice Department Preparation of Bill Material, Box 1, Legislative Background, Civil Rights Act of 1964, p. 12, LBJL; William J. Kendrick to Henry Wilson, 20 July 1965, Equal Opportunity, Office Files of Henry Wilson, Box 7, LBJL; House Committee on Education and Labor, General Subcommittee on Labor, *Equal Employment Opportunity, 1965*, 89th Cong., 1st sess., 1965, 101–15.

23. Memorandum, Lee C. White to Johnson, 5 October 1965. *Civil Rights During Johnson*, part 1, reel 5; William L. Taylor to Lee C. White, 8 December 1965, *Civil Rights During Johnson*, part 1, reel 11; Memorandum, Katzenbach to Califano, 9 October 1965, LE/HU, WHCF, Box 65, LBJL; Memorandum, Katzenbach to Califano, 13 December 1965, LE, WHCF, Box 65, LBJL; Ramsey Clark to Charles L. Schultze, 21 March 1966, LE/HU 2–1, WHCF, Box 66, LBJL; Memorandum, W.H. Rommel to Harry McPherson, 22 April 1966, LE/HU 2–1, WHCF, Box 66, LBJL.

24. Memorandum, Ramsey Clark to Joseph Califano, 1966 Task Force Report, Legislative Background, Civil Rights Act of 1964, LBJL; Memorandum, Roy Wilkins to Johnson, 29 December, 1966, *Civil Rights During Johnson*, part 1, reel 11; Memorandum, Harry C. McPherson, Jr. to Johnson, 30 December 1966, *Civil Rights During Johnson*, part 1 reel 11; Ramsey Clark to Humphrey, 17 February 1967, *Civil Rights During Johnson*, part 1, reel 10; Ramsey Clark to Humphrey, 17 February 1967, *Civil Rights During Johnson*, part 1, reel 10; Graham, *Civil Rights Era*, 262–73; Douglas S. Massey and Nancy A. Denton, *American Apartheid: Segregation and the Making of the Underclass* (Cambridge: Harvard University Press, 1993), 192–94.

25. Memorandum, Ramsey Clark to Joseph Califano, 1966 Task Force Report, Legislative Background, Civil Rights Act of 1964, LBJL; Memorandum, Steve Pollak to James Gaither, 30 October 1968, *Civil Rights During Johnson*, part 1, reel 10.

26. Reps. William F. Ryan, Philip Burton, John Conyers Jr, Edward R. Roybal, and Charles C. Diggs to Johnson, 20 June 1968, *Civil Rights During Johnson*, part 1, reel 7; Background Paper on Organization and Procedures of Equal Employment Opportunity Commission After Transfer of Functions Under Executive Order 11246, *Civil Rights During Johnson*, part 1, reel 10.

27. Skrentny, *Ironies of Affirmative Action*, 178–82; Stephen Skowronek, *The Politics Presidents Make: Leadership from John Adams to George Bush* (Cambridge: Harvard University Press, 1993), 43–45; Frymer and Skrentny, "Coalition-Building"; Dean J. Kotlowski, *Nixon's Civil Rights: Politics, Principle, and Policy* (Cambridge: Harvard University Press, 2001).

28. Alexander to Nixon, 8 April 1969, FG 109, WHCF, Box 1, NPM; Reps. Donald M. Fraser, John Brademas, James C. Corman, and Don Edwards to Nixon, 27 June 1969, Ex HU 2, WHCF, Box 2, NPM.

29. Ramsey Clark to Charles L. Schultze, 21 March 1966, LE/HU 2–1, WHCF, Box 66, LBJL; Memorandum, Nixon to John Mitchell, 13 February 1969, Ex FG 109, WHCF, Box 1, NPM; Memorandum, Arthur Burns to Nixon, 15 March 1969, Ex LE, WHCF, Box 1, NPM; Alton Frye to Daniel P. Moynihan, 24 March 1969, Gen HU 2–2, WHCF, Box 18, NPM; Memorandum, Peter Flanigan to Jerris Leonard, 29 April 1969, Ex FG 109, WHCF, Box 1, NPM.

30. Proposed Draft of Presidential Message to Congress, Equal Employment Opportunity, Ex SP 2–3, WHCF, Box 26, NPM; Memorandum, William H. Brown III to Daniel P. Moynihan, 29 April 1969, Ex SP 2–3, WHCF, Box 26, NPM; Memorandum, Robert J. Brown to Ken Cole, 30 April 1969, Ex SP 2–3, WHCF, Box 26, NPM; Memorandum, Moynihan to Cole, 30 April 1969, Ex SP 2–3, WHCF, Box 26, NPM; Memorandum, Jerris Leonard to Bryce N. Harlow, 28 April 1969, Ex SP 2–3, WHCF, Box 26, NPM; Memorandum, Ken Cole to John Ehrlichman, 1 October 1970, FG 109, WHCF, Box 1, NPM.

31. Memorandum, Ken Cole to Arthur Burns, Pat Moynihan, Jerris Leonard, Jim Keogh, John Mitchell, 30 April 1969, Ex SP 2–3, WHCF, Box 26, NPM; Memorandum, Steve Hess to John Ehrlichman, EEOC, Office Files of Bradley Patterson, Box 29, NPM; Memorandum, Jerris Leonard to John Ehrlichman, [22 October 1969], FG 109, WHCF, Box 1, NPM.

32. Memorandum, Arthur F. Burns to Nixon, 8 August 1969, Ex HU 2–2, WHCF, Box 17, NPM; Memorandum, Richard T. Burress to John D. Ehrlichman, 19 November 1969, HU 2–2, WHCF, Box 17, NPM; Clayton Willis to Ronald Ziegler, 18 August 1969, FG 109, WHCF, Box 1, NPM; Transcript, Today Show Interview with William H. Brown III, 15 August 1969, FG 109, WHCF, Box 1, NPM; James K. Batten, "Equal Employment Boss: Slaying a Dragon With a Pea-Shooter," *Miami Herald*, 23 October 1969, 8-B (attached to Clayton Willis to Ronald Ziegler, 31 October 1969, FG 109, WHCF, Box 1, NPM).

33. Memorandum, Ken Cole to John Ehrlichman, 1 October 1970, FG 109, WHCF, Box 1, NPM; Confidential Memorandum, Ken Cole to file, 9 November 1970, Ex LE, WHCF, Box 3, NPM; Memorandum, Leonard Garment to John

Ehrlichman, 27 November 1970, FI 4/FG 109, WHCF, Box 26, NPM; Graham, *Civil Rights Era*, 433; *Congressional Quarterly Almanac* 26 (1972), 710–12.

34. Memorandum, William H. Brown III to Leonard Garment, 5 November 1970, FI 4/FG 109, WHCF, Box 26, NPM.

35. Memorandum, Tom Stoel to Garment, 16 January 1971, EEOC, Office Files of Bradley Patterson, Box 29, NPM; Confidential Memorandum, Cole to Garment, 17 February 1971, CF HU 2, WHCF, Box 35, NPM; Memorandum, Ken Cole to John Ehrlichman, 1 October 1970, FG 109, WHCF, Box 1, NPM; Memorandum, Laurence Silberman to Garment, 17 February 1971, EEOC, Office Files of Bradley Patterson, Box 29, NPM; Memorandum, Charles Perry to Leonard Garment, 22 February 1971, EEOC, Office Files of Bradley Patterson, Box 29, NPM; Memorandum, Silberman to Cole, 6 April 1971, FG 109, WHCF, Box 1, NPM.

36. Graham, *Civil Rights Era*, 439–43; *Congressional Quarterly Almanac* 28 (1972), 247–56, 2-S–9-S.

37. Graham, *Civil Rights Era*, 443; Tom Wicker, "The Same Old Story," *New York Times*, 10 February 1972, p. 43.

38. Skrentny, *Ironies of Affirmative Action*, 225; Graham, *Civil Rights Era*, 439–45.

39. There remained a final conflict between the EEOC and the Civil Rights Division of the Justice Department over the transfer of functions, which was resolved only with some difficulty in 1974.

40. Cabell Phillips, "Franklin Roosevelt Jr. to Head Equal Job Opportunity Agency," *New York Times*, 11 May 1965, p. 1; Memorandum, John W. Macy Jr. to Marvin Watson, 3 August 1965, FG 655, WHCF, Box 380, LBJL; Memorandum, Bill Moyers to Franklin D. Roosevelt Jr., 21 August 1965, FG 655, WHCF, Box 380, LBJL; E. W. Kenworthy, "Senate Restores Job Agency Funds," *New York Times*, 13 August 1965, p. 14; *Congressional Record*, 89th Cong., 1st sess., 1965, 111, pt. 15: 20961; Graham, *Civil Rights Era*, 179. Roosevelt did run for governor in 1966 on the Liberal Party line and received half a million votes (around 8 percent).

41. Skrentny, *Ironies of Affirmative Action*, 123–24; Graham, *Civil Rights Era*, 239–40.

42. Aaron Wildavsky, *The Politics of the Budgetary Process*, 4th ed. (Boston: Little, Brown, 1984).

43. Memorandum, Patterson to Garment, [May 1972], EEOC, Office Files of Bradley Patterson, Box 29, NPM.

44. Memorandum, Dwight Ink to Charles Perry, 22 February 1971, EEOC, Office Files of Bradley Patterson, Box 29, NPM; Memorandum, Dean to Garment, 26 February 1971, EEOC, Office Files of Bradley Patterson, Box 29, NPM; Graham, *Civil Rights Era*, 435–36.

45. Memorandum, Garment to Cole, 24 May 1972, EEOC, Office Files of Bradley Patterson, Box 29, NPM.

46. John Cramer, "EEOC Is Badly Run, Violates Law, CSC Says," *Washington Evening Star and Daily News*, 21 May 1973 (CF FG 109, WHCF, Box 23, NPM); Memorandum, Ethel Walsh to William H. Brown III, 22 May 1973, CF FG 109, WHCF, Box 23, NPM.

47. Graham, *Civil Rights Era*, 445.

48. The data reported on EEOC caseloads were calculated from figures reported in the EEOC's annual reports. The annual number of charges received is reported each year. The annual number of charges resolved includes all cases on which the commission finished its work, either by completing an investigation and issuing a determination of probable cause or no cause, finishing a conciliation process, or transferring or deferring the case to a state EEO agency. The cumulative backlog is simply the running total of the difference between these two figures.

49. Richard P. Young and Jerome S. Burstein, "Federalism and the Demise of Prescriptive Racism in the United States," *Studies in American Political Development* 9 (1995): 1–54.

50. J. David Greenstone and Paul E. Peterson, *Race and Authority in Urban Politics: Community Participation and the War on Poverty* (New York: Russell Sage Foundation, 1973); James A. Morone, *The Democratic Wish: Popular Participation and the Limits of American Government* (New York: Basic, 1990), chap. 6; James W. Button, *Blacks and Social Change: Impact of the Civil Rights Movement in Southern Communities* (Princeton: Princeton University Press, 1989).

51. Sovern, *Legal Restraints on Racial Discrimination in Employment* (New York: Twentieth Century Fund, 1966), 73–75; Alfred W. Blumrosen, *Black Employment and the Law* (New Brunswick, N.J.: Rutgers University Press, 1971), 83–89, 149–55.

52. Judith Stein, *Running Steel, Running America: Race, Economic Policy, and the Decline of Liberalism* (Chapel Hill: University of North Carolina Press, 1998), 113. See also Herman Belz, *Equality Transformed: A Quarter-Century of Affirmative Action* (New Brunswick, N.J.: Transaction, 1991), 29.

53. Blumrosen, *Black Employment and the Law*, 66–79; Graham, *Civil Rights Era*, 193–97, 239–43.

54. Memorandum, Clifford L. Alexander Jr. to Loyd Hackler, 28 December 1967, FG, WHCF, Box 380, LBJL; Memorandum, Clifford L. Alexander Jr. to Henry Fowler, 12 April 1968, HU 2–1, WHCF, Box 44, LBJL; Stein, *Running Steel*, 118; Dirksen to Bryce Harlow, 7 April 1969, CF FG 109, WHSF/WHCF, Box 23, NPM; Memorandum, Flanigan to Cole, 14 April 1969, CF FG 109, WHSF/WHCF, Box 23, NPM; Memorandum, Garment to Flanigan, HU 2–2, WHCF, Box 17, NPM; Memorandum, Flanigan to Bill Timmons, 9 April 1970, HU 2–2, WHCF, Box 17, NPM.

55. Stein, *Running Steel*, 111–13; Graham, *Civil Rights Era*, 251–54.; Skrentny, *Ironies of Affirmative Action*, 127–33.

56. *Griggs v. Duke Power Company*, 420 F.2d. 1225 (4th Cir. 1970); *Griggs v. Duke Power Company*, 401 U.S. 424 (1971); Graham, *Civil Rights Era*, 385–86; Richard A. Epstein, *Forbidden Grounds: The Case Against Employment Discrimination Laws* (Cambridge: Harvard University Press, 1992), 193–94; Belz, *Equality Transformed*, 52–53; Andrew Kull, *The Color-Blind Constitution* (Cambridge: Harvard University Press, 1992), 204–5.

57. Blumrosen, *Black Employment and the Law*, 144–49; Stein, *Running Steel*, 102–5, 112; Belz, *Equality Transformed*, 28–29; Graham, *Civil Rights Era*, 250–

54, 385; Jack Greenberg, *Crusaders in the Courts: How a Dedicated Band of Lawyers Fought for the Civil Rights Revolution* (New York: Basic, 1994), 418–20.

58. Alexander M. Bickel, *The Least Dangerous Branch: The Supreme Court at the Bar of Politics*, 2d ed. (New Haven: Yale University Press, 1986), 247. See also Gerald N. Rosenberg, *The Hollow Hope: Can Courts Bring About Social Change?* (Chicago: University of Chicago Press, 1991).

59. Theda Skocpol, Marshall Ganz, and Ziad Munson, "A Nation of Organizers: The Institutional Origins of Civic Voluntarism in the United States," *American Political Science Review* 94 (2000): 527–46; Skrentny, *Ironies of Affirmative Action*, 114–17; Graham, *Civil Rights Era*, 110–13; Paul Burstein, *Discrimination, Jobs, and Politics: The Struggle for Equal Employment Opportunity in the United States since the New Deal* (Chicago: University of Chicago Press, 1985).

60. Kull, *Color-Blind Constitution*; Graham, *Civil Rights Era*; Stephan Thernstrom and Abigail Thernstrom, *America in Black and White: One Nation, Indivisible* (New York: Simon and Schuster, 1997), 423–40.

61. Commission for Racial Equality, *First Annual Report, 1977*, Parliamentary Papers HC 529, 1977/78, vol. 49 (London: Her Majesty's Stationery Office, 1978), 112.

62. Commission for Racial Equality, *Annual Report, 1978*, Parliamentary Papers HC 128, 1979–80, vol. 12 (London: Her Majesty's Stationery Office, 1979), 20–21; Christopher McCrudden, "Anti-Discrimination Goals and the Legal Process," and Peter Sanders, "Anti-Discrimination Law Enforcement in Britain," in *Ethnic Pluralism and Public Policy: Achieving Equality in the United States and Britain*, ed. Nathan Glazer and Ken Young (Lexington, Mass.: D. C. Heath, 1983), 56–59, 77.

63. The data reported in figure 8.2 were compiled from CRE Annual Reports.

64. John Wrench and Tariq Modood, "The Effectiveness of Employment Equality Policies in Relation to Immigrants and Ethnic Minorities in the UK," International Migration Paper No. 38 (Geneva: International Labour Office, International Migration Branch, 2001), 43–44.

65. House of Commons, Home Affairs Committee, Race Relations and Integration Sub-Committee, "The Operation and Effectiveness of the Commission for Racial Equality," *Sessional Papers, 1980–81*, 11 May 1981, vol. 26, 91.

66. Sanders, "Anti-Discrimination Law Enforcement in Britain," 79–81; Commons, "Operation and Effectiveness," 11 May 1981, p. 79. The data on formal investigations are from the CRE's annual reports.

67. Commission on Racial Equality, *Annual Report, 1986* (London: Her Majesty's Stationery Office, 1987), 7.

68. Steven M. Teles, "Positive Action or Affirmative Action? The Persistence of Britain's Antidiscrimination Regime," in *Color Lines: Affirmative Action, Immigration, and Civil Rights Options for America*, ed. John David Skrentny (Chicago: University of Chicago Press, 2001); Commission for Racial Equality, *Annual Report, 1984* (London: Her Majesty's Stationery Office, 1985), 13–14; Commission for Racial Equality, *Annual Report, 1985* (London: Her Majesty's Stationery Office, 1986), 15; Wrench and Modood, "The Effectiveness of Employment Equality Policies," 50–61.

69. "10 Promotions, four resignations in Callaghan reshuffle," *Times*, 15 April 1976, pp. 1–2; "Mr Callaghan accused on racial harmony," *Times*, 17 April 1976, p. 2; "Alex Lyon 'invited sacking'," *Observer*, 18 April 1976, p. 3; "Former minister tells of clash with civil servants over immigration," *Times*, 26 April 1976, 2; "Callaghan denial of change in race relations policy," *Times*, 27 April 1976, p. 3; "Mr. Lyon describes how reform attempts were frustrated," *Times*, 10 May 1976, p. 3; Alex Lyon, "Race: Why we must act now," *Sunday Times*, 23 May 1976, p. 16; Roy Jenkins, *A Life at the Centre* (London: Macmillan, 1991), 443; Ira Katznelson, *Black Men, White Cities: Race, Politics and Migration in the United States, 1900–1930, and Britain, 1948–1968* (Chicago: University of Chicago Press, 1968), 181; Gary P. Freeman, *Immigrant Labor and Racial Conflict in Industrial Societies: The French and British Experience, 1945–1975* (Princeton: Princeton University Press, 1979), 58, 126.

70. Martin MacEwen, "Anti-Discrimination Law in Great Britain," *New Community* 40 (1994): 353–70; Chris Boothman and Martin MacEwen, "The British Commission for Racial Equality as an Enforcement Agency," in *Anti-Discrimination Law Enforcement: A Comparative Perspective*, ed. Martin MacEwen (Aldershot: Avebury, 1997); Anthony M. Messina, *Race and Party Competition in Britain* (Oxford: Oxford University Press, 1989), 134. See also Sven Steinmo, *Taxation and Democracy: Swedish, British, and American Approaches to Financing the Modern State* (New Haven: Yale University Press, 1993).

71. Commons, "Operation and Effectiveness," 30 March 1981, p. 26.

72. Commons, "Operation and Effectiveness," 30 March 1981, pp. 63–65.

73. Commons, "Operation and Effectiveness," 22 June 1981, pp. 224–26, 233.

74. Commons, "Operation and Effectiveness," 30 March 1981, p. 68; 13 July 1981, pp. 243–44.

75. MacEwen, "Anti-Discrimination Law in Great Britain," 363–67; Ray Honeyford, *The Commission for Racial Equality: British Bureaucracy and the Multiethnic Society* (New Brunswick, N.J.: Transaction, 1998), 67–72.

76. Tariq Modood, "Ethnicity and Political Mobilisation in Britain," in *Ethnicity, Social Mobility, and Public Policy in the United States and the United Kingdom*, ed. Glenn Loury, Tariq Modood, and Steven Teles (Cambridge: Cambridge University Press, 2005); McCrudden, "Anti-Discrimination Goals and the Legal Process," 68–71; Martin MacEwen, *Tackling Racism in Europe: An Examination of Anti-Discrimination Law in Practice* (Oxford: Berg, 1995), 194–96; L. Lustgarten and J. Edwards, "Racial Inequality and the Limits of the Law," in *Racism and Antiracism: Inequalities, Opportunities and Policies*, ed. Peter Braham, Ali Rattansi, and Richard Skellington (London: Sage, 1992); John Edwards, *Positive Discrimination, Social Justice, and Social Policy: Moral Scrutiny of a Policy Practice* (London: Tavistock, 1987), 28–31; Elaine Dubourdieu, "The Theory and Practices of 'Positive Discrimination'," in *Discourse on Inequality in France and Britain*, ed. John Edwards and Jean-Paul Révauger (Aldershot: Ashgate, 1998), 95.

77. See Wendy Ball and John Solomos, eds., *Race and Local Politics* (London: Macmillan, 1990). On local developmental politics, see Paul E. Peterson, *City Limits* (Chicago: University of Chicago Press, 1981).

78. Commons, "Operation and Effectiveness," 1 June 1981, pp. 124–25.

79. Ken Young, "Approaches to Policy Development in the Field of Equal Opportunities," in *Race and Local Politics*, ed. Ball and Solomos; Gideon Ben-Tovim, John Gabriel, Ian Law, and Kathleen Stredder, *The Local Politics of Race* (Houndmills: Macmillan, 1986).

80. Grant McConnell, *Private Power and American Democracy* (New York: Knopf, 1966); Katznelson, *Black Men, White Cities*; Robert C. Lieberman, *Shifting the Color Line: Race and the American Welfare State* (Cambridge: Harvard University Press, 1998).

81. Ian Forbes and Geoffrey Mead, *Measure for Measure: A Comparative Analysis of Measures to Combat Racial Discrimination in the Member Countries of the European Community* (Southampton: Equal Opportunities Study Group, University of Southampton, 1992), 36–37; Jacqueline Costa-Lascoux, "French Legislation Against Racism and Discrimination," *New Community* 20 (1994): 376–78; Régine Dhoquois, "Idéologie conciliatrice et répression des récalcitrants dans l'inspection du travail (1892–1970)," and Philippe Auvergnon, "Débats et idées sur l'Inspection du travail sous la Vᵉ République," in *Inspecteurs et inspection du travail sous la IIIᵉ et IVᵉ République*, ed. Jean-Louis Robert (Paris: Documentation Française, 1998).

82. Jacqueline Costa-Lascoux, "Des lois contre le racisme," in *Face au Racisme*, ed. Pierre-André Taguieff (Paris: La Découverte, 1991); Commission Nationale Consultative des Droits de l'Homme, *La lutte contre le racisme et la xénophobie, 1998* (Paris: Documentation Française, 1999), 313–15. The EEOC data are from the EEOC's Annual Reports. The courts data were compiled by Sean Farhang from records of the Administrative Office of the United States Courts. Both the EEOC and courts data include all forms of discrimination under federal jurisdiction, not just claims of racial discrimination.

83. David Stuart Blatt, "Immigration Politics and Immigrant Collective Action in France, 1968–1993" (Ph.D. diss., Cornell University, 1996); Sidney Tarrow, *Power in Movement: Social Movements, Collective Action and Politics* (Cambridge: Cambridge University Press, 1994), 177–79; Don Dignan, "Europe's Melting Pot: A Century of Large-Scale Immigration Into France," *Ethnic and Racial Studies* 4 (1981): 148–50; Catherine Wihtol de Wenden, *Les immigrés et la politique: Cent cinquante ans d'évolution* (Paris: Presses de la Fondation Nationale des Sciences Politiques, 1988), 137–42; Freeman, *Immigrant Labor and Racial Conflict*, 78–92; Patrick Weil, *La France et ses étrangers: L'aventure d'une politique de l'immigration, 1938–1991* (Paris: Calmann-Lévy, 1991), 69–71; Michèle Lamont, *The Dignity of Working Men: Morality and the Boundaries of Race, Class, and Immigration* (New York: Russell Sage Foundation; Cambridge: Harvard University Press, 2000); Patrick R. Ireland, *The Policy Challenge of Ethnic Diversity: Immigrant Politics in France and Switzerland* (Cambridge: Harvard University Press, 1994), 71–72; Jonathan Marcus, *The National Front and French Politics: The Resistible Rise of Jean-Marie Le Pen* (New York: New York University Press, 1995), 52–55; Françoise Gaspard, *A Small City in France*, trans. Arthur Goldhammer (Cambridge: Harvard University Press, 1995), 120–31; Taguieff, ed., *Face au racisme*; Pierre-André Taguieff, "L'antiracisme en crise: Eléments d'une critique réformiste," in *Racisme et modernité*, ed. Michel Wieviorka (Paris:

La Découverte, 1993); Vincent Geisser, *Ethnicité républicaine: Les élites d'origine maghrébine dans le système politique français* (Paris: Presses de la Fondation Nationale des Sciences Politiques, 1997); Philippe Bataille, *Le racisme au travail* (Paris: La Découverte, 1997).

84. Commission Nationale Consultative des Droits de l'Homme, *La lutte contre le racisme*, 314–15; F. H. Lawson, A. E. Anton, and L. Neville Brown, *Amos and Walton's Introduction to French Law*, 3rd ed. (Oxford: Oxford University Press, 1967), 7–12; Frank Dobbin and John R. Sutton, "The Strength of a Weak State: The Rights Revolution and the Rise of Human Resources Management Divisions," *American Journal of Sociology* 104 (1998): 441–76; Bataille, *Le racisme au travail*, 121–31; François Vourc'h, Véronique de Rudder, and Maryse Tripier, "Racisme et discriminations dans le travail: Une réalité occultée," *L'Homme et la société* 121 (July–December 1996): 145–59.

85. See Peter Bachrach and Morton S. Baratz, "Decisions and Nondecisions: An Analytic Framework," *American Political Science Review* 57 (1963): 632–42.

86. Kull, *Color-Blind Constitution*, 191. See also Thernstrom and Thernstrom, *America in Black and White*, 424–27; Graham, *Civil Rights Era*.

CHAPTER NINE

1. King's speech at the March on Washington of 28 August 1963 is widely anthologized. The peroration, including the pertinent passage, appears in David J. Garrow, *Bearing the Cross: Martin Luther King, Jr., and the Southern Christian Leadership Conference* (New York: William Morrow, 1986), 283–84. King recycled this locution in the dedication of his 1964 book, *Why We Can't Wait* (New York: Mentor, 1964), v.

2. Nathan Glazer, *Affirmative Discrimination: Ethnic Inequality and Public Policy* (New York: Basic, 1975); Arthur M. Schlesinger, Jr., *The Disuniting of America: Reflections on a Multicultural Society* (New York: Norton, 1991); Todd Gitlin, *The Twilight of Common Dreams: Why America Is Wracked by Culture Wars* (New York: Metropolitan Books, 1995); Shelby Steele, *The Content of Our Character: A New Vision of Race in America* (New York: St. Martin's, 1990).

3. Nathan Glazer, *We Are All Multiculturalists Now* (Cambridge: Harvard University Press, 1997), 125–27.

4. Theda Skocpol, "African Americans in U.S. Social Policy," in *Classifying by Race*, ed. Paul E. Peterson (Princeton: Princeton University Press, 1995).

5. R. Kent Weaver and Bert A. Rockman, "Assessing the Effects of Institutions," Richard Gunther and Anthony Mughan, "Political Institutions and Cleavage Management," and Arend Lijphart, Ronald Rogowski, and R. Kent Weaver, "Separation of Powers and Cleavage Management," in *Do Institutions Matter? Government Capabilities in the United States and Abroad*, ed. R. Kent Weaver and Bert A. Rockman (Washington, D.C.: Brookings Institution, 1993).

6. E. E. Schattschneider, *The Semisovereign People: A Realist's View of Democracy in America* (New York: Holt, Rinehart and Winston, 1960); William H. Riker, *The Art of Political Manipulation* (New Haven: Yale University Press, 1986). See also James Madison's *Federalist Papers*, nos. 10 and 51.

7. Sidney Tarrow, *Power in Movement: Social Movements, Collective Action, and Politics* (Cambridge: Cambridge University Press); Edwin Amenta, *When Movements Matter: The Impact of the Townsend Plan and U.S. Social Spending Challengers* (typescript, New York University, 2002); Theda Skocpol, *Diminished Democracy: From Membership to Management in American Civic Life* (Norman: University of Oklahoma Press, 2003); Elisabeth S. Clemens, *The People's Lobby: Organizational Innovation and the Rise of Interest Group Politics in the United States, 1890–1925* (Chicago: University of Chicago Press, 1997); Mancur Olson, *The Logic of Collective Action: Public Goods and the Theory of Groups* (Cambridge: Harvard University Press, 1965); Schattschneider, *Semisovereign People*.

8. Gunnar Myrdal, *An American Dilemma: The Negro Problem and Modern Democracy* (New York: Harper and Brothers, 1944).

9. Examples on the Left include Derrick Bell, *Faces at the Bottom of the Well: The Permanence of Racism* (New York: Basic, 1992); Andrew Hacker, *Two Nations: Black and White, Separate, Hostile, Unequal* (New York: Scribner's, 1992). On the Right, see Thomas Sowell, *Civil Rights: Rhetoric or Reality?* (New York: William Morrow, 1984); Stephan Thernstrom and Abigail Thernstrom, *America in Black and White: One Nation, Indivisible* (New York: Simon and Schuster, 1997); Jim Sleeper, *Liberal Racism* (New York: Viking, 1997). For defenses of race consciousness, see Glazer, *We Are All Multiculturalists Now*; Stephen Steinberg, *Turning Back: The Retreat from Racial Justice in American Thought and Policy* (Boston: Beacon, 1995); K. Anthony Appiah and Amy Gutmann, *Color Conscious: The Political Morality of Race* (Princeton: Princeton University Press, 1996).

10. *Grutter v. Bollinger*, 539 U.S. 306 (2003). This was the case concerning the university's law school. The other case [*Gratz v. Bollinger*, 539 U.S. 244 (2003)], in which the court struck down the university's undergraduate admissions policy because it applied race-conscious standards too mechanistically and impersonally, is less significant because it did not contradict *Grutter*'s central holding that race-conscious approaches are allowable. See Marta Tienda, Kevin T. Leicht, Teresa Sullivan, Michael Maltese, and Kim Lloyd, "Closing the Gap? Admissions and Enrollment at the Texas Public Flagships before and after Affirmative Action" (typescript, Princeton University, 2003), available at http://www.texastop10.princeton.edu/publications/tienda012103.pdf.

11. Anatole France, *Le lys rouge*, in *Œuvres* (Paris: Gallimard, 1987), 2:399.

12. Robert C. Lieberman, *Shifting the Color Line: Race and the American Welfare State* (Cambridge: Harvard University Press, 1998); see also Ira Katznelson and Sean Farhang, "The Southern Imposition: Congress and Labor in the New Deal and Fair Deal," *Studies in American Political Development* 19 (2005); Alexander Keyssar, *The Right to Vote: The Contested History of Democracy in the United States* (New York: Basic, 2000).

13. Martin Gilens, *Why American Hate Welfare: Race, Media, and the Politics of Antipoverty Policy* (Chicago: University of Chicago Press, 1999).

14. James Smith and Finis Welch, "Black Economic Progress after Myrdal," *Journal of Economic Literature* 27 (1989): 519–64; James J. Heckman and Brook S. Payner, "Determining the Impact of Federal Antidiscrimination Policy on the Economic Status of Blacks: A Study of South Carolina," *American Economic Review*

79 (1989): 138–77; James J. Heckman, "The Central Role of the South in Accounting for the Economic Progress of Black Americans," *American Economic Review* 80 (1990): 242–46; John J. Donohue III and James Heckman, "Continuous Versus Episodic Change: The Impact of Civil Rights Policy on the Economic Status of Blacks," *Journal of Economic Literature* 29 (1991): 1603–43; Harry J. Holzer and David Neumark, "What Does Affirmative Action Do?" *Industrial and Labor Relations Review* 53 (2000): 240–71; William G. Bowen and Derek Bok, *The Shape of the River: Long-Term Consequences of Considering Race in College and University Admissions* (Princeton: Princeton University Press, 1998); William Julius Wilson, *The Declining Significance of Race: Blacks and Changing American Institutions* (Chicago: University of Chicago Press, 1978); William Julius Wilson, *The Truly Disadvantaged: The Inner City, the Underclass, and Public Policy* (Chicago: University of Chicago Press, 1987), 109–18.

15. Kenneth Prewitt, "The Census Counts, The Census Classifies," in *Not Just Black and White: Historical and Contemporary Perspectives on Immigration, Race, and Ethnicity in the United States*, ed. Nancy Foner and George M. Fredrickson (New York: Russell Sage Foundation, 2004); Melissa Nobles, *Shades of Citizenship: Race and the Census in Modern Politics* (Stanford: Stanford University Press, 2000); David I. Kertzer and Dominique Arel, eds., *Census and Identity: The Politics of Race, Ethnicity, and Language in National Censuses* (Cambridge: Cambridge University Press, 2002).

16. Desmond King, *Making Americans: Immigration, Race, and the Origins of the Diverse Democracy* (Cambridge: Harvard University Press, 2000); Mae M. Ngai, "The Architecture of Race in American Immigration Law: A Reexamination of the Immigration Act of 1924," *Journal of American History* 86 (1999): 67–92; Matthew Frye Jacobson, *Whiteness of a Different Color: European Immigrants and the Alchemy of Race* (Cambridge: Harvard University Press, 1998); Gary Gerstle, *American Crucible: Race and Nation in the Twentieth Century* (Princeton: Princeton University Press, 2001); Daniel J. Tichenor, *Dividing Lines: The Politics of Immigration Control in America* (Princeton: Princeton University Press, 2002); Glazer, *We Are All Multiculturalists Now*; John D. Skrentny, *The Minority Rights Revolution* (Cambridge: Harvard University Press, 2002).

17. Under the Census's new multiple-race option, available for the first time in 2000, 12.3% reported their race as black alone and 12.9% as black in combination with one or more other races. Latinos (of any race) were 12.5%. The Census Bureau estimates that by 2002 the Latino population was larger than the black population no matter how the black population is counted. U.S. Census Bureau, Population Division, *National Population Estimates, Characteristics*, table NA-EST2002-ASRO-04 (2003); U.S. Bureau of the Census, *Population Projections of the United States by Age, Sex, Race, and Hispanic Origin: 1995 to 2050*, Current Population Reports, P25–1130 (Washington, D.C.: U.S. Government Printing Office, 1996), 12; Aristide R. Zolberg and Long Litt Woon, "Why Islam Is Like Spanish: Cultural Incorporation in Europe and the United States," *Politics and Society* 27 (1999): 5–38.

18. Latinos are also the only group whose median benefits have experienced absolute declines, although the general trend is still upward, if gradually. Social Security benefit data are from the Annual Statistical Supplement of the *Social*

Security Bulletin. See also Bernard Wasow, "Setting the Record Straight: Social Security Works for Latinos" (New York: Social Security Network/Century Foundation, 2002); Eric Rodriguez, "Social Security Reform: Issues for Hispanic Americans," Submitted to U.S. House of Representatives, Committee on Ways and Means, Subcommittee on Social Security (Washington, D.C.: National Council of La Raza, 1999).

19. U.S. Bureau of the Census, *Current Population Survey, Annual Demographic Supplement* (various years); Albert M. Camarillo and Frank Bonilla, "Hispanics in a Multicultural Society: A New American Dilemma?" in *America Becoming: Racial Trends and Their Consequences*, ed. Neil J. Smelser, William Julius Wilson, and Faith Mitchell (Washington, D.C.: National Academy Press, 2001), 110–14.

20. U.S. Department of Health and Human Services, *Indicators of Welfare Dependence: Annual Report to the Congress* (various years).

21. Eric Rodriguez and Kaydee Kirk, "Welfare Reform, TANF Caseload Changes, and Latinos: A Preliminary Assessment," Issue Brief No. 3 (Washington, D.C.: National Council of La Raza, 2000).

22. Labor market data are from the U.S. Bureau of Labor Statistics. See also Camarillo and Bonilla, "Hispanics in a Multicultural Society," 112–13. These aggregate data, it should be noted, conceal substantial variation among Latinos by country of origin, immigration status, and sex. Evelyn Nakano Glenn, *Unequal Freedom: How Race and Gender Shaped American Citizenship and Labor* (Cambridge: Harvard University Press, 2002); Claire Gonzales, *The Empty Promise: The EEOC and Hispanics* (Washington, D.C.: National Council of La Raza, 1993), 3–9; Alfred W. Blumrosen and Ruth G. Blumrosen, *The Reality of Intentional Job Discrimination in Metropolitan America—1999* (Rutgers University, 2002, available at www.eeo1.com), xv. The Blumrosens measure the risk of discrimination by comparing firm-level employment patterns of minorities and women with average levels of employment for each group in the same industry and metropolitan area for the same occupational category. Firms are deemed to discriminate if their employment level of a particular group is more than two standard deviations below the relevant mean. They outline their estimation procedure in chap. 5 and appendix C.

23. Skrentny, *The Minority Rights Revolution*, chap. 4; Gonzales, *The Empty Promise*, 13–25.

24. Douglas S. Massey and Nancy A. Denton, "Hypersegregation in U.S. Metropolitan Areas: Black and Hispanic Segregation along Five Dimensions," *Demography* 26 (1989): 373–91; Douglas S. Massey and Nancy A. Denton, *American Apartheid: Segregation and the Making of the Underclass* (Cambridge: Harvard University Press, 1993), 77, 112–14; Nathan Glazer and Daniel P. Moynihan, *Beyond the Melting Pot: The Negroes, Puerto Ricans, Jews, Italians, and Irish of New York City*, 2d ed. (Cambridge: MIT Press, 1970); Camarillo and Bonilla, "Hispanics in a Multicultural Society," 130–31.

25. Glenn, *Unequal Freedom*; Linda Gordon, *The Great Arizona Orphan Abduction* (Cambridge: Harvard University Press, 1999); Neil Foley, *The White Scourge: Mexicans, Blacks, and Poor Whites in Texas Cotton Culture* (Berkeley: University of California Press, 1997); Clara E. Rodr,guez, *Changing Race: La-*

tinos, the Census, and the History of Ethnicity in the United States (New York: New York University Press, 2000); Rodney E. Hero, *Latinos and the U.S. Political System: Two-Tiered Pluralism* (Philadelphia: Temple University Press, 1992); Rodney E. Hero, *Faces of Inequality: Social Diversity in American Politics* (New York: Oxford University Press, 1998); Jan E. Leighley, *Strength in Numbers? The Political Mobilization of Racial and Ethnic Minorities* (Princeton: Princeton University Press, 2001); Paul Frymer and John David Skrentny, "Coalition-Building and the Politics of Electoral Capture in the Nixon Administration: African-Americans, Labor, Latinos," *Studies in American Political Development* 12 (1998): 131–61; Paul Frymer, *Uneasy Alliances: Race and Party Competition in America* (Princeton: Princeton University Press, 1999); Rodolfo O. de la Garza and Louis DeSipio, eds., *From Rhetoric to Reality: Latino Politics in the 1988 Elections* (Boulder, Col.: Westview, 1992); Rodolfo O. de la Garza and Louis DeSipio, eds., *Ethnic Ironies: Latino Politics in the 1992 Elections* (Boulder, Col.: Westview, 1996); Rodolfo O. de la Garza and Louis DeSipio, eds., *Awash in the Mainstream: Latino Politics in the 1996 Elections* (Boulder, Col.: Westview, 1999); Rodolfo O. de la Garza, Louis DeSipio, F. Chris Garcia, John Garcia, and Angelo Falcon, *Latino Voices: Mexican, Puerto Rican, and Cuban Perspectives in American Politics* (Boulder, Col: Westview Press, 1992); Earl Shorris, *Latinos: A Biography of the People* (New York: Norton, 1992); Michael Jones-Correa, *Between Two Nations: The Political Predicament of Latinos in New York City* (Ithaca: Cornell University Press, 1998); Francisco E. González, "Latinos and American Political Development: A Looming Problem for Democratization in the United States?" (Typescript, Nuffield College, Oxford, 2004).

26. Zolberg and Woon, "Why Islam Is Like Spanish."

27. Christopher Allen and Jørgen S. Nielsen, *Summary Report on Islamophobia in the EU after 11 September 2001* (Vienna: European Monitoring Centre on Racism and Xenophobia, 2002).

28. See *Le Monde*, 14 July 1998.

29. *Le Monde*, 3 May 2002, 24 October 2002.

30. Council Directive 2000/43/EC, *Official Journal of the European Communities*, L 180, 19 July 2000, 22–26; Stephan Leibfried and Paul Pierson, eds., *European Social Policy: Between Fragmentation and Integration* (Washington, D.C.: Brookings Institution, 1995); Andrew Geddes and Virginie Guiraudon, "The Emergence of a European Union Policy Paradigm Amidst Contrasting National Models: Britain, France and EU Anti-Discrimination Policy," *West European Politics* 27 (2004): 334–53.

31. See Bob Herbert, "Keep Them Out!," *New York Times*, 7 December 2000, A39, and Colbert I. King, "Ghosts in Florida," *Washington Post*, 9 December 2000, A29, reprinted in *Bush v. Gore: The Court Cases and the Commentary*, ed. E. J. Dionne, Jr., and William Kristol (Washington, D.C.: Brookings Institution, 2001), 240–42, 248–50; Political Staff of the *Washington Post, Deadlock: The Inside Story of America's Closest Election* (New York: Public Affairs, 2001), 74–77, 158–59; *Shaw v. Reno*, 509 U.S. 630 (1993); *Georgia v. Ashcroft*, 539 U.S. 461 (2003); Abigail M. Thernstrom, *Whose Votes Count? Affirmative Action and Minority Voting Rights* (Cambridge: Harvard University Press, 1987); Lani Guinier, *The Tyranny of the Majority: Fundamental Fairness in Representative De-*

mocracy (New York: Free Press, 1994); Charles Cameron, David Epstein, and Sharyn O'Halloran, "Do Majority-Minority Districts Maximize Substantive Black Representation in Congress?" *American Political Science Review* 90 (1996): 794–812; David Lublin, *The Paradox of Representation: Racial Gerrymandering and Minority Interests in Congress* (Princeton: Princeton University Press, 1997); David T. Canon, *Race, Redistricting, and Representation: The Unintended Consequences of Black Majority Districts* (Cambridge: Harvard University Press, 1999); Katherine Tate, *Black Faces in the Mirror: African Americans and Their Representatives in the U.S. Congress* (Princeton: Princeton University Press, 2003).

32. Randall Kennedy, *Race, Crime, and the Law* (New York: Pantheon, 1997); Loïc Wacquant, "Deadly Symbiosis: When Ghetto and Prison Meet and Mesh," *Punishment and Society* 3 (2001): 95–133; Angela Behrens, Christopher Uggen, and Jeff Manza, "Ballot Manipulation and the 'Menace of Negro Domination': Racial Threat and Felon Disenfranchisement in the United States, 1850–2002," *American Journal of Sociology* 109 (2003): 559–605.

33. Randall Robinson, *The Debt: What America Owes to Blacks* (New York: Dutton, 2000); Michael C. Dawson, *Behind the Mule: Race and Class in African-American Politics* (Princeton: Princeton University Press, 1994); Dalton Conley, *Being Black, Living in the Red: Race, Wealth, and Social Policy in America* (Berkeley: University of California Press, 1999). For a highly polemical statement of the case against reparations and a rather tendentious account of the rising temperature of the debate, see David Horowitz, *Uncivil Wars: The Controversy over Reparations for Slavery* (San Francisco: Encounter Books, 2002).

34. Rebecca M. Blank, "An Overview of Trends in Social and Economic Well-Being, by Race," in *America Becoming*, ed. Smelser, Wilson, and Mitchell; Council on Economic Advisors, *Changing America: Indicators of Social and Economic Well-Being by Race and Hispanic Origin* (Washington, D.C.: U.S. Government Printing Office, 1998); Joe Soss, Sanford F. Schram, Thomas P. Vartanian, and Erin O'Brien, "Setting the Terms of Relief: Explaining State Policy Choices in the Devolution Revolution," *American Journal of Political Science* 45 (2001): 378–95; Lael R. Keiser, Peter R. Mueser, and Seung-Whan Choi, "Race, Bureaucratic Discretion, and the Implementation of Welfare Reform," *American Journal of Political Science* 48 (2004): 314–27; Kenneth Finegold and Sarah Staveteig, "Race, Ethnicity, and Welfare Reform," in *Welfare Reform: The Next Act*, ed. Alan Weil and Kenneth Finegold (Washington, D.C.: Urban Institute Press, 2002); Pamela Loprest, "Who Returns to Welfare?" New Federalism Series B, No. B-49 (Washington, D.C.: Urban Institute, 2002); Lawrence Bobo, James R. Kluegel, and Ryan A. Smith, "Laissez-Faire Racism: The Crystallization of a Kinder, Gentler Antiblack Ideology," in *Racial Attitudes in the 1990s: Continuity and Change*, ed. Steven A. Tuch and Jack K. Martin (Westport, Conn.: Praeger, 1997); Lawrence D. Bobo and Ryan A. Smith, "From Jim Crow Racism to Laissez-Faire Racism: The Transformation of Racial Attitudes," in *Beyond Pluralism: The Conception of Groups and Group Identities in America*, ed. Wendy F. Katkin, Ned Landsman, and Andrea Tyree (Urbana: University of Illinois Press, 1998).

35. Christopher Edley, Jr., *Not All Black and White: Affirmative Action and American Values* (New York: Hill and Wang, 1996); *Hopwood v. Texas*, 78 F.3d 932 (5th Cir. 1996).

36. Rogers M. Smith, *Civic Ideals: Conflicting Visions of Citizenship in U.S. History* (New Haven: Yale University Press, 1997).

37. Jennifer L. Hochschild, "Affirmative Action as Culture War," in *The Cultural Territories of Race: Black and White Boundaries*, ed. Michèle Lamont (Chicago: University of Chicago Press; New York: Russell Sage Foundation, 1999), 346; Neil A. Lewis, "Court Vacancies: Some on the Right See a Challenge," *New York Times*, 24 June 2003, p. A1.

38. Thernstrom and Thernstrom, *America in Black and White.*

39. William J. Clinton, "Commencement Address at the University of California San Diego in La Jolla, California, June 14, 1997," in *Public Papers of the Presidents: William J. Clinton, 1997* (Washington, D.C.: U.S. Government Printing Office, 1998), 1: 739–40. See also William J. Clinton, Executive Order 13050, *Federal Register* 62, no. 116 (17 June 1997), 32987–88.

40. *One America in the 21st Century: Forging a New Future*, President's Initiative on Race, Advisory Board's Report to the President (Washington, D.C.: U.S. Government Printing Office, 1998).